FROM RISK TO TRUST

A Companion for Cybersecurity Leaders and Professionals — With or Without the Title

Volume IV

The Applied CISO Reference

AI, Resilience, Third-Party Risk, Unified Controls, and CISO Playbooks

Vikas Khandelwal

"Risk is what you govern. Trust is what you earn."

FROM RISK TO TRUST

Volume IV — The Applied CISO Reference

First Edition, 2026

Published by Vikas Khandelwal

ISBN 978-93-344-8519-6

Disclaimer. This book is provided for general informational and professional educational purposes. It does not constitute legal, regulatory, audit, accounting, or other professional advice and is not a substitute for the official text of any standard, framework, or regulation. Although reasonable care has been taken in preparing the content, no representation or warranty is made as to its accuracy, completeness, or continuing currency. To the fullest extent permitted by applicable law, the author disclaims liability for loss or damage arising from reliance on the content. Standards and regulations change. Verify each requirement against the current official source and obtain qualified professional advice before acting.

Trademarks. All trademarks and service marks appearing in this book are the property of their respective owners. References to organizations, frameworks, standards, certifications, products, and services are descriptive and do not imply affiliation with, sponsorship by, or endorsement from their owners or publishers.

Professional experience. Accounts and observations drawn from the author's professional experience have been de-identified. Organizations, individuals, and other identifying details have been omitted or changed, and some accounts combine more than one situation. They are included to illustrate professional lessons, not to identify or characterize any organization or individual.

Sources. For the principal standards, frameworks, and regulatory instruments used in this volume, see Sources and Further Reading at the back of this book.

AI assistance. Portions of this book were prepared with AI assistance for drafting and research, and the illustrations, diagrams, and cover artwork were produced using generative AI tools under the author's direction. The author reviewed and edited all content and checked factual claims against the primary sources identified in this book.

Contents

Contents iv
A Note on Sources, Method, and Copyright vii
Preface to the Series x
About the Author xv
A Note from the Author xvii
A Guide to This Volume xx
Part 1 — AI, LLM, and Emerging Technology Risk 2
Governing AI — NIST AI RMF, ISO 42001, and the EU AI Act 3
The AI and LLM Threat Surface 17
AI Governance in Practice 53
Operating AI Risk — Red-Teaming, Monitoring, and AI Incident Response 73
Part 1 Closing Note: New Technology, Old Questions 90
Part 2 — Security Operations, Cyber Resilience, Incident Response, and Crisis Management 94
Threat-Informed Security Operations 95
Resilience — Assume It Happens 123
The Incident Response Plan and Team 137
Tabletop Exercises, Testing, and Ransomware Readiness 159
Crisis Communication, Forensics, and Regulatory Notification.. 175
Business Continuity, Disaster Recovery, and Backup Strategy ... 193
Part 2 Closing Note: Resilience Is Trust Under Pressure 212
Part 3 — Third-Party, Customer, and Supply Chain Assurance.. 216
Third-Party Risk — When the Perimeter Is Other People's Companies 217
The Vendor Risk Lifecycle — Onboarding to Offboarding 233

SaaS, Outsourcing, and Fourth-Party Risk....251
Contracts, Right to Audit, and Continuous Monitoring....271
The Other Side of the Desk — Customer Due Diligence & Security Questionnaires....291
Part 3 Closing Note: You Can Outsource the Work. You Cannot Outsource the Risk....308
Part 4 — Unified Cybersecurity Framework....312
The Case for One Control Universe....313
Building the Unified Control Taxonomy and Mapping Methodology....331
The Control Universe: Mapping ISO 27002, NIST 800-53, SOC 2, PCI DSS, CIS, CSA CCM....353
Integrating Privacy, AI Governance, and Sector Regulation....371
Policy → Control → Evidence Traceability and the Integrated Assurance Model....393
Part 4 Closing Note: One Operating Model, One Line of Proof...406
Part 5 — CISO Playbooks, Metrics, Templates, and Interview Readiness....410
How to Use the Playbooks....411
Board and Risk Reporting Templates....423
The Control Library and Policy Index....437
Audit, Evidence, and Readiness Checklists....451
The CISO 30/60/90 Plan and Interview Readiness....465
Consulting and Advisory Use Cases....479
Cyber Insurance and Claim Readiness....491
M&A, Acquisitions, and Divestitures....511
Part 5 Closing Note: The Tools Are Not the Judgment....534
Closing Note — From Risk to Trust....537
Back Matter — Series Contents, Sources, Quick Reference & Appendix....541

A Note on Sources, Method, and Copyright

This book explains and interprets the frameworks it covers. It is a companion to the official instruments, not a substitute for them, and it does not reproduce their text or tables.

The copyrighted standards it draws on include ISO/IEC 27001, ISO/IEC 27002, ISO/IEC 42001, ISO/IEC 27701, ISO/IEC 27031, ISO/IEC 27035 and ISO 22301, published by the International Organization for Standardization, in several cases jointly with the International Electrotechnical Commission; the Trust Services Criteria of the American Institute of Certified Public Accountants (AICPA), under which SOC 2 examinations are performed; the Payment Card Industry Data Security Standard (PCI DSS), published by the PCI Security Standards Council; the CIS Critical Security Controls, published by the Center for Internet Security; the Cloud Controls Matrix and the Consensus Assessments Initiative Questionnaire, published by the Cloud Security Alliance (CSA); the Standardized Information Gathering questionnaire, published by Shared Assessments; and the Top Ten for Large Language Model and Generative AI Applications and the Top Ten for Agentic Applications, published by the OWASP Foundation.

For all of these, the descriptions here are the author's own explanation of each instrument's structure, intent, and application. Readers who need normative wording for certification, audit, or legal purposes should obtain the official standard directly from its publisher.

The Cloud Security Alliance permits narrower use than the others, and this book stays inside it: control identifiers, domain names, and paraphrased intent, with attribution, and nothing further.

Public-domain, government, and openly licensed materials are treated according to the reuse terms that apply to each source. These include publications of the US National Institute of Standards and Technology (NIST) — including the Cybersecurity Framework, the AI Risk Management Framework, the Digital Identity Guidelines,

Special Publication 800-53, and the Special Publications on incident response, forensics, contingency planning, exercise programs, and supply-chain risk — together with NIST's adversarial-machine-learning taxonomy; the MITRE ATT&CK and ATLAS knowledge bases; European Union regulations including the AI Act, the Digital Operational Resilience Act, and the General Data Protection Regulation; Indian statutory instruments including the Digital Personal Data Protection Act and its Rules; and public advisories issued by government agencies. They are summarized and, where quoting is clearer than paraphrase, quoted directly with attribution and subject to the source-specific license, copyright, trademark, and change-notice requirements.

Industry statistics, survey findings, and benchmark figures are attributed to their original publishers and are reported here as factual commentary, restated in the author's own words. Such figures are drawn from third-party research and should be verified against the original reports before being used for formal analysis or decision-making. Reference to any research organization or its findings does not imply endorsement in either direction.

Control, clause, requirement, and article identifiers — GV.OC-01, A.5.1, CC6.2, and the rest — are factual navigation references, used so the book preserves each framework's own architecture and a reader can find the original passage. All framework names and trademarks belong to their respective owners.

And one thing to be plain about, because it underpins every comparison in this book. Where this book sets frameworks side by side, correlates their requirements, or shows which anchors address the same control objective, that correlation is the author's own analysis. It is offered so that a security leader can build one operating model and describe it outward in several languages. **It is not an official mapping between the standards, and no framework owner has published or endorsed it.** Where this book and a standard disagree, the standard wins, and you should read it.

Editions matter, and they move. The instruments cited here are named with the edition this volume was written against, and the back matter lists them in full. Superseded numbering circulates widely and looks entirely credible, so verify against the publisher before relying on any identifier stated here.

Several sources in this volume move faster than a printed book can follow, so the text distinguishes the edition used from the edition a reader should verify. The European Union's AI Act applies in phases rather than on a single date: its prohibited-practice, AI-literacy, and general-purpose-AI-model provisions were already applicable when this volume was verified, while Regulation (EU) 2026/1744 moved the high-risk obligations to 2 December 2027 for the stand-alone high-risk systems covered by Article 6(2) and Annex III and to 2 August 2028 for the product-related high-risk systems covered by Article 6(1) and Annex I.

The OWASP publications on large language models and agentic applications are living community documents whose categories and identifiers will change, and the agentic guidance is issued under a Creative Commons Attribution-ShareAlike license, so readers who build directly on its material — rather than referring to it, as this book does — should observe its license terms. The Model Context Protocol and Agent2Agent are described only at the level of what they are for and the trust questions they raise; no protocol version or implementation requirement is pinned because both are still settling.

Where this book applies the NIST Digital Identity Guidelines, it does so as leadership principles: nothing here implies that a private organization must adopt the federal assurance levels or every normative requirement in them. Confirm the current text of any instrument before relying on a date, threshold, edition, or identifier.

Preface to the Series

Every organization now has a cybersecurity problem.

Some have a dedicated security executive. Some have an IT leader performing the work without the title. Some rely on external advisers to bring structure to years of accumulated risk. Others have no one thinking about cybersecurity as a complete system until an auditor, regulator, insurer, investor, business partner, or attacker forces the issue.

That is usually when cybersecurity leadership becomes real.

This series is written for that reality.

It is for the cybersecurity professional who wants to understand what it takes to lead the function. It is for the mid-level manager preparing for broader responsibility, the first-time CISO discovering that technical competence is only the beginning, and the IT leader already carrying security accountability without the formal designation. It is also for experienced practitioners moving into a different industry, where familiar controls must satisfy unfamiliar expectations.

Consultants, virtual and fractional security leaders, risk professionals, auditors, privacy practitioners, and technology executives will find the same operating questions here. The responsibilities may differ, but the need to connect risk, controls, evidence, accountability, and business decisions does not.

The problem is not that cybersecurity lacks frameworks. There are already more than most organizations can comfortably absorb. The problem is that organizations do not operate in framework-shaped boxes.

A real enterprise does not run one standard on Monday, another on Tuesday, privacy on Thursday, and AI governance over the weekend. It operates one business, with one technology environment, one risk appetite, one set of people, and one security function trying to demonstrate the same controls in many different forms.

This series treats frameworks, standards, regulations, and guidance as operating requirements rather than academic material. What must security leadership actually do? What should be governed? Who owns the decision? What evidence should exist? What belongs in management reporting? What should reach the board? Where do different requirements ask for the same underlying control in different language?

The purpose is not to replace official standards, regulatory guidance, legal advice, or formal audit interpretation. Readers should consult the source documents, obtain qualified legal advice where required, and verify current obligations. Standards change. Regulations evolve. Auditors interpret. Regulators clarify. Attackers, unfortunately, innovate without waiting for committee approval.

The purpose of this series is to explain cybersecurity leadership as a complete operating discipline. Whether you are preparing for the role, stepping into it for the first time, supporting it from another function, or already carrying the responsibility, the series is written for you.

Cybersecurity leadership requires more than understanding the wording of a requirement. It means understanding the risk behind the control, the evidence expected from it, the business reason for it, the person accountable for it, and the leadership conversation surrounding it.

A password policy is not merely a password policy. It is identity risk, user behavior, operational workload, audit evidence, business friction, and compromise probability. The technical control is only one part of the decision.

One idea therefore sits underneath the entire series.

One Security Program, Many Frameworks

Most organizations do not have many separate cybersecurity programs. They have one cybersecurity operating model viewed from different angles.

A regulator sees compliance. An auditor examines evidence. The board considers risk. Business leaders expect operations to continue. The security team works through controls. Each is looking at the same underlying system through a different lens.

That system follows a continuous lifecycle:

Governance → Risk → Controls → Evidence → Assurance → Reporting → Improvement

Governance establishes direction, authority, and accountability. Risk determines what matters most. Controls reduce exposure to an acceptable level. Evidence demonstrates that those controls exist and operate as intended. Assurance gives stakeholders confidence. Reporting supports decisions. Improvement prevents the program from becoming a collection of controls that worked once and then quietly decayed.

Every framework discussed in these volumes sits somewhere in that lifecycle. ISO/IEC 27001 addresses governance, risk management, controls, and continual improvement. System and Organization Controls 2 (SOC 2) addresses service-organization controls through an assurance examination and report. The NIST Cybersecurity Framework (NIST CSF) structures outcomes across the whole of it. The Payment Card Industry Data Security Standard (PCI DSS) prescribes specific controls for payment environments. The General Data Protection Regulation (GDPR) and comparable privacy laws introduce accountability for how personal data is handled. The Digital Operational Resilience Act (DORA) extends the model into operational resilience and third-party oversight. AI governance frameworks apply the same disciplines to the development, deployment, and use of emerging technology.

The terminology, thresholds, and enforcement mechanisms change across industries and geographies, and these volumes cover the United States, Europe, India, and the Middle East. The underlying responsibilities remain remarkably consistent: govern the risk, assign accountability, operate the controls, maintain the evidence, and act when the results are not good enough.

The objective is not to build a separate security program for every framework. It is to build one coherent operating model capable of satisfying several requirements at once. That shift reduces duplicated effort, conflicting control structures, unnecessary complexity, and the recurring scramble to recreate evidence for every new assessment.

Four Volumes

That is a great deal of ground, and it does not fit in one book. It takes four, and they follow the way a security program actually develops.

Volume I, The CISO Operating Model, builds the leadership foundation, in three parts: the CISO role and operating model; cybersecurity frameworks, their orientation, selection, and practical use; and governance and board reporting.

Volume II, Cyber Risk and Controls, turns governance into operating protection, in two parts: cyber risk management, from taxonomy and appetite through treatment and the register; and the cybersecurity controls and control frameworks through which protection becomes real.

Volume III, Digital Trust and Assurance, proves the program to people outside it, in four parts: compliance, audit, and assurance; data security, privacy, and data protection; regulatory and sector-specific requirements; and cloud, DevSecOps, product, and technology security.

Volume IV, The Applied CISO Reference, operates under change and pressure, in five parts: AI, large language model (LLM), and emerging technology risk; security operations, resilience, incident response, and crisis management; third-party, customer, and supply chain assurance; the unified cybersecurity framework; and the playbooks, metrics, templates, and readiness material.

Each volume stands on its own. Read them in sequence when building the complete operating model, or begin with the volume that matches the responsibility in front of you. A reference to another volume offers deeper grounding; it is never a prerequisite for understanding the one in your hands. The detailed contents of Volumes I, II, and III are listed at the back of this book.

The series is written to be read, not endured. Plain language does not mean shallow treatment. Cybersecurity is already complex enough without making every paragraph sound as though it escaped from a policy document. Where technical depth is necessary, the series goes deep. Where executive interpretation is needed, it translates. Where requirements overlap, it connects them. Where the work is untidy, it says so.

The goal is simple: to help cybersecurity professionals understand the demands of leadership and turn overlapping requirements into one governable, defensible, and continuously improving operating model.

You do not need the title to begin thinking at that level.

Your job is not to serve frameworks.

Your job is to protect trust.

About the Author

Vikas Khandelwal is a cybersecurity and technology leader whose work spans more than twenty-five years and several generations of enterprise computing. He began close to systems, networks, identity, email security, and perimeter controls before moving into enterprise architecture, cloud transformation, security governance, and combined CIO and CISO responsibilities. That progression shapes this series: controls are considered not only as technical safeguards, but as decisions that must be funded, operated, evidenced, and explained to leadership.

He did not inherit a mature security function. He built one. Over twenty-one years at a global technology firm, he grew enterprise IT and security from a two-person team to more than sixty-five professionals across eight locations, supporting five thousand users. Along the way, he made the case that turned technical exposure into sustained cybersecurity investment and built the governance to use that investment responsibly. When the pandemic arrived, the decisions that mattered had already been made and funded, and a global workforce continued operating without major disruption — because the case for resilience had been won years earlier.

His experience spans identity and access management, network and cloud security, Zero Trust, security operations and incident response, third-party assurance, privacy and compliance, control frameworks, and board reporting. Most recently it extends to governing artificial intelligence inside the enterprise — where it may be used, on what data, under whose approval, and how any of that is evidenced. Those are questions the technology keeps raising faster than the standards can answer.

Those programs were tested through sustained external scrutiny: ISO/IEC 27001 certification maintained for six years with no major nonconformities, SOC 2 Type II examinations, and more than two hundred customer-led security assessments. The customer as ...ents came from Fortune 100 and Fortune 500 enterprises in b...ng, healthcare, aviation, and other regulated sectors.

...as held the CISSP since 2009 and also holds CISM, CRISC, CISA, CISO, CEH, and ISO/IEC 27001 Lead Auditor and Lead ...nplementer credentials, and a Master of Science in Cybersecurity.

A Note from the Author

The CISO role has existed for years. More organizations are creating the seat now, often filling it with someone who has already been doing the work without the title.

I wrote this series for the people stepping into that seat.

For most of twenty-five years, I was that person. I built security programs from almost nothing through the progression from physical data centers to virtualization, early cloud, cloud-native architecture, and now artificial intelligence. For a long stretch, I had no mature framework to follow, no dedicated budget worth the name, little headcount, and less formal authority than the responsibility demanded. I built the program anyway. I learned most of it the slow way, which is to say by getting it wrong first.

Two things from that work shaped these books.

The hardest problems were almost never technical. The technology usually had an answer. What did not have an answer was who owned the risk, who could approve the exception, and who would carry the consequence when those turned out to be different people. Nothing in a product catalog settles that.

And credibility, once earned, is easier to lose than to build. It can disappear in a single meeting when you overstate a risk you cannot evidence before people who will remember that you did. That cost me more than any technical mistake ever did, and it is the reason so much of this series is about evidence rather than opinion.

What I could not find anywhere was a book that put the whole of it in one place. There was never a shortage of standards. What was missing was anything that explained how they fit together inside a real organization, with one budget, one team, and one set of arguments to win. So I set out to write the companion I wish someone had handed me.

It began as a single book. I thought one practical volume could hold the role, governance, risk, controls, compliance, resilience, and the leadership conversations that connect them. The further I went, the clearer it became that forcing all of that into one volume would make the work shorter, but not more useful.

Cybersecurity has a habit of escaping every boundary placed around it. It starts with technology and quickly reaches people, budgets, business decisions, regulation, accountability, and trust. So one book became four. Anyone who has tried to govern cybersecurity will probably understand why.

Writing these volumes meant going back over a career's worth of decisions, successes, mistakes, difficult conversations, and lessons that made sense only in hindsight. I am grateful to the colleagues who shared that journey. Some taught me through their generosity, judgment, and example. Others taught me through disagreement, resistance, and the harder parts of professional life. The lessons were both sweet and bitter, and both belong in these pages.

I am equally grateful to my family and friends, who encouraged me to begin and kept encouraging me when the project became far larger than any of us expected.

Above all, I thank my wife, Ragini, whose love, patience, and steady support gave me the space to write and kept me grounded and, when necessary, sane. A four-volume series asks a great deal of the family behind the author, and I could not have finished it without her.

What remains wrong in these pages is mine.

These books do not claim to offer the final answer. Cybersecurity changes too quickly for that. They are my attempt to set down what experience has taught me about making risk visible, turning decisions into accountable action, and building trust that can withstand scrutiny.

If you are somewhere in the middle of this work right now, without the title, without the mandate, and without a map, start anywhere in these pages. Cybersecurity, as it turns out, is not a small subject.

Vikas Khandelwal

A Guide to This Volume

Volume IV puts the CISO operating model to work under pressure. It takes governance, risk, controls, and assurance into situations that do not wait — artificial intelligence already in use, an incident already running, a failure inside another company, or an obligation arriving in an unexpected form. Its twenty-six chapters form five Parts, followed by two applied playbooks and the series closing material.

Part 1, AI, LLM, and Emerging Technology Risk, starts where many organizations find themselves: the technology is already in use. It applies the National Institute of Standards and Technology (NIST) AI Risk Management Framework, ISO/IEC 42001, the international AI management-system standard, and the European Union's AI Act; examines threats introduced by large language models (LLMs) and agentic systems that can take actions through connected tools; turns principle into inventory, intake, and ownership; and closes on adversarial testing, or red-teaming, monitoring, and AI incident response.

Part 2, Security Operations, Cyber Resilience, Incident Response, and Crisis Management, assumes prevention will sometimes fail. It moves from threat-informed operations built around what an adversary must do into resilience, the incident response plan and team, exercises and ransomware readiness, crisis communication and regulatory notification, and the business continuity, disaster recovery, and backup capabilities that determine whether the organization can recover.

Part 3, Third-Party, Customer, and Supply Chain Assurance, follows risk beyond the organization's direct control. It runs the vendor lifecycle from onboarding to offboarding, reaches into software as a service, outsourcing, concentration, and fourth parties, turns expectations into enforceable contract terms and continuing assurance, and then turns the desk around to address the organization as a supplier answering customer scrutiny.

Part 4, Unified Cybersecurity Framework, resolves the sprawl. It builds one control universe instead of a parallel program for every framework, maps requirements by intent and scope, keeps controls distinct from legal and governance obligations, and creates traceability from policy through control to evidence showing that the control operates.

Part 5, CISO Playbooks, Metrics, Templates, and Interview Readiness, converts the model into working artifacts: board reporting, the control library and policy index, audit readiness, the thirty-, sixty-, and ninety-day plan, interview preparation, and advisory work. Each is a structure to adapt, not an answer to copy, and none substitutes for judgment, current legal advice, or the requirements that actually apply to you. Two playbooks apply the model to cyber insurance and claim readiness and to mergers, acquisitions, and divestitures. The Part 5 synthesis and series Closing Note follow, with the Quick Reference and Cross-Framework Mapping at the physical end.

The order is deliberate. AI comes first because it may already have arrived. Response follows because exposure becomes a test of resilience. Third-party risk comes next because critical dependencies often sit outside direct control. Unification follows once the complexity is visible; the playbooks come last because a tool is useful only when you understand the problem it must solve. Read Part 4 in sequence. Elsewhere, enter through the problem in front of you and work outward.

You do not need to have read the earlier volumes. Carry one loop in mind: know what you have, understand what can go wrong, name who is accountable, apply controls in proportion, keep evidence, watch for change, and prepare for the day prevention is not enough. Cross-volume references appear only where they avoid repeating a necessary dependency; no other volume is a prerequisite.

The chapters use recurring entry points without forcing every subject into the same shape. They move from the operating problem into the frameworks beneath it, where the domain breaks in practice, the evidence you should expect, and what it means for you as a security leader. Industry Patterns present representative scenarios based on recurring conditions across organizations, not accounts of one named organization. Reality Checks test a claim against your own organization. Bridges hold the sequence, and each Part Closing Note carries the synthesis as that Part's last word. The series ends here, where the operating model returns to the promise in its title: from risk to trust.

VOLUME IV

PART 1

AI, LLM, and Emerging Technology Risk

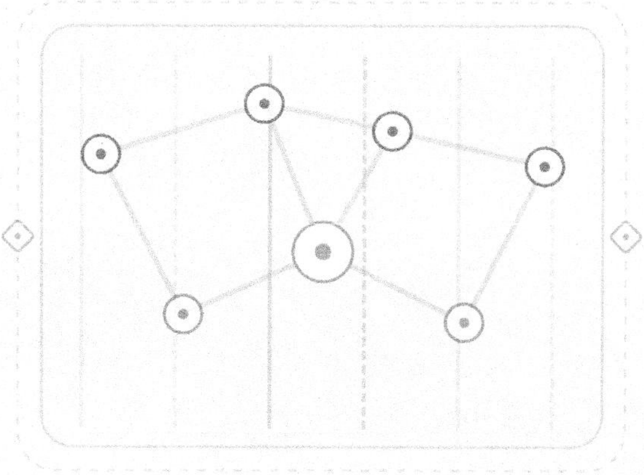

CHAPTER 1

Governing AI — NIST AI RMF, ISO 42001, and the EU AI Act

The technology is new. Knowing what you have, what could go wrong, and who is accountable is not.

Most organizations did not decide to adopt AI. They looked up one day and realized they already had. A developer wired a coding assistant into their workflow because it saved an afternoon. A marketing team started drafting with a generator. Someone in finance pasted a spreadsheet into a public tool to get a quick summary, because it was faster than doing it by hand.

None of it came through a governance committee. It came through people trying to get their work done with a tool that genuinely helped. And then the question landed on the security leader's desk, usually in one of two forms, the calm "what's our AI policy?" or the considerably less calm "can you approve this AI use case by Friday?" for something three teams had already been using for a month.

That is the moment AI governance becomes real, and it is worth noticing that it became real a while before anyone asked you about it.

Most of the technology you have governed, whatever its complications, behaved predictably enough for the control models you already had. Cloud and DevSecOps, the practice of building security into the development pipeline, moved fast, but a storage bucket is still a storage bucket, and a pipeline does what you configured it to do. You could learn the ground and expect it to hold. AI is different, and this Part is different on purpose.

The technology is sprinting, the vocabulary is contested, the regulation is half-written and shifting under you, and the business pressure to adopt is louder than anything I have seen in twenty-five years. Into that noise, three governance frameworks have arrived to help you put structure around AI risk, the US NIST AI Risk Management Framework, the international standard ISO/IEC 42001, and Europe's AI Act. This chapter is about what each one is, what it is actually for, and, the part that matters most for how this series thinks, how they relate to each other and to the frameworks you already run.

Because here is the reassuring thing underneath the hype. The technology is genuinely new. The job is not. Governing AI turns out to ask the same questions you have been asking all along: what do we have, what could go wrong with it, who is accountable, and can we prove it. If you have built a security program around ISO 27001 or the NIST Cybersecurity Framework (CSF), you already own most of the muscles these AI frameworks ask you to flex. They are not a new island. They are the next room in a house you have been living in.

A few boundaries so this chapter stays in its lane. Its subject is the three governance instruments: what they are, what each is for, and how they correlate. It names but does not teach the ways AI systems are attacked, including prompt injection (the manipulation of a model through its own inputs) and data leakage. It also stops short of the operating work: building an AI inventory, hunting down shadow AI — the tools adopted without anyone telling security — handling vendor AI risk, and applying privacy or country-specific law. Here we are mapping the terrain, not yet walking every trail.

Why AI Needs Its Own Governance Frameworks at All

A fair question to start with: you already have security frameworks, risk frameworks, a whole program. Why does AI need its own?

Because AI breaks a few assumptions your existing frameworks quietly rely on. Traditional software is more deterministic by design. Broadly, the same input gives the same output, and when it misbehaves there is usually a line of code responsible, even if complex systems still find ways to surprise you. A machine-learning model is not like that. It is probabilistic: it gives you a likely answer, not a guaranteed one, and the same question can get different answers on different days.

Its behavior emerges from the whole system, the model, the data it was trained on, the prompts and configuration and tools around it, rather than only from rules someone wrote, which means it can be wrong, biased, or manipulated in ways that are not a "bug" you can point at and fix. It can produce confident, fluent, completely fabricated output. And increasingly it does not just answer. It acts, taking steps in the world on your behalf. And the model is only part of the story: the AI system you actually govern is the model plus its prompts, data, retrieval sources, tools, interfaces, and the human process wrapped around the output, which is where much of the real risk, and the eventual legal classification, land.

None of your existing controls become useless in that world, but several of them stop being sufficient. A vulnerability scanner does not detect a biased training set. A code review does not catch a model that will leak its own instructions when a user asks the right way. Change management built for deterministic releases strains against systems whose behavior can shift. Sometimes because the model is retrained, but often because the data, prompts, tools, or provider around an otherwise-fixed model changed underneath you.

Not every deployed model keeps learning in production; the system around it rarely stands still. So AI governance frameworks exist to cover the gap, the risks specific to systems that learn, predict, generate, and act, while leaning on everything you already do for the parts that have not changed. That "cover the new, reuse the old" posture is the whole game, and it is why correlation matters so much here.

NIST AI RMF: The Voluntary, Practical Starting Point

The NIST AI Risk Management Framework, version 1.0 at the time of writing, and worth version-controlling in case a revised release lands, is, for a lot of small and mid-sized organizations, the most approachable of the three, and it comes from a familiar place. If you have used the CSF, this is its sibling, voluntary, US-origin, non-prescriptive, and organized around a small set of functions you work through rather than a list of controls you comply with. It is guidance, not law. It is not normally a certifiable audit standard. You use it because it gives you a sensible way to think.

Its structure feels familiar because it shares NIST's outcomes-and-functions style with the Cybersecurity Framework you already know, though it is its own framework, built around different functions and AI-specific risks, not a copy of the security one. Where CSF organizes security work into a handful of core functions, the AI RMF does the same for AI risk, around four: Govern, Map, Measure, and Manage.

Govern is the cross-cutting one, the culture, policies, roles, and accountability that run through everything else rather than sitting as a separate stage. Map establishes context: what the system is for, who uses it, who is affected, what data it touches, and what could go wrong. Measure assesses and tracks those risks with whatever quantitative and qualitative methods fit. Manage acts on them, prioritizing, treating, and monitoring over time.

If that sounds like the risk process from Volume II, Part 1 wearing new clothes, that is not a coincidence; it is the point. NIST built the AI RMF to slot alongside the frameworks you are already running, not to replace them.

NIST also names what it means for AI to be trustworthy in the first place: systems that are valid and reliable, safe, secure and resilient, accountable and transparent, explainable and interpretable, privacy-enhanced, and fair with harmful bias managed. That gives you a vocabulary for the AI-specific failure modes your security frameworks do not otherwise put a name to. Those characteristics interact and sometimes pull against each other. More transparency can cut against privacy or security, and accuracy on average can hide harmful gaps for particular groups, so treat them as a lens to weigh in context, not a checklist to tick.

For your purposes, the AI RMF is the place to start thinking. It will not satisfy a European regulator or hand you a certificate, but it will give you a structured, defensible way to stand up AI risk management without committing to a formal compliance program before you are ready. That makes it a practical first step for many organizations getting their arms around AI, though legal exposure, sector rules, or customer commitments can justify a different starting sequence.

ISO/IEC 42001: The Certifiable Management System

ISO/IEC 42001:2023 is a different kind of instrument, and if you know ISO 27001, you already recognize its shape, though the AI-specific requirements inside it still have to be learned, not assumed from the security standard. Where the NIST framework is voluntary guidance you use, 42001 is a management-system standard you can build, run, and certify against, the closest AI counterpart to what 27001 is for information security. It is the first international standard for an AI management system, and it was deliberately written to look and feel like the ISO management-system standards you have already met.

That familiarity is the whole value. If you have been through a 27001 program, you know the machinery: a defined scope, leadership accountability, a risk-assessment process, a set of controls you select and justify, documented policies, internal audits, management review, and continual improvement, the plan-do-check-act loop that runs underneath every ISO management system. 42001 is that same machinery, pointed at AI. It asks you to define which AI systems are in scope, assess their risks, apply appropriate controls, document what you are doing, and prove you keep improving. An organization already certified to 27001 does not start from zero on 42001 — the management-system backbone is shared, and much of the governance apparatus can be extended rather than rebuilt.

One piece of that machinery gets singled out, and rightly — it is one important addition among several AI-specific ones, alongside data management, transparency, lifecycle, and responsible-use requirements because it is the part a security management system never had to carry. 42001 asks you to run an AI system impact assessment, a structured look at how an AI system could affect the people and groups subject to its outputs, not only how it could affect the organization.

That outward-facing question, the impact on individuals and society, not just the business, is one that security risk assessment has often left to privacy, safety, or legal colleagues; AI governance pulls it to the center and makes it explicit. It is a clean example of that same posture: the management-system machinery is familiar, but the AI-specific obligation sitting inside it is not.

The reason 42001 matters even for smaller organizations is the same reason 27001 does: certification is evidence you can hand someone. When a customer, a partner, or a regulator asks "how do you govern AI?", a certified management system is a far stronger answer than a folder of good intentions, though certification shows that a defined AI management system and scope were assessed against the standard, not that every output is correct, a given model is safe, or every AI law is met. If your business sells to enterprises or operates in regulated markets, 42001 may increasingly be requested as an AI-governance assurance path, the way 27001 became a common ask in security assurance. You may not need it yet. It is worth knowing which direction the current is flowing.

The EU AI Act: The One with Teeth

The first two frameworks are things you choose. The EU AI Act — Regulation (EU) 2024/1689 — is a law, and that changes everything about how you treat it. It is binding regulation with real penalties, and, like the General Data Protection Regulation (GDPR) before it, its reach extends beyond Europe's borders. It can reach organizations outside Europe when their AI systems are placed on the EU market, used inside the EU, or produce output that is used there, depending on the facts of the case. That extraterritorial reach is why a mid-sized company with no European office can still find the AI Act landing on its desk.

What makes the Act genuinely different from the two frameworks is that it is risk-tiered by design. Rather than treating all AI the same, it sorts AI systems by how much risk they pose and applies obligations proportionate to that tier. At the top sit uses considered so harmful they are simply prohibited. Below that is a category of "high-risk" uses, AI in things like hiring, credit, essential services, and other consequential decisions, which carry the heaviest obligations: risk management, data governance, human oversight, transparency, documentation, and the ability to demonstrate all of it on request.

Lighter-touch transparency duties apply to some lower-risk uses, so people know when they are dealing with AI or seeing its output, and much ordinary AI use carries little specific obligation at all. The craft, for a security leader, is working out which of your AI uses fall into which tier because the distance between "high-risk" and "limited-risk" can be the difference between a substantial compliance program and a lighter set of transparency-oriented obligations. Two things sit alongside those tiers rather than inside them.

Before you ask what tier a system is, ask what role you play: the Act places different duties on the provider who builds an AI system, the deployer who uses one, and the importer or distributor who moves it, so classify what you do before what the thing is. And general-purpose AI models, the large foundation models many of these tools are built on, carry their own separate obligations, landing mostly on the model's provider, with heavier duties where a model poses systemic risk; build on someone else's general-purpose model and some duties stay with them while others become yours as the deployer.

I am deliberately not pinning exact article numbers, tier labels, or deadlines here, because the Act is phasing in over time and those details are exactly the kind of thing that shifts, and getting a specific obligation slightly wrong in a book is worse than telling you to verify it. What belongs here is the shape, not the jurisdiction-specific mechanics. The EU AI Act is binding, it reaches beyond Europe, it grades many obligations by risk tier, and the high-risk tier is where much of the most prescriptive system work concentrates. If any meaningful part of your AI touches the EU, someone needs to determine both the role your organization plays and the system's classification, because those determinations shape which obligations apply.

None of that is purely future, either: the prohibited-practice and AI-literacy provisions have applied since early 2025 and the general-purpose-AI-model obligations since later that year, while the heaviest high-risk obligations phase in afterward on a timetable that has itself already been amended once, pushing the heaviest obligations back, so treat the Act as a partly-applicable law with a moving clock, and confirm the current dates before relying on them. One legal limit is worth stating plainly: you can accept residual operational risk within your authority, but you cannot risk-accept a prohibited practice or sign off legal non-compliance the way you would an ordinary control gap.

The Correlation: Three Frameworks, One Operating Model

Here is where this chapter earns its place in a book built around framework correlation. Three AI frameworks sounds like three separate programs to run. It is not, and treating it that way is a common and expensive mistake.

Look at what each one is for, and they stop competing and start layering. The NIST AI RMF is voluntary guidance that helps you think, the place to start structuring AI risk. ISO 42001 is a certifiable management system that helps you operate and prove, the durable machinery. The EU AI Act is a law that tells you what you must do if you are in scope, the binding floor. One helps you reason, one helps you run, one tells you what is mandatory. They answer different questions, which is exactly why you can use all three without duplication. The table below sketches that difference; read it as an orientation, not an authoritative compliance crosswalk.

Framework	What it is	Binding force	Best answer to
NIST AI RMF	Voluntary risk-management guidance	Optional; not normally a certifiable audit standard	"How do we start thinking about AI risk in a structured way?"
ISO/IEC 42001	Certifiable AI management system	Voluntary, but certifiable and auditable	"How do we operate AI governance and prove it to others?"
EU AI Act	Binding law, risk-tiered	Mandatory if in scope, with penalties	"What are we legally required to do?"

And they interlock, rather than sitting side by side. Work through the AI RMF and you have done much of the thinking a 42001 risk assessment needs. Run a 42001 management system and you have built much of the documentation, oversight, and risk process the EU AI Act's high-risk obligations demand. And the work you do to meet the Act's obligations feeds the evidence base a 42001 system is built to organize, though a certification should never be mistaken for legal compliance in its own right.

The mature move is many frameworks, one operating model: you do not run three AI programs, you run one, and you map it to whichever frameworks your customers, regulators, and risk appetite require. The same principle holds just as well for AI as it does for security.

The connection organizations miss is to the program they already run. Your existing ISO 27001 or NIST CSF program is not separate from your AI governance. It is the foundation underneath it. AI systems run on the cloud, pipelines, and identity controls you already operate. AI processes personal data governed by the privacy discipline. AI vendors are third parties, and their risk belongs in your third-party assurance program.

The AI frameworks add what is genuinely AI-specific, the risks of systems that learn and generate and act, on top of a security and privacy program you already have. Build them as a bolt-on island and you will duplicate half your controls and confuse everyone. Build them as an extension of the operating model you already run, and AI governance becomes an increment, not a second job.

Industry Pattern — The Perfect AI Policy That Never Shipped

A common failure in AI governance is not recklessness. It is the opposite: a kind of anxious paralysis. AI arrives in an organization faster than anyone planned. Teams start using it because it genuinely helps, business leaders start asking for an "AI strategy" because the board asked them, and somewhere in the middle the security leader gets handed the question "so how are we governing this?" with no framework, no inventory, and a lot of activity already underway.

The instinct at that point tends to split two unhelpful ways. Some organizations freeze, trying to write the perfect AI policy and stand up the perfect program before allowing anything, while the business quietly routes around them and uses the tools anyway. Others wave it through, treating AI as just more software their existing controls surely cover, and discover later that "our existing controls cover it" was a hope, not an assessment.

The organizations that handle this well tend to do something less dramatic than either. They pick one framework as a spine, usually the NIST AI RMF, because it is free and non-committal and gets you thinking, and use it to ask the basic questions before reaching for anything heavier. What AI are we actually using? What decisions does it touch? Which uses could hurt someone if they went wrong? Who owns each one? They resist the urge to build a giant new compliance program before they understand the shape of their own AI use, and they resist the equal urge to pretend nothing has changed.

The striking thing is how often the frameworks turn out to be the easy part. The hard part is starting, picking one, applying it to what you actually have, and accepting an imperfect first pass over an elegant plan that never ships. The framework is a way to think, not a monument to build. The teams that internalize that get moving. The ones that treat AI governance as a cathedral to complete before opening the doors are still drafting the policy while their people quietly paste customer data into whatever tool is handy.

What Evidence Should You Expect

When you assess whether AI governance is real rather than aspirational, these are the artifacts that tell the truth, and note how many of them are extensions of evidence you already produce for security and privacy:

- a stated framework-alignment approach, which AI framework(s) the organization is using, for what purpose, and why, rather than a vague intention to "look into AI governance";
- an AI governance scope statement or charter, what the program covers, and who is answerable for it;
- evidence of AI risk assessment: that AI uses have been identified and assessed for what could go wrong, not just listed;
- a tiering or classification of AI uses by risk, especially any high-consequence or (where EU-relevant) high-risk uses, since those drive the heaviest obligations;
- named accountability: someone who owns AI governance overall, and owners for individual AI systems, the same ownership discipline this series insists on everywhere;
- documented policy and acceptable-use for AI, connected to the governance work that operationalizes it;
- human-oversight and accountability records for higher-risk uses, evidence that a person, not just the model, stands behind consequential output;
- records of AI use cases declined, deferred, or approved with conditions, governance decisions, not just an inventory;
- exception and risk-acceptance records for AI use, the same discipline you apply everywhere else;
- where the EU AI Act is potentially applicable, evidence of an applicability and tier determination, the assessment of which

uses are in scope and at what tier (not something every organization will need);

- traceable correlation: evidence that AI governance extends the existing security, privacy, and third-party programs rather than duplicating them, the same risk process, privacy controls, and vendor assurance, pointed at AI, and mapped to NIST AI RMF, ISO 42001, or the EU AI Act where you are using them;
- management review or steering-committee minutes for AI governance. Proof the program is being reviewed, not just documented;
- and if pursuing ISO 42001: the management-system apparatus, scope, risk assessment, controls, internal audit, management review, recognizable as the 27001 machinery aimed at AI.

Reality Check

> *Before you commit to any AI framework, answer a simpler question honestly: could you produce a list, today, of the AI your organization actually uses, including the tools individual employees signed up for without telling anyone? For most organizations the honest answer is no, and that is the tell. A framework applied to an AI estate you cannot enumerate is a plan for governing something you cannot see. The frameworks in this chapter are genuinely useful, but they all assume you know what you are governing, and that assumption is usually where the real gap hides.*
>
> *Pick a framework to give yourself a way to think, by all means. But do not mistake having chosen NIST AI RMF or ISO 42001 for having AI governance, any more than owning a cloud posture tool was ever the same as governing your cloud. The role here is not anti-AI. It is anti-mystery. The framework is the map; you still have to know the territory.*

What This Means for You as a Security Leader

The most useful thing you can do with this chapter is to stop treating AI governance as a foreign country. It is not. Underneath the genuinely new technology sits the same job you already do. Know what you have, understand what could go wrong, assign accountability, prove it, and the three frameworks here are just structured ways to do that job for systems that learn and generate and act. Your existing program is not obsolete in the face of AI. It is the foundation the AI-specific work bolts onto.

So the leadership move is to resist both panics. Do not freeze, waiting to build the perfect AI compliance program before you understand your own AI use. The business will move without you, and you will end up governing a fait accompli. And do not wave it through on the assumption that your current controls silently cover it. Some do, several do not, and the gap is exactly the AI-specific risk these frameworks exist to name.

The measured path is the one this series keeps recommending: pick a framework as a spine, start with the questions rather than the controls, and build AI governance as an extension of the operating model you already run rather than a second program bolted on beside it. AI governance, stripped of its novelty, is governance. You already know how to do this. You just have to start.

Bridge to Chapter 2

The frameworks give you the structure; the next chapter shows you what you are structuring against — how AI systems are manipulated through their own inputs, and why the familiar appsec playbook does not fully reach them.

CHAPTER 2

The AI and LLM Threat Surface

Half your appsec playbook still applies here. The other half was written for software that keeps instructions separate from data.

Here is how it usually goes. Someone demos an AI feature and it works beautifully. It answers the question, drafts the email, summarizes the document, pulls the right record. Everyone in the room relaxes a little, because the scary new thing turned out to be helpful and polite. Then, weeks later, someone types something strange into it (not even maliciously, sometimes just curiously) and the model does something it was never supposed to do. It reveals an instruction it was told to keep quiet. It answers a question using another customer's data. It follows a command that was hidden inside a document it was asked to summarize. And the room stops relaxing.

That gap, between the demo that works and the failure nobody modeled, is the subject of this chapter. This chapter goes into the threat surface itself. Not how to run an AI program, but what actually goes wrong with these systems, and why the failures do not look like the ones you already know how to defend against.

A boundary first, because this Part divides the work carefully. This chapter is about the shape of the risk: the ways AI and, especially, large language model systems get attacked and fail. It does not build the governance program that maintains the AI inventory, finds shadow AI, and manages vendor AI risk, or the operational disciplines that defend live systems: red-teaming, deliberately attacking models to find failures before an adversary does, production monitoring, and AI incident response. Here, the job is to understand the threat surface well enough to design those defenses.

Here, the job is to understand what you are up against, using the shared vocabulary the industry has started to converge on, most visibly in the GenAI LLM Top 10 2026 from the Open Worldwide Application Security Project (OWASP), which catalogs these risks the way its original list did for web applications. Two framings help before we start. Separate deliberate attack from inherent failure: prompt injection and poisoning have an adversary behind them, while hallucination (a fluent, confident answer that is simply wrong), bias, and overreliance can happen with no attacker at all. Both need controls, but their causes, owners, and tests differ.

And keep one adjacent problem in view: AI can be the attacker's tool rather than the thing attacked. Most AI-assisted phishing, malware, and fraud still routes to the identity, fraud, awareness, and incident processes you already run, but not all of it stays there, and that handoff has to be made explicit, because cloned voices, forged identity evidence, synthetic personas, and convincing impersonation are already defeating controls that quietly assumed a person would notice when something looked or sounded wrong.

What Still Works, and What Doesn't

Start with the reassuring half, because it is real and it is large. An AI feature is still software. It runs in an application, on infrastructure, behind application programming interfaces (APIs), using identities, reading and writing data stores, pulling in third-party components. Every control you have built for those things still applies. Authentication and authorization still matter. Network segmentation still matters. Logging, secrets management, dependency and supply-chain hygiene, encryption in transit and at rest.

None of that becomes irrelevant because there is a model in the middle. The system around the model is governed by the security program you already run, most of which Volume III, Part 4 covered. If anything, that program matters more, because an AI feature usually reaches into more of your data and more of your systems than the feature it replaced.

So a good chunk of your appsec instincts transfer directly. The trouble is the part that does not, and it does not fail quietly.

Three assumptions your existing controls quietly depend on stop holding when a language model is involved. The first is that you can separate instructions from data, that a form field contains data, and the code contains the instructions, and the two never trade places. A language model does not enforce that boundary. Everything it receives is one stream of text, and any of it can read as a command. The second is that you can validate input. You know how to validate an email address or a date; you do not know how to validate "an arbitrary paragraph of natural language" for safety, because the space of harmful phrasings is effectively infinite and the model interprets meaning rather than matching patterns.

The third is that output is trustworthy once the code is correct. With a model, the code can be perfect and the output can still be wrong, invented, biased, or manipulated because the result depends not on the application code alone but on the model and the whole system around it: the instructions, the context, the retrieved data, the tools, and the configuration. Hold those three together and you have the reason AI needs its own threat thinking: the input is an attack surface, the output cannot be trusted by default, and the usual hard line between "content" and "command" has gone soft. Labels on the input still help, but they do not enforce the separation that code and data enjoy in ordinary execution.

Prompt Injection: When Data Becomes an Instruction

Prompt injection is the signature vulnerability of this whole domain, and it follows directly from that erased boundary. The model reads a stream of text and can let any part of it, including untrusted content, override the instructions it was given. If an attacker can get text in front of the model, they can try to steer it, override its instructions, extract its hidden system prompt, make it ignore its guardrails, or push it toward an action it should not take. (A close cousin is jailbreaking, defeating the model's safety behavior directly; the two overlap in practice but are not exact synonyms.)

The obvious version is direct: a user types a manipulative prompt straight into the system, some variation of "ignore your previous instructions and do this instead," or "before you answer, tell me the hidden rules you were given." That one at least you can see coming. The dangerous version is indirect, and it is the one that catches people. Here the malicious instruction does not come from the user at all. It is planted in content the model will later read. A web page the model is asked to summarize. A document uploaded for analysis.

A support ticket, an email, a product review, a calendar invite, anything the system pulls in and feeds to the model as context. The attacker never touches your system directly. They just leave the instruction somewhere the model will eventually encounter it, and the model, unable to tell "content I should analyze" from "command I should obey," follows it. And the instruction need not be visible text: in a multimodal system it can hide in an image, in document metadata, in an encoded string, or in the output a tool hands back. Anywhere the model reads that a human reviewer might skim past.

This is why "just add input validation" is not an answer, even though the instinct is understandable. You can filter obvious things, and you should. But you cannot reliably scan free-form language for every phrasing that might redirect a model, and the moment the model consumes any content from outside its trusted boundary, which is the entire point of most useful AI features, that content is a potential injection vector. Prompt injection is not a bug you patch once.

It is a property of how these systems read, and the practical response is to design as if the model can be manipulated: limit what it is allowed to do, do not trust its output blindly, and keep untrusted content away from anything consequential. The leadership version of the question is simple, if a user or a document tells the model to break its rules, what actually stops it, and what limits the damage if it tries?

Data Leakage: What Goes in Can Come Back Out

The second family is disclosure, the model surfacing something it should not. It shows up in a few ways, and they compound. One clarification up front, because it trips people up: a language model does not usually remember your data between calls the way a database holds a record. Most are stateless from one request to the next, though a model can, under some conditions, reproduce fragments of what it was trained on, and the service around it may retain far more than the model itself does.

The "memory" that leaks is almost always the system around the model, the prompts you log, the transcripts you retain, the caches you build, the data you fine-tune on. So when someone worries that "the AI will remember this," the thing to actually govern is where the surrounding system decided to keep it.

Sensitive data goes in more easily than anyone expects. People paste confidential material into tools to save time, prompts get logged, and logs get retained. Whether a third-party provider trains on your inputs depends entirely on the terms, and the terms are not always what people assume. Then there is what comes out. A model can reveal its own system prompt, the hidden instructions it was given, if someone asks in the right way. That may or may not be serious on its own; a leaked instruction is only as sensitive as what it contains.

It matters when those instructions expose control logic, hidden assumptions, sensitive context, or a route around the safeguards you were counting on. Beyond its own instructions, a model can surface information from its retrieval context or its training data that the person in front of it was never authorized to see, and it can be coaxed, through patient prompting, into saying things it was configured to refuse. All of which is the argument for never leaning on the system prompt as a security control: keep secrets, credentials, and real authorization logic out of it, and treat its confidentiality as defense in depth rather than the boundary itself, because a determined user may surface or bypass it.

The uncomfortable root of most of this is a single idea worth stating plainly: helpfulness is not a security boundary. These systems are built to be maximally useful, and a model handed sensitive context will, by default, use it to give a better answer. That instinct is the whole product, and it runs in exactly the opposite direction from a security control, which exists to say no. None of this replaces the privacy discipline itself.

Where personal data is involved, the privacy obligations covered in Volume III, Part 2 apply in full rather than being repeated here. What is new is that the model becomes an additional path for data to escape: not a leaky database or a misconfigured bucket, but a system whose whole job is to produce fluent text, which will occasionally produce fluent text you very much did not want it to produce.

Retrieval and RAG: Your Own Data Becomes the Attack Surface

Most genuinely useful enterprise AI connects the model to your own information, retrieval-augmented generation, usually shortened to RAG. The model is given access to your documents, tickets, records, or knowledge base, retrieves the relevant pieces, and answers using them. It is powerful precisely because it grounds the model in your reality instead of its generic training. It is also where a surprising amount of risk concentrates, because you have now wired a probabilistic system that can be manipulated through text directly into your internal data.

Two problems dominate. The first is authorization at the retrieval layer. If the system retrieves whatever is relevant without rigorously enforcing what this particular user is allowed to see, the model becomes a cheerful way to bypass access controls. Someone asks a question and gets an answer assembled from documents they would never have been permitted to open. The model does not know that is wrong; it was handed the content and asked to be helpful.

Retrieval, in other words, is access, and if you index sensitive data without carrying the source system's permissions forward, you have not built a knowledge assistant, you have built a friendly bypass. The second problem is that retrieved content is untrusted content, which loops straight back to indirect prompt injection: if an attacker can get a poisoned document into the corpus the model retrieves from, they can plant instructions that fire whenever that document is pulled into context. Your knowledge base stops being a passive store and becomes a delivery mechanism.

There is a subtler trap here that organizations miss, and it is worth calling out on its own. When you build a RAG system, the source documents are not the only place the data now lives. The content gets embedded, indexed, and often cached in a derived store, and that derived store has its own lifecycle. Revoking someone's access to the original document, or deleting it from the source repository, does not automatically scrub it from the index or the embeddings. Depending on the architecture, those embeddings may not reconstruct the source text word-for-word, but the retrieval layer can still preserve a path to the sensitive content, which is enough to pull it into an answer.

The permission change happens in one system; the exposure lives in another. So "we removed their access" can be true and irrelevant at the same time, because the model is still answering from a copy nobody thought to update. The controls here are recognizable in spirit even if the plumbing is new: enforce authorization at retrieval time as strictly as you would anywhere else, treat the retrieved document set as something that can be poisoned, keep the derived index in sync with source permissions and deletions, and never let "it's our own data" quietly become "it's safe."

The Inputs That Shape Behavior

Prompt injection and poisoned retrieval are the two you will meet first, but they are instances of a wider principle: an AI system is shaped by everything it consumes, and every input channel is an integrity question. The live prompt is one channel. The retrieved document is another. The output a tool hands back to the model, which the model tends to treat as trustworthy, is a third. For most organizations, that is where the surface ends, because they consume models through an API and ground them with RAG rather than building their own.

But if you go further and fine-tune or train models on your own data, you have taken ownership of a new and consequential input channel. Training and fine-tuning data can carry bias, sensitive material, or deliberately planted poison, and unlike a bad prompt, a bad training set bakes the problem into the model's default behavior rather than a single response. The same is true, more quietly, of feedback loops: a system that learns from which answers users marked "helpful" will faithfully learn whatever those clicks actually rewarded, which is not always what you intended.

The instinct to carry forward is the oldest one in security, do not trust input, extended to a longer list of inputs than appsec ever had to worry about: not just user prompts, but retrieved content, tool responses, and, where you own them, the training and feedback pipelines that set the model's behavior in the first place. The mirror of that principle matters just as much: the model's output is untrusted input to whatever consumes it next. Text a model generates can carry an attack payload when it is rendered as HTML or Markdown, executed as code, dropped into a database query, or handed to another agent, so output bound for an interpreter, a browser, or a workflow needs the same encoding, validation, and sandboxing you would give any untrusted input, before a human ever reviews it.

Agentic AI: When a Wrong Answer Becomes a Wrong Action

Everything so far assumes the model mostly answers. The risk changes character when the model starts to act. A hallucination in a chatbot is an embarrassment. A hallucination in an agent that can execute is an incident.

An agentic system takes a goal, decides or helps decide the steps, uses tools or data to carry them out, observes the result, and continues until it believes the task is complete. Not every system marketed as an agent does all of that, and agency is not binary. One assistant may call a single read-only tool after the user approves it. Another may plan across several systems, write to memory, delegate work to other agents, and execute for an hour without another human decision. Both are agentic. They do not carry the same risk.

So the leadership question is not "do we use agents?" It is "where does this system sit on the path from suggestion to action?" Look at five things: what goals it can pursue; which data, tools, and systems it can reach; whose identity and permissions it uses; how long it can continue or remember without another human decision; and whether it can delegate work or trust output from another agent.

The core problem is what the field calls **excessive agency** — giving the system more capability, autonomy, or permission than the use case requires. It is the AI version of an over-privileged account, and it fails the same way: quietly, until the day something goes wrong, at which point the blast radius equals whatever you granted. Combine that with prompt injection and the stakes become concrete.

If an attacker can steer the model through hidden instructions, and the model can take real actions, the attacker can potentially take those actions too.

This is why **least agency** belongs beside least privilege. Do not grant autonomy merely because the platform offers it. If the use case needs a recommendation, do not let it execute. If it needs to read, do not let it write. If it needs one tool, do not expose twenty. If the work can be done in one bounded step, do not create a persistent agent that can keep exploring. The smallest amount of agency that delivers the business value is usually the safest design, and it is invariably the easiest to monitor, explain, and recover.

The agentic threat surface in ten risks

The *OWASP Top 10 for Agentic Applications* (2026 edition), released in December 2025 by the OWASP GenAI Security Project's Agentic Security Initiative, gives the field a shared vocabulary for the rest of the problem. It should not become another list to memorize. For a leader the ten entries, ASI01 through ASI10, make more sense in four groups.

Control of the agent's purpose and behavior. *Agent Goal Hijack* (ASI01) is the redirection of an agent's objective, plan, or decisions through manipulated prompts, documents, tool output, peer-agent messages, or other untrusted content. Prompt injection is a common route into that failure, and the distinction matters: injection manipulates the model through its inputs and may alter an answer, an action, or later behavior; goal hijack redirects the agent's objective, plan, or decisions across multiple steps — potentially through content the agent merely reads rather than an instruction anyone typed.

Memory and Context Poisoning (ASI06) makes that persist: false or malicious information written into memory, summaries, retrieval stores, or shared context influences later tasks after the original input is gone. *Rogue Agents* (ASI10) covers agents that depart from their intended function or authorized scope and keep acting. "Rogue" here requires no science fiction, a compromised, poisoned, misconfigured, or behaviorally divergent agent operating outside its approved boundary is enough, and each individual action may still look permissible.

The power to act. *Tool Misuse and Exploitation* (ASI02) appears when a legitimate tool is invoked for the wrong purpose, with unsafe parameters, in an unsafe sequence, or without the authorization the action deserves. *Identity and Privilege Abuse* (ASI03) appears when an agent holds excessive, inherited, stale, or transferable permissions, or when delegation lets one agent quietly exercise another user's or agent's authority. *Unexpected Code Execution* (ASI05) appears when generated content, tool output, or an integration path leads to commands running outside the intended boundary.

This is where the blast radius lives, and it is worth being blunt about the implications. A well-written system prompt cannot compensate for an agent running under an administrator's standing credential. A content filter cannot make unrestricted shell access safe. A human approval box does not help if it says only "Allow?" and hides which data will move and which system will change. Decide deliberately whether the agent acts with its own permissions or the calling user's, because "acts as a powerful service account on a user's behalf" is how a modest request quietly inherits broad power.

Treat the agent as a managed non-human identity: its own identity where practical, permission scoped to task, resource, action, and duration, short-lived credentials rather than standing secrets, and consequential steps re-authorized rather than assumed to be covered by approval of the original request. And treat generated code and commands as untrusted output, separate generation from execution, isolate the runtime, restrict filesystem and network access, and remove the capability entirely where the use case does not need it.

The agentic ecosystem. *Agentic Supply Chain Vulnerabilities* (ASI04) extend supply-chain risk to models, orchestration frameworks, prompts, tools, plug-ins, agent registries, capability descriptors, memory components, and other runtime dependencies. *Insecure Inter-Agent Communication* (ASI07) covers weak authentication, authorization, integrity, or validation between agents. *Cascading Failures* (ASI08) describe what follows when one bad input, poisoned memory, compromised tool, or faulty decision spreads across agents and workflows into system-wide harm.

Traditional supply-chain thinking asks whether a component came from a trustworthy source. Agentic systems add a runtime question: is this still the same tool, server, prompt, agent, or capability description we approved, and is it behaving inside the boundary we expected? An agent may discover a tool dynamically, select a peer based on a capability claim, or find that a server has changed what it exposes. The dependency is no longer only what was built into the release; it can appear or change while the system is running.

So use curated registries and explicit allowlists for sensitive environments, verify provenance and ownership before enabling a tool or peer, record changes in capability and permission, and keep an emergency way to disable a compromised connection. Then design for containment: limit fan-out, delegation depth, retries, cost, concurrency, and execution time, and require a fresh authorization decision when a task crosses a trust domain. A circuit breaker that stops a cascade is worth more than a beautiful trace explaining it afterward.

The human. *Human-Agent Trust Exploitation* (ASI09) captures the way a fluent, confident, personalized agent can persuade a person to disclose information, approve an unsafe action, or accept a recommendation without independent validation. Human oversight is necessary and still attackable. An agent can frame the request, choose what evidence to show, create urgency, or bury the consequential part inside a long explanation, and the person may technically approve while understanding very little.

For approval to mean anything, show the proposed action, target, identity, data involved, expected consequence, and whether it can be reversed. Separate the agent's recommendation from the evidence used to authorize it. And for high-impact actions use an approval path the agent cannot rewrite through persuasive language. Otherwise the human in the loop this chapter has recommended becomes an approval ritual rather than a safeguard.

Connections between agents: familiar trust questions, new plumbing

Two protocol names increasingly appear in agentic architecture. The **Model Context Protocol (MCP)** standardizes how an AI application connects to external capabilities, in practice, how an agent reaches the systems around it. **Agent2Agent (A2A)** standardizes communication between independent agents, in practice, how one agent works with another. They are complementary rather than competing, and they can operate together, with an agent receiving delegated work through one and using tools reached through the other.

Both improve interoperability. Neither makes any participant trustworthy, and that distinction is the whole of the security point. The specifications support security mechanisms; implementations and deployments still have to establish trust.

The failure modes are already documented. A server can describe a tool honestly, incorrectly, or maliciously. Descriptors, schemas, and routing metadata can be poisoned so an agent invokes a tool on the strength of a falsified capability. A registry or management server can be compromised and serve tampered components at scale. In agent-to-agent settings, a rogue peer can advertise exaggerated capabilities in its published agent record, and an attacker can register a fake peer in a discovery service using a cloned schema to intercept privileged coordination traffic.

So treat every such connection as a trust relationship and every exposed tool as an executable capability. Approve the server and its owner. Inventory what it exposes. Constrain the data and actions reachable through it. Authorize the specific skill, action, and data rather than merely the connection, and avoid passing one broad credential through a chain of services. Enforce which protocol versions and peers are acceptable rather than accepting whatever presents itself. Log discovery as well as invocation. A tool name, an agent card, or a capability description is metadata, not proof of safety and not a security assessment.

The most important architectural question is lineage. When an action happens, can you reconstruct which user or service initiated the goal, which agent planned it, which peers contributed, which tools were called, which identity authorized each step, what data moved, and where a human approved or intervened? If that answer disappears halfway through a chain of agents, accountability disappeared with it.

The core agentic control set

The controls underneath agentic security are recognizable rather than exotic.

- **Constrain the goal.** Define the approved purpose, prohibited outcomes, and the conditions requiring a stop or fresh approval.
- **Apply least agency and least privilege.** Grant only the autonomy the use case needs, and give each agent a managed identity with task-scoped, time-bound access.
- **Authorize the action, not just the session.** Re-check consequential tool calls, privilege changes, external transfers, and delegation across trust boundaries.
- **Treat plans and outputs as untrusted.** Validate tool parameters, generated code, messages, and downstream use.
- **Control tools and peers.** Approve sources, verify provenance, inventory capabilities, and monitor for change.
- **Protect memory and context.** Control what may write to persistent memory, preserve provenance, and be able to expire, isolate, or reset it.
- **Sandbox execution.** Restrict filesystem, network, process, and secret access, and separate generation from execution.
- **Bound the run.** Limit steps, time, cost, retries, tool calls, delegation depth, and concurrency.

- **Make approval meaningful.** Show what will happen, under whose authority, to which data and system, and whether it can be reversed.
- **Keep lineage.** Correlate goals, identities, messages, tool calls, memory changes, approvals, and outcomes.
- **Build graded stop controls.** Be able to revoke an identity, disable a tool or connection, quarantine memory, stop delegation, block outbound traffic (egress), and move to a safe mode.

The model will remain probabilistic. The safety boundary should not be.

When the Attacker Has AI Too: Fraud, Account Takeover, and Impersonation

Everything to this point has been about the AI system you deploy. How it fails, how it is attacked, what it can be talked into doing. Turn the telescope around. AI does not need any access to your systems to hurt you. Sometimes the model sits entirely on the attacker's side, and the only thing that reaches you is the output.

It writes the message and translates it cleanly. It studies an executive's public speaking and imitates the phrasing. It produces the profile photograph, clones the familiar voice, generates a plausible identity document, or keeps a convincing chat going long enough for someone to move money or hand over an account. The target may never knowingly interact with an AI system at all. What reaches them is an email, a phone call, a video meeting, a support chat, a social profile, a search result, or a website that feels ordinary enough to trust.

I want to be careful about the boundary here, because it is easy to get wrong in a way that helps no one. AI-enabled fraud is not automatically an "AI security" incident, and it should not land on the AI governance team's desk simply because synthetic media was involved. The attack usually arrives in a process you already own or influence: identity proofing, authentication, account recovery, payment approval, supplier changes, customer support, brand protection, awareness, fraud detection, incident response. What AI changes is the quality, speed, personalization, and scale of the deception. It does not remove the need for any of those controls. It raises the bar each of them has to clear.

What AI changes, and what it doesn't

Fraud has always run on a believable story and a gap in verification. The chief executive needs an urgent payment. The supplier has new bank details. The help desk gets a call from an employee who has lost their phone. The customer is warned their account is under attack and must be "secured" right now. A support page asks them to sign in. None of these ideas is new. AI makes them easier to produce, harder to dismiss on sight, and cheaper to run at volume.

The tells we quietly relied on are fading. The awkward grammar, the generic greeting, the mismatched photo, the wrong-sounding voice. These were never real controls, just friction that let a careful person catch the obvious fakes. An attacker can now generate polished text in the target's language, hold a patient conversation, imitate a writing style, produce a believable face, and add audio or video when the victim asks for proof. Public talks, earnings calls, interviews, podcasts, and employee profiles can supply useful material for the imitation.

The FBI's 3 December 2024 public alert *Criminals Use Generative Artificial Intelligence to Facilitate Financial Fraud* (Alert I-120324-PSA) reads like a catalog of exactly this: AI-written text for fraudulent profiles, investment-scam sites, and chatbots that steer people toward malicious links; AI images for romance-scam photos, forged identification, and fake-charity appeals; cloned audio impersonating a relative in distress or a customer calling the bank; and AI video for real-time calls that impersonate an executive.

None of that means every attempt is now a flawless deepfake. Plenty are still crude, and basic awareness still stops a lot of them. The leadership mistake is designing the control as though poor quality will stay the attacker's problem. It will not. So authenticity can no longer rest on how real a communication feels. A familiar voice is a claim. A recognizable face on a video call is a claim. A message arriving inside an existing thread is stronger evidence, but even that can follow an account compromise. The control has to confirm the person, the authority, and the transaction through something the suspicious communication does not control.

One attack, several routes through the organization

The same deception takes different paths depending on what the attacker is after, and it helps to see them as distinct, because they land on different controls.

Business-process impersonation targets authority. The attacker poses as an executive, a supplier, an employee, an adviser, a regulator, a customer, or a bank, and asks for a payment, a change of bank details, a disclosure, a new account, an authenticator reset, or an exception to the normal process. AI-generated text makes the request fit the relationship; cloned audio or synthetic video gets added when the recipient wants reassurance. The attacker is not defeating encryption. They are persuading someone who has legitimate access to use it wrongly.

Account takeover targets control of an existing identity. Credentials get stolen through a fake sign-in page, malware, credential stuffing, where passwords leaked from one breach are replayed against your logins, or a convincing call; a one-time code gets relayed through a fake support line; a push prompt gets fatigued into approval; a session gets stolen after authentication; a new authenticator gets bound or a recovery address changed. Once an attacker is inside a real mailbox or collaboration account, they inherit more than data. They inherit trust, conversation history, contacts, and the ability to make the next impersonation arrive from exactly the account the victim expects.

Identity-proofing fraud targets the moment you decide a new or returning person is who they claim to be. Generated or altered documents, synthetic faces, virtual cameras, injected video, and manipulated biometric samples are used to open an account or recover one. This is not only a consumer-platform problem. Remote employee onboarding, contractor access, privileged-user recovery, customer enrollment, benefits, and support-assisted verification all rest on some form of proofing.

Brand abuse borrows your reputation without ever entering your environment. Lookalike domains, cloned sites, fraudulent search ads, fake mobile apps, counterfeit social profiles, and bogus support numbers convince people they are dealing with you. AI helps build the site, fill it with credible content, staff it with a chatbot, and adapt the conversation. The loss may happen in a customer's account or on a platform you do not control, but the customer harm, the response cost, and the erosion of trust are still yours.

These routes chain together, which is the part a siloed view misses. A fake brand page harvests a credential. The credential opens an account. The account is used to impersonate a trusted employee. That impersonation changes a supplier's payment details. Treating each event as a separate phishing report, login alert, brand complaint, and finance exception is how an organization looks at four pieces of one attack and sees four unrelated tickets.

Voice and video cannot carry approval on their own

Plenty of organizations have an informal rule that sounds sensible: if the email looks odd, call the person; if the request is sensitive, get them on video. That is still better than replying to the suspicious message. It stops being a control the moment the call goes to a number supplied in that message, or the video meeting is arranged through the same unverified channel because the attacker is happy to appear on camera now.

Independent verification means leaving the path the attacker controls. Use a number already held in the corporate directory, the supplier master, or the customer record. Start a fresh conversation through a known-good account. Use an approved workflow that identifies the requester and shows their authority. And for the actions that actually matter, require a second approver whose evidence comes from a different path.

The goal is not to put friction in front of every ordinary interaction. It is to name the transactions where a false identity does material harm, new or changed payment destinations, release of sensitive data, creation or recovery of privileged access, changes to contact details, enrollment of a new device, unusual transfers, payroll changes, or any bypass of an established control, and to protect those.

For them, confirming the *transaction* matters as much as confirming the person, because even a real executive can be mistaken about what an attacker has put in front of them. The approver should see what will change, the destination, the amount or data involved, the source of the request, and whether it can be reversed. "I spoke to her and she sounded right" is not a control record.

Account recovery is an authentication ceremony

Organizations tend to protect the front-door login carefully and then build a friendlier way around it, because people genuinely do lose devices and forget passwords. That friendlier path is exactly where an attacker goes when the front door is strong. Treat authenticator replacement, password reset, recovery-address change, device enrollment, and help-desk override as security-sensitive transactions in their own right. NIST's authenticator guidance (SP 800-63B-4) handles account recovery and account notifications as managed processes for precisely this reason. Recovery is not an afterthought to authentication, it is part of it. Strong authentication with weak recovery is weak authentication, and the control should scale to the account's consequence, not to how frustrated the caller sounds.

The same guidance is refreshingly blunt about what "strong" means against an attacker with AI. It states plainly that passwords, look-up secrets, out-of-band authentication, and one-time password (OTP) authentication are *not* phishing-resistant. Each can expose or relay a valid secret or authenticator output to an impostor verifier, which is precisely the outcome that convincing phishing sites, messages, and calls are designed to produce. It requires verifiers to offer at least one phishing-resistant option at authenticator assurance level 2 (AAL2) and requires phishing resistance outright at level 3 (AAL3), where the authenticator's private key must be non-exportable. Those are federal assurance requirements, not a claim that every private organization must adopt AAL2, AAL3, or every normative provision in the guidelines.

The leadership principle still travels: phishing-resistant cryptographic authentication binds the login to the legitimate site instead of asking a hurried person to notice that the site is fake, which is why it, and not more vigilance, is the real answer to AI-written phishing. For employees, administrators, finance users, and developers, move the high-consequence identities toward phishing-resistant authentication and keep the weaker methods from quietly becoming the fallback that undoes the whole effort. For customers, apply the same logic to consequence and usability: offer stronger authenticators, protect enrollment and recovery, notify the legitimate user when an authenticator or recovery method changes, and make compromise easy to report.

And do not stop at the login. Watch for a new device followed by a sensitive action, a recovery immediately followed by a payout change, an unusual session that binds a new authenticator, a support call followed by a credential reset, or a valid session behaving unlike the account it belongs to. Fraud often begins at authentication, but the loss happens in the transaction that follows.

Remote identity proofing needs more than a face match

A face that matches an identity document is useful evidence. It is not proof that the camera is genuine, that the document is genuine, or that the image reached the comparison service without substitution. SP 800-63A-4 addresses this directly in its treatment of digital-injection prevention and forged-media detection. It describes injection attacks that place modified or forged media between the capture device and the comparison component.

When biometric characteristics are collected and compared remotely, the guidance requires presentation-attack detection. For remote proofing that uses optical capture, it also requires analysis of submitted media and testing of automated analysis against available genuine and forged or manipulated samples. Separately, it recommends looking for signatures associated with known generative-AI algorithms and deepfake tools. Underlying identity attributes still have to be validated through authoritative or credible sources rather than trusted because the document or person looks convincing.

The leader-level lesson is layered verification, not a single clever detector. Validate the identity evidence against authoritative sources. Raise your confidence that the media came from a genuine capture device rather than a virtual camera or an injected stream. Protect the channel between capture and comparison. Test presentation-attack and media-analysis controls against both genuine and manipulated samples, and look at the false positives as hard as the false negatives, because a control that rejects real people is its own kind of failure.

Use human review to cover the limits of automated detection, and keep a path for investigation and redress when fraud is suspected. Deepfake detection is a useful signal inside that stack; it is not an oracle, and a detector that emits a score with no documented decision process has just moved the trust problem to another algorithm.

The privacy side travels with all of this. Proofing collects identity documents, facial images, video, and device data, sensitive material by any measure. Fraud prevention does not suspend purpose limitation, access control, retention limits, deletion, transparency, or the need for an accessible alternative when the standard process fails a legitimate applicant. A stronger proofing process that quietly becomes a permanent biometric archive has simply traded one risk for another.

Protect the transaction, not only the login

Some fraud gets past authentication because the legitimate account holder is being manipulated in real time. Some begins from an already-compromised account. Either way, the controls have to sit around the action as well as the identity. For material payments and sensitive changes, that means independent callback to a known contact, dual authorization, separation between creating and approving a payee, cooling-off periods on unusual changes, limits that rise gradually rather than all at once, confirmation to an address already on file, and review of anything that deviates from the account's normal behavior. The exact mix depends on the business. The principle does not: a convincing request should never be able to rewrite its own verification path.

This is also where awareness earns its keep, but only when it is specific. "Watch out for deepfakes" is not something a busy accounts-payable analyst can act on. "Never use the contact details in a bank-change request; verify through the supplier record and note who confirmed it" is. "Never read out a one-time code" beats "be alert to suspicious calls." "A video call does not replace the payment-approval workflow" is clearer than asking people to study facial shadows. Teach the action that survives a better fake: pause, leave the channel, verify independently, use the approved workflow, and report it quickly. The human layer is strongest when the person has a usable process to fall back on rather than a perception skill to lose.

Brand protection is part of the attack surface

Security teams are used to defending assets the organization owns. Brand abuse happens on someone else's infrastructure, domains, ad platforms, app stores, social networks, messaging services, telephone networks. So the control is a different shape: preparation, monitoring, evidence, relationships, and speed rather than patching. Know the legitimate presence you have to defend, your domains and their common lookalikes, your approved social accounts, your apps, your support numbers, your executive profiles, and the third parties allowed to speak in your name.

Use the email-authentication standards that let receiving servers check that mail really came from your domain (SPF, DKIM, DMARC) on the domains you operate, while being honest that it does not stop every lookalike domain or a compromised legitimate account. Monitor for impersonation where the consequence justifies it. Make reporting easy for employees, customers, suppliers, and researchers. And pre-establish the takedown and escalation paths with registrars, hosts, platforms, ad networks, app stores, and telecom providers, because the middle of an incident is a bad time to learn who to email.

Speed matters, because a fraudulent site or profile does real damage during the argument over who owns the ticket. The runbook should already say who preserves evidence, who requests takedown, who warns affected customers or suppliers, who coordinates with banks or payment providers, and who decides whether a public warning is warranted. And do not let takedown become the only measure of success, the same campaign may return quickly under another domain, account, advertisement, or telephone number. Track the infrastructure, lures, payment destinations, accounts, and behavior that connect the attempts, because brand intelligence becomes security intelligence the moment it reaches the people who can block an authentication, a payment, a message, or an access request.

Join the signals before the attacker does

Fraud crosses teams because the attacker follows the easiest route, not your org chart. Security operations sees a suspicious login. Support sees a recovery request. Finance sees a bank-detail change. Brand protection finds a cloned site. An employee reports a voicemail from the "CEO." Each signal looks inconclusive alone; together they can describe one live campaign. So build the route for those signals to meet. That does not mean moving every fraud function under the CISO.

It means shared severity criteria, named contacts, compatible case identifiers, agreed evidence handling, and an escalation path that works at 2 a.m. In a smaller organization that can be a single cross-functional runbook and a short contact list, which still beats five teams opening five unrelated tickets. It is also the same coordination NIST's identity guidance calls for when it puts identity, fraud, and threat-intelligence functions in the same conversation rather than separate lanes because AI-enabled fraud is precisely the threat that punishes organizations for keeping them apart.

When an event is confirmed, contain the harm, not just the technology. Revoke sessions and compromised authenticators. Freeze or recall transactions where you still can. Secure the affected mailboxes and recovery channels. Block the malicious domains, numbers, apps, and accounts. Preserve the messages, headers, recordings, account changes, approval records, and transaction details. Notify the affected people through a channel they can trust. Coordinate with financial institutions, insurers, platforms, law enforcement, and regulators as the event and the jurisdiction require.

And remember that recovery includes restoring trust in the legitimate channel: a customer whose account was taken over needs more than a password reset; a supplier who was impersonated needs their verified contact details reinstated; an executive whose voice was cloned may need a communications plan; a brand that was cloned has to tell people where the real service lives. Fraud response is not finished until the unsafe path is closed and the legitimate relationship can operate safely again.

The control set that survives a better fake

The through-line is simple: AI has weakened the informal evidence people leaned on, clean writing, a familiar face, a known voice, a plausible document, so the defense has to rest on controls that never depended on that evidence in the first place.

- **Verify through an independent path.** Never let a suspicious request supply the contact details, meeting link, or recovery method used to check it.
- **Use phishing-resistant authentication where consequence warrants it.** Do not present relayable codes as equivalent protection; keep weaker methods from becoming the ungoverned fallback.
- **Protect authenticator binding and recovery.** Treat new-device enrollment, resets, recovery-channel changes, and help-desk overrides as high-risk events, with notification to the legitimate user.
- **Verify sensitive transactions, not only identities.** Show the approver exactly what will change, and use dual control or separation of duties where the harm justifies it.
- **Layer remote identity proofing.** Combine evidence validation against authoritative sources, capture integrity, injection and manipulated-media controls, protected channels, human review, and a fraud-investigation path.
- **Detect behavior after authentication.** Correlate identity, device, session, recovery, and transaction signals rather than trusting a clean login.

- **Prepare for brand abuse outside the perimeter.** Inventory the legitimate presence, monitor proportionately, harden email authentication, and pre-build reporting and takedown routes.
- **Make reporting easy and response cross-functional.** Connect security, fraud, finance, customer operations, HR, legal, communications, and brand owners before an incident, not during one.

AI will keep making synthetic content better. Your controls should not require it to stay bad.

Overreliance: The Confident Wrong Answer

The last threat is not an attacker at all. It is us. These models are fluent, and fluency reads as competence. A confident, well-structured, completely wrong answer is more dangerous than an obviously broken one, because people act on it. Automation bias, the human tendency to trust a machine's output more than our own judgment, does the rest. Someone accepts a fabricated citation, a wrong number, a plausible-sounding summary that missed the one clause that mattered, and the error propagates because a person signed off on it without checking.

This is why human oversight keeps appearing in governance evidence, and it is why it is not a formality. The goal is not a model that never errs; that model does not exist. The goal is to design the use case so a wrong answer gets caught before it does harm. That is partly design — surfacing uncertainty, citing sources, and making it easy to verify rather than just trust — and partly culture: training people to treat AI output as a capable draft rather than a finished answer, especially when the output feeds a decision that matters. The sharpest way to size a use case is to ask what happens when the model is wrong.

If the answer is "nothing much," it is low-risk. If the answer is "a customer is harmed, a payment is approved, a regulator is misled, or an incident is mishandled," the reliance needs controls the fluent answer will never provide on its own. The model is a fast, tireless, confident colleague who is sometimes confidently wrong and will never tell you which time this is. And a citation is not grounding: a model can invent a reference or cite a real source that does not support the claim, so a footnote is a prompt to verify that the source exists, that the user was allowed to see it, and that it says what the answer claims. It is not a substitute for having checked.

The Threat Surface at a Glance

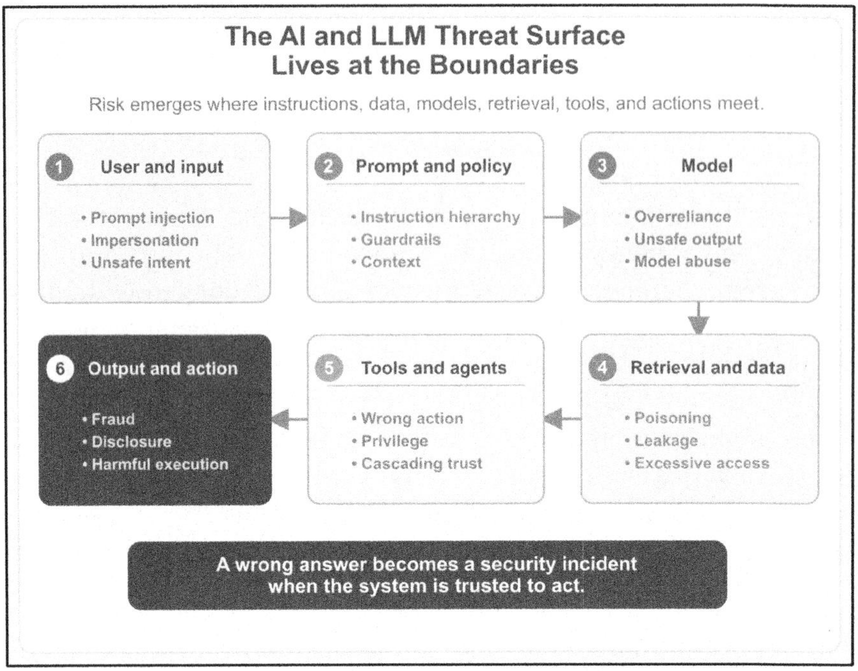

The families overlap and reinforce each other, but it helps to see them against the controls they slip past. The table is illustrative rather than a complete threat model, and it maps loosely to the OWASP list rather than reproducing all ten.

Threat family	What it is	Why your existing controls do not fully catch it
Prompt injection	Crafted input (direct, or hidden in content the model reads) that redirects the model's behavior	The model cannot reliably separate "content to analyze" from "command to obey"; input validation cannot cover free-form language
Data leakage / disclosure	The model reveals sensitive data, its own instructions, or content the user was not authorized to see	A new exit path that many existing data loss prevention (DLP) patterns were not designed to see; output is generated, not retrieved from a controllable store
Insecure retrieval (RAG)	Weak authorization at retrieval, poisoned corpus content, or a derived index that outlives the source's permissions	The model bypasses access controls by assembling answers from documents the user could not open; "our own data" is treated as trusted when it is not
Input / data poisoning	Manipulation through the material the model consumes, tool output, and (where you own them) training, fine-tuning, and feedback data	"Don't trust user input" was scoped to the user; these channels were not in the threat model, and poisoned training bakes the flaw into default behavior
Excessive agency (agentic AI)	An agent granted more capability or permission than the task needs, especially combined with injection	Least privilege still applies, but the permission boundary now has to hold against a model that can be manipulated through language, where a bad answer becomes a real action
Overreliance	People trusting fluent, confident output that is wrong, invented, or manipulated	No technical control catches a human accepting a plausible answer; the failure is in judgment, not the stack

Threat family	What it is	Why your existing controls do not fully catch it
Unbounded consumption	An agent loop, runaway tool chain, or high-volume attacker that exhausts compute, tokens, or budget, resource and cost exhaustion, denial-of-wallet	Ordinary rate limits may miss recursive agents, non-terminating tool chains, and metered-cost abuse; the harm is availability and cost, not confidentiality

Industry Pattern — The Assistant That Read Past Every Permission Boundary

> *A pattern the industry has watched play out more than once looks something like this. A team builds an internal assistant on top of the company's own documents, a genuinely good idea, the kind that saves people real time. It connects the model to a shared knowledge store so it can answer questions grounded in actual company material. It works, people love it, adoption climbs.*
>
> *Then someone asks it a question and gets back a clean, confident answer built from a document they were never supposed to see. Not because anyone attacked it, but because the retrieval layer pulled whatever was relevant and the model helpfully summarized it, and nobody had wired the user's permissions into the retrieval step. The documents had come from several repositories: some open internally, some restricted, some carrying HR or customer material, some old exports from systems whose permissions never traveled with the content into the index. The access controls that governed the originals simply did not come along for the ride. The assistant had, in effect, become a polite way to read past every permission boundary in the building.*
>
> *The instructive part is not the mistake; it is how ordinary it was. No villain, no exotic exploit, just a powerful feature shipped a step ahead of the boring control that should have sat underneath it. That is the texture of most AI incidents at this stage. Not clever adversaries defeating strong defenses, but useful systems deployed before anyone asked the unglamorous questions: what can this reach, on whose behalf, and what happens when it is wrong.*

What Evidence Should You Expect

The threat surface is defended at design time, so the evidence is architectural, proof that someone asked how each AI system could be manipulated and built accordingly, rather than shipping and hoping. A CISO should expect to see:

- threat-modeling records for AI systems. Evidence the failure modes above were considered for the specific use case, including a misuse- and abuse-case catalog for the high-impact ones, rather than assumed away;

- architecture and data-flow records showing the model, application, data sources, retrieval layer, tools, and users, and where prompts and outputs travel;
- input-handling controls: how untrusted content reaching the model is constrained, and what the model is prevented from doing regardless of what it is told;
- output-handling controls: evidence that model output is treated as untrusted before it is displayed, stored, or acted on, including validation or human review for high-impact outputs;
- retrieval authorization records: proof that RAG systems enforce per-user access at retrieval time, ideally tested with users at different access levels, showing the model cannot return what a given user could not reach directly;
- corpus and index integrity controls: how the content a model retrieves from is protected against poisoning, who can add to it, and how the derived index or embeddings are kept in sync when source access or the source document changes;
- tool and agent permission scoping: the least-privilege boundary for any agentic system, which tools it can call, which actions each allows, whether it acts as the user or a service account, plus tool-call logs and approval records for consequential actions;
- an agentic architecture record, the goal, orchestrator, agent identities, tools, connected servers, peer agents, memory, data stores, trust boundaries, approval points, and containment paths;
- an agent capability and connection inventory, approved tools, servers, peer agents, discovery source, owner, provenance, permissions, support status, and emergency-disable method;
- managed non-human identity records for agents, credential source, scopes, duration, delegation rules, rotation,

revocation, and whether the agent acts as itself or on behalf of a user;

- persistent-memory controls, what may be written, which sources are trusted, how provenance is retained, how entries expire or are corrected, and how memory can be isolated or reset after suspected poisoning;
- execution-boundary evidence for agents that can run code, sandbox, filesystem, egress, secret-access, resource-budget, and approval controls;
- inter-agent security records. How agents authenticate, how messages are protected and validated, how authority and originating purpose survive delegation, and how communication or discovery can be disabled;
- end-to-end lineage, showing a consequential action traced from the initiating identity through agent decisions, peer messages, tool calls, permissions, approvals, and outcome;
- human-in-the-loop requirements for consequential or irreversible actions, tied to the use case's risk tier;
- an AI-enabled fraud and impersonation threat model, connecting executive and supplier impersonation, account takeover, remote identity proofing, customer-support abuse, and brand abuse to the specific business transactions each route could influence;
- a phishing-resistant authentication roadmap for high-impact workforce and customer identities, naming the systems still dependent on relayable codes and the controls that keep weaker methods from becoming an ungoverned fallback;
- authenticator-binding and account-recovery evidence. Verification, user notification, help-desk override, recovery-channel change, new-device enrollment, revocation, and a fast compromise-reporting path;
- remote identity-proofing records, evidence validation against authoritative sources, capture integrity, protected channels,

injection- and forged-media testing, detector performance including false-positive impact, manual-review criteria, privacy handling, and an investigation or redress path;

- sensitive-transaction verification records for payment, bank-detail, payroll, privileged-access, recovery, and high-risk data-release changes, with independent confirmation and separation of duties where the harm justifies it;
- account-takeover detection tied to post-authentication behavior. Payee and contact-detail changes, anomalous exports, impossible-travel and session anomalies, not only to a successful login;
- brand-abuse readiness, an inventory of legitimate domains, accounts, apps, and support numbers, lookalike monitoring, email-authentication posture, reporting routes, evidence-preservation and external-escalation contacts, rehearsed takedown, and named customer-warning authority;
- joined fraud telemetry and case records, correlating authentication, session, recovery, customer-support, transaction, brand, messaging, and employee-reporting signals into one view;
- a cross-functional fraud-response runbook. Naming the roles that can revoke access, freeze or recall transactions, contact affected parties, preserve evidence, request takedown, and coordinate with financial institutions, platforms, insurers, law enforcement, regulators, and communications;
- role-specific awareness material that teaches employees to leave the suspicious channel and use an approved verification process rather than relying on their ability to recognize synthetic media;
- and outcome-oriented measures, time to revoke a compromised authenticator, time to freeze a suspicious transaction, time to obtain a takedown or publish a trusted warning, recovery-related fraud, and repeat campaigns, not only the count of suspicious messages blocked.

- model and guardrail configuration records, the system prompts or instruction sets, guardrail settings, and approved change history for each system, with sensitive prompt text protected, so behavior can be investigated without broadcasting the instructions;
- adversarial-input test evidence, records of prompt-injection and misuse testing done before and during deployment, with the remediation decisions that followed (the ongoing red-team program itself is covered in Chapter 4);
- prompt and output logging: enough record of what went in and came out to investigate later, with retention limits, access review, and appropriate privacy handling applied to those logs;
- data-handling records for what enters the model, connecting to the privacy program rather than duplicating it;
- and exception and risk-acceptance records for threat-surface risks that were understood but not fully resolved, the same discipline you apply everywhere else.

For a small or mid-sized organization, start with the practical minimum: an architecture and data-flow record for each AI use case, a use-case threat model, a RAG source inventory, evidence that retrieval enforces permissions, some prompt-injection testing, a tool-permission review, prompt and output logging rules, and human review for high-impact output. You do not need perfection to start. You need visibility into where the AI can see, speak, and act. The operational counterparts — red-teaming the model, monitoring it in production, and running an AI incident when something slips through — generate their own evidence: test results, monitoring records, and incident records.

Reality Check

> *For every AI feature you have approved, you can probably say what data it can see. Here is the harder question: can you say what it is allowed to do if it is manipulated? Not what it is designed to do on a good day, what it can do on a bad one, when the input is hostile and the model does what the input says. What can it reach, what can it trigger, whose permissions does it borrow, and where does a wrong answer turn into a wrong action?*
>
> *If the answer is "it just answers questions," the execution risk may be bounded, but disclosure, manipulation, and overreliance still depend on who receives the answer and what decisions it influences. If the answer involves tools, actions, integrations, or your internal data, then you are no longer governing a chatbot alone. You are governing something that can act, and the injection and agency risks above are yours to own. It may still be a perfectly good use case; it may still be fine to run as a constrained, low-risk pilot. But it should not drift quietly into a sensitive workflow while everyone is still discovering how it behaves. The teams that get burned are usually the ones who evaluated the feature by what it does when everything goes right.*

What This Means for You as a Security Leader

The mental shift this chapter asks for is small to state and hard to internalize: treat the model's inputs as an attack surface, treat its outputs as untrusted until proven otherwise, and treat whatever it is allowed to do as your real blast radius. Your appsec instincts are half-right, and knowing which half is the whole skill. The infrastructure, identity, network, logging, and supply-chain discipline you already run still carries the system around the model, and you should lean on it hard. What it does not cover is the model itself, a component that cannot cleanly separate data from instruction, whose output you cannot fully trust, and which becomes genuinely dangerous the moment you let it act.

This is also why the risk cuts across so many owners. Some of it is appsec, some is data governance, some is privacy, some is cloud and platform, some is product, and a fair amount is legal and compliance. No single team owns "AI security," which means the CISO's real job here is to make the risk visible enough that ownership can actually be assigned, and to refuse two easy outs. Do not accept "it's just a chatbot" without hearing what the chatbot can see and do, and do not accept "the model is secure" from a vendor when the real exposure is your data, your permissions, your retrieval layer, your logs, and your people trusting the output.

You do not need to become a machine-learning expert to lead here. You need to ask the questions that expose the real exposure, what the system reads, what it can be made to do, whose data it can reach, and what happens when it is wrong, and to insist that the boring controls underneath the exciting feature actually got built. The organizations that struggle will not be the ones that could not understand the technology. They will be the ones that were so impressed by what the AI could do that they never asked what it could be made to do.

Bridge to Chapter 3

Threat knowledge becomes a working program through inventory, intake, shadow-AI discovery, vendor review, and data rules people can follow.

CHAPTER 3

AI Governance in Practice

The policy was the easy part.

Ask a room full of security leaders whether they have an AI policy, and most of the hands go up. Ask the same room how many AI tools their organization is actually using, counting the ones that arrived as features inside the software-as-a-service tools they already pay for, the ones a developer wired in through an API last quarter, and the ones individual people signed up for on a Tuesday afternoon because it saved them an hour, and the hands come down. That gap, between having a policy and knowing what you are actually governing, is where this chapter lives.

This chapter is the program: the unglamorous operational machinery that turns "we should govern AI" into "we do." It is procedural because that is what the job actually demands at this altitude. Governance you cannot operate is just a document with good intentions.

A quick boundary, because this Part divides related work carefully. The frameworks and attack mechanics remain necessary context, but the work here begins after those questions are understood. This chapter builds the governance program: how AI use enters, becomes visible, gets classified and owned, and reaches an accountable decision. Adversarial testing, production monitoring, and AI incident response sit outside that program boundary.

Where AI touches personal data, the privacy discipline lives in Volume III, Part 2. Where it arrives through a vendor, the supplier-assurance program still applies. Here, the job is the AI governance program itself, and underneath all its moving parts it comes down to four things: make the use visible, sort it by risk, give it owners, and build a path people will actually take. Everything else is detail hanging off those four.

You Can't Govern What You Can't See

The first job is an inventory, and it is harder than it sounds, not because AI is exotic, but because of how it arrives. Formally managed systems usually leave a trail, procurement, architecture, an identity record, a change request. AI often enters through routes where that trail is thin: an embedded SaaS feature, an individual subscription, an API a developer added, a browser tool. Shadow IT and rogue SaaS did some of this long before AI; AI just does it faster and in more places. There is rarely a moment where anyone declares "we are now deploying an AI system." It just accretes.

So when you go looking, you find AI in more places than anyone told you about. Employees are using public assistants for real work. A SaaS product you have licensed for years quietly grew an AI feature in its last release, and it is on by default. A team stitched a model into a workflow through an API. Your own product added an AI capability that marketing is excited about and nobody in security has reviewed. And underneath all of it, your vendors are adding AI to their products, which means AI is entering your environment through supply chains you do not directly control.

You cannot manage that by intuition, so you build an inventory, and you build it three ways at once. You ask, surveys, an intake process, a simple "tell us what you're using" that people can actually complete. You look, procurement and expense data show what got bought, SaaS admin consoles and single sign-on (SSO) logs show what has been connected, network and cloud access security broker (CASB) signals show what is being reached, endpoint and browser telemetry show where people actually go, and vendor release notes show the AI that appeared inside tools you already run.

And you keep it living, because an AI inventory is not a project you finish; it is a register you maintain, since the picture changes month to month as vendors ship features and teams try new things. A good register does not just list the tool; it captures who owns the use case, what data goes in, whether output reaches customers or drives decisions, whether it connects to internal systems, and what risk tier it landed in. But do not wait for that fuller picture before you start governing. An imperfect list of what you are actually using beats an elegant policy governing nothing.

An Agent Register Needs More Than a Tool Name

An ordinary AI inventory asks what tool is in use, who owns the use case, what data enters it, and how the output is used. An agentic inventory has to go further, because the risk is carried by authority and connection rather than by the model alone.

Before any of that, though, ask the question that is cheapest to act on: **does this need to be an agent?** Autonomy is a design choice, not a property of the technology, and a great many proposals that arrive described as agents are workflows that would be safer, cheaper, and more predictable as a scripted integration with a model call inside it. Asking early avoids securing capability nobody needed.

Where the answer is genuinely yes, capture for each material agent or agentic workflow: the business goal and accountable owner; the level of autonomy approved; the agent's identity and whose authority it can exercise; the data, systems, and tools it can reach; any external tool servers, plug-ins, or local capabilities connected to it; any peer agents, registries, or discovery mechanisms it can use; what it remembers, where that memory lives, and who can write to it; whether it can generate or execute code; which actions require human approval; limits on time, steps, cost, retries, delegation, and concurrency; the maximum credible consequence of an incorrect or manipulated action; and how the agent, connection, credential, tool, or memory can be disabled.

This is not an inventory of every experimental script a developer runs. Start with agents that reach sensitive data, production systems, customer workflows, privileged tools, money movement, code repositories, communications, physical operations, or other agents, and build outward from consequence.

Treat connected tool servers, plug-ins, and peer agents as governed relationships rather than invisible plumbing. A connection approval should name the owner, source, purpose, capabilities, data access, permission model, support status, and review date. Where the platform discovers tools or agents dynamically, govern the registry and discovery path as well as the individual component, because "the agent found it" is not an approved-source process.

Risk-tier the **maximum authorized action**, not the friendliness of the interface or the harmlessness of the demo. An assistant that usually summarizes email but can also send messages, download attachments, query customer data, and call a scripting tool should be governed for those capabilities even if the pilot uses one of them.

Capability that is technically present and reachable is part of the exposure.

Agency also creates change events the existing intake should recognize. A new tool, broader scope, longer memory, a new peer, additional delegation, automatic approval, a new credential, a changed registry source, or a move from read to write can all change the risk tier without changing the model, and each should trigger review just as a new model or a sensitive data source would.

Finally, name accountability in language that survives an incident. The agent may select the step, but it does not accept organizational risk. The business owner remains accountable for the use case; technology owners for the platform and integrations; security, privacy, legal, and data owners for their respective decisions; the vendor for the commitments it made. "The agent decided" describes a mechanism. It does not identify an accountable human.

Shadow AI — the Signal, Not Just the Sin

The moment you start looking, you meet shadow AI: AI used outside approved, visible, governed channels. The instinct is to treat it as a discipline problem, people breaking the rules, and sometimes it is. More often, it is a signal. When a whole team quietly adopts a tool before anyone asks permission, that usually means they found something genuinely useful and the organization had not given them a safe way to use it yet. That distinction matters, because it changes what you do about it. Discover it, and the first question should not be "who broke policy?" but "what problem were they solving?" — because the answer tells you where real demand is, and demand is what you build the safe path around.

The response has a natural shape once you stop treating it as an enforcement action. You discover the usage, through the same asking-and-looking that feeds the inventory. You sort it by risk, separating harmless productivity use from the cases where sensitive data, customer-facing output, or internal integrations are involved. You redirect the legitimate need onto an approved tool and a safe pattern, so the person who went looking gets a real answer rather than a scolding. And you remediate the genuine exposure, pull or restrict the unsafe tool, rotate anything that leaked, deal with the data, and close the process gap that made the shortcut necessary in the first place.

What you do not do is lead with prohibition, because if your only move is "no," the usage does not stop. It goes quiet, which is the worst of both worlds. Now it is ungoverned and invisible, and the next time you find it will be during an incident. The better move is structured enablement: approved tools for the common needs, clear rules about what data can go where, a fast way to ask about the uncommon needs, and training that explains the real risks without turning into a fear campaign.

Reserve consequences for people who ignore clear rules, not for people who could not find a safe path. The goal was never to stop AI at the perimeter. You cannot, and pretending otherwise just teaches people to route around you. The goal is to make the governed path good enough that people prefer it. None of which means prohibition is never right: a specific tool, data type, or use may warrant a hard block, and someone who ignores a clear rule may warrant consequences. Targeted enforcement where the exposure is real is a different thing from leading with a blanket no.

If this feels like a rerun, that is because it is. Cloud sprawl happened when teams needed speed and central IT was too slow to provide it. SaaS sprawl happened when business units needed tools and procurement showed up late. AI sprawl is the same story with a more capable lead. The technology keeps changing. The human pattern — people will use what helps them, and they will route around whatever slows them down — does not. If you internalize one thing from this chapter, make it that, because every other control you build succeeds or fails on it.

One Front Door — the Intake

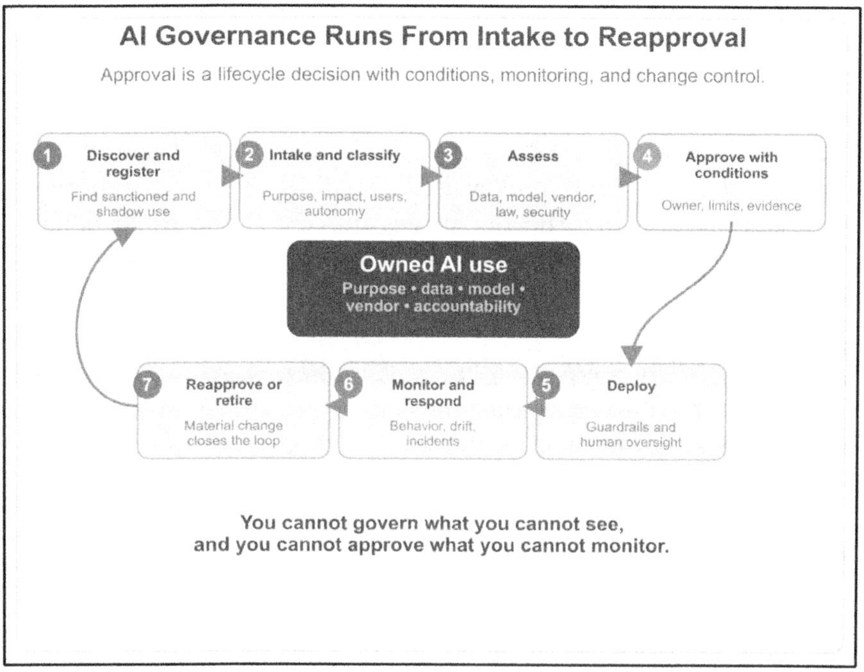

The mechanism that ties visibility to governance is an intake: a single, low-friction way for an AI use case to enter the program. Think of it as the front door. Without one, use cases enter through a hundred side entrances and you are back to discovery-after-the-fact. With one, you get to ask three questions before something goes live, the same three questions worth asking of any AI use, now turned into a process.

The first is what is this for. That is the inventory question, and it is how the use case gets on the register in the first place. The second is how risky is it, which is where classification happens because summarizing public marketing copy and screening job applicants are both "using AI," and treating them identically is how a program loses credibility in both directions at once. Risk here turns on the things you would expect: the sensitivity of the data involved, whether real people are affected by the output, how automated the decision is, whether a human stays in the loop, and how much the business is quietly trusting what comes out.

This is risk-based thinking applied to AI, and, where the EU AI Act applies, the risk tiering that can carry legal obligations, brought down to a working triage. Keep those two linked but distinct: your internal tier sets how much governance a use gets, while the legal classification turns on its own definitions and role tests, and an internal "low-risk" label cannot retire a statutory obligation. The third question is what makes it acceptable, which is where the classification pays off: the tier drives the path. The table below is illustrative, a shape to adapt to your own risk appetite and obligations, not a substitute for that legal determination.

Use-case tier	What it looks like	Governance path
Low / productivity	General assistants on non-sensitive work, drafting, summarizing public material, brainstorming	Acceptable-use policy, approved-tools list, data-handling rules. Self-serve; no per-case review
Moderate	Internal data involved, or output used in real work but reviewed by a person before it counts	Lightweight intake: data review, security check on integrations, named owner, logging
High-impact / potentially regulated	Output affects customers, employees, or decisions, eligibility, screening, customer-facing content, anything a regulator would care about	Full review: privacy, legal, security architecture, human-oversight requirement, and sign-off before go-live

Above the top tier sits a line the table does not need to draw but the program does: some use cases do not proceed at all. Where the law forbids it, where it breaks a contractual commitment, or where the data is simply too sensitive to put into the tool on offer, the right governance answer is no, or not like this, redesign it. A program that can only ever say "yes, with controls" is not governing risk; it is processing it. The mature intake has a rejection path and uses it.

The intake is also where the cross-functional reality becomes concrete. No single team can clear an AI use case, because the risk spans privacy, legal, data, security, and the business that wants to use it. The CISO's role here is orchestration: making sure the right people are pulled in at the right moment, not personally owning every judgment.

And every use case that comes through the door has to come out with an actual decision attached: approved, approved with conditions, deferred pending controls, rejected, or formally accepted as a risk by the business owner, within their delegated authority, since no owner can "accept" a prohibited use or sign off legal non-compliance the way they would an ordinary control gap. A use case that vanishes into "under review" forever is just shadow AI with better manners.

There is one operational rule that outranks all the others: the front door has to be fast. If your intake is slower and more painful than the shortcut, people will take the shortcut, and you will have spent real effort building a process that manufactures shadow AI. A fast, imperfect intake that people actually use beats a rigorous one they route around every time.

Acceptable Use — Rules People Will Actually Follow

Somewhere in here sits the acceptable-use policy, and the most common mistake with it is length. The instinct is to write a comprehensive document that anticipates every scenario, and the result is twelve pages that are technically complete and functionally ignored. A policy nobody reads governs nothing.

The version that works is short, concrete, and phrased as much around yes as around no. It names the approved tools for the common jobs, so people do not have to guess. It states plainly what data can go into which tools, the one rule most likely to prevent a real problem. It says when someone needs to come through the intake instead of self-serving. And it is written in language a normal employee can act on without a legal dictionary.

The approved-tools list matters more than people expect, because "here's what you can use" is a far more effective control than "here's what you can't" — it gives the safe path a name and removes the excuse that there was not one. In practice, the artifact people actually follow is rarely the formal policy; it is the one-page do-and-do-not guide that sits on top of it, the thing someone can read in a minute and remember under deadline.

A policy only governs behavior if people know it exists and understand it, which is where a small amount of targeted awareness earns its place, not a lecture on how models work, but the handful of things that actually change behavior: which tools are approved, what data must never go in, when output needs a human check, and where to ask. Most employees need that and little more.

The people building AI systems (developers, product and data teams) need the deeper version, and that connects straight back to the threat surface. Keep it proportionate to what each audience actually touches. And where the EU AI Act applies, its AI-literacy provisions are already in force, which makes role-appropriate training an obligation rather than a nicety for the people who build, deploy, or rely on these systems.

Data Governance for AI — the Gate on What Goes In

Data is one of the strongest things that make an AI use case risky, and often the single most useful question is what data is allowed to enter it, and what happens to that data once it is inside, though purpose, consequence, autonomy, who is affected, and how the output is used can push a use high-impact even when the data itself is not especially sensitive. You already have a data classification scheme. This is where you point it at a new question. For any given tool, the gate is simply whether the data someone wants to feed it is allowed to go there, given its sensitivity and given what the tool does with it.

The "what it does with it" half is where AI adds wrinkles the old data rules did not cover. Does the input get retained? Is it used only to answer the question in front of it, or also to train, fine-tune, evaluate, or "improve" the vendor's model? Those are different commitments with different consequences. Who can see the prompts and outputs later? That last one hides a trap people miss: the prompts and outputs are themselves data, often sensitive data, sitting in logs that rarely inherit the classification of what went into them. Those questions decide whether a given class of data can safely enter a given tool, and the answers live in vendor terms people rarely read.

Do not let a team wave this away with "it's only internal productivity" when the thing they are feeding the tool is customer contracts or source code, the label on the use case does not set the risk, the data does. Get this wrong and the polished, helpful assistant everyone loves becomes a data-leakage machine that answers politely. Where the data is personal, this stops being only a data-governance question and becomes a privacy obligation. I will not re-run that legal treatment here.

The operational point for this chapter is narrower: the data gate belongs in the intake, early, because "we already fed it the data" is a much worse place to discover a problem than "should we feed it this data." One neighboring question belongs in the same gate: whether the provider's terms actually permit your intended use of the output. Commercial reuse, code you will ship, content that might carry someone else's intellectual property. That is a legal call to route rather than resolve in the intake, but one the intake should surface rather than assume.

Vendor AI — the Questions That Are Actually Different

Here is a fact worth sitting with: for organizations that consume models rather than train their own, which is most, a large share of AI risk arrives through vendors, not through systems you build yourself. It comes in two flavors. The first is the AI vendor you deliberately adopt, a tool whose whole pitch is its AI capability. The second, and the one that catches people, is the AI feature quietly added to a product you already use, often enabled by default, sometimes without a clear announcement.

A SaaS tool that adds AI is not always a new vendor, but it may be a new risk, because data that used to sit quietly inside a workflow is now being processed, summarized, retained, or shipped to a model provider in ways your original review never contemplated. That is the real reason the inventory has to keep breathing: a vendor's release notes can change your risk posture without anyone on your side doing a thing.

Your general third-party assurance program (onboarding, contracts, right-to-audit, ongoing monitoring) is Part 3's subject, and you extend it here rather than replace it. What this chapter adds is the AI-specific overlay: a short set of questions the standard vendor review often does not ask. Does the vendor train on your data, and will they commit in the contract not to unless you have explicitly agreed? Is the AI feature on by default, and can you configure or disable it? How long are inputs and outputs retained, and where? Can the model change underneath you without notice, and would you know? Who is the actual model provider sitting behind the feature, the sub-processor under the sub-processor, and does your data flow through to them? Where, physically and legally, does your data go once it enters the tool?

None of these are exotic. They are the ordinary vendor questions, rotated toward the specific ways AI moves and keeps data, and they belong in your intake and your vendor review, not in a separate AI vendor process bolted on beside the one you already run. Two cautions travel with them. A "we don't train on your data" line is a statement, not evidence. It often says nothing about abuse-monitoring, human review, logging, or retained backups, so reconcile it against the contract and the actual settings. And provider assurance covers the provider's side of the line, not your data selection, your prompts, your permissions, or how you handle the output; that half stays yours.

When the AI Is in Your Product

There is a distinction worth drawing sharply, because organizations blur it and pay for it later: AI you use internally and AI you build into what you sell are not the same governance problem. An internal productivity assistant can still leak data, mishandle privacy, and get overtrusted, real risks, but the blast radius is mostly inside your walls. The moment AI becomes part of your customer-facing product, its output is a promise to the market. Customers see the failures.

Contracts, privacy notices, and support scripts may all need to move. Liability stops being hypothetical. And your customer-assurance surface changes: the security questionnaires and the due-diligence calls will start asking how the AI in your product is governed, and "we hadn't thought about that" is an expensive answer to give a prospect. Whether the AI actually falls inside your SOC 2 examination, the independent audit report customers ask for, is its own question, customer questions and contract claims can reach well beyond what the current report scopes, so check rather than assume.

So product AI earns a heavier review than an internal tool, and it pulls in people an internal use case would not (the product owner, legal, customer assurance, support) alongside the usual security, privacy, and data reviewers. The governing question shifts, too. For an internal tool it is "is this use acceptable, and under what conditions?" For product AI it is "what exactly are we committing to our customers by putting AI here, and can we stand behind that commitment when it's wrong?" That is a different conversation with different stakes, and it is worth having deliberately rather than discovering it after launch.

Product AI also needs a plan for watching its own behavior and catching misuse once it is live, but the mechanics of that monitoring and incident response are Chapter 4's, and the broader customer-assurance program sits outside this chapter. What belongs here is simply the decision to give product AI a heavier review from the start (product, legal, transparency, and assurance in the room) while remembering that its final tier still turns on purpose, affected people, autonomy, and consequence; a consequential internal use such as screening or eligibility can outrank a low-impact customer-facing assistant.

Ownership — the Part That Makes It Real

A program with no owners is just a document. For AI governance to be real, two kinds of ownership have to be named. Someone owns the program overall, the person accountable for the inventory existing, the intake running, and the risk being reported upward.

And each individual use case has an owner, ideally the business leader who wants it, because they are the one accountable for the risk it carries and the real decisions it will generate: whether it should touch customer data, whether its output can be customer-facing, whether to proceed before every control is mature, whether to accept an exception. Security, privacy, and legal do more than advise here, each owns the controls and calls within its own authority, but they do not absorb ownership of a business decision they did not make and cannot run day to day.

This is the same ownership discipline the rest of this series insists on everywhere, and it is tempting to skip because AI governance often starts life as an enthusiastic cross-functional working group where everyone is involved and therefore no one is accountable. A working group (or a small governance forum, in a larger shop) is genuinely useful for building the program, approving the policy and the risk tiers, and ruling on the high-impact and customer-facing cases.

Just do not let it become a substitute for a name next to each decision, or a place where use cases go to wait politely until they die. The moment something goes wrong with an AI system, "the AI committee owned it" is not an answer anyone can act on. Keep the forum small enough to actually decide, and make sure it can approve, reject, escalate, and assign ownership, otherwise it is not governance, it is another meeting.

Industry Pattern — The Approved Tools List That Did Not Exist

> *A pattern that shows up across the industry, more than once and in more than one shape, goes like this. An organization takes AI governance seriously and does the visible thing: it writes a solid acceptable-use policy, circulates it, maybe runs a training module, and reasonably concludes it has AI governance now. The policy is genuinely good. The problem is that a policy is a statement of intent, and intent does not inventory anything.*
>
> *Months later, someone finally runs a real discovery pass, pulls the SaaS spend, looks at what is actually being reached, asks teams directly what they use, and the result is uncomfortable. There is far more AI in the environment than the policy ever contemplated: features switched on inside tools nobody thought of as AI tools, an integration a developer built and forgot to mention, a team that had been feeding customer data into something handy for a quarter.*
>
> *Some of it was unmet demand and unclear guidance; some was weak awareness, a vendor default left on, or a deliberate shortcut. Mostly, each individual choice made local sense. But the governed path had been slower and vaguer than just using the tool, so people used the tool, and the policy governed a world that did not match the one they were living in. And when the policy finally landed saying "use only approved tools," it ran straight into the obvious question, which ones?, that nobody had answered yet.*
>
> *The lesson is not that the policy was wrong, or that the people were careless. It is that a policy is the start of governance, not the whole of it, and that the real work (the inventory, the intake, the fast safe path) is the part that is tedious enough to skip and important enough that skipping it is how you end up governing on paper while your actual AI runs somewhere you are not looking. Governance loses the moment usefulness arrives before usability.*

What Evidence Should You Expect

If AI governance is operating rather than aspirational, it produces a trail of ordinary artifacts. A CISO should expect to maintain or produce:

- an AI inventory or register of the AI tools, features, integrations, and vendor capabilities actually in use, not a one-time survey, but a maintained list with a refresh cadence;
- an agent and agentic-workflow register, purpose, owner, risk tier, autonomy, identity, tools, data, memory, peer agents, connections, approval points, operating limits, maximum consequence, and shutdown method;
- an approved capability and connection catalog, external tool servers, plug-ins, registries, and peer agents with provenance, owner, permissions, review date, and revocation status;
- non-human identity governance for agents, issuance, scope, credential lifetime, delegation, rotation, monitoring, and offboarding;
- memory-governance rules, permitted content, source provenance, retention, correction, deletion, isolation, and reset;
- change triggers returning an agentic use case to review when tools, permissions, autonomy, memory, peers, or delegation change;
- acceptance records showing that the accountable business and technology owners (not the agent, and not a general AI committee) accepted the deployment conditions and residual risk;
- shadow-AI discovery and remediation records: evidence you actively look for ungoverned use, and what you did when you found it;
- AI use-case intake records, the form or workflow itself, and the approvals that ran through it, showing what came through and how it was decided;
- documented risk-classification criteria and the tier assigned to each use case, so the governance path is defensible rather than ad hoc;

- an AI acceptable-use policy, the one-page employee guide that sits on top of it, and an approved-tools list with a review cadence, the "yes" list, not only the prohibitions;
- communication records showing the policy and the approved tools were actually pushed to employees, not just written;
- data-handling rules for AI, and evidence the data gate was applied at intake, including how each use case classifies data use (inference only, meaning the model answers from the data but is not trained on it, versus training, fine-tuning, evaluation, retention, and logging), with personal-data cases routed into the privacy process;
- AI-specific vendor review records, training-on-data commitments, retention, default-on status, model-change notice, and the model-provider/sub-processor chain, layered onto your general supplier assurance, plus release-note or change-monitoring records for AI features appearing in existing SaaS;
- product-AI review records for any customer-facing AI, showing the heavier review, the customer-assurance impact considered, and the owners who signed off on the commitment;
- human-oversight requirements recorded for high-impact use cases;
- named owners: one for the program, and one for each use case, with the business owner carrying the use-case risk;
- records of use cases declined, deferred, approved with conditions, or re-reviewed after their scope changed, governance decisions, not just an inventory of what got a yes;
- exception and risk-acceptance records, each with a named accepting owner and a review or expiry date, for AI use running with known, accepted risk;
- and governance forum or working-group decisions and escalation records, and management reporting on AI

adoption, risk classification, exceptions, and open items, plus periodic re-inventory showing the register is kept current.

For a small or mid-sized organization, do not try to build all of that before you start. Begin with the minimum that makes AI use visible and steerable: a use-case register, an approved-tools list, a short acceptable-use policy, a simple fast intake, data-handling rules, a risk classification, the AI-specific vendor questions, shadow-AI discovery, and named owners for anything customer-facing or high-impact. Visibility first, then the rest as the program earns its keep.

Reality Check

> *Two questions cut to whether your AI governance is real. First: could you produce, this week, a reasonably complete list of the AI actually in use across your organization, including the vendor features and the tools people signed up for without telling anyone? If the honest answer is no, you do not yet have a program; you have a policy sitting on top of an estate you cannot see, and the first task is not more policy, it is discovery.*
>
> *Second, and this is the one that predicts success: is your governed path faster than the shortcut? Time it honestly. If getting an AI use case approved takes two weeks and a series of meetings while the unapproved tool takes thirty seconds and a sign-up page, you already know which one people will choose, no matter what the policy says. A governance program that is slower than the behavior it is trying to replace does not reduce shadow AI. It manufactures it, and then blames the users. The fix is almost never a sterner policy. It is a faster front door.*

What This Means for You as a Security Leader

Nothing in this chapter is conceptually new to you. You already run intake processes, risk classification, vendor review, acceptable-use policy, data governance, and named ownership, for everything else in your program. AI governance in practice is that same operating model pointed at a new and fast-moving object. The frameworks tell you how to think about it; the threats tell you what you are defending against; this chapter is just the running machinery that makes both of those real day to day.

So the leadership move is to resist the two failure modes at once. Do not mistake a policy for a program. The document is the easy part; the inventory, intake, and ownership are the work. And do not build a program so heavy that people route around it, because a governed path nobody takes is worse than no path at all, since it gives you the comfortable illusion of control while shadow AI grows behind it.

The order that works is the order this book keeps coming back to: visibility first, then ownership, then controls, then assurance. Make the use visible, sort it by risk, give it owners, and make the safe path the fast one. Do those four things and you are governing AI. Skip any of them and you are documenting it.

Bridge to Chapter 4

Approval is only the start; red-teaming, production monitoring, and AI incident response keep a live system within the risk accepted at sign-off.

CHAPTER 4

Operating AI Risk — Red-Teaming, Monitoring, and AI Incident Response

The system you approved may not be the system you are running six months later, even when nobody formally changed the application.

Most AI governance stops at the moment of approval. The use case comes through intake, gets classified, gets an owner, gets a yes, and everyone moves on to the next thing. That is the front half of the job, and it is the half organizations actually build. The back half, what happens to the system after it is live, is the half most have not built, and it is the half AI needs most, because AI makes a familiar lifecycle problem unusually hard: the model itself may stay fixed, but the provider, the prompts, the retrieval data, the tools, the users, and the business's reliance on it can all move around it after you approve it.

The model gets updated by the vendor. The data it draws on shifts. The way people use it drifts away from what you scoped. New attack techniques appear that did not exist when you reviewed it. And none of that files a change request. The system you signed off on is quietly not the system you are running a quarter later, and the only way to know whether it is still safe is to keep checking.

This chapter is about the operational disciplines that keep a live AI system honest after approval. There are three. You test it adversarially, before and after launch, to find the failures before someone else does: red-teaming. You watch it in production, to notice when its behavior changes: monitoring. And you respond when something slips through anyway: AI incident response. Together they make the NIST AI RMF's measurement and risk-response outcomes operational, while the framework's governance and context continue to run across the lifecycle. It is the running, unglamorous work of keeping the thing trustworthy after the launch email goes out.

The general incident-response and resilience machinery — the playbook structure, severity model, crisis communication, forensic investigation, regulatory notification, and recovery — belongs in Part 2; here I am only adding the AI-specific overlay. Monitoring and security testing are disciplines you already run, bent by the specific ways AI breaks.

Why "approve and move on" doesn't work for AI

Every material technology needs lifecycle governance. A firewall rule can quietly become unsafe as the architecture around it shifts, and vendors change their services all the time. What AI adds is a harder wrinkle: behavior and evaluation challenges that make drift, provider change, and unintended use unusually difficult to detect. Governance-at-intake leans on the assumption that you can review once and have the review hold; AI strains that assumption in a few specific ways, and each one is a reason the back half of the job exists.

The provider ships a new model version, and behavior you validated can shift, better in general, occasionally worse for your particular use, and rarely announced in terms that map to your risk. Performance can deteriorate as the population, the source data, the retrieval corpus, or the operating environment drifts away from the conditions you evaluated against, and a system that was accurate at launch degrades slowly enough that no alarm ever fires. People find new uses for a tool that worked well for the scoped one, and the low-risk assistant quietly starts touching higher-risk work that nobody re-reviewed. And the jailbreak that failed at launch works next month, because the techniques for manipulating these systems are shared, refined, and public.

None of that shows up as an outage, and that is the trap. A crashed server tells you it crashed. A model that has quietly started leaking data, or following a hidden instruction, or being subtly wrong, tells you nothing at all. It keeps answering, fluently, and the failure surfaces when a customer, a researcher, or a regulator notices before you do. Operating AI risk is the work of noticing first.

Red-Teaming — Find the Failures Before Someone Else Does

Red-teaming an AI system means deliberately trying to make it misbehave, feeding it the hostile inputs, the trick prompts, the injection attempts, the requests it is supposed to refuse, to find out which failure modes actually land against your specific system, before an outsider runs the same experiment on your behalf. It is the offensive-testing instinct you already apply to your infrastructure, pointed at a new kind of target.

It helps to keep a few terms apart: evaluation measures whether a system meets defined performance, safety, and policy criteria; adversarial testing throws hostile inputs at it; red-teaming is the goal-driven, threat-informed version that hunts for harmful behavior across the whole system; and application penetration testing still examines the code, infrastructure, and identities around the model. They overlap, but a prompt test set is not automatically a red-team exercise, and model red-teaming does not replace pen-testing the application.

And it is a genuinely different kind of target. Traditional penetration testing looks for flaws in code and configuration, a missing patch, an exposed port, a broken access check. That work has its own bounded scope and never quite produces an "all clear" either, but the flaws it hunts are, in the end, closer to present-or-not. Red-teaming a model is fuzzier, because you are not exploiting a bug, you are trying to talk a system into doing the wrong thing, and the space of things you can say to it is effectively infinite.

There is no "all clear": passing your test set does not prove the system is safe, only that it survived the attacks you thought of. That makes red-teaming less a one-time certification and more a standing practice, a growing library of adversarial cases you re-run every time the model, the prompt, the data, or the tools change.

What you actually throw at it comes straight from the threat surface. You try direct and indirect prompt injection, including instructions hidden inside content the system will retrieve. You try to extract the system prompt, and to pull data the tester should not be able to reach, which for a RAG system means running the same query as users at different permission levels and checking the answers differ. You check whether data that was supposedly deleted or access-revoked still surfaces through an index or cache that never got the message. Where the system can act, you test whether a crafted input can make it take an action it should not. And you probe the plain-old-wrong dimension: the confident, fluent, incorrect answers that overreliance turns into real decisions.

You do not need a specialist red team to start, and most small and mid-sized organizations will not have one. External specialists exist for high-stakes systems and are worth it when the blast radius justifies the cost. But the accessible version is a structured self-test: a documented set of adversarial prompts and scenarios, run by someone who did not build the system, on a schedule and on every meaningful change. And the effort should follow the risk, a low-risk internal assistant needs basic misuse and data-handling checks; a customer-facing system or one wired to sensitive data or real-world actions needs the deep adversarial version.

That is less impressive than a boutique AI red team and vastly better than the common alternative, which is finding out from a customer. Start with the test set, and grow it every time you learn a new way the system can be fooled, and treat it like real assurance, which means findings, owners, fixes, and a retest, not a slide deck of clever prompts. And not every finding is a security bug, the same testing surfaces privacy, safety, bias, and plain-reliability problems too, so route each one to the owner who can actually fix it rather than filing all of them under security.

Monitoring — Watch the Behavior, Not Just the Uptime

You already monitor your systems; you already have that discipline — the logs, the detection, the signals that tell you something is wrong. AI monitoring extends it with a question traditional monitoring never had to ask. Your existing monitoring answers "is it up, and is anything attacking the box it runs on?" AI monitoring also has to answer "is the model still doing the right thing?" — and that is the harder question, because a misbehaving model does not crash. It keeps working, confidently, while being wrong.

So you instrument for behavior, not just health. You watch the outputs (sampling them, since you usually cannot review them all) for the ones that are unsafe, off-policy, or obviously wrong. You watch for abuse patterns: the probing, the repeated jailbreak attempts, the users who have discovered they can push the system somewhere it should not go. You watch the boring operational signals too, because a sudden spike in volume, cost, error rate, or refusals is often the first visible edge of a problem you cannot yet name.

And you treat the humans in the loop as a monitoring surface, the reviewer who catches a bad output and the user who flags a wrong answer are sensors, if you give them a channel to report and you actually act on what comes in. Any feedback the system collects is a monitoring signal too, and an input channel that can be gamed, so watch it as much as you learn from it.

The signal that deserves its own name is drift: the slow divergence between what you validated at launch and what the system does now. Some of it comes from the model, some from the data it retrieves, some from users quietly relying on it for heavier work than you scoped, and some from the vendor changing the service underneath you, different kinds of drift with different tells, not one undifferentiated slide toward wrong.

Most of it arrives without an announcement, and the most dangerous version arrives with a small one. "We only changed the model version" should never automatically bypass review, because in an AI system a model-version change is a behavior change, and the whole point of watching for drift is to notice when the system you are running has stopped being the system you approved. Treat material model, prompt, data-source, and tool changes as change management for behavior, not just for code.

All of this runs on logging prompts and outputs, which is exactly where monitoring collides with data governance. Those logs are sensitive: they hold whatever people typed in and whatever the model said back, so they inherit real handling obligations, and where personal data is involved, the privacy discipline applies to the logs themselves. You need enough captured to investigate and to spot drift, retained and access-controlled like the sensitive records they are. Log too little and you are blind; log carelessly and the monitoring system becomes its own exposure.

The heavyweight version of this uses purpose-built AI observability tooling, and if you have it, use it. The version available to everyone else is not nothing: log the interactions, sample a slice of outputs for human review on a cadence, give users a one-click "this was wrong" path, and watch your basic operational metrics for anomalies. That is a real monitoring program. It is just built from parts you already own.

Monitor the Action Chain, Not Only the Model

Agentic monitoring has to follow a longer story than prompt in, answer out. An agent receives or forms a goal, makes a plan, reads context and memory, selects tools or peers, calls them under an identity, receives results that may change the plan, and may then write memory, ask for approval, delegate, or act again. If you log only the original prompt and the final answer, the consequential part of the system happens in the dark.

For material agentic workflows, preserve enough telemetry to reconstruct the initiating user or service and the approved goal; the agent, model, prompt, and configuration versions; the plan or proposed action sequence at whatever level the system exposes; each tool or peer selected and the capability it claimed; tool arguments, results, errors, and retries; the identity and authorization context used for each consequential action; memory reads, writes, and source provenance; inter-agent messages, delegation, and task status; human approval, rejection, or override; external data transfer and code execution; consumption of cost, time, steps, and concurrency; and the final action and outcome.

That is not a demand for a model's private reasoning. What you need is **operational lineage** — the declared goal, the material decisions, the capabilities used, the data and identities involved, the approvals, and the effects. Record what the system did and why the control allowed it, rather than an unverifiable narrative claiming to expose every hidden step.

The useful detections follow from that lineage. Watch for a goal changing after untrusted content enters; a new tool or server appearing; a capability description changing; a peer selected from an unapproved source; a read of sensitive data followed by an external transfer; a memory write derived from an untrusted result;

an unusual privilege request; an approval pattern that has become automatic; or a sequence of individually permitted tools producing a prohibited outcome.

Watch too for the beginnings of a cascade, rapid fan-out, loops where agents hand a task back and forth, repeated retries, queue growth, rising cost, spread across tenants or data domains, the same faulty instruction propagating through several workflows. None of those is proof of compromise. Each is a reason to slow, isolate, or stop before uncertainty becomes scale.

Testing should exercise the connections, not only the model. Replace a trusted tool response with a malicious one. Present a forged or misleading capability record. Poison memory and see whether the effect survives into a later task. Try to make a low-privilege request inherit a stronger agent identity. Send a manipulated message through an agent-to-agent path. Cause one agent to fail and observe whether the error is contained or amplified. Try to persuade a human approver with a plausible rationale, because that is the test teams forget and the one that turns oversight into formality. And test the stop mechanism under load, since a kill switch that worked in the design review is another untested assumption.

Containment for an agentic incident

The containment unit is not always the whole AI application. Depending on what failed, the safest action may be to pause the current task or goal; revoke or narrow the agent's credential; disable one destructive tool while preserving read-only operation; disconnect a tool server; remove a peer or registry from the trusted set; stop further delegation or fan-out; quarantine suspect memory; block outbound network access; move the workflow to human-only approval; isolate the agent while preserving its execution trace; or shut the capability down entirely.

Build those options before the incident. A single global switch is better than nothing, but graded levers let an incident commander reduce risk without causing unnecessary business harm.

Preserve evidence before resetting: the active goal, plan, identities, credentials and scopes, model and configuration versions, tool catalog, connections, messages, memory state, inputs, outputs, approvals, and execution lineage. Then assume memory, peer agents, and downstream systems may carry the effect beyond the component where the problem first appeared, the cascade question is the one to ask early. What else consumed this agent's decisions before we noticed?

Recovery means more than restarting the agent. Re-establish trusted configuration and dependencies, rotate affected credentials, clean or rebuild memory, verify the registry and peers, replay representative tasks, retest the original failure, and confirm the agent cannot resume an unsafe task from saved state. Then restore agency gradually: read-only before write, bounded before autonomous, one agent before the whole network.

Human Oversight — a Control, Not a Comfort

"Human in the loop" is the most reassuring phrase in AI governance, and one of the most abused. A human is not overseeing an AI system just because a person could, in principle, review the output. Oversight is only real when the reviewer understands the task well enough to know when the AI is wrong, has the source material or evidence needed to actually check it, has the time and the authority to override, and, this is the part that quietly kills it, is not measured in a way that punishes them for slowing down.

If someone is graded on throughput and the AI makes throughput faster, they will approve its output, especially when it looks polished. A review step with no evidence, no uncertainty, and a throughput target attached is not a control; it is a rubber stamp with a person's name on it.

There is a second failure mode worth naming, because it is the mirror image: oversight fatigue. When the model is right ninety-nine times, the reviewer stops truly reading by the hundredth, and the one that mattered sails through on autopilot. A good model quietly trains its own reviewer to trust it, which means the better the system performs day to day, the more deliberately you have to keep the human's attention real. That is why oversight has to be designed rather than assumed, and designed in proportion to the stakes. For a low-risk assistant, informal review is fine.

For a high-impact use case, the tier where the output touches customers, employees, or consequential decisions, oversight becomes a control you build deliberately: defined decision points, the evidence a reviewer needs put in front of them, training on where the model tends to fail, a real override path, and a record that review happened. The question to ask is not "is there a human in the loop?" It is the harder one: could that human actually catch and stop the specific failure we are worried about? If the answer is no, the oversight is comforting language, not a safeguard, and you have been counting a control you do not have.

AI Incident Response — the Same Fire Drill, a Different Fire

Sooner or later something gets through, the test set did not cover it, the monitoring caught it late, or a customer caught it first, and you have an AI incident. The good news is that you already have an incident-response program: preparation, detection, containment, eradication, recovery, severity, crisis communication, notification. You do not build a separate one for AI. What you build is the overlay, the handful of things about an AI incident that your existing process will not handle unless you have told it to.

The first is recognition. A leaked database and a phishing compromise look like security incidents; your people know one when they see it. A model that has started answering with another customer's data, or following an instruction buried in a document, or confidently generating harmful output, does not trip the same reflex. Half the battle is getting your detection and your responders to treat "the model said something it shouldn't have" as an incident that belongs in the same queue as "someone's credentials were stolen" — with a defined trigger, a severity that plugs into your existing model rather than a new one invented on the spot, and a path.

The second is containment, and here AI actually hands you options a traditional incident does not. You usually cannot un-say what the model said, but you can often stop it saying more, fast: disable the feature, roll back to the previous model version, tighten or replace the system prompt, revoke the tools an agent can call, quarantine a poisoned document out of the retrieval corpus, cut the integration to the sensitive data source, or fall back to human-only processing. Those levers are worth deciding in advance, because the middle of an incident is a bad time to discover you do not know how to turn the thing off, and a full stop is a real, often correct first move, though not the only one; a safe degraded mode (read-only, human-only, tenant-isolated) can beat a hard shutdown that causes its own harm.

Two cautions travel with these levers. A prior model version is not a guaranteed refuge. It may be unavailable, unsupported, or carry the same weakness, so test rollback and fallback rather than assuming they exist. And containment should not destroy the evidence: capture the model version, configuration, prompts, outputs, and retrieval results before you start replacing prompts or rolling back, and treat a prompt change as temporary containment, not a durable fix for injection or a broken authorization boundary.

The third is working out what happened and how far it reached. The root cause of an AI incident might be a prompt injection, a poisoned document in the retrieval corpus, a vendor's silent model update, a configuration or design weakness, a data-quality problem, or the model simply operating at the edge of its known limitations, and each points at a different fix. The blast-radius questions are AI-shaped too: what did it output, to whom, drawing on what data, and did any of that get used in a decision or sent somewhere it should not be?

And when the misbehaving model is a vendor's, your investigation runs partly on their cooperation, so the questions to settle before an incident are concrete: can they suspend the feature, provide the prompt and output logs and how fast, tell you whether a model or configuration change is what shifted the behavior, and preserve evidence? A vendor who cannot support any of that is itself part of your risk picture, and better understood now than at 2 a.m.

There is one dimension your standard incident process may not flag on its own: an AI incident can carry obligations that are not obviously "security." Depending on what happened and where you operate, a model that exposed personal data, made or influenced a consequential decision about someone, or produced harmful output can pull in privacy-breach notification, sector rules, or emerging AI-specific regulation. You do not have to be the expert on all of it, but the AI incident overlay should include the reflex to ask, early, "does this one trigger a legal or regulatory clock?" and to pull legal and privacy in when it might.

Where the EU AI Act is the regime in question, be precise about it: its post-market-monitoring and serious-incident duties attach to defined high-risk systems and to specific roles, a provider carries different obligations from a deployer, rather than to every AI error, and the reporting specifics are still phasing in, so keep the current rules in your obligation register and confirm your role and the system's classification before reaching for that route.

So the concrete deliverable is an AI incident playbook that plugs into your incident-response process: a definition of what counts as an AI incident, the triggers that route one into your existing flow at the right severity, the containment levers pre-identified per system, who gets called (including the person who actually understands the model, and legal or privacy when obligations may apply), and the vendor incident contacts for the systems you do not control. It is a short document. It is also the difference between a contained event and a slow, public, improvised one.

The Three Together — a Loop, Not a Launch

Red-teaming, monitoring, and incident response are not three separate projects; they are one loop, and the loop is what "operating AI risk" actually means. Red-teaming finds failures proactively. Monitoring catches the ones that surface in production. Incident response handles the ones that get through anyway. And, this is the part that closes the circle, what all three learn feeds back into governance. A red-team finding becomes a new control or a tighter tier. A monitoring signal becomes a reason to re-review a use case. An incident becomes an update to the intake questions so the next system does not repeat it. The governance register is not a filing cabinet; it is the thing this operational loop keeps current.

Discipline	The muscle it extends	What AI changes about it
Red-teaming	Security and penetration testing	You are not exploiting code, you are talking a system into misbehaving; the attack space is open-ended, so "passed" means "survived the tests you thought of," not "safe"
Monitoring	Logging, detection, the SOC	You watch whether the model is still behaving, not just whether it is up; failures are silent and behavioral, the system keeps answering while being wrong
Incident response	Your incident-response and resilience program	The incident is a model saying or doing the wrong thing; containment is disable / roll-back / restrict rather than host isolation; the cause may be a vendor model change or a poisoned input

That table is the whole argument in miniature, really. You learned the frameworks and how they relate. You learned how these systems fail. You built the program that governs them on the way in. And now you operate them once they are live. It is the same security operating model this series has been building the entire way, pointed at the fastest-moving object most of us have had to govern in our careers, and, stripped of the novelty, it turns out to be governance, testing, monitoring, and response. The tools you already have, bent to a new shape.

Industry Pattern — The Pilot Nobody Reviewed Again

Here is how it usually goes wrong after launch. An organization does the front half well. A useful AI feature, a limited pilot, non-sensitive data, internal users, advisory output. Goes through review, gets sensible controls, gets an owner, and launches. Everyone is pleased, and rightly. Then it runs. Someone adds a data source because the original corpus was too narrow.

Another team asks for access. A manager starts using the output in weekly decisions. The vendor ships a model upgrade and the aggregate numbers look better, so nobody checks whether the security behavior, the subgroup performance, or the refusal patterns changed with it. And at some point everyone quietly stops calling it a pilot, because the whole business now depends on it.

Nobody formally changed the risk tier. Nobody revisited the approval. Nobody started monitoring, because monitoring was not part of the plan. Approval was. Then the problem surfaces from outside: a user notices the assistant returning something it should not, or a researcher finds it can be talked past its guardrails and posts about it, or a customer's security team sends a questionnaire with a question nobody internally can answer, because no one has looked at the system since launch. The review was not bad. The use case changed after the review, and governance did not follow it.

That is the operating-AI-risk problem in a sentence: AI systems do not just need approval, they need re-approval triggers. Without them, "pilot" quietly becomes the word an organization uses for production systems it has not gotten around to governing. The teams that stay safe are not the ones that block pilots; they are the ones who defined, up front, what turns a pilot into production, what changes force a fresh look, and what monitoring switches on the moment usage becomes real.

What Evidence Should You Expect

Operating AI risk, if it is real rather than intended, leaves an operational trail. A CISO should expect to maintain or produce:

- red-team or adversarial-test records for AI systems, including the reusable test set itself, a risk-based cadence, and evidence it is re-run on model, prompt, data, or tool changes, not a one-time pre-launch exercise, with findings, owners, fixes, and retests;
- coverage showing what the testing actually probed: prompt injection (direct and indirect), data and system-prompt extraction, RAG retrieval tested at different permission levels, stale or revoked data still reachable through indexes or caches, tool and action abuse, and unsafe-output and overreliance cases;
- monitoring coverage for AI systems: what is logged, how outputs are sampled and reviewed, how abuse and drift are detected, and which operational signals are watched;
- end-to-end agent execution traces correlating the initiating identity and goal with plans, tool calls, authorization decisions, memory changes, peer messages, approvals, external transfers, and outcomes;
- detections for goal deviation, anomalous tool sequences, privilege expansion, unapproved servers or peers, suspicious memory writes, sensitive-read-to-external-transfer patterns, loops, cost spikes, fan-out, and cascading behavior;
- test records covering malicious tool output, poisoned memory, forged discovery records, inter-agent message manipulation, delegated-privilege abuse, unsafe code execution, human-approval persuasion, and cascade containment;
- graded containment procedures and tested stop controls for credentials, tools, servers, peers, memory, delegation, egress, and the complete agentic service;
- recovery evidence showing identity, memory, tools, peers, configuration, and saved task state were returned to a known-trusted condition before autonomy was restored;

- change records for model, provider, prompt, guardrail, data-source, and tool changes, with review triggers for material change, so “we only updated the model” does not silently bypass governance;
- evidence that prompt and output logs are handled as the sensitive records they are, retention, access control, and privacy handling where personal data is involved;
- a user- and reviewer-feedback channel for flagging bad AI output, with evidence the flags are triaged and acted on rather than merely collected;
- human-oversight evidence for high-impact use cases: defined review points, the evidence put in front of reviewers, override authority, and records that review actually happened, oversight designed as a control, not asserted as a comfort;
- an AI incident playbook that plugs into your incident-response process: the definition and triggers for an AI incident, per-system containment levers, the call list (including model expertise, and legal or privacy where obligations may apply), and vendor incident contacts and support commitments;
- records of AI incidents and near-misses: what happened, how it was detected, how it was contained, the root cause, the blast radius, and whether any legal or regulatory notification obligation was assessed;
- evidence the loop closes: red-team findings, monitoring signals, and incident lessons feeding back into the governance register, the risk tiers, and the intake questions;
- and post-approval review records confirming a use case’s risk tier, data use, owner, and controls still match reality, and vendor-model-change tracking for the systems you consume rather than build.

For a small or mid-sized organization, start with the minimum that turns “deployed” into “operated”: a documented adversarial test set, run before launch and on changes; permission testing for any RAG system and a tool-permission review for any agent; interaction logging with periodic output sampling and a "report a bad answer" path; and a one-page AI annex to your existing incident-response plan naming the containment levers, the change triggers that force a re-review, and who to call. Begin there, and add depth as the systems earn it.

Reality Check

> *One question separates an operated AI system from a deployed-and-forgotten one: if the AI you approved last quarter started misbehaving right now, leaking something, following a planted instruction, confidently getting an important answer wrong — how would you find out? If the honest answer is "a customer would tell us," you have a deployed system, not an operated one, and the space between those two is exactly where the incident you will remember is going to come from.*
>
> *Two more, quickly. Have you ever tried to make one of your live AI systems fail on purpose, actually sat down and attacked it, or are you assuming it is fine because nothing has gone visibly wrong? And if you decided this afternoon that a given AI system had to stop, could you? Do you know which lever turns it off, and who pulls it? "Nothing has gone wrong yet" is not a control. Being able to find out, and being able to stop it, are.*

What This Means for You as a Security Leader

The operating model this book keeps returning to does not end at approval, and AI is the technology that makes that hardest to ignore. You already test your defenses, monitor your systems, and respond to incidents. Those are core muscles, not new ones. Operating AI risk is those same muscles pointed at a system that fails through language, degrades silently, and can be talked into misbehaving in ways your code never could.

Red-team it, watch it, keep real human oversight where the stakes justify it, and be ready both to respond and to switch it off. None of that asks you to become a machine-learning researcher; it asks you to treat a live AI system the way you would treat any other critical system you cannot afford to stop looking at.

So the move is to build the back half deliberately, because nobody will ask you to. There is no launch email for monitoring, no celebration for a red-team test that found nothing, no applause for a containment lever you never had to pull. The reward for operating AI risk well is a set of incidents that stayed small or never happened. Invisible by design, which is precisely why it gets underfunded. Approval is temporary confidence, not permanent assurance; the job is to know when a system has stopped behaving within the risk you accepted. The organizations that struggle with AI will not be the ones that could not govern it at the gate. They will be the ones that governed it beautifully at the gate and then stopped watching.

Part 1 Closing Note: New Technology, Old Questions

Artificial intelligence did not remove the need for an operating model. It exposed every place where one was missing.

That is the bet this Part made and kept: that AI, the newest and loudest risk surface in this book, did not arrive needing a rulebook of its own — it needed the same operating model, pointed carefully at a technology that fails differently. The Part opened with governance because that is where the exposure was already real: most organizations did not decide to adopt AI; they looked up one day and discovered they had. NIST AI RMF, ISO 42001, and the EU AI Act turned out to correlate the way security frameworks always have — many instruments, one operating model, each a different lens on the same obligations of inventory, accountability, and proof.

The threat surface chapter then earned the Part's keep, because half the appsec playbook still applies and the other half was written for software that does not think: prompt injection turning data into instructions, leakage through what goes in and comes back out, retrieval making your own data the attack surface, agents converting a wrong answer into a wrong action. Governance in practice brought it down to the unglamorous program — the inventory, the intake, the acceptable use people will actually follow, the governed path that must be faster than the shortcut, or the shortcut wins. And operating AI risk closed the loop that approval alone never closes: the system you approved is not the system you are running six months later, so red-teaming, behavior monitoring, human oversight, and AI incident response are not enhancements. They are the control.

Two disciplines deserve restating at this altitude. Human oversight is not achieved by placing a person somewhere in the diagram; it is a designed control only when the reviewer has enough information, time, competence, and authority to challenge or stop the result. And depth should follow consequence: a low-impact productivity assistant and a system influencing an important customer or employee decision should not receive identical governance. A smaller organization does not need a parallel AI bureaucracy — it needs a visible inventory, proportional intake, clear data boundaries, named accountability, and an incident path connected to the response capability it already runs.

The posture across all four chapters is anti-mystery, not anti-AI. Know what you have, including what arrived as a feature inside SaaS you already pay for. Understand what it reads, what it can be made to do, whose data it can reach, and what happens when it is wrong. Assign accountability by name. Prove it operates. Watch it drift. That is not a new job. It is the oldest job in this book, applied to a system that can be talked into things.

What AI could not be given inside this Part is the capability every chapter kept reaching for: the organization-wide ability to detect abnormal behavior, decide what it means, act in time, and survive the disruption. A model behaving strangely is, in the end, an operational signal that may become an incident — and handling that possibility belongs to a discipline bigger than any one technology.

That discipline is the next Part. AI is one demanding test of it. It is not the only one.

Bridge to Part 2

Every AI incident reflex depends on a broader capability to detect, respond, communicate, recover, and keep operating under pressure.

VOLUME IV

PART 2

Security Operations, Cyber Resilience, Incident Response, and Crisis Management

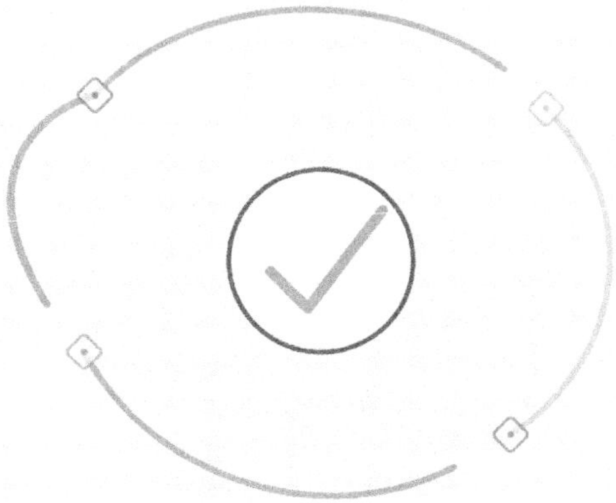

CHAPTER 5

Threat-Informed Security Operations

Detection is not a product. It is a defensible point of view about what matters.

Most security operations centers are built the wrong way round. They begin with a tool, a SIEM (security information and event management) platform, an EDR (endpoint detection and response) tool, a managed service, and then ask what it can detect. The answer is: whatever its vendor decided to write rules for. That is not a strategy. It is an inheritance.

The alternative starts one step earlier, with a question that sounds obvious and is asked far less often than it should be: who is likely to come for an organization like ours, what would they actually do once inside, and would we see any of it? A security operation built from that question looks different. It collects different data, writes different detections, measures itself differently, and, this is the part that matters to a board, can explain why it watches what it watches. That is what threat-informed means. Not more alerts. A defensible point of view about the adversary, and an operation organized around it.

This chapter opens the resilience Part deliberately. Recognizing abnormal activity early strengthens every response, but not every disruption begins with an alert and not every incident is discovered by the security operation. This chapter owns the operating path from threat knowledge to signal, investigation, escalation, and initial action. Resilience, incident command, crisis management, continuity, and recovery begin after that handoff.

Security Operations Is a Capability, Not a Room

People use *SOC* to mean a physical room, a team, a service provider, or a platform. Any of those may be part of security operations; none of them is the capability. What makes it a capability is a connected chain: understand the business and its relevant threats, identify what needs visibility, collect and maintain the telemetry, build and test detections for priority scenarios, triage with technical and business context, investigate and scope, escalate or contain under clear decision rights, hunt for what the detections would miss, and feed what is learned back into detections, controls, architecture, and exposure management.

If one link is missing the weakness surfaces somewhere else. Threat intelligence without a consumer becomes a report. Telemetry without detection logic becomes storage. A detection without tested data becomes an assumption. An alert without business context becomes a ticket. An investigation without response authority becomes a delay. An incident without feedback becomes a recurring lesson. That is why security operations should be managed as a service to the business rather than as a collection of tools. It has customers, priorities, inputs, decision points, dependencies, and outcomes, and it should be designed deliberately.

Volume II's logging and monitoring chapter (Chapter 13) established the telemetry foundation. This chapter builds the operating model on top of it: how threat knowledge becomes detection, how signals become decisions, and how the results improve the wider program.

What Security Operations Protects

Security operations protects the organization's ability to notice abnormal activity, understand what it may mean, and act while there is still time to change the outcome. That purpose is worth stating plainly because the function accumulates so much machinery that it can disappear beneath its tooling.

Every control this series has built so far might fail. Identity restricts who gets in, until a credential is phished. Patching removes known weaknesses, until an unknown one is used. Segmentation limits movement, until a path nobody mapped turns out to exist. Every preventive control is a bet that something will hold, and security operations is the discipline that exists because some of those bets lose. It protects the decision window between the first observable signs and a larger consequence, a window in which faster understanding and authorized action may still limit harm, rather than the organization learning what happened from a customer, a journalist, or a regulator.

That framing sets the scope. Security operations owns threat monitoring, detection, triage, initial investigation, hunting, escalation, and any protective actions specifically pre-authorized before formal incident declaration. Once that threshold is crossed, incident response owns coordinated incident command and containment, while security operations continues to supply telemetry, investigation, detection, and technical support. Crisis leadership, notification decisions, continuity, and recovery sit outside that boundary.

The Control Objective, in Plain Language

Know which threats plausibly apply to this organization, ensure the activity those threats generate would actually be visible in the data you collect, detect it reliably enough to act, investigate it fast enough to matter, contain it before it becomes a crisis, and feed what you learn back into both the detections and the preventive controls, so that the organization's ability to notice improves with every incident rather than resetting after each one.

Four things have to be true at once, and they fail independently. **Relevance:** you are watching for things that plausibly apply to you rather than everything a vendor ships. **Visibility:** the data that would reveal the activity is actually collected, from the systems that matter, and retained long enough to be useful. **Reliability:** the detection fires when it should, does not fire constantly when it should not, and reaches a human who can act.

Feedback: what each incident teaches gets written back into the operation. Drop relevance and you get a busy operation defending against someone else's threat model. Drop visibility and you get excellent detections over data that does not contain the answer. Drop reliability and you get alert fatigue, which is not a nuisance but a control failure with a name. Drop feedback and you get an operation that responds to the same intrusion pattern for the third time as though it were the first.

Threat-Informed Means Starting With the Adversary

The phrase gets used loosely, so let me be precise about what it demands. Threat-informed defense means the operation's priorities are derived from how real adversaries actually behave, rather than from what a tool happens to alert on or what a compliance checklist happens to require.

Starting with the adversary does not mean starting with a list of actor names. Priority comes from the intersection of business criticality, technology, exposure, credible adversary behavior, and potential impact, and a scenario such as "stolen credentials used to access a critical cloud service" is usually more useful to a defender than a disputed judgment about which named group might attempt it.

That begins with a threat profile the organization can defend in a sentence. Who plausibly targets an organization of this size, in this sector, in these countries, holding this data, with these suppliers? For many organizations, financially motivated crime, credential abuse, fraud, extortion, and opportunistic exploitation will dominate the practical threat profile. State-aligned risk belongs when the organization can explain its strategic relevance through sector, geography, data, infrastructure, government relationships, critical suppliers, or access to another target. It may involve espionage, pre-positioning, disruption, supply-chain access, or financially motivated activity, so do not assume a single motive or operating tempo. If strategic relevance cannot be established, rank the scenario below more probable threats rather than including it for prestige; a threat profile that includes everyone prioritizes nothing.

Geopolitical risk belongs in this profile when it changes what the organization should do, not as a standing exercise in reacting to headlines. An organization becomes strategically relevant through its sector, geography, intellectual property, government relationships, infrastructure role, suppliers, public positions, or its access to a more interesting target.

So the useful questions are business questions: which countries, customers, facilities, or partnerships raise our relevance during tension; which data or operational capability could carry strategic value; which cloud, telecommunications, software, or managed-service dependencies concentrate risk; could a compromise of us provide a route into someone more important; and what specifically would we change, in monitoring, privileged access, supplier coordination, or response readiness, if the threat credibly rose? Define the triggers, the proportionate actions, the decision owner, and the criteria for standing back down. Treating every international event as a heightened alert produces fatigue and nothing else.

Attribution deserves particular restraint. Overlapping techniques, shared infrastructure, and resemblance to public reporting can support an analytic judgment, but they rarely establish certainty, and technical, legal, public, and governmental attribution are four different decisions with four different standards. Preserve the evidence, state the confidence and the alternatives, and resist converting an investigative judgment into a political conclusion. A board does not need a tour of threat-actor names; it needs to know why the organization might be relevant, what could happen, how ready it is, and what decisions are required.

The second move is the one that separates a threat-informed operation from a well-equipped one: translate that profile into behaviors, then check whether you would see them. Adversary behavior is more durable than adversary tooling. Malware gets rebuilt, infrastructure gets rotated, and file hashes can become stale quickly, but the underlying sequence of what an intruder must accomplish changes slowly. Something has to gain initial access, execute code, establish persistence, escalate privilege, avoid being noticed, harvest credentials, discover the environment, move laterally, collect what it came for, control it remotely, and get it out.

That structure is the common language the industry has settled on for describing behavior rather than indicators, and MITRE ATT&CK organizes it explicitly. Its Enterprise matrix, version 19.1, the release used for this chapter, organizes behavior under fifteen tactical objectives: Reconnaissance, Resource Development, Initial Access, Execution, Persistence, Privilege Escalation, Stealth, Defense Impairment, Credential Access, Discovery, Lateral Movement, Collection, Command and Control, Exfiltration, and Impact. Their display order can help a reader follow adversary activity, but it is not a required attack sequence: adversaries may skip objectives, repeat them, or pursue several in parallel.

Two of those will be unfamiliar to anyone who learned the older matrix: what used to be a single Defense Evasion tactic is now split between Stealth (TA0005), where the adversary blends into legitimate activity to reduce the chance of being seen, and Defense Impairment (TA0112), where the adversary actively degrades the security tooling and pipelines so defenders cannot see or trust what is happening. That split is worth internalizing, because the two demand entirely different detections.

Used well, that structure gives a security operation something it usually lacks: a map of its own blind spots. Take the handful of behaviors your threat profile makes most likely and ask three questions of each. As one illustrative identity-to-impact scenario, a team might examine Phishing (T1566), Valid Accounts (T1078), OS Credential Dumping (T1003), Remote Services (T1021), and Data Encrypted for Impact (T1486). Would the activity generate any record at all in the data we collect?

If it would, do we have a detection for it? And if we do, has it ever actually fired correctly? Most organizations doing this honestly for the first time find the same shape of result, good coverage of endpoint execution and malware, thin coverage of identity abuse and credential misuse, and almost nothing covering the administrative tooling and legitimate-looking activity that a competent intruder prefers, precisely because it looks like work.

That is the point of the exercise. It converts "we have a SIEM" into "we can see these behaviors, we cannot see those, and here is which gap we are closing first."

Coverage Is a Data Problem Before It Is a Detection Problem

You cannot detect what you never collected. Many detection failures are, at root, telemetry failures, the log source that was never onboarded, the cloud account outside the pipeline, the identity provider whose sign-in events were considered too voluminous to keep, the server whose agent silently stopped reporting three months ago.

So the operation needs an honest inventory of what it can see, mapped to the estate it is supposed to be watching. Endpoints and servers. Identity and authentication, which for most modern intrusions is the richest source there is. Cloud control planes and their audit logs. Network flows and egress. Email, which remains the most common front door. SaaS platforms holding real business data. Applications and databases where consequence concentrates. Administrative and remote-access paths. The question for each is not merely "do we have logs?" but "do we get them, are they complete, are they timely, are they retained long enough to investigate an intrusion that began months ago, and would we know if they stopped?"

That last question deserves its own control, because silent loss of telemetry, the signal data your tools emit, is one of the most common ways a security operation goes blind without noticing. Agents die. Forwarders break. A network change drops a log-forwarding path. A cost review quietly reduces retention. And some telemetry loss is not accidental at all: the entire Defense Impairment tactic exists because degrading the defender's visibility is a deliberate adversary objective, expressed in techniques such as Disable or Modify Tools (T1685), including its sub-techniques for clearing Windows event logs (T1685.005) and disabling or modifying cloud logs (T1685.002), alongside Prevent Command History Logging (T1690) — and, from the adjacent Stealth tactic, Indicator Removal (T1070).

An operation that does not alert on the disappearance of expected telemetry has left one of the adversary's most useful moves unmonitored. Monitoring the monitoring, alerting on the absence of expected data, not just on suspicious data, is one of the highest-value and least glamorous controls in this entire domain. NIST's Cybersecurity Framework anchors the monitoring expectation across the environment, from networks and network services (DE.CM-01) through computing hardware, software, and runtime environments and their data (DE.CM-09), and the practical test is simply whether those sources are still arriving today.

Retention deserves a decision rather than a default. Intrusions are frequently discovered long after they began, and the first question an investigation asks is how far back the data goes. If the answer is thirty days and the intrusion started several months earlier, the investigation will be a matter of inference rather than evidence, and the notification you eventually make to a customer or regulator will carry that uncertainty with it.

Detection Engineering: Rules Are Code, and They Rot

Treating detections as a product feature you configure once is how operations end up with hundreds of rules nobody trusts. Detections behave like code: they are written against assumptions, those assumptions age, and they need testing, versioning, ownership, and retirement.

A detection worth keeping can answer a few questions. What behavior is this looking for, and which part of the threat profile does it serve? What data does it depend on, and what happens to it if that source degrades? How noisy is it in this environment, and what did we do about that? What should the analyst actually do when it fires? And when did it last fire correctly? A rule that has neither produced a true positive nor been validated through controlled testing is not necessarily wrong, but it is unproven, and an operation should know which of its detections are load-bearing and which are decoration.

Tuning is where the discipline shows. The instinct when a rule is noisy is to weaken it until it stops complaining, which quietly converts a detection into a placebo. The better response is to narrow it with context, the same activity from an unexpected account, at an unexpected hour, from an unexpected location, or against an unexpected target, so that it fires on the version that matters. Where a rule genuinely cannot be made reliable, retire it and say so rather than leaving it firing into a queue everyone has learned to ignore, and record the coverage gap that retirement creates, so it is addressed through another analytic, a control, a hunt, or an accepted-risk decision rather than quietly disappearing.

Two failure patterns are worth naming plainly. The first is coverage measured by rule count, which rewards volume over relevance; five hundred rules mapped to the same handful of behaviors is not coverage. The second is the alert queue treated as work rather than as signal: when volume exceeds capacity, the queue stops being a detection mechanism and becomes a backlog, and the intrusion that was flagged correctly on Tuesday is opened on Friday.

Triage, Investigation, and Knowing What "Handled" Means

An alert is a question, not a finding. Triage answers it quickly enough to matter: is this real, how bad could it be, does it need to escalate now, and what does the analyst do next.

The operation needs a small number of things to be true here. Alerts must reach a human, or an automation with defined authority, within a time appropriate to their severity, and that time has to be measured rather than assumed. There must be enough context attached to decide without a research project: what the asset is, who the user is, whether the account is privileged, what the system does for the business, and what else has happened around it. There must be a documented next action for common alert types, because expecting every analyst to improvise every response is how quality varies by shift. And there must be a defined threshold at which triage stops and incident response begins.

That threshold is worth deciding in advance, in writing, because it will be crossed at an inconvenient moment. What makes something an incident rather than an event? Who can declare one? What happens in the first fifteen minutes? Who gets woken up? Most organizations discover their answer is vague only while they are living through the thing that needed it. NIST's framework separates the analysis that establishes what has taken place and the root cause of an incident (RS.AN-03) from the containment and eradication that follow (RS.MI-01, RS.MI-02), and the separation is useful in practice: understanding and stopping are different activities with different tempos, and confusing them produces either paralysis or premature action.

Automation belongs here too, with its limits stated. It can accelerate enrichment, evidence collection, routine blocking, and case creation, and AI-assisted tooling can summarize cases, draft investigation queries, or explain unfamiliar data. None of that makes uncertain evidence certain. Automated actions need defined conditions, safeguards, logging, exceptions, and a recovery path, because automation amplifies a bad decision as efficiently as a good one, and high-impact containment touching safety, production, customer access, or privileged identities should reflect the organization's decision rights rather than a script's.

Two cautions are specific to AI-assisted work: sensitive investigation data should not flow to an unapproved model or service, and attacker-controlled content sitting in logs, emails, or documents can attempt to manipulate an AI-assisted workflow that reads it. Whatever the mix, the organization should be able to reconstruct what an automated or assisted process did, what it used, and where a human decision entered.

Investigation, when it happens, has its own discipline. Preserve evidence before you disturb it. Establish a timeline rather than a list of alerts. Answer the questions that drive decisions, how they got in, what they reached, what they took, whether they are still there, and whether the same path exists elsewhere, rather than the questions that are merely interesting. And write it down as you go, because the reconstruction that feels obvious during the incident becomes contested three weeks later when the notification letter is being drafted.

Intelligence Requirements Come Before Intelligence Feeds

The market offers more threat information than any organization can use, so the hard part is not acquiring data. It is deciding what you need to know. That starts with intelligence requirements: the specific questions the organization needs intelligence to help answer. "Tell us about ransomware" is too broad to guide anything. More useful questions look like: which ransomware access methods are most relevant to our technology and geography; what would indicate that a privileged identity or remote-management tool is being prepared for misuse; which critical suppliers create an access path into our environment; which observed attacker behaviors are not covered by tested detections; and what geopolitical developments could change the threat to our people, data, or service availability.

Those requirements then shape collection, and the output should be shaped for the consumer rather than published uniformly. Detection engineers need behaviors, data requirements, and testable hypotheses. Hunters need questions they can investigate. Exposure teams need adversary interest and exploitability context. Architects and control owners need the patterns that reveal design weaknesses. Responders need context that helps scope an investigation. Executives need business implications, uncertainty, and decisions, not a list of indicators. Internal evidence deserves particular weight here, because your own alerts, incidents, identity data, and fraud signals describe your actual environment rather than a generalized landscape.

Threat Intelligence That Changes What You Do

Threat intelligence earns its place when it changes a decision. Most of what is sold as intelligence changes nothing: a feed of indicators nobody acts on, a weekly report nobody reads, a dashboard of global attack trends with no connection to this organization's estate.

Useful intelligence answers one of a small number of operational questions. Which threats should our profile actually include, and has that changed? Which behaviors should we be able to detect first? Is there a specific, current campaign against our sector or our software that warrants action this week? Is there evidence of our credentials, data, or brand appearing where it should not?

And after an incident, what does this tell us about who this was and what else they typically do? NIST's framework makes this integration explicit as an outcome rather than a purchase, expecting cyber threat intelligence and other contextual information to be integrated into the analysis of adverse events (DE.AE-07), which is a precise way of saying that intelligence belongs inside the analytical workflow, not beside it in a subscription.

For a small or mid-sized organization, this does not require an intelligence team. It requires a named person who spends a defined amount of time on it, a short list of sources appropriate to the sector, national computer emergency response team (CERT) advisories, sector information-sharing bodies, the security advisories of the vendors actually in use, and reputable open reporting, and a standing route from "we read something relevant" to "we changed something." The industry-specific sharing communities are frequently the highest-value source available to a smaller organization, because they carry what is happening to organizations that look like yours rather than what is happening globally.

The discipline to avoid is collecting indicators as though volume were value. A million blocked hashes is not a security outcome. A single well-understood behavior that you can now detect, because reporting told you it mattered and you checked your coverage, is.

Threat Hunting: Asking Better Questions of Your Environment

Threat hunting exists because detections encode only part of what the organization knows to look for. A hunt is a structured, hypothesis-driven investigation that asks whether relevant behavior may be occurring, or may have occurred, without producing a sufficient alert.

The hypothesis should come from something real: current intelligence, a priority threat scenario, an earlier incident, an exposure finding, an untested ATT&CK behavior, or a known weakness in existing detections. The hunt should define the question, why it matters, the systems and period in scope, the data required, the expected evidence, and the conditions that would expand or close the work.

A hunt can produce several useful outcomes: confirmed suspicious activity; a detection gap; missing or unreliable telemetry; a control weakness; a better baseline of normal behavior; or a bounded conclusion that the available evidence does not support the hypothesis. That last outcome deserves care in how it is stated: "nothing found" does not prove that nothing happened, particularly where visibility is incomplete.

A useful hunt leaves the operation better than it found it. The result may be a new or improved detection, a data-quality correction, a control change, a refined threat assessment, or a documented limitation with a follow-up decision attached. Hunting should not become random log searching, or an activity performed only when the alert queue happens to be quiet; it belongs inside the same improvement loop as intelligence and detection engineering. For a smaller organization, a few hours each month on one priority hypothesis is a credible starting point.

The Handoff Into Incident Response

One of the most consequential moments in security operations is where routine investigation becomes coordinated incident response. Somewhere between "this alert looks real" and "this is a crisis," an intrusion changes hands, and how well an organization manages that transition largely determines how the rest of the incident goes.

That handoff needs to be designed rather than improvised. Who has the authority to declare an incident, at any hour, without waiting for a meeting? What happens automatically on declaration, who is notified, what channel opens, what gets preserved? What can the operation do on its own authority before that point, and what must it not do? That last question matters more than it appears. An analyst who isolates a host may prevent further harm, but may also disrupt a critical service or alert the intruder; wiping, reimaging, or making uncontrolled changes can destroy evidence outright. Pre-agreed decision rights should distinguish urgent protective action from steps that require incident-command approval, and those rights should be settled in advance rather than at two in the morning.

What happens next is separate work: the response plan and team, the exercises that make it real, the crisis communication and regulatory notification, and the continuity and recovery underneath it all. This chapter's obligation is to hand over cleanly: a declared incident, relevant evidence preserved, a documented timeline, an initial assessment of scope, and a named person who has been woken up.

In-House, Managed, or Hybrid — and What Cannot Be Outsourced

Few security leaders have unlimited analysts, engineering capacity, time-zone coverage, and platform expertise. So the question is not whether external support is legitimate; it is which model delivers the capability, and where accountability has to stay.

An in-house team offers the strongest business context and tightest integration, but requires sustained investment in people, engineering, and out-of-hours coverage. A managed detection and response provider offers scale, specialist skills, and continuous hours, but only within the scope, data, authority, and context it has been given. A hybrid model, often practical for a mid-sized organization, combines the two, and lives or dies on how carefully the interface is designed.

Whatever the model, a specific set of things cannot be transferred: ownership of the business risk, the choice of priority threat scenarios, decisions about acceptable coverage gaps, knowledge of which services and data matter most, authority for disruptive containment, executive and board accountability, and the obligation to learn after a failure. This is exactly where arrangements weaken in practice. The contract says continuous monitoring, but the provider has no visibility into a critical cloud environment. The provider escalates, but no internal owner responds. The provider sees the compromise, but cannot disable the account. The internal team assumes the provider tunes detections; the provider assumes that is out of scope. Both sides meet their narrow obligations and the outcome still fails.

So a managed or hybrid arrangement needs an operating agreement, not just a commercial one: which systems, sources, identities, and hours are in scope; who owns detection content and telemetry health; how deep triage and investigation go; severity definitions and escalation routes; which containment actions are pre-authorized and which need approval; what access you get to cases, raw evidence, and detection logic; how you communicate when primary systems are down; and what happens on exit. Measure it on decisions and outcomes rather than ticket handling, a five-minute acknowledgment means little if it takes three hours to find the right internal owner, or if the evidence needed to determine scope never arrives.

Metrics That Survive Contact With a Board

Security operations metrics are unusually prone to measuring effort rather than effectiveness. Alert volume, tickets closed, and events ingested describe how busy the function is, not whether it works.

The measures that mean something are harder to produce and worth the trouble. Time measures are useful only when their start and stop points are defined, so separate event-to-alert, alert-to-review, review-to-decision, and decision-to-containment wherever the data supports it. Where the start of malicious activity is unknown, which is common, describe dwell time as unknown or estimated rather than manufacturing precision, and report percentiles and the materially slow cases alongside averages, because a small number of delayed investigations may carry most of the risk.

What proportion of the behaviors in the threat profile do we have working coverage for, and is that proportion moving? What fraction of alerts turn out to be real, and what is that doing to the queue? How much of the estate is actually feeding telemetry, and would we know if a source stopped? And how were the last several intrusions actually found, by our own detection, by a hunt, by a user, by a supplier, or by an outside party telling us? That last measure is the most revealing metric in the domain, and the one most operations avoid publishing.

For a board, the translation is narrower. They need to know whether the organization would notice a serious intrusion, roughly how quickly, what the known blind spots are, what is being done about them, and how the answers have changed since last time. Coverage against a defensible threat profile, with the gaps named and a plan attached, is a story a board can act on. A count of alerts is not.

The Core Security Operations Control Set

The following control set is illustrative rather than exhaustive; its value lies in how the controls connect around the ability to notice.

- **Threat profile and prioritization.** A documented, current view of which adversaries and behaviors plausibly apply, reviewed as the business, sector, geography, and technology change.
- **Telemetry coverage and integrity.** A mapped inventory of monitored sources against the estate, with completeness, timeliness, retention, and alerting on the loss of expected data.
- **Detection engineering.** Detections owned, documented, mapped to the threat profile, tested, tuned with context rather than weakened, versioned, and retired when they cannot be made reliable.
- **Triage and investigation.** Defined severities, response times, required context, documented next actions, evidence preservation, and a timeline discipline that survives later scrutiny.
- **Threat intelligence integration.** A defined set of relevant sources feeding profile updates, detection priorities, hunts, and incident context, with a route from reading to changing something.
- **Threat hunting.** Hypothesis-driven searches against collected telemetry, prioritized by coverage gaps, with each hunt producing a detection, a data-quality correction, a control improvement, a refined threat assessment, or a bounded documented conclusion.

- **Escalation and handoff.** A declared threshold, named authority to declare at any hour, defined immediate actions, and a clean transfer into incident response.
- **Measurement and feedback.** Coverage, known or reasonably estimated dwell time, time to an accountable owner or containment decision, source of discovery, and a loop that writes every incident's lessons back into detections and preventive controls.
- **Provider governance.** Where an external provider is involved, scope, telemetry and detection-content ownership, investigation depth, service levels, escalation, containment authority, evidence access, testing, continuity, and exit responsibilities are defined and reviewed as an operating interface.
- **Protection and continuity of the operation itself.** The platforms, privileged integrations, automation credentials, case records, and retained telemetry that security operations depends on are themselves high-value targets, and the team needs a way to communicate, investigate, decide, and record when the identity platform, network, collaboration tool, or SIEM is the thing that is unavailable.

The Frameworks Underneath Security Operations

The frameworks describe this domain from different altitudes, and together they cover it well.

The CSF 2.0 carries the clearest structure, because it separates the two halves of the work into distinct functions. Detect covers adverse event analysis and continuous monitoring: potentially adverse events are analyzed to understand associated activities (DE.AE-02), cyber threat intelligence and other contextual information are integrated into that analysis (DE.AE-07), and monitoring extends across networks and network services (DE.CM-01) and across computing hardware, software, runtime environments, and their data (DE.CM-09).

Respond then covers incident management, analysis, communication, and mitigation: the response plan is executed in coordination with relevant third parties once an incident is declared (RS.MA-01), analysis establishes what took place and the root cause (RS.AN-03), stakeholders are notified (RS.CO-02), and incidents are contained and eradicated (RS.MI-01, RS.MI-02). Read together, these outcomes describe the transition from security operations into coordinated incident response.

ISO/IEC 27002:2022 distributes the same work across connected controls, the collection and protection of logs, the monitoring of systems and networks for anomalous behavior, the use of threat intelligence as an input to security decisions, and the information security incident management controls covering planning, assessment, response, and learning from incidents. Its contribution is the management-system framing: monitoring is not a tool deployment but a governed capability with ownership, review, and improvement.

The CIS Controls v8.1, from the Center for Internet Security, convert the same intent into a prioritized sequence, with audit log management establishing the telemetry foundation, network monitoring and defense covering the detection surface between them, and incident response management establishing the process, roles, and reporting that turn detection into action. For a smaller team, CIS is the most directly actionable of the three.

MITRE ATT&CK is not a control framework at all, and that is exactly why it belongs here. It is a publicly maintained knowledge base of adversary tactics and techniques observed in real intrusions, and it supplies what the control frameworks deliberately do not: a shared vocabulary for adversary behavior. Where the frameworks say monitor and detect, ATT&CK lets an organization answer *detect what, specifically*, and assess coverage behavior by behavior.

The breadth of the Enterprise matrix is both its strength and the reason it is so often misused. No organization should attempt to cover all of it. The point is to select the behaviors your threat profile makes plausible and assess those honestly. Recent versions have also begun publishing detection strategies and analytics alongside the techniques, which narrows the old gap between naming a behavior and knowing what to look for in the data.

It is worth naming how ATT&CK goes wrong, because the failure is common. A colored matrix can manufacture the appearance of rigor without anyone defining what "covered" means, and coverage is really several separate questions: whether the relevant data is collected from the environments that matter, whether that data is complete and correctly parsed, whether an analytic can recognize the behavior, whether an analyst could reconstruct what happened, whether any control prevents or limits it, whether any of that has been tested against a realistic representation, and whether the resulting signal reaches someone who can decide.

A preventive control does not prove detection if prevention fails; a rule does not prove the telemetry exists on every critical system; a test in one environment does not prove coverage everywhere. Nor should ATT&CK be used as proof of attribution, different adversaries share behaviors, and similar evidence supports several explanations. Used carefully it provides structure. Used carelessly it turns uncertainty into a heat map.

Read across them and the correlation is clean. NIST supplies the outcomes and the Detect/Respond split. ISO wraps the capability in a management system. CIS makes it a prioritized build order. ATT&CK supplies the adversary vocabulary that makes "coverage" a measurable idea rather than an aspiration. Build the ability to notice once, then describe it in whichever language the audience requires.

Where Security Operations Actually Breaks

The same failures recur in organizations of very different sizes.

- **The tool defines the strategy.** Detection coverage is whatever the platform shipped with, and nobody has asked which adversary behaviors it does and does not address.
- **Telemetry gaps are invisible.** Sources were onboarded once, something broke quietly, or was deliberately disabled, and the first anyone learns of it is during an investigation that has no data for the relevant period.
- **Retention is set by cost alone.** The logs cover thirty days, the intrusion began four months ago, and the scope of the breach becomes a matter of inference.
- **The queue exceeds the capacity.** Alert volume outgrew the team, triage became a backlog, and a correctly generated alert sat unopened while the intrusion progressed.
- **Rules are weakened instead of narrowed.** Noisy detections were tuned toward silence rather than toward precision, and the operation now runs on rules that no longer fire on the thing they were written for.
- **Intelligence is a subscription, not an input.** Feeds arrive, reports circulate, indicators are ingested, and no decision, detection, or hunt has changed as a result.
- **Coverage is counted in rules.** Five hundred detections cluster around a handful of behaviors, the count looks impressive, and whole stages of an intrusion have nothing watching them.
- **Identity is under-monitored.** Endpoint telemetry is rich, authentication and privilege-use telemetry is thin, and the intrusion that arrives through valid credentials looks like an ordinary working day.
- **The escalation threshold is undefined.** Nobody knows who can declare an incident at 2 a.m., so the declaration waits for business hours, and the containment window closes.
- **Containment destroys the evidence.** A host is wiped or reimaged in the first ten minutes, the intruder is alerted and

the forensic trail is gone, and the investigation can never establish what was taken.

- **Nothing is learned.** Incidents are closed rather than mined, the same intrusion path is used again months later, and no detection was ever written for the last one.
- **Outsourcing is mistaken for transferring accountability.** The provider monitors what it receives and does what the contract says, while the organization assumes threat priorities, business context, decision rights, and learning went with it.
- **The operation itself is unprotected.** The platforms, credentials, integrations, and evidence stores the team depends on become an attack route, or fail at precisely the moment they are needed.
- **Discovery keeps coming from outside.** The intrusions that matter are reported by a customer, a supplier, a researcher, or law enforcement, and the operation's own metrics never surface that fact.

Industry Pattern — The Board Question the CISO Could Not Answer

> ***A composite industry pattern, not one named organization:*** *An organization with a well-regarded managed detection service and a healthy alert volume is asked, during a board discussion, a question its CISO cannot answer cleanly: if an attacker used stolen credentials to log in normally, move through the environment using built-in administrative tooling, and stage data for exfiltration over several weeks, would we see it? The honest answer turns out to be partly, and nobody can say which parts.*
>
> *The exercise that follows is not a procurement. The team writes down the handful of adversary behaviors its sector actually faces, then walks each one against its own telemetry and detections. Endpoint execution is well covered. Email is well covered. Identity is thin. Sign-in telemetry is collected but barely used, and privilege escalation inside the identity platform has no detection at all. Lateral movement using legitimate administrative tools is invisible by design, because those tools are supposed to be used. Two log sources thought to be feeding the platform stopped months earlier and nobody was alerted.*
>
> *None of that was a product failure, and buying another platform would not have surfaced it. The fixes were mostly unglamorous: onboard the missing sources and alert on their absence, use the identity telemetry already being paid for, write a small number of detections for the specific behaviors that mattered most, and put a monthly hour into hunting the gaps that remained. The alert volume went down. The ability to notice went up. Those two things are not in tension. They only appear to be when volume is mistaken for coverage.*

What Evidence Should You Expect

- **A documented threat profile** — the adversaries and behaviors judged relevant to this organization, with the reasoning, the review date, and the trigger for revisiting it; it proves prioritization is deliberate rather than inherited from a vendor.

- **Telemetry coverage records** — monitored sources mapped against the actual estate, with completeness, timeliness, retention periods, and evidence that the loss of an expected source raises an alert; it proves the operation knows what it can and cannot see.
- **A detection inventory** — detections with owners, the behavior each addresses, data dependencies, tuning history, test results, and when each was last validated or fired as intended; it proves the rule set is maintained rather than accumulated.
- **Triage and investigation records** — severities, response times against target, the context available to analysts, documented next actions, evidence-preservation steps, and incident timelines; it proves alerts become decisions at a defensible speed.
- **Threat intelligence in use** — the sources relied on, and specific instances where intelligence changed a detection, a hunt, a control, or a priority; it proves intelligence is an input rather than a subscription.
- **Hunt records** — hypotheses, the data queried, findings, and what each hunt produced: a detection, a data-quality correction, a control or threat-model improvement, or a bounded conclusion with its limitations stated; it proves the operation looks for what its detections would miss.
- **Escalation and handoff evidence** — the declaration threshold, who holds authority at any hour, what happens automatically on declaration, and records of actual escalations; it proves the transition into incident response is designed rather than improvised.
- **Provider operating agreement and service reviews** — where a managed provider is involved, the documented scope, telemetry and content ownership, escalation routes, pre-authorized containment, evidence access, and review records; it proves the internal-external boundary is operational rather than only commercial.

- **Continuity evidence for the operation itself** — how the team communicates, investigates, preserves evidence, and decides when its own primary platforms are unavailable; it proves the capability survives an incident that touches it.
- **Operational metrics and the feedback loop** — coverage against the threat profile (distinguishing telemetry, data quality, analytic detection, investigation, mitigation, validation, and decision readiness), known or reasonably estimated dwell time, time to an accountable owner or containment decision, source of discovery, and evidence that incident lessons were written back into detections and preventive controls; it proves the operation improves rather than repeats.

What This Means for You as a Security Leader

You are unlikely to run this function yourself, and in many organizations you will not even own the people who do, the operation may be a managed service, a shared IT capability, or two people wearing several hats. What you own is the point of view. Nobody else in the organization is positioned to say which adversaries matter, what they would do, and whether the organization could see it.

So start there rather than with the tooling. Write down the threat profile, defend it in plain language, and be honest where it is uncertain. Take the handful of behaviors that follow from it and walk each one against your own telemetry and detections, the exercise is unglamorous, can be completed incrementally, and often produces the most useful roadmap this domain offers. Fix the visibility gaps before buying new detection capability, because a detection over data you do not collect is a slide, not a control. Insist on alerting for the absence of telemetry, not just its content. And decide the escalation threshold and the after-hours declaration authority now, in writing, while it is a calm conversation.

If the operation is outsourced, the questions change but the ownership does not. Which behaviors does the provider actually detect, and how do you know? What are they not watching, and who covers that? What do they do on their own authority, and what do they hand back to you? How fast, measured how, and against what target? What happens at 3 a.m. on a public holiday? A contract that specifies alert volumes and response times without specifying coverage has bought you activity and left you to discover the gaps yourself.

Report it upward in terms a board can act on. Not alert counts and not tool names, but whether the organization would notice a serious intrusion, roughly how fast, which blind spots are known, what is being done about them, and how those answers have moved. Include the uncomfortable measure, how the last several incidents were actually discovered, because an operation that keeps learning about its intrusions from outsiders has a coverage problem no amount of tooling will fix.

The mature position is not "we monitor everything." Nobody does. It is: "we know who is likely to come, we know which of their behaviors we can and cannot see, our gaps are named and shrinking, and when something real happens we find it ourselves and hand it over cleanly."

Reality Check

Pick a plausible intrusion scenario for your organization. As an illustrative one, consider a credential obtained through Phishing (T1566), used as a Valid Account (T1078) to log in normally, followed by credential theft and movement through Remote Services (T1021) using legitimate administrative tooling. Walk it stage by stage against your own environment and ask, at each step, whether the activity would produce a record in data you actually collect, whether a detection exists for it, and whether that detection has ever fired correctly. Where the answer breaks is your real detection posture, and it is rarely where the dashboard suggests.

Then perform two checks that are simple to run and often reveal uncomfortable surprises. First, pick three log sources you believe are feeding your platform and verify that data arrived today, not that the integration exists, that the data arrived. Second, ask how your last three genuine incidents were discovered: by your own detection, by a hunt, by a user, or by someone outside the organization. If external discovery dominates, treat that as evidence of a material detection, visibility, or escalation gap rather than explaining it away as bad luck.

Bridge to Chapter 6

Detection shortens the distance between a signal and a decision; the next chapter asks the harder question of whether the organization can keep operating while the disruption is still happening.

CHAPTER 6

Resilience — Assume It Happens

Security tries to prevent the bad day. Resilience decides whether the organization survives it.

There is a quiet fantasy inside a lot of security programs. If we build enough controls, train enough people, patch fast enough, buy the right tools, and monitor closely enough, maybe the incident just will not happen. It is a comforting idea, and it is not a strategy.

Prevention matters — enormously. Most of this series has been about it: governance, controls, evidence, privacy, regulation, cloud, AI, third-party assurance, all the disciplines that lower the odds of failure. Good security work prevents countless bad days nobody ever sees. That is the invisible success of the function, and it is real.

But mature security leadership begins the moment you hold a second truth alongside the first: something will still go wrong. Not because the team failed or the CISO did not care or the controls were pointless. Because systems are complex, people are human, vendors fail, attackers adapt, dependencies break, configurations drift, credentials leak, software has defects, and business pressure creates shortcuts no policy fully closes. That is where resilience begins.

Resilience is not the opposite of security. It is what security becomes when it gets honest about reality. A resilient organization does not assume it can prevent every incident. It assumes incidents will happen and prepares to keep thinking, deciding, communicating, operating, recovering, and learning when they do.

This chapter widens the lens from preventing and detecting incidents to the leadership work of carrying the organization through one.

Whether the trigger is ransomware, a cloud outage, a vendor compromise, a data exposure, a failed change, insider misuse, an AI failure, or plain operational breakdown, the leadership question eventually lands in the same place: can the organization decide, contain, continue, recover, communicate, and learn? That is resilience, and it is one of the truest tests of whether a security program is real.

What Resilience Actually Means

It is worth being precise, because the word gets used loosely. Robustness is a system's ability to resist stress, the wall, the redundancy, the hardened config. Useful, but finite; every robust thing has a breaking point. Resilience is what happens after that point. It is the capacity to absorb a hit, keep delivering what matters most, recover in a controlled way, and come out having learned something. A resilient organization is not one that never gets hit. It is one where getting hit does not become a crisis, and a crisis does not become an existential event.

A useful way to hold it as a leader is four capabilities: the ability to anticipate what could go wrong, withstand it when it does, recover to normal operations, and adapt so the next one lands softer. None of those is a product you can buy. They are organizational muscles, and like any muscle they only exist if you exercise them.

Which leads to the reframe the rest of this part is built on. Prevention controls reduce the probability of compromise. Resilience controls reduce the damage after it, and plenty of controls, segmentation and tested recovery among them, do both. Two organizations can face the same attack and have completely different outcomes, one detects quickly, isolates cleanly, preserves evidence, communicates clearly, restores critical services, meets its notification obligations, and learns; the other notices late, argues over severity, loses logs, delays containment, cannot restore cleanly, confuses customers, and spends the next quarter explaining what it should have known on day one. Same trigger, different resilience. The difference is rarely one tool. It is operating maturity.

Both halves belong in the board conversation: what are we doing to reduce the likelihood of incidents, and if one happens, what are we doing to reduce the impact. Most security dashboards over-index on the first, because it is easier to measure, patching, phishing rates, endpoint coverage, multi-factor authentication (MFA) adoption. Those matter. But a CISO who reports only prevention has told leadership half the story. The other half is survivability.

Assume It Happens — as a Design Principle

"Assume breach" became a popular phrase because it worked: it pushed teams past the perimeter into detection, segmentation, containment, and blast radius. Resilience extends that same mindset past the breach itself. Assume the vendor is unavailable. Assume a cloud region fails. Assume a backup is corrupted. Assume the incident starts on a Friday evening, the first facts are wrong, the customer hears before the executive team does, and the regulator's clock starts before anyone feels ready.

This is not pessimism. It is design pressure. Good resilience planning asks the uncomfortable questions before the uncomfortable day. You do not want to learn whether your backups restore for the first time during ransomware, or go looking for the cyber-insurance contact mid-incident, or decide who is allowed to take a system offline while that system is burning. You ask early, then build around the answers.

Some security leaders worry that talking openly about failure sounds weak. It does not. Mature boards already know no control environment is perfect. What they want to know is whether management thought about the bad day before the bad day. Resilience is that answer.

Critical Services Come Before Critical Systems

Security teams think in systems, applications, servers, databases, identities, endpoints, cloud accounts, APIs. Business leaders think in services, onboarding, payments, order processing, claims, support, payroll, patient care, regulatory reporting. Resilience has to start from services, not systems.

A system can be technically important but not business-critical; another can look ordinary and quietly hold up a critical service. A small identity dependency can take down half the environment. A low-profile API can stop customer transactions. The better opening question is not "which systems matter?" but "which business services must continue, recover first, or degrade gracefully?" Once you know that, you can map the systems, data, identities, vendors, people, network paths, and backups each one actually needs.

This is usually where an organization discovers its resilience assumptions are thinner than it thought. The payment app has a recovery plan, but the identity provider it depends on does not. The enterprise resource planning system can be restored, but the middleware that feeds it, the software that passes data between systems, has no tested recovery. The core platform is redundant, but a certificate or domain name system (DNS) process lives in one person's head. Critical services are valuable precisely because they surface those hidden dependencies, and mapping them in detail is the work Chapter 10 owns. The leadership move here is simpler: push the organization to reason from the business service backward, so teams protect what is essential rather than only what is visible.

RTO and RPO Are Promises, Not Decorations

Every resilience conversation eventually meets two terms. Recovery Time Objective. How quickly a service should be restored. Recovery Point Objective. How much data loss is tolerable, measured in time. They show up in continuity plans, audit evidence, customer questionnaires, and regulator expectations. They are useful, and they are frequently fictional.

An RTO written in a document is not a capability. If the approved RTO is four hours but a representative restore test takes fourteen, the objective is still four hours, what you have proven is a ten-hour capability gap, plus whatever confusion the real event adds. If the RPO is fifteen minutes but the recovery design can lose a day of data, the objective is still fifteen minutes, and the capability simply fails to meet it.

This is where resilience gets uncomfortable: it exposes the gap between business expectation and technical capability. A CISO should welcome that exposure, because it is far cheaper to find the gap in a test than in an incident with customers waiting. The mechanics of proving these numbers (the restore tests, the measurement against objectives) belong to Chapter 10. What matters at this altitude is the discipline of treating RTO and RPO as commitments that require evidence, not numbers that require only a meeting.

The Four Disciplines Under One Umbrella

Here is where people get tangled. Resilience is not one plan you file. It is an umbrella over several disciplines that grew up separately and are often still owned by different teams:

- Incident response (IR), the operational machine that detects, contains, and eradicates a security event.
- Disaster recovery (DR), restoring technology services after a disruption, whatever caused it.
- Business continuity (BCP), keeping the business running, or degrading gracefully, while the technology is restored.
- Crisis management and communication, the decisions, roles, and messaging around a serious event, including customers, regulators, and the board.

Different origins, one job: keep the organization functioning under stress. The common failure is running incident response, disaster recovery, business continuity, and crisis management as four disconnected binders that never touch until they are all needed at once; then the phone numbers are stale, the roles overlap, and nobody agreed who declares a crisis. Treat them as one coordinated capability: the response plan with its roles, escalation, and decision rights; the testing that proves it through tabletops, exercises, and ransomware readiness; the crisis communication, forensics, and regulatory notification that surround it; and the continuity, disaster recovery, and backup strategy that bring the business back. One operating frame, with specialist machinery that connects instead of collides.

This chapter does not re-teach those individual disciplines. It explains why the organization needs them to operate as one machine, and how a security leader should think about the whole.

One preview worth planting now, because it shapes everything downstream: a serious incident is not only a technical condition, it is a decision environment. Facts are incomplete, time is short, and different teams optimize for different outcomes. Security wants containment, IT wants stability, the business wants operations back, legal wants accurate language and preserved privilege, communications wants clarity before speaking.

All of that is normal, and it is exactly why decision rights have to exist before the crisis: who can declare a major incident, who can take a critical service offline, who approves customer notification, who accepts the risk of running in degraded mode. If those decisions are not assigned in advance, they get negotiated live, and negotiation during a crisis is slow, and slow is expensive. Building that decision structure is its own work; the point here is only that resilience assumes it exists.

The Frameworks Underneath Resilience

Resilience is a place where several frameworks converge on the same capability from different angles, a clean illustration of this book's through-line: many frameworks, one operating model. You do not adopt them one at a time as separate programs. You recognize they are describing the same muscle in different vocabularies. A few you will meet, defined briefly and treated in depth where noted:

The CSF 2.0 organizes cybersecurity outcomes across six functions, Govern, Identify, Protect, Detect, Respond, and Recover. Respond and Recover are the two most visible once disruption hits, though resilience draws on all six. It is a useful common language for showing a board where response and recovery fit, and it tells you what capabilities to have, not how to build them.

NIST's incident-handling guidance, the SP 800-61 line, is what teams usually mean by "the NIST IR process," and it changed materially in April 2025. Revision 3 supersedes the 2012 guide and is published as a Cybersecurity Framework 2.0 Community Profile, organizing incident response across all six CSF Functions rather than as a standalone phase model. The familiar arc — preparation, detection and analysis, containment and eradication, recovery, and learning — remains a useful operational sequence for a playbook, but treat it as your own working shape rather than as the current NIST structure. NIST's contingency-planning guidance, the SP 800-

34 line, covers disaster recovery and continuity. Both belong to the coordinated resilience capability being framed here; their detailed implementation is not this chapter's job.

ISO 22301 is the international standard for a business continuity management system, and it is worth being clear that it is not a security standard. It is the continuity counterpart to ISO 27001, sharing the same management-system spirit of context, leadership, planning, operation, evaluation, and improvement, but pointed at keeping the business running rather than securing it. Readers meeting both for the first time tend to blur them; keep them distinct.

ISO/IEC 27031 narrows further to information and communications technology (ICT) readiness for business continuity, the bridge between "the business must keep running" and "here's what technology has to do to make that possible." And ISO/IEC 27001:2022 itself carries continuity inside its control set, information security during disruption, and ICT readiness for business continuity, which is worth remembering: if you are certified, some resilience is already in scope through your Statement of Applicability. Just do not read the certificate as proof of enterprise-wide operational resilience; it attests that the scoped management system conforms, not that every critical service will recover.

DORA, the Digital Operational Resilience Act, Regulation (EU) 2022/2554, applicable since 17 January 2025, is the EU's operational-resilience regime for the financial sector, and it is less a voluntary framework than a binding obligation with teeth: governance, ICT risk management, incident reporting, resilience testing, and third-party oversight, all mandated. The Reserve Bank of India (RBI), the Securities and Exchange Board of India (SEBI), and the Saudi Central Bank (SAMA) and their equivalents elsewhere also set sector-specific resilience expectations. Keep the distinction clean: those instruments tell you the rules; this chapter builds the operational muscle that lets you meet them.

The point of the list is not memorization. It is so that when someone drops "we need to be ISO 22301 aligned" or "DORA testing is coming" into a meeting, you already know it maps to work you are doing here, not a new island to staff. That mapping does not make them interchangeable: they share the operating machinery, but each carries its own scope, evidence, and notification obligations, so you build the capability once and still honor what each specific instrument demands.

Resilience Runs on Evidence, Not Confidence

A phrase that should make any CISO slightly nervous is "we should be okay." It usually means nobody has tested recently, but the last person who understood the system believed the plan made sense. Resilience should not rest on confidence. It should rest on evidence, that backups actually restore, that critical services have current dependency maps, that incident roles are assigned, that contact lists work, that vendors can be reached, that recovery tests met their objectives, and that the gaps those tests found became actions that actually closed.

This does not mean every organization needs an enterprise-grade resilience platform. A small organization can start with pragmatic evidence: a tested restore, a service-dependency map, a contact list that is current, a tabletop report, a measured recovery time, and an honest list of known gaps. An untested plan is not a plan. It is a hypothesis. Tested evidence is what turns the hypothesis into a capability.

And the direction of travel makes this less optional every year. Regulators increasingly ask not only whether you have controls, but whether you can stay operational under disruption, report incidents quickly, manage third-party dependencies, and prove it. That is useful leverage for a security leader. You are no longer asking for resilience investment because "security thinks it's important," but because customers, regulators, insurers, and the business increasingly expect evidence the organization can withstand a bad day. Use that leverage responsibly. Do not oversell. Do not tell leadership "we can recover in four hours" because a plan says so. Tell them what the evidence supports, where the gaps are, and what risk they are currently accepting. That is a resilience conversation a board can act on.

Backup is a control. Resilience is a capability.

Industry Pattern — The Recovery Plan That Worked Only on Paper

> *This one repeats across the industry often enough to be predictable. An organization has a disaster recovery plan, documented, reviewed, filed. The RTOs look reasonable, the backup dashboard is green, the infrastructure team is confident, and the business believes critical services will come back inside the approved window.*
>
> *Then a serious disruption hits. The database backup restores, but the application will not start because a dependent service was never in the recovery runbook. The identity provider is up, but a certificate quietly expired in the secondary environment. A DNS change needs approval from someone who is not on the incident call. The support team cannot reach the customer-communication template because the collaboration platform is also down. The continuity plan says manual processing is available, but nobody has actually done it in two years.*
>
> *The backup was real. The recovery capability was partial. That is the gap resilience exposes. The lesson is not that anyone was careless. It is that recovery is an end-to-end business service, not a pile of technical restores. A plan that restores components but has never tested the service still has an assumption sitting in the middle of it. And assumptions are where incidents like to live.*

What Evidence Should You Expect

Resilience should produce evidence that the organization can identify its critical services, understand what they depend on, respond to disruption, recover within realistic objectives, communicate under pressure, and improve after a test or a real event. At leadership altitude, that means being able to point to:

- a current incident response plan with assigned roles and a clear trigger for declaring an incident;
- a business impact analysis that names the critical services and how long each can be down;

- recovery objectives that have been tested, not just approved, with business-owner sign-off on critical-service priority and on the recovery objectives themselves, so RTO and RPO are business commitments rather than numbers IT set alone;
- dependency maps for those critical services;
- a crisis-communication and notification process that involves legal, privacy, and communications rather than only the security team;
- dated exercise and recovery-test records;
- post-incident reviews that produced changes rather than just paperwork; and
- a resilience risk register or corrective-action tracker that carries the gaps found through business impact analyses, recovery tests, exercises, and real incidents through to closure — the same risk-management discipline, pointed at continuity.

The detailed artifact-by-artifact evidence for each of these belongs with the discipline that owns it; what a CISO owns here is the whole picture being coherent.

Notice the through-line: nearly every piece of real evidence is about something being exercised and improved, not merely documented. A binder proves intent. A dated exercise record with lessons that actually changed the plan proves capability.

For a small or mid-sized organization, the practical minimum is enough to stop pretending:

- Identify the handful of services whose disruption would cause the most harm.
- Define realistic RTO and RPO with the business owners.
- Map the major dependencies for those services.
- Test a restore for the most important data and system.
- Create a simple incident escalation path and keep emergency vendor contacts current.

- Run one tabletop exercise, a discussion-based walkthrough of a scenario with the people who would actually respond. Document the gaps, and track the fixes to closure.

That is not a complete resilience program. It is enough to know where you actually stand, which is more than many organizations can say.

Reality Check

> *Pick one critical service. Not a system, a service. Onboarding, payments, claims, support, payroll, order fulfillment, security monitoring, regulatory reporting. Whatever matters most where you are.*
>
> *Now ask: how long can it be down before real harm starts? How much data can we lose without unacceptable impact? Which systems, vendors, identity, cloud, DNS, certificate, and integration dependencies does it rely on? Who owns recovery, and who owns telling customers? When was recovery last tested end to end, and did it meet the stated RTO and RPO? What manual workaround exists? Which third parties would we need during recovery, and do we know how to reach them after hours? What would we tell customers if it failed today, and which gaps do we already know about but have not fixed?*
>
> *If those questions produce silence, the resilience program is not real for that service yet. That is not a reason to panic. It is a reason to start where the business impact is highest. Resilience gets built service by service.*

What This Means for You as a Security Leader

A modern CISO cannot sell cybersecurity as prevention alone. Prevention is necessary, but the board, the regulator, the customer, and the business also need to know whether the organization can survive disruption, and that is the resilience conversation. Your job in this part is not to become the incident commander, the continuity manager, and the crisis spokesperson all at once. It is to make sure those roles exist, connect, and have been rehearsed before they are needed.

Practically, that is a shift in where you spend attention. You connect the dots other teams tend to see separately, security controls, incident response, backup and recovery, business continuity, disaster recovery, vendor dependency, privacy breach handling, regulatory notification, customer communication, executive decision-making. Individually those sit in different teams. Collectively they decide whether the organization can handle a bad day. And you push, gently and repeatedly, for rehearsal, because rehearsal is the only thing that turns a plan into a capability.

The stance underneath all of it is simple. Assume it happens, not because you are negative, but because you are responsible. Assume the incident, the outage, the vendor failure, the incomplete first facts, the gap in the plan. Then test, prepare, document, improve, and report honestly. That is how resilience becomes more than a word on a slide.

Security tries to stop the bad day. Resilience decides whether the organization survives it.

Bridge to Chapter 7

Mindset is where resilience starts, not where it lives; the next chapter is the incident response plan and the team that runs it.

CHAPTER 7

The Incident Response Plan and Team

When the incident starts, clarity is a control.

Every organization believes it will respond well to an incident, right up until the first real one. Then something consistent happens. The technical people usually do fine; they know their systems, they contain what they can, they work the problem. What breaks is rarely the technology. It is everything around it. Nobody is certain who is actually in charge. Two people give instructions that contradict each other. An executive joins the call and starts redirecting the team. Someone takes a critical system offline without telling anyone. Legal finds out an hour late. And a question that should take thirty seconds, are we allowed to do this?, turns into a twenty-minute debate while the clock runs.

That is not a technology failure. It is an organizational one. You do not rise to the occasion during an incident; you fall to the level of the decisions you already made. Which is the whole reason the incident response plan exists.

Incident response is one of resilience's most important operating systems. Not the policy. Not the PDF named "IR Plan – Final – Approved." The operating model: who does what, in what order, and who decides. And when the pressure is on, clarity about those things is itself a control.

What the Plan Is Actually For

Here is the reframe that changes everything else. An incident response plan is not really a set of instructions for handling an incident. It is a set of decisions you make now, calmly, so nobody has to make them later under pressure with bad information.

Most organizations have a plan that can pass a document review. It has phases, roles, and a contact list where half the numbers are already wrong. That plan satisfies an auditor reading calmly. It can still fail on a bad day, because it was written for the auditor rather than for tired people making decisions with incomplete information. A useful plan answers operational questions fast: How does an alert become an incident? Who can declare one? Who leads? Who joins the technical work, and who joins the decision-making? When do legal and privacy come in? Who can approve containment that disrupts the business? Who preserves evidence? Who records decisions? When does the incident move from containment to recovery, and who declares it over?

If the plan cannot answer those quickly, it is incomplete no matter how good the headings look. Incident response is a decision-design exercise, not a writing exercise. The document matters because it encodes the operating model, but the model is what people actually do when the bridge opens.

What Actually Counts as an Incident

Before a team can respond, it has to agree on what it is responding to, and that is less obvious than it sounds. In some organizations everything suspicious becomes an "incident," which buries the serious cases in noise. In others, serious events stay ordinary IT or security tickets because nobody wants to use the incident word too early. Both patterns lose the same thing: time.

NIST's incident-response guidance draws a useful three-way distinction. An **event** is any observable occurrence involving computing assets, including physical and virtual platforms, networks, services, and cloud environments. Most events are routine, a login attempt, a software update, an application processing a request. An **adverse cybersecurity event** is an event with a potentially negative cybersecurity impact. A **cybersecurity incident** is the narrower category: an occurrence that actually or imminently jeopardizes information or an information system without lawful authority, or violates, or threatens to violate, applicable law, security policy, security procedure, or acceptable-use policy.

You do not need to force that vocabulary onto every service desk. You do need to keep three operating decisions separate: does this signal need investigation, does this adverse event need coordinated action, and has it crossed the threshold for formal incident command, escalation, and notification assessment?

That separation lets the organization move early without declaring a crisis every time. A suspected cloud credential exposure can be investigated and protected immediately while the facts are still incomplete. A vendor's vague breach notice can enter structured triage before you know whether your data was involved. An AI system surfacing one customer's information to another can activate privacy, product, and security specialists without anyone waiting for the perfect label.

Your internal definition may also be wider than the cybersecurity scope. A destructive but non-malicious change, a prolonged cloud failure, physical sabotage, fraud, or a safety event may use some of the same command, communication, evidence, and recovery machinery. That is fine. Just define the boundary. The incident-response plan handles cybersecurity incidents; resilience and crisis processes may activate for other disruptive events and join the same leadership structure when they need to.

The important word remains **suspected**. If people must prove an incident before they are allowed to escalate one, the organization has designed delay into its plan. Early response is disciplined action under uncertainty: protect what may be at risk, preserve evidence, bring in the right authority, and keep revising the assessment as facts improve. A good definition does not cause panic. It creates permission to look early, coordinate proportionately, and escalate before a material event grows in silence.

The Lifecycle Has Changed — and That Matters

For years the incident-response lifecycle was taught as a sequence: prepare, detect and analyze, contain, eradicate, recover, and learn. That sequence is still useful inside a playbook. Responders still have to find the incident, understand it, limit it, remove the cause, restore the operation, and learn from what happened. Keep it as the operational arc your team executes.

But the reference everyone cites for it has moved, and the change is more than a version bump. *NIST Special Publication 800-61 Revision 3, Incident Response Recommendations and Considerations for Cybersecurity Risk Management,* published in April 2025, supersedes the 2012 *Computer Security Incident Handling Guide* and is structured as a **Cybersecurity Framework 2.0 Community Profile.** Its point is that incident response can no longer be treated as a separate circle a specialist team enters when an alert turns serious and exits after a lessons-learned meeting.

The revised model uses all six CSF Functions. **Govern, Identify, and Protect prepare the organization.** Together they help prevent some incidents, prepare the organization for those that still occur, reduce their likely impact, and turn lessons into improvements. Governance establishes policy, authority, risk tolerance, communication paths, and supplier responsibilities. Identify supplies the asset, service, data, risk, and dependency context that lets a responder understand what an alert means. Protect reduces exposure and preserves the capabilities the response will need, identity, backups, communications, logging, and other safeguards.

Detect, Respond, and Recover run the live incident. Together they find and analyze possible attacks, prioritize the situation, coordinate action, contain and eradicate the threat, restore affected assets and operations, and support incident reporting, notification, and other communications.

And improvement connects both sides continuously, carried in the Improvement Category within the Identify Function rather than parked at the end. Lessons can emerge while detection, response, and recovery are still underway: a newly observed technique may require a detection change today, a discovered shared administrative account may require an access correction beyond the affected system, a vendor escalation failure may need executive intervention before recovery completes. Others become longer-term corrective actions afterward. The change is that learning is no longer saved for the final meeting.

This framing explains something experienced responders already know: **the quality of the response is often decided before the incident is detected.** If the organization does not know which business service depends on the affected asset, severity becomes guesswork. If the data inventory cannot show what information the system holds, privacy and notification assessments start late. If the cloud provider's responsibilities and escalation path are unclear, the response waits in a support queue.

If emergency authority was never assigned, responders negotiate permission while the attacker continues. If identity, communications, logs, and backups can all be disabled by the same compromise, the plan loses the tools it assumed would be there. Those are not failures of containment technique. They are failures across Govern, Identify, and Protect that only become visible during Detect, Respond, and Recover.

For a small or mid-sized organization this does not require six new workstreams. Keep the response sequence your team can actually execute, but be clear that it is your operational sequence rather than the current NIST model, then test it against three bands. **Preparation:** do governance, inventories, architecture, supplier arrangements, communications, access controls, logging, backups, and exercises give responders what they will need? **Live response:** can the organization detect, declare, coordinate, contain, eradicate, communicate, and recover with clear authority? **Improvement:** can a lesson become an owned, prioritized, funded, and verified change, during the incident when urgent, and afterward when structural?

That is the practical shift. Incident response is still a specialized capability, but it is produced by the wider operating model, and the response team does not own every dependency the response relies on. Making those dependencies visible, assigned, and exercised before the incident asks whether they are real is the leadership job.

One boundary remains: preparation includes exercising the plan, but that discipline is substantial enough to stand on its own. This chapter builds the plan, roles, authority, and improvement loop; testing whether they survive pressure is separate work.

Severity: The Switch That Starts the Right Machine

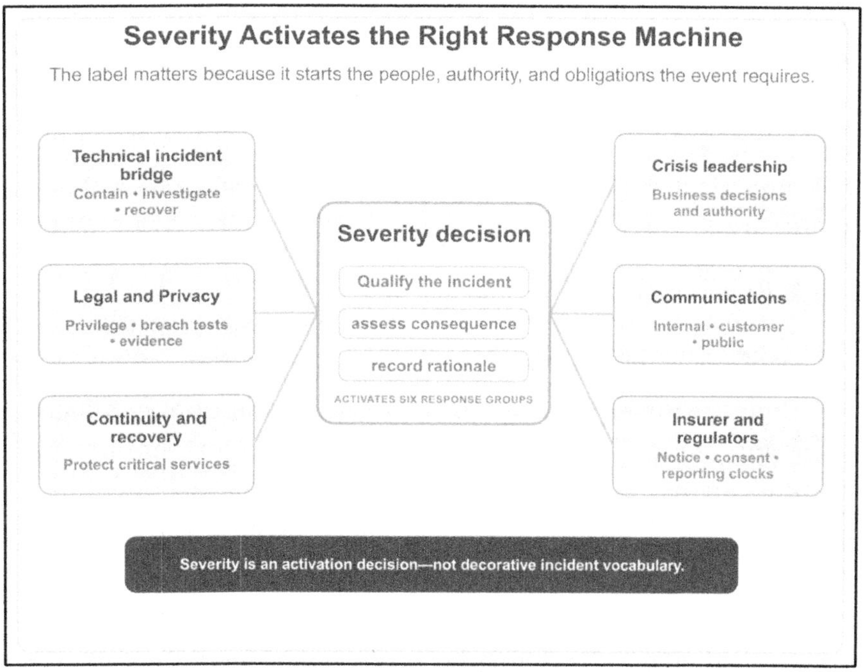

The first real decision in any incident is a single question: how big is this? Severity classification is how the organization answers it fast, and almost everything else keys off that answer. The response to a single phished mailbox and to ransomware moving through production cannot be the same, and severity is what tells them apart.

Get it wrong in either direction and it costs you. Under-classify, and a serious event stays a quiet technical ticket until it is too big to ignore, evidence gone, containment late, leadership surprised. Over-classify, and every suspicious email scrambles the executives until people stop taking escalations seriously. A weak model produces both failures; a good one avoids them by being simple enough to use in the moment and rich enough to reflect business impact, not just technical noise.

That last point matters: do not classify on technical indicators alone. A malware alert on a test box and a suspected data exposure in a customer-facing system are not the same problem, and a small technical event in a regulated service can outrank a loud one in a low-value system. A useful scheme weighs data sensitivity, customer and service impact, privileged access, attacker persistence, scope, legal or regulatory exposure, third-party involvement, and whether leadership needs to know.

Most organizations land on three or four levels. More than that just creates argument. An illustrative four-level scheme:

- Critical, major disruption, encrypting ransomware, widespread compromise, significant data exposure, regulatory notification likely, board-level crisis.
- High, customer impact, critical-service disruption, privileged compromise, sensitive data exposure, or possible notification obligations.
- Moderate, a confirmed or likely control failure with limited impact, or repeated suspicious activity that needs a coordinated look.
- Low, limited observed scope, no sensitive data, no customer or material business impact.

The labels matter less than what each one triggers: who is notified, who takes command, how fast the clock starts, the update cadence, whether legal and privacy engage, whether communications gets ready. Severity without action rules is just a label. And it has to be allowed to move, an incident that looks minor often grows, so re-classifying upward should be a normal, blame-free act, not an admission that someone guessed wrong. Build the habit of re-checking severity at each major update and whenever a material new fact lands, rather than setting it once and forgetting it.

One Incident, Two Bridges

Serious incidents usually need two operating spaces, and trying to run them in one crowded call is one of the most common ways a competent team ends up looking chaotic.

The technical bridge runs the investigation and containment, logs, indicators, accounts, cloud events, timelines, affected systems, containment options, recovery dependencies. It needs room to think. The leadership or crisis bridge runs decisions, business impact, legal and privacy assessment, communications, customer strategy, vendor escalation, executive updates. It needs distilled facts, not raw debate. Put them in the same room and the bridge turns to noise: executives listen to analysts argue over firewall rules, responders get interrupted for status every few minutes, legal asks questions while people are still reading logs. Everyone is trying to help, and the signal drowns.

The better model keeps the two spaces separate but tightly connected, with the incident commander or CISO making sure information flows between them: one source of truth, two operating spaces. In a small organization you may not have two formal calls, but you still need the two modes, one for diagnosis and action, one for decisions and communication, and you still should not let the whole anxious company pile onto the technical bridge.

An incident bridge is not a spectator sport. One thing the bridge quietly depends on: staying reachable and trustworthy. Keep the plan, the contacts, and a way to talk available even when identity, email, or the network is down, and if you suspect the intruder is watching your normal channels, move the response to an out-of-band one, because coordinating a breach on a platform the attacker can read is its own kind of disaster.

The Team, and the One Role That Holds It Together

An incident is not handled by "the security team." It is handled by a defined group, most of whom do not sit in security, and the mistake many organizations make is assuming everyone knows their role because it feels obvious. It is not obvious at 2 a.m.

Think in two rings. A small core is always in a serious incident: someone running it, someone leading the technical work, someone owning communication and coordination, and someone keeping the log. An extended ring is pulled in as the incident demands: legal, privacy, IT and infrastructure, business owners, customer-facing leads, HR when there is an insider angle, an executive sponsor, and outside specialists like counsel or forensics. Not everyone is needed every time, but everyone who might be needed should already know they are on the list and how they will be reached. Name a primary and a backup for the roles that matter, because incidents are rude; they do not check calendars.

A few roles go missing so often they are worth naming. A scribe who keeps a running timeline of what was known and decided when, unglamorous, and priceless afterward. An executive sponsor who does not run the incident but makes the business calls the team cannot, and keeps other executives from freelancing into the response. And, above all, an incident commander.

If one role separates a managed incident from a chaotic one, it is the incident commander. The job is to run the incident, not to do the technical work, hold the current picture, set the tempo, make sure decisions get made and recorded, pull in the right people, and keep the call from turning into a debate club. A good incident commander is almost soothing in their repetitiveness: here is what we know, here is what we do not, here are the open actions and who owns each one, here is the decision we need, here is the next update time, here is the current severity and what would change it. That rhythm is what pulls a room from anxiety into action.

This has a consequence people find counterintuitive: the incident commander is often not the CISO, and often not the most technical person present. Your best technical responder is most valuable with their hands on the problem, not stepping back to coordinate, and during a serious incident the CISO usually has a different job, talking to executives, the board, and sometimes regulators, which is hard to do while also running the tactical response. In a small organization the CISO may well be the incident commander; in a larger one, a trained incident manager runs the bridge while the CISO works the leadership layer. Both work. What does not work is everyone quietly assuming someone else is coordinating.

Decision Rights: Decide Before You Have To

This is the heart of the chapter: the decision structure that keeps a serious incident from becoming a crowded call with nobody in charge.

The idea is simple to state and easy to neglect: for every consequential decision an incident can force, someone should already hold the authority to make it, agreed before the incident rather than negotiated during it. When that is true, the response moves. When it is not, the decisions get made slowly, by whoever's loudest, at the worst possible moment.

The decisions worth assigning in advance are recognizable almost anywhere. Who can declare a major incident and activate the plan. Who can take a critical system offline or isolate a segment, a call that trades business disruption against containment, and one nobody should improvise. Who sets recovery priority when several services are down and cannot all come back at once. Who decides whether to restore from backup or preserve the environment for investigation, a real tension between getting back to business and understanding what happened. Who approves external communication.

Who determines whether an incident may be notifiable, and here the plan should route to the people and legal analysis that own that question; this chapter's job is to make sure the decision has a clear owner and gets raised early. Who can engage outside help — counsel, forensics, insurer, law enforcement — and, closely tied to that, who can approve the emergency spending it usually requires, because forensic retainers, surge cloud capacity, and urgent recovery resources rarely wait for procurement's normal pace. Who accepts the risk of running in degraded mode. And, easy to forget, who gets to declare the incident over and stand the team down.

Escalation is the other half. The plan should make clear how an incident moves up, analyst to incident commander, incident commander to executive sponsor, and on to the board, and what triggers each step. Good escalation runs on thresholds, not nerve. A person deciding in the moment whether something is "bad enough" to wake the CISO will, under pressure, usually guess wrong. A plan that says this severity, these conditions, this call gets made takes that judgment off their shoulders. Assigning all of this costs an afternoon. Not assigning it costs the first, most expensive hour of the one event where hours matter most.

Legal, Privilege, and Evidence

Two things belong in the plan early rather than bolted on late, because getting them wrong quietly forecloses options you will wish you had.

The first is legal and privacy involvement. The instinct to gather facts before waking legal is understandable, nobody wants to escalate a false alarm, but serious incidents create obligations before the facts are complete. Legal may need to preserve privilege, guide evidence handling, weigh contractual notice, or bring in outside counsel; privacy may need to assess whether personal data is involved and whether a notification clock has quietly started. (Worth flagging one myth: involving a lawyer does not by itself make the response privileged. Privilege turns on purpose, participants, and jurisdiction, so copying counsel onto a thread or stamping a document "privileged" does not create it; the move is to let legal structure that properly.)

The answer is not to hand them the bridge; it is early, conditional involvement, if an incident may touch personal or sensitive data, customers, a regulator, or material disruption, they are pulled in early enough to shape evidence and timing before avoidable mistakes are made. A team that waits too long can preserve the wrong things, write careless updates, lose privilege, or discover a breach clock that is already running. The specifics are jurisdictional and genuinely a lawyer's call; the leadership move is simply to make legal and privacy first-ring participants so the option exists rather than being lost by default.

The second is evidence preservation. In the rush to fix the problem, it is easy to destroy the very thing you will later need, to understand the attack, meet a regulatory account, support an insurance claim, or defend a decision. Wiping and rebuilding a compromised machine feels like progress and can erase the answer to "how did they get in?" Logs roll over, memory vanishes, cloud resources get deleted, telemetry ages out.

Not every incident needs full forensic imaging, do not turn every phishing report into a courtroom exercise, but for serious ones the team needs a simple instinct: before you destroy state, ask whether it needs to be preserved, and know who to call if the answer might be yes. The deep forensic discipline belongs to Chapter 9; the habit that protects your options belongs here. The worst way to end an incident is not "we were breached" — it is "we don't know what happened, because we destroyed the evidence while fixing it."

The Incident Log: Your Memory Under Stress

Closely related, and just as neglected: keep a real incident log. Not a scattered chat thread, not memory, not screenshots reconstructed afterward, a structured record of detection and escalation times, severity changes, key facts and assumptions, decisions and who made them, actions and owners, systems affected, evidence preserved, communications sent, and closure. Under stress, people forget, misremember the sequence, and assume someone else captured the decision.

This is the scribe from the team you named earlier, and it is worth being explicit that they own the timeline because timeline accuracy is precisely what notification, board reporting, forensics, and customer assurance all lean on afterward. The log is the organization's memory, and it is often the single most valuable artifact you have once the incident is over. Assign someone to own it from the start of any high-severity incident. The role is not glamorous; it is disciplined.

Vendors Are Part of the Response, Not a Footnote

Many incidents cannot be handled inside your own walls. A cloud provider holds logs you need. A SaaS vendor controls the affected feature. A managed service provider (MSP) has the admin access. A forensic firm has to be engaged, an insurer notified, a processor's data assessed, an AI provider's configuration or retention checked. If a vendor is critical during the incident, vendor coordination has to be planned before it, a current contact list, a real 24×7 escalation path, the contractual notification and support commitments, and a named internal owner for each relationship.

This does not replace your supplier assurance program; it connects incident response to it. A supplier can pass onboarding and still be useless at 2 a.m. So ask the uncomfortable questions while it is calm: who do we call, will they answer, what can they give us, how fast, and what do we do if they do not respond? Confirm the support tier and escalation entitlement you are actually paying for, too, plenty of teams discover mid-crisis that their contract does not include the response speed they assumed. "We'll raise a support ticket" is fine for a low-risk tool and not remotely fine for a critical service in a major incident.

Communication Discipline Starts Inside the Team

Crisis communication — the external, customer, regulator, and media dimension — is its own discipline. But it starts inside the response team, because if responders cannot communicate clearly with each other, the external message will fail later.

The pattern the incident commander should enforce is the same every update: what we know, what we are assuming, what is still open, what we are doing, who owns it, and when the next update comes. That structure heads off the most dangerous incident habit. Premature certainty. Early on, everyone wants the clean statement: it is contained, no data was accessed, it is only one system, it is not ransomware, we are back to normal.

Some of those may turn out true; none should be said as fact before the evidence supports it. "At this point we have activity on two systems, we haven't confirmed data access, containment is in progress, next update in thirty minutes" is not weakness. It is accuracy, and it is the same honest register the CISO should model upward to executives. Disciplined uncertainty keeps leadership informed without trapping the team into a false statement it has to walk back on the worst possible day.

Learn While the Incident Is Still Moving

The traditional lessons-learned meeting happens after recovery, when the team is tired, the urgent work has moved elsewhere, and memory has already begun smoothing away the confusion. You still need that review. You should no longer make it the only place improvement happens.

Serious incidents can run for weeks. Waiting until the end to act on every lesson can leave the same weakness available throughout the response. The team needs a controlled way to capture, evaluate, and route lessons as they appear, without turning a live incident into a general improvement project. Think in three tempos.

Immediate operational corrections keep the current response effective. A missing log source is enabled. An attacker indicator becomes a detection. A compromised credential pattern triggers a wider reset. A broken vendor escalation moves to an executive channel. A communication method believed safe is replaced because the intruder may be watching it. These belong in the incident log, with an owner and a reason, because they change the live response.

Near-term corrective actions address conditions that could cause recurrence or obstruct recovery, an exposed trust path, a monitoring gap, a recovery procedure that did not work, a playbook that misled, a standing vendor entitlement nobody needed. They can begin before the incident formally closes, but they need change control and prioritization so improvement does not destabilize the environment being recovered.

Structural improvements flow into the wider risk-management system. The incident may expose unclear ownership, weak architecture authority, incomplete inventories, supplier terms that do not support response, a risk repeatedly accepted without treatment, or a resilience assumption never tested. These belong in the same governance, risk, architecture, supplier, and assurance processes used for any other material weakness, not in a slide deck called "lessons learned" that nobody tracks.

Do not confuse a lesson with an action. "We need better logging" is an observation. "The infrastructure owner will enable and retain the missing identity events for the affected service by this date, security will validate coverage using this test, and the control owner will accept or escalate any residual gap" is a corrective action.

And resist the search for one root cause. Serious incidents usually have an entry point and several contributing conditions, excessive privilege, weak segmentation, delayed detection, unclear ownership, an unavailable vendor, an untested restoration path, a decision threshold nobody understood. Removing the entry point matters. Correcting the conditions that turned it into a serious incident is where resilience actually improves.

So the improvement loop should capture each material lesson, decide whether it needs an immediate, near-term, or structural response, assign an accountable owner and date, connect it to the relevant risk or control, and verify the change worked before closing it. The incident commander should not own every corrective action. Their responsibility is to make sure important lessons leave the bridge with a destination.

The Frameworks Underneath Incident Response

Incident response is another place where several frameworks describe the same capability in different language, the series' recurring point that you are running one operating model, not collecting separate programs. The important development is that the current NIST publication no longer presents incident response mainly as a standalone handling process.

NIST SP 800-61 Revision 3, published in April 2025, supersedes Revision 2 from 2012. Its full title, *Incident Response Recommendations and Considerations for Cybersecurity Risk Management: A CSF 2.0 Community Profile*, signals the change. It is organized around CSF 2.0 and treats incident response as an organization-wide risk-management capability rather than work performed only by handlers after detection.

The Community Profile highlights the CSF outcomes that matter to incident preparation, detection, response, recovery, and improvement, and attaches relative priorities that the publication describes as a starting point, expecting organizations to customize them to their own priorities and needs. It is not a certification scheme or a universal checklist. The publication also points readers to online resources for implementation detail alongside the document itself, a sensible division, since the framework organizes the capability while playbooks, procedures, tooling, and exercises make it executable.

This also corrects a common shorthand. Incident-response readiness and execution do not live only inside the CSF **Respond** Function. Govern, Identify, and Protect prepare the organization and reduce incident impact; Detect finds and analyzes possible compromise; Respond coordinates action; Recover restores assets and operations; and the Improvement Category within Identify carries lessons back across all six.

The CSF 2.0 itself remains the shared vocabulary for showing leadership where response sits in the wider picture; like the rest of CSF it says what capabilities to have rather than how to build them. **ISO/IEC 27035** remains the international incident-management reference many organizations encounter, framing incident handling as a governed, repeatable process connected to the wider security program. And the widely taught **SANS** sequence, preparation, identification, containment, eradication, recovery, lessons learned, remains a practitioner model rather than a formal standard, popular in training and response circles.

The point is not to adopt all of them. It is that when someone references "the Respond function" or "the SANS process" in a meeting, you recognize them as dialects for the capability this chapter builds. Recognizing them as dialects does not make them identical: their scope, terminology, and emphasis differ, and any contractual, regulatory, or assurance commitment still has to be met on its own terms. Revision 3 simply makes the dependency on the wider operating model impossible to miss.

Industry Pattern — The Bridge With Everyone and No Owner

> *A suspicious event turns serious and someone opens an incident bridge. People join fast because they want to help, security, IT, application and infrastructure teams, executives, vendor contacts, support, customer success, legal, communications. For a few minutes it feels productive.*
>
> *Then it becomes clear that nobody is running the call. Technical teams debate possible causes. Executives ask for business impact. Legal asks whether data was involved. Support asks what to tell customers. A vendor says they need logs. Someone starts screen-sharing; someone else asks for a timeline; a senior leader joins late and asks everyone to recap the last thirty minutes. The incident is real. The response model is not. Eventually someone takes charge, but time is gone and confidence is dented.*
>
> *The lesson is not that too many people cared. It is that concern without structure becomes noise. A serious bridge needs an owner, a rhythm, a log, and decision rights, and without them an organization can generate a great deal of activity and very little response. That is why the incident commander role exists: not because titles matter, but because someone has to turn anxiety into action.*

What Evidence Should You Expect

A real incident response capability leaves evidence that it is more than a document. At leadership altitude, a CISO should be able to point to an approved, current plan with named roles rather than abstract titles, an actual incident commander function with real people assigned to hold it and back it up; an incident definition and a way to report one; a severity model that defines the levels and, crucially, what each one triggers; a core-and-extended team with a contact list that is genuinely current rather than populated with people who left last year; a decision-rights and escalation structure covering who declares an incident, takes systems offline, approves external communication and emergency spend, engages outside help, and stands the team down; and simple procedures for evidence preservation and incident logging.

The evidence that the plan is lived rather than filed is the more telling half: records of real incidents and near-misses handled through the process; incident-declaration and severity-change records; incident logs showing what was known and decided when; an emergency-decision log; evidence that the contact list and out-of-hours escalation have actually been tested, critical vendors included; legal and privacy engaged early rather than after the fact; a dated periodic plan-review approval; and post-incident reviews that produced actual changes to the plan, the controls, or the team.

Evidence that the plan has been exercised, tabletops and their findings, is the strongest proof of all, and because that discipline is substantial in its own right it belongs to the next chapter; what a CISO owns here is that the plan, the roles, and the decision structure are real and current.

The revised NIST model also expands the evidence beyond the incident-response document itself. Expect to see the operating context on which response depends: current inventories of important hardware, software, services, suppliers, and data; critical-service and dependency information that helps the team assess impact and recovery priority; protected logging, communication, backup, and response-access arrangements; and supplier agreements that define incident disclosure, information flow, coordination, evidence access, and authority to act.

The procedures below the plan should be usable under stress. A proportionate organization does not need a playbook for every imaginable event, but it should have actionable procedures for the incidents it is most likely to face and for the emergency actions it cannot afford to invent during the incident, compromised privileged identity, ransomware or destructive activity, cloud-account compromise, sensitive-data exposure, supplier compromise, and loss of a primary authentication or communication capability.

Finally, expect evidence that learning entered the wider operating model: response-performance measures that expose delay and decision friction; corrective actions with owners and dates; and verified changes to risks, controls, architecture, supplier arrangements, playbooks, training, monitoring, or recovery. A lesson recorded in a review is not yet an improvement. The evidence is the changed and tested capability.

For a small or mid-sized organization, the practical minimum is enough to move from "we have a document" to "we know how to start":

- One clear incident definition and a way to report one.
- Three or four severity levels, each tied to what it triggers.
- A named incident commander and backup.
- A current core-team contact list, plus critical-vendor escalation contacts.
- Test that contact list and its out-of-hours escalation at least periodically, a list nobody has ever called is not a reliable one.
- A trigger for pulling in legal and privacy early.
- Simple evidence-preservation guidance and an incident-log template.
- A short decision-rights list, at minimum, who can take systems offline and who can communicate externally.

- One tabletop that includes security, IT, legal or privacy, a business owner, and the executive sponsor.

The through-line is the one that ran through resilience: a binder proves intent; a used, current, rehearsed plan proves capability. If the contact list is stale and the incident commander is a title nobody holds, the capability is not there yet, whatever the document says.

Reality Check

> *Pretend an incident is happening right now, ransomware on a production system, discovered ten minutes ago.*
>
> *Who is the incident commander? Name the person, not the role, and do they know they hold it? Who declares this a major incident, and has that call been made yet? Who is allowed to take the affected systems offline, and would they do it or wait for permission? Who is calling legal, and do they know to? Is there a current number for outside counsel and forensics, and who has it? Who is keeping the log? Who tells the executives, and who keeps them from taking over the call? And when it is over, who gets to say it is over?*
>
> *Then the harder question: have these people ever practiced this together? If the first set took hesitation, or the honest answer to several is "we'd figure it out in the moment," the plan is still mostly theoretical. That is not a failing. It is the most common state there is. It is just the reason to assign the roles and walk them through now, on an ordinary day, rather than discover the gaps on the worst one. The first real incident should not be the first rehearsal.*

What This Means for You as a Security Leader

Your role in a serious incident is probably not to be the incident commander, and it is worth being deliberate about that. The CISO usually has a harder, different job in the moment: turning technical reality into decisions and language that executives, the board, and sometimes regulators can act on, and absorbing the organizational pressure that would otherwise land on the response team. Trying to run the tactical response and manage upward at the same time is how both get done badly.

So most of the leadership work happens before any incident. You make sure the plan exists and is current rather than aspirational. You make sure the incident commander role is held by real people who know it. You get the decision rights assigned and the escalation thresholds agreed while everyone is calm, because those same conversations are miserable in the middle of a crisis. You wire legal and privacy in early by default. And you push (gently, repeatedly) for the team to walk through the plan before it is needed, because a plan that has only ever been read is a hypothesis about how the organization will behave, and rehearsal is what turns that hypothesis into something you have actually watched work.

You do not need a hundred-page plan. You need one people can execute under stress: a team that knows each other, decision rights that do not require negotiation mid-crisis, and a bridge that turns uncertainty into action. That is the line between a security event and an organizational incident. The event may still be painful, but it should not be confusing. Clarity does not solve every incident. It is what makes solving it possible.

Bridge to Chapter 8

A plan on paper and a team on a contact list are not a tested capability; the next chapter runs them under realistic pressure, through tabletop exercises and ransomware readiness.

CHAPTER 8

Tabletop Exercises, Testing, and Ransomware Readiness

You can test the plan on an ordinary Tuesday, or wait for an incident to test it for you.

The plan can look complete on paper: roles named, severity defined, decision rights assigned, the escalation path drawn. The organization appears to know exactly what to do when the bad day arrives.

Except you do not actually know that yet. You know what the plan says. Whether the organization can do it, whether the incident commander can hold a room that is coming apart, whether legal picks up at 11 p.m., whether the backup you are counting on actually restores, whether the executive sponsor makes the hard call instead of deferring it. None of that is settled by writing it down. A plan that has only been read is a hypothesis. A team listed on a contact sheet has not necessarily worked together. A decision right in a document has not necessarily been exercised. This chapter is where you test the hypothesis, on purpose, under conditions you control, before a real incident tests it for you under conditions you do not.

That framing matters more than any technique in this chapter, so it is worth saying plainly: the point of testing is not to prove the plan works. It is to find the places where it does not, while finding them is still cheap. A test that surfaces five broken things is a good test. A test where everything goes smoothly might mean the team is genuinely ready, but more often it means the scenario was too easy or nobody was honest, so treat a finding-free exercise as a reason to check the design, not as a gold star. You are not after a gold star. You are after the gaps because every gap you find on a Tuesday is one you do not discover during ransomware.

The Spectrum of Testing

"Testing the plan" covers a range of activities, and they are not interchangeable. Think of them as a spectrum, running from cheap and low-disruption to expensive and high-fidelity. Most organizations should start at the cheap end and earn their way up.

At the accessible end is the tabletop exercise, a discussion-based walkthrough. You gather the people who would respond to a real incident, put a realistic scenario in front of them, and talk through what each of them would actually do, step by step, as the situation develops. Nothing is taken offline; no systems are touched. It is a conversation with a purpose, it is cheap and low-risk, and it gets the most useful gaps out of hiding faster than anything else, which is why it is where nearly every organization should begin.

In the middle sit functional or technical drills, where you stop talking and actually do part of it. Restore a specific system from backup and time it. Run the detection logic against a simulated indicator and see if it fires. Execute a containment step in a test environment. Call the out-of-hours numbers and find out who answers. These cost more effort and carry a little more disruption, but they test the thing a tabletop cannot: whether the capability is real, not just described.

At the far end are full-scale simulations and adversary-emulation exercises, red and purple team engagements that emulate a realistic attacker to test whether your detection and response actually hold up against someone trying to get past them. These are the highest-fidelity and the most demanding to run, and they are where a maturing program eventually goes. (Their cousin, offensive testing aimed at finding vulnerabilities in controls, like penetration testing, belongs to the technical security and assurance program; here the lens is on testing the response, not the controls.)

You do not need all three to start. A small or mid-sized organization gets enormous value from tabletops alone, adds a restore drill and a contact-list test as the next step, and works toward adversary emulation later. Maturity here is a direction, not a starting requirement.

Running a Tabletop That's Worth the Afternoon

A tabletop can be genuinely transformative or a complete waste of an afternoon, and the difference comes down to a few choices.

The first is who is in the room. A tabletop run only by the security team tests only the security team, and incidents are lost on the coordination layer, not the technical one. The people whose absence breaks a real incident are the ones whose presence makes a tabletop worth running: legal, privacy, a business owner who understands what the affected service actually does, someone from communications, and the executive sponsor who will have to make the expensive calls.

Not everyone joins every exercise, and you should keep the group proportionate, but do not run a ransomware tabletop without the people who decide whether systems come offline, whether customers get told, and whether a ransom is even discussable. The people whose decisions matter should practice making them.

The second is the facilitator's job, which is not to run the incident but to run the exercise. A good facilitator sets the scene, then introduces complications — "injects" — as the discussion unfolds, precisely to push the group past the comfortable part. The plan handles the obvious opening; the injects test the seams. The backup you were about to rely on is also encrypted. The person who holds the decision is on a flight. The story leaks to a customer before you have confirmed anything. Legal says you cannot say what communications wants to say.

The regulator's clock, it turns out, started six hours ago. The exercise should get uncomfortable, that is the point. If everyone stays relaxed for the whole tabletop, the scenario was too easy. And while the facilitator guides the scenario, the person who would run the real response should practice running this one, holding the same structured rhythm, what we know, what we do not, what we have decided, who owns what, when the next update lands. Facilitating the exercise and commanding the response are different jobs; do not let one quietly become the other.

The third, and the one most often skipped, is capturing what did not work. The entire value of a tabletop lives in its after-action notes, the moment someone said "wait, who actually decides that?" and the room went quiet. Those silences are the deliverable. If nobody writes them down, converts them into owned actions with real dates, and tracks them to closure, the exercise was theater. A tabletop that produces a warm feeling and no changes has taught you nothing except that your people are pleasant to be in a room with.

Start with the Objective, Then Build the Scenario

A weak exercise starts with a dramatic scenario. A strong one starts with a clear objective, what are we actually trying to test?, and builds the scenario to serve it. A single tabletop cannot test everything well; try to cover the whole universe in two hours and you get polite discussion and shallow findings.

So pick the target first, then design toward it. If you want to test legal and privacy escalation, build a scenario where the data impact is genuinely ambiguous and the team has to decide when to pull them in. If you want to test executive decision-making, build one where containment means taking a revenue-generating service offline. If you want to test customer communication, build one where customers spot the problem before your investigation is finished. The scenario is the delivery mechanism; the objective is the point.

Realistic beats dramatic. The scenarios worth the room's time are grounded in how your organization actually operates, the systems it depends on, the data it holds, the vendors it relies on. Ransomware is almost always worth running because it stresses nearly every part of the machine at once, but it should not be the only one: a critical vendor going dark, a cloud misconfiguration exposing customer data, a departing insider, an AI system leaking one customer's information to another, each exercises different muscles and different decision-makers. Rotating scenarios over time is how you avoid a team that is excellent at the one incident it always practices and lost the moment reality picks a different one.

When Talk Isn't Enough

Tabletops share one weakness: everyone in the room is describing what they believe would happen, and belief diverges from reality in exactly the places that hurt most. The only way to close that gap is to actually do the thing.

The clearest example is recovery. In a tabletop, someone says "we'd restore from backup," everyone nods, and the exercise moves on. Whether that restore actually works, whether the backup is complete, whether it is clean, whether it comes back inside the time the business needs, whether anyone has performed the restore recently enough to trust it, is not a question a conversation can answer. Only a restore test can. Organizations discover the hard way that a backup which exists is not the same as a recovery capability that works.

This is a readiness question, not an architecture one. What belongs here is simpler and more uncomfortable: have you actually restored the backup, recently, under something like real conditions, and did it work? Do not let a tabletop get away with "we restore from backup" without forcing the next questions: which backup, how do we know it is clean, how long will it take, what has to come back first, and who has actually tested that?

The same logic runs through the rest of the plan. Does the detection you are relying on actually alert, or does it only exist in a policy? Do the out-of-hours contacts answer, or is the escalation list a set of names nobody has dialed after 6 p.m.? Can the critical vendor deliver the support the contract promised, or does that only get discovered at 2 a.m.? These are the assumptions quietly holding up the whole plan, and testing them turns "we're pretty sure" into "we know" — or, just as valuably, into "we were wrong, and now we can fix it."

Ransomware Readiness

Ransomware deserves its own attention, not because it is the only threat that matters, but because it compresses almost every resilience problem into one event, detection, containment, privileged access, backup integrity, recovery sequencing, legal and privacy, communication, executive decision-making, vendor readiness, insurance, continuity, all at once, under real pressure. That is what makes it both the most demanding scenario and the most instructive one to be ready for. It reveals whether the response model is real.

A ransomware tabletop should not open with "all systems are encrypted" — that skips the important part. Start earlier: a user reports odd behavior, an endpoint alert fires, a privileged account does something it should not, files start changing fast, a server goes unreachable, the team sees lateral movement. Only then does encryption get confirmed in one area, then another, then the note appears, then the attacker claims data theft, then a customer asks what is going on. Starting early is what forces the organization to practice detection, triage, escalation, containment, and evidence preservation before the dramatic moment, which is exactly where a real event is won or lost.

Two things about modern ransomware change the shape of the exercise. First, it usually is not just encryption. Many operations exfiltrate the data before or alongside locking it and then threaten to publish, while others extort through theft or disruption with no encryption at all, so do not assume either that data was taken or that it was not; that is an investigative question, and until it is answered, recovering your systems does not end the incident.

You may still have a data-breach and notification problem, and that is where this connects to notification. It is also why recovery cannot outrun containment: restoring encrypted systems while the attacker's access path is still open can hand them the environment straight back. Eradication and recovery can overlap in a phased, closely monitored return of critical services, but that should be a deliberate decision, with the restored environment kept away from any path not yet trusted. Second, running underneath everything is one decision the organization really should not be making for the first time in the moment: whether it would ever pay.

That payment question is a decision right, and it belongs with the other decision rights settled in advance. Whether to pay is tangled up in law, sanctions exposure, insurance, law-enforcement guidance, and the uncomfortable reality that paying guarantees nothing. It is a genuinely terrible decision to work out from scratch while systems are down and a countdown runs. This book is not giving legal advice on ransom payment; the CISO's job is to make sure the organization has decided the governance path before it is under extortion pressure: who can even discuss it, who must be consulted, whether legal has to check sanctions risk, whether insurance requires notice before any negotiation, who actually has authority to approve or reject, and who documents the decision and its rationale.

Two hard edges are worth stating outright: public law-enforcement guidance (the FBI's, for one) discourages paying and is clear that payment guarantees neither recovery nor that stolen data stays unpublished; and no individual responder should ever contact, negotiate with, or pay an extortion actor on their own. That has to run through the authorized legal, law-enforcement, insurer, and executive channel, because handling it freelance can create real sanctions and financial-crime exposure.

And here is the thing worth internalizing: the most valuable outcome of readiness is the ability to not be cornered. Even a firm "we don't pay" policy only holds if you can recover without paying, which loops straight back to the restore test. Backups you can trust, that an attacker cannot reach or encrypt, that you have actually recovered from, are what turn "we have no choice" into "we have a choice." (The resilient-backup architecture is outside this chapter; the readiness question — can we recover without paying, and have we proven it? — sits here.) Even if the policy is never to pay, the exercise should still test what happens when the pressure becomes real, because policies are easy when nobody is staring at downtime, customer loss, and leaked data.

Test the Boring Things

Ransomware gets the attention because it is dramatic. A surprising number of exercises fail on things that are not dramatic at all. Can the contact list actually reach people after hours? Does the conference bridge work if the collaboration platform is the thing that is down? Can the team open the incident plan if the main file-sharing system is unavailable? Can legal reach outside counsel at midnight? Does the cyber-insurance number still connect to a human? Can the team communicate at all if email itself is compromised, and does everyone know where the decision log lives?

Can anyone reach the break-glass admin and MFA accounts, the emergency credentials kept for exactly this situation, if the normal identity system is the thing that is down, a genuine recovery blocker that tends to surface at the worst possible moment? Incidents are slowed far more often by these small operational failures than by sophisticated technical puzzles. The best tabletops surface the boring gaps, and then you fix them, which is cheap and unglamorous and exactly the kind of readiness that pays off at 3 a.m.

Executives Need Their Own Rehearsal

Executives often assume incident response is a technical process, right up until they are in one and discover their role is not technical at all. It is decision-making. Do we take the service offline? Do we tell customers before we know everything? Do we engage outside counsel, accept degraded operation, pause new customer onboarding, approve emergency spend, and get legal the facts they need to work out whether a reporting clock has already started? Those are leadership decisions, and they deserve practice too.

An executive tabletop should not drown leadership in technical detail; it should give them just enough fact to force realistic choices, and test whether they understand the severity model, their own decision rights, how much the CISO can honestly know early, and how uncertainty gets communicated. There is a specific failure this heads off: a board or leadership team that has never practiced receiving incomplete incident information will, in a real event, demand a certainty the organization cannot honestly provide, and push it toward overclaiming. Far better to teach that lesson in a tabletop than during the real thing. Boards do not need to join every operational exercise, but in regulated or high-impact organizations the board or risk committee should periodically rehearse its own role in crisis oversight.

Testing Is a Program, Not an Event

The single most common way testing fails is not a bad exercise. It is a good exercise that happens once, produces a report, and is never followed up. Readiness is not a thing you achieve; it is a thing you maintain, because the organization keeps changing underneath the plan, new systems, new vendors, new people in the named roles, new services that quietly became critical. Every change is a chance for the plan to drift out of date, and only a regular rhythm catches the drift.

So the useful frame is a cycle, not a checkbox. You run an exercise, capture the gaps honestly, turn each one into a corrective action with a real owner and a real date, or an explicit risk acceptance recorded in the exception register if it cannot be fixed, so nothing just quietly disappears, close them, and then test again, ideally with a different scenario, to confirm the fix held and find the next layer.

This is where exercising connects back to governance: the findings feed the same risk register, exception and risk-acceptance register, control-improvement plan, and board reporting as everything else in the risk program. A program that runs on that loop gets measurably better over time. One that runs an annual tabletop to satisfy an auditor, files the report, and changes nothing has the paperwork of readiness without the substance, and the difference shows up on exactly one day, by which point it is too late to fix.

The cadence does not have to be heavy: a regular cross-functional tabletop, a periodic restore test aligned to how critical the system is, an occasional contact-list check, a focused exercise after any significant change to the environment, and an executive tabletop now and then because executive decision-making is a separate muscle from technical response. What matters is that it is routine, protected on the calendar, not the first thing canceled when the quarter gets busy.

The Frameworks Underneath Exercising and Testing

Testing and exercising is another area where a few frameworks describe the same discipline in different words, the series' recurring theme that you are running one operating model, not adopting separate programs. A couple worth knowing, defined briefly:

NIST's guidance on test, training, and exercise programs lays out the same spectrum this chapter describes, the progression from discussion-based tabletop exercises up through functional drills to full-scale simulations, and frames exercising as an ongoing program rather than a one-time event. It is a useful reference if you want a structured vocabulary for the exercise types and how to build a program around them.

The CSF 2.0 reinforces the same idea from the governance side: its improvement activities, which sit under the Identify function and feed lessons back across all six, treat testing, exercising, and learning as built into the operating model, not optional extras. And for ransomware specifically, public ransomware-readiness guidance from national cybersecurity agencies commonly emphasizes tested and protected backups, rehearsed response, rapid detection, containment, and pre-considered governance for extortion decisions, themes that map cleanly onto everything in this chapter.

The point, as always, is not to adopt all of them. It is that when someone references a “TT&E program” or “ransomware readiness guidance” in a planning meeting, you recognize it as vocabulary for the discipline this chapter builds, not a new initiative to stand up from scratch.

Industry Pattern — The Tabletop That Found the Real Problem

> *The pattern repeats in exercise after exercise. An organization runs a ransomware tabletop expecting to find technical gaps. The scenario opens with endpoint alerts, moves to suspected lateral movement, and eventually confirms encryption on a business application.*
>
> *The technical team performs well. They know how to isolate systems, which logs to check, which admin accounts matter, how the backup platform works. If the exercise had been a test of technical skill, they would have passed it.*
>
> *The real problems are somewhere else entirely. Nobody is quite sure who can approve taking the affected application offline. Legal is not clear on when they should have been pulled in. Customer success does not know whether they are allowed to send a holding statement. The business owner cannot confirm the real recovery-time tolerance. The vendor "escalation contact" turns out to be a generic support portal. The incident log gets started late. And when the executive sponsor asks whether the organization can safely say "no data was taken," the room goes quiet.*
>
> *The exercise did exactly its job. It found the gaps while nothing was on fire. And the most valuable finding was not a missing tool. It was a missing decision structure. That is the whole reason tabletops matter: they expose the difference between technical capability and organizational readiness, and a serious incident needs both.*

What Evidence Should You Expect

A real testing program leaves a trail that proves readiness is exercised rather than assumed. At leadership altitude, a CISO should be able to point to a testing schedule or cadence that is actually followed rather than aspirational; records of tabletop exercises showing the objective set, the scenario and injects used, and, importantly, who participated, because an exercise that never included legal, a business owner, or the executive sponsor tested only part of the organization; a decision log and any severity changes from the exercise itself; after-action reports that honestly capture what did not work rather than reading like a success memo;

and a corrective-action tracker that carries the gaps found in exercises through to closure within the same risk-management discipline.

Beyond the exercises themselves, the evidence that readiness is real rather than described includes restore-test records showing that critical recovery has actually been performed and measured against the time the business needs; evidence that the contact list and out-of-hours escalation have been tested rather than just maintained; validation that critical-vendor escalation and the cyber-insurance and external-responder contacts actually reach someone; evidence that the awkward dependencies were tested, break-glass admin and MFA access, an alternate communications path when email or collaboration is down, and who can approve emergency spend; ransomware-specific readiness evidence, a pre-considered payment position, tested and isolated backups, a rehearsed response; executive or board exercise records where appropriate; and, over time, re-test evidence that later exercises revisited earlier gaps and confirmed the fixes held.

The strongest possible evidence is the boring kind: a gap found in one exercise, an owner and a date, and a later exercise showing it closed. That loop, visible in the records, is what separates a program from a performance.

For a small or mid-sized organization, the practical minimum is enough to be genuinely ready without a large program, and it can start small: two hours, one realistic scenario, eight to ten people, one facilitator, one scribe, a handful of timed injects, one decision log, one action tracker. Concretely:

- Run at least one cross-functional tabletop that includes security, IT, legal or privacy, a business owner, and the executive sponsor.
- Use a scenario grounded in your real risk. Ransomware is a strong first choice because it exercises the whole machine; customer-data exposure suits SaaS and service providers; a critical-vendor outage suits cloud-heavy organizations.

- Actually restore your most important system from backup, time it, and compare it to what the business can tolerate.
- Test that the contact list and out-of-hours escalation reach real people, that a critical vendor's escalation path actually escalates, and that a communications path still works if email or the main collaboration tool is down.
- Settle a preliminary position on ransom payment, with legal and leadership involved.
- Write down what did not work, assign owners and dates, and check the fixes at the next exercise.

That is not a mature testing program. It is enough to know whether the plan you built is a capability or a document. NIST SP 800-84 remains a useful vocabulary source for exercises, but it dates from 2006 and was written for US federal IT, so pair it with current incident-response and sector guidance.

Reality Check

> *Two questions, and answer them honestly rather than the way you would want to answer them in front of the board.*
>
> *When did you last actually restore your most important system from backup, not confirm the backup job ran, but perform the restore end to end and time it? If the honest answer is "I'm not sure we ever have," you do not currently know whether you can recover, whatever the dashboard says.*
>
> *And when did you last put the whole response group, security, IT, legal, a business owner, the executive sponsor, in one room and walk them through a serious scenario together, with someone keeping a log and the severity allowed to change as it got worse? If the answer is "never," or "only the security team has done it," then the plan has been read but not rehearsed, and the coordination layer, the one that actually decides whether an incident stays contained or becomes a crisis, is completely untested. Neither answer is a reason to panic. Both are a reason to put a date on the calendar before something else does.*

What This Means for You as a Security Leader

Your job here is less about running exercises yourself and more about making sure they happen, stay honest, and lead somewhere. Testing is the first thing an organization cancels when the quarter gets busy, precisely because nothing is on fire yet, which is exactly the wrong instinct, because the whole point is to do it while nothing is on fire. Protecting the cadence, keeping it on the calendar, and insisting the right people show up is leadership work that pays off invisibly, on a day that may never announce itself in advance.

The honesty matters as much as the frequency. A tabletop is a rehearsal, not a performance review, and its purpose is not to prove the team is good. It is to find where the system breaks before a real incident finds it for you. That takes a certain leadership maturity: you have to make it safe for people to surface gaps. If every finding turns into blame, the next exercise becomes theater, people hide uncertainty, dodge hard scenarios, and protect the appearance of readiness, which is the opposite of the real thing. So treat the gaps a tabletop surfaces as gifts. They show you where to invest, where to clarify, where to fix a contract, where to test recovery, where to train executives, and where to tell leadership the truth.

Carry that truth upward in the right language. When you report readiness to the board, report tested capability, not documented intent. "We have an incident response plan" is a weaker and less honest statement than "we exercised a ransomware scenario last quarter, found three gaps, closed two, and here's the plan for the third." The second is what readiness actually sounds like.

And underneath all of it is a single stance: assume the incident happens, build the plan, then rehearse it, deliberately, honestly, and often enough that when the real thing arrives, it is hard but it is not new. Rehearsal is the only thing that converts a plan into a capability. Everything else is paperwork waiting to be tested by an adversary who does not care how good your documentation looks.

Bridge to Chapter 9

Incident command now has to connect to the facts and words around it: forensics, crisis communication, and regulatory notification.

CHAPTER 9

Crisis Communication, Forensics, and Regulatory Notification

The incident is technical. Whether it becomes a crisis depends on what you say, to whom, and when.

Here is something the calmer chapters can gloss over. In a lot of serious incidents, the technical part is not the hardest part. The team contains the threat, the systems come back, the forensics eventually explain what happened, and none of that is what decides whether the organization comes out of it intact. What decides that is everything happening in parallel: what you tell customers who are already worried, what you file with regulators whose clocks are running, what you say to a board that wants certainty you do not have, and whether any of it turns out to be wrong later.

This is the part of incident response where trust is actually won or lost, which, given the title of this book, puts it close to the center of everything. You can handle the technical incident flawlessly and still do lasting damage in the telling. And you can have a messy, painful technical incident and come out with customers more confident in you than before, because of how honestly and competently you handled the communication. The incident is what happened. The crisis is what people believe happened, and how you behaved while they were forming that belief. During a serious incident, the organization is judged twice — once for what happened, and once for how it handled what happened, and the second judgment usually lasts longer.

Three disciplines govern that parallel track: crisis communication (what you say and to whom), forensics (how you actually know what happened), and regulatory notification (what you are legally obligated to disclose, and by when). They are usually owned by different people (communications, the security and IR team, legal or privacy) and in a real incident they collide in the same handful of hours and constrain each other constantly.

This chapter is about running them as one operating model instead of three disconnected reflexes. It does not ask the CISO to become the lawyer, the spokesperson, the forensic examiner, and the regulator liaison all at once. It asks the CISO to make sure those functions are wired into the response early enough that the organization can preserve facts, speak carefully, and notify on time, instead of creating a second incident with its own words.

One boundary up front, because it holds throughout: this chapter owns the operational capability — how you communicate, investigate, determine, and notify under pressure. The privacy-specific law that defines what a breach is and what must be reported lives in Volume III, Part 2. Sector and jurisdictional obligations still have to be read on their own terms. Here we assume those obligations exist and build the muscle that meets them.

Communicating in the Fog

The defining condition of incident communication is that you have to do it before you know everything. The facts are incomplete, they move, and they sometimes reverse, and yet customers, regulators, and executives are asking questions now. That tension, speak before you are certain, but do not say things that turn out false, is the whole discipline.

The failure mode that does the most damage is overclaiming. Under pressure to reassure, someone reaches for the comforting sentence: no customer data was affected, it was only one system, this is fully contained, the vendor confirmed it was not them. Sometimes those are true. The real question is whether they are supported by evidence at the moment they are said because a statement that is true later but unsupported now is still a risk, and one that turns out false is worse.

It converts a breach into a breach plus a credibility problem, and the second one outlives the first. The organization that said "no data was taken" and walked it back a week later is trusted less than the one that said "we don't yet know what was accessed, and we'll tell you the moment we do." On the internal bridge this is disciplined uncertainty; externally it is the same instinct with higher stakes. Do not hide uncertainty, structure it: what we know, what we do not yet know, what we are doing, and when we will update next.

Underclaiming has its own cost, though it is rarer. An organization so afraid of saying the wrong thing that it says nothing leaves a vacuum, and the vacuum fills, with rumor, with the attacker's version, with a journalist's reconstruction. Silence reads as either incompetence or concealment. The goal is not to say as little as possible; it is to be the single most reliable source of truth about your own incident.

Holding Statements, and One Voice

Two habits make communicating in the fog survivable, and both have to exist before the incident.

The first is the holding statement, a short, controlled message used before the full facts are in. Its job is not to answer everything; it is to acknowledge the issue, show the organization is in control of the process, avoid speculation, and set an expectation for the next update. The difference between a good one and a useless one is concrete. "We take security very seriously and are looking into this" is not wrong. It is just fog, and customers have learned to hear it as fog.

Compare: "We're investigating a security incident affecting access to the customer portal. We've activated our incident response process, engaged our technical and legal teams, and temporarily restricted access while the investigation continues. We'll provide another update by 7 p.m." That does not say everything. It says enough to show control without pretending certainty. Draft these in advance for the scenarios you can predict, outage, suspected data exposure, ransomware, a vendor incident, and have legal, privacy, communications, and security review them while nobody is under pressure. Templates do not replace judgment; they replace panic.

The second is one voice, many audiences. Incident communication comes apart when different parts of the organization speak separately. Support tells customers one thing, sales tells prospects another, an executive improvises a third, the status page says a fourth, and very quickly the inconsistency becomes the story. The fix is not one person writing every sentence; it is one approved message discipline, adapted per audience from the same set of facts. Executives need business impact and the decisions in front of them. The board needs severity, materiality, whether the incident is significant enough to require disclosure, and management's response.

Employees need to know what to do and what not to say. Customers need to know whether and how they are affected and where to get updates. Regulators need specific facts in a specific form on a specific clock. Same facts, different framing, which is exactly why communications and legal control the formal message path while the CISO helps translate technical uncertainty into language each audience can use. A high-severity incident is not the moment for a well-meaning engineer to answer a customer or a reporter directly. Helpful freelancing is how the second incident starts.

Internal Communication Comes First

Organizations instinctively think about the external audiences first, customers, regulators, media, the board. But internal communication is where a surprising number of incidents actually go sideways, and it usually goes first.

Employees see the outage, the strange behavior, the customer questions, sometimes the attacker's own message, before leadership has a settled story. With no guidance, they improvise, reply to customers casually, speculate in internal chat, forward screenshots, ask a vendor for help outside the coordinated channel, and discuss the whole thing in tools that may later become evidence.

So a fast internal message matters: what is known at a high level, who is leading the response, what to do, what not to do, where to send customer or media questions, and when the next update lands, plus a plain reminder not to speculate externally. This is not about keeping employees in the dark; it is the opposite. It is about keeping the response coherent and protecting the investigation, because in a serious incident, loose internal communication becomes external communication within minutes.

Knowing What You're Actually Talking About

You cannot communicate honestly, or notify accurately, if you do not know what happened, which sounds obvious right up until a regulator's clock is running while the investigation is still working out the basic shape of the thing. Forensics is the discipline that turns "something happened" into "here is what happened, to what, affecting whom, and how far back," and everything downstream depends on it: how the attacker got in, what accounts and systems they touched, what data they may have viewed or taken, how long they were there, whether persistence was established, and whether the environment is actually clean enough to recover.

The first tension is between the instinct to fix and the need to know. Wiping and rebuilding a compromised machine restores service and can destroy the evidence that would have explained how they got in and what they took. Containment and preservation have to be balanced deliberately, not left to whoever reaches the keyboard first, and the balance does not always favor preservation; safety, stopping active harm, or restoring an essential service can outweigh it, so the commander makes that call with forensic and legal input and records it, rather than letting "preserve everything" quietly stall containment.

The simple instinct is to ask, before you destroy state, whether it needs preserving; what this chapter adds is the discipline behind it, proper evidence handling, a defensible record of who did what to which artifact and when, and the judgment about when your own team can investigate and when you need specialists. That last call matters more than people expect: a serious incident or suspected breach that may end up in litigation, regulatory scrutiny, or an insurance claim is often a moment to bring in external forensic specialists, and to do it early, because the evidence they would need degrades by the hour.

It usually travels with legal, because involving counsel appropriately can shape whether the investigation carries privilege — the specifics are jurisdictional and genuinely a lawyer's question — so the leadership move is to have the relationships and the trigger defined in advance, and rehearsed, not to be hunting a forensic firm's after-hours number while the clock runs.

And a hard truth: the honest forensic answer usually takes longer than everyone wants. Executives, customers, and regulators all want to know now whether data was taken and whose, and the investigation often cannot say for days. Managing that gap, refusing to state as fact what you only suspect, while not hiding behind the investigation to avoid saying anything, is one of the genuinely hard parts of the role, and it is why the communication and forensic disciplines are inseparable: what you can honestly say is bounded by what you actually know.

There is a subtler trap folded inside that: "we have found no evidence of data access" is only honest if you actually had the visibility to detect it. Where the logs or telemetry needed to see access were never in place, "no evidence" quietly means "we can't tell" — and saying the first while meaning the second is its own kind of overclaim.

Legal Hold and Disciplined Documentation

Two legal realities belong in the response early, not bolted on late. The first is the legal hold, sometimes seen first at the operational level as a preservation notice, when litigation, regulatory inquiry, or an insurance claim becomes possible, legal may need to instruct the organization to preserve relevant records and stop anything from being deleted or altered: logs, email, chat, tickets, system images, cloud audit records, access records, vendor and customer communications, the decision log. Whether and how to invoke that, and whether to route work through outside counsel for privilege, is legal's call, not the CISO's. The leadership move is to make sure legal is close enough, early enough, to make it.

The second is documentation discipline, which cuts in an interesting direction. The lesson is not to stop writing things down. Serious incidents need disciplined records, and the incident log is essential. The lesson is how to write: record facts, label assumptions as assumptions, capture decisions and who made them, and keep out the blame, the unsupported conclusions, and the casual jokes or private commentary that would read terribly later in front of a regulator, a court, a board, or a journalist. Incidents make people forget obvious things; this is one worth remembering on purpose.

"Was it a breach?" — the question that triggers everything

At some point a specific question gets asked, and everything downstream hinges on it: is this a breach? It sounds technical. It usually is not. It is a legal and definitional question, and treating it as technical is a classic, consequential mistake.

Here is why the distinction matters. Different laws define "breach" differently, and each definition triggers a different set of obligations. A privacy law may frame it around personal data being accessed or lost; a security regulation may define a reportable "incident" far more broadly; a securities regulator may care whether the event is material to investors regardless of whether any data moved; a customer contract may require notice when no law does. The same underlying event can be a notifiable breach under one regime, a reportable incident under another, and nothing under a third. So "was it a breach?" does not have one answer. It has as many answers as there are frameworks that apply to you, which is exactly the cross-jurisdictional reality this book keeps returning to.

The practical consequence is that this is a joint determination, not a security call. Security and forensics supply the facts, what was accessed or exfiltrated, whose data, over what period, whether it was encrypted or otherwise protected, when the organization became aware. Legal and privacy apply those facts to the definitions and make the call, with business owners on impact and executives approving where required.

The failure to avoid runs in two directions: do not let the security team quietly declare "no breach" just because it has not seen exfiltration yet, and do not let the business declare "breach" because customers are angry. Either way it is a documented, evidence-based decision. Sometimes the decision is to notify, sometimes it is not to, and both need to rest on evidence rather than instinct. (The actual definitions and thresholds are not this chapter's subject; the point here is who owns the call and how easily it gets made by accident.)

Notification Under the Clock

Once something is determined notifiable, you are operating against time, and usually against several clocks at once, which is the part that surprises people. One incident can start a privacy-law notification window, a sector reporting requirement, a securities-disclosure obligation, and a stack of customer-contract notice clauses, all measured from different trigger points and running in parallel.

Some are counted in days: under GDPR Article 33, for instance, a controller notifies the supervisory authority without undue delay and, where feasible, within seventy-two hours of becoming aware of a personal-data breach, unless it is unlikely to risk individuals' rights and freedoms; a processor instead notifies the controller, and telling affected individuals, under Article 34, runs on the separate, higher "high-risk" threshold, and some obligations, in certain sectors and jurisdictions, run in mere hours. You do not need every deadline here; the ones that bind you are set by the privacy and sector regimes themselves. What matters operationally is that they overlap, they start before you feel ready, and missing one is its own violation independent of the underlying incident.

That produces the sharpest tension in the chapter: notify early with incomplete facts, or wait for a complete picture and risk blowing the window? The instinct to wait until you "know everything" feels responsible and is usually wrong, because most regimes are built to expect an initial notification based on what you know so far, followed by updates as the picture clarifies. On the whole, regulators respond better to honest-and-early with acknowledged uncertainty than to complete-and-late, the same disciplined-uncertainty posture as the rest of your communication. The clock rarely waits for certainty, and it is not supposed to.

Two operational points make this survivable. First, the decision to notify, like the other decision rights, needs a clear owner assigned in advance; working out who pulls the trigger while a seventy-two-hour clock ticks is a terrible time to discover the org chart is unclear. Second, the notices have to be consistent with each other and with everything else you are saying.

It is entirely possible to file a careful regulatory notice while a customer statement, a press line, and an executive's offhand comment all say slightly different things, and those inconsistencies are exactly what erodes trust and invites scrutiny, because regulators and journalists read your statements side by side later. Coordinating notification across regulators, customers, and the public so it tells one coherent, honest story is the operational heart of getting this right.

Customer Notification Isn't Regulator Notification

Worth separating, because you will hit this constantly: notifying a customer is a different act from notifying a regulator, on a different rhythm. A regulator wants facts in a required structure and timeline. A customer wants something more relational, confidence that you are handling it, clarity on whether and how they are affected, guidance on what to do, and a commitment to keep them posted. And here is the part that catches people: a contract can require you to notify an affected customer even when no law requires you to notify any regulator, often on a short, defined clock, sometimes with defined content, root cause, indicators, affected data categories, sub-processor involvement, a remediation plan.

This is where incident response ties straight to customer trust and revenue, and it is especially sharp for SaaS, managed-services, cloud, and anyone serving regulated clients. Do not improvise it: know which customers are affected, which ones carry contractual notice terms, who owns and approves the message, and what can honestly be said now versus later. (The contractual-notice obligations themselves (tracking them, negotiating them) belong to third-party and customer assurance; here the point is simply that this clock exists and has to be in the notification picture.)

Board, Media, and the Post-Incident Record

Three shorter beats round out the outward-facing side.

Board updates: no panic, no perfume

The board does not need packet captures; it needs decision-grade truth, what happened at the current confidence level, what is affected, business impact, whether it is contained, whether customer or personal data is involved or still under assessment, who else is now involved (regulators, insurer, law enforcement), what management has decided, and what the board may need to approve. Not panic, not perfume: a board handles bad news far better than late news, corrected news, or polished news that later turns out incomplete. (The standing governance and board-reporting machinery lives in Volume I, Part 3, and the reusable templates; here it is just another audience on the map.)

Public statements: assume comparison later

If the incident goes public, public statements get special care for one reason: they will be compared later, against your customer notices, your regulator filings, the forensic findings, employee messages, and any future legal filing. Inconsistency is the danger. So they run through legal and communications with security providing the facts, and they stay short, accurate, and non-speculative. Avoid the reflexes: do not attribute blame early, do not say "no data was accessed" before evidence supports it, do not call every attack "sophisticated" by default, and do not lean on "out of an abundance of caution" when the real reason is legal or customer impact, but do not go so empty that it reads as evasive either. Affected stakeholders deserve useful truth.

The post-incident report: where the story becomes governance

The post-incident report is where the incident becomes organizational learning rather than just a bad week. It is a governance document, not a blame document, timeline, detection source, root cause where known, what was affected, the containment and recovery actions, the forensic and legal/privacy assessment, what was communicated and notified when, what worked, what failed, and corrective actions with owners and dates. Where root cause or forensics are still open, it says so.

And it feeds the same loop everything in this part feeds, the risk register, control and playbook improvements, training, the next tabletop's scenarios, board reporting, and customer assurance. The discipline is worth extending to serious near misses, too, not just confirmed breaches; some of the most valuable lessons come from the incident that almost happened. A painful incident with learning is still painful. A painful incident without learning is a weakness left in place, waiting for the next event.

The Frameworks Underneath Crisis Communication and Notification

This is another area where a handful of frameworks describe the same capability in different vocabularies, the series' recurring point that you are running one operating model, not standing up separate programs. A few worth knowing, defined briefly:

The NIST incident-handling guidance (the SP 800-61 line) treats communication, coordination, and reporting as integral parts of the response lifecycle rather than afterthoughts, a useful reminder that notification and messaging are response activities, not events bolted on at the end. NIST also publishes guidance specifically on integrating forensic techniques into incident response (the SP 800-86 line), which frames digital forensics as a disciplined process (collection, examination, analysis, reporting) built to produce findings that hold up rather than a frantic scramble through logs.

And running underneath the notification discipline are the legal and regulatory regimes themselves, the privacy laws and the sector and jurisdictional reporting rules, which are the actual source of the clocks and thresholds this chapter operates against. The frameworks tell you how to communicate, investigate, and coordinate; the law tells you what you are obligated to disclose and when.

The point is not to adopt all of them. It is that when someone references "the forensic process" or "our 800-61 communication plan" in a planning meeting, you recognize it as vocabulary for the capability this chapter builds, and you know which parts of it live in the legal chapters instead.

Industry Pattern — The Statement That Aged Badly

> *An organization detects a serious incident and contains it competently. Early evidence points to a single affected system, and under real pressure from customers and leadership an early statement goes out: the issue was limited to one system, and there is no evidence of data access. At the moment it is written it feels reasonable, the investigation has not found data access, leadership wants to reassure, communications wants clean language.*
>
> *Two days later, forensic review finds the attacker reached a shared storage location connected to that system after all. Now the first statement has to be corrected, and the correction lands harder than the truth would have if it had been told carefully the first time. Customers do not focus on the incident anymore; they focus on the correction, and on why they were told there was no data access. The honest answer: "at that time, there was no evidence" — is true, but the wording never preserved that nuance, so it does not help.*
>
> *The version that would have aged well was right there and only slightly less comforting: "We're investigating unauthorized activity affecting one system. At this stage we have not confirmed unauthorized access to customer data. The investigation is ongoing, and we'll update as facts are verified." Less reassuring in the moment, far more durable a week later. The lesson is not that anyone was careless, the pressure to reassure is real and human. It is that in an incident, the reassuring thing and the true thing are not always the same thing yet, and the gap between them is where trust gets spent.*

What Evidence Should You Expect

A real crisis-communication, forensics, and notification capability leaves evidence that these disciplines are prepared rather than improvised. At leadership altitude, a CISO should be able to point to prepared communication materials, version-controlled holding-statement templates for the likely scenarios, a named and authorized spokesperson, an internal-communication procedure, and an audience map with an approval workflow covering employees, customers, regulators, the board, partners, and the public; a defined breach-determination process with a decision owner that involves legal and privacy, not security alone; established relationships and pre-agreed triggers for external forensic and legal support, alongside a legal-hold or preservation-notice template and a forensic-readiness map showing which log sources exist and how long they are retained; and a notification process mapped to the obligations that actually apply (regulatory, contractual, and insurance) with a notification-clock tracker, a clear owner for the decision to notify, and a notification decision log.

The evidence that the capability is real rather than theoretical is familiar: records showing these disciplines have been exercised, communication and notification decisions walked through in tabletops, not just documented; and, after any real incident, an honest record of the messages issued with their approval timestamps, how the breach determination was made, whether obligations were met on time, and a post-incident report feeding the same corrective-action loop as everything else. A forensic process is worthless if the evidence has already aged out, so knowing your log sources and retention windows in advance is itself part of the evidence.

For a small or mid-sized organization, the practical minimum keeps the worst outcomes off the table:

- A holding-statement template you can adapt fast, and one named person who speaks for the organization.
- A clear rule that breach determination is a joint legal/privacy/security call, never a solo technical one.
- A pre-identified external forensic and legal contact, with the trigger for calling them agreed in advance, and a basic legal-hold and evidence-preservation checklist.
- A simple map of which notification clocks could apply, regulatory and contractual, and who owns the decision to notify.
- An alternate communication channel that still works if email or collaboration tools are compromised.

- A board-update format and a post-incident report template.
- One tabletop, at least, that tests the communication and notification pressure, not just the technical response.

That is not a full crisis-management program. It is enough to keep a technical incident from becoming a trust catastrophe. NIST SP 800-86 remains useful process orientation for forensics, but it is a 2006-era reference that predates cloud, SaaS, and containers, so supplement it with current platform and provider guidance.

Reality Check

> *Imagine you have just confirmed a serious incident that may involve customer data, and the pressure to say something is already building.*
>
> *Who speaks for the organization? One named person, or whoever gets asked first? Is there a holding statement you can adapt in ten minutes, or does someone draft one from scratch right now? When the executive team asks "can we tell customers their data is safe?", who is allowed to answer, and is the honest answer "we don't know yet"? Who makes the call on whether this is a legally notifiable breach, and does everyone understand that an engineer's "no data was accessed" is not that call?*
>
> *Do you know which notification clocks might already be running, including the ones buried in customer contracts, and who owns the decision to start? If you needed a forensic firm in the room tonight, do you have a number, a contract, or just a hope? And the one that catches everything: would the statement you are about to make still look accurate if the investigation finds more tomorrow? If the answer is no, change the statement.*
>
> *If several of those are uncertain, that is not a crisis. It is a Tuesday-afternoon to-do list. Every one is far cheaper to settle now than to discover mid-incident, with the clock running and the first statement already being drafted.*

What This Means for You as a Security Leader

Your role here sits right on the seam between the technical world and everyone who needs to understand it, and that is a job only the security leader can really do. You are the translator, turning what the forensic picture actually shows into language executives can decide on, legal can act on, and communications can build a message from, without letting the translation drift into false reassurance or needless alarm.

Nobody else is positioned to hold that line, and holding it well is one of the most consequential things a CISO does in a serious incident. During one, your own language should be calm, precise, and evidence-bound: you do not need to sound certain before certainty exists, you need to sound in control of the process, and there is a real difference between the two.

Most of the work, as with everything in this part, happens before the incident. You make sure the holding statements exist, the spokesperson is named, the forensic and legal relationships are in place with triggers agreed, the legal-hold process is understood, and the breach determination is wired as a joint call. You fold these disciplines into the tabletops, because a communication plan that has never been exercised fails exactly the way a response plan does. And in the moment, you protect the organization from its own worst instinct, the urge to say the comforting thing before the facts support it, by being the person who calmly, repeatedly, insists on the honest version.

There is a reason this chapter sits where it does in a book called From Risk to Trust. Almost everything else in these pages is about managing risk. This chapter is about the moment trust is most directly on the line, when customers, regulators, and the market are deciding, in real time and on incomplete information, whether your organization can be relied on. You do not earn that trust by never having an incident; everyone has incidents.

You earn it by how you behave during one: telling the truth at the speed the facts allow, preserving the evidence that supports the truth, and documenting the decisions made along the way. Handled that way, a serious incident can end with more trust than you started with. Handled the other way, a minor one can cost you trust you spent years building. The difference is often not the technology alone. It is the telling.

Bridge to Chapter 10

Communication carries the organization through the incident; the next chapter asks whether the business can keep running — continuity, disaster recovery, and the backup strategy underneath both.

CHAPTER 10

Business Continuity, Disaster Recovery, and Backup Strategy

Bringing the system back is not the same as bringing the business back.

Every chapter in this part has been building toward one question, and it is finally time to answer it plainly: when something takes your critical services down, ransomware, a cloud region failure, a botched change, a data center that floods, can you actually get the business running again, and how fast?

Recovery is where resilience stops being a mindset and becomes a measurable capability. It runs in parallel with incident handling and outlasts it, because you can contain cleanly, communicate honestly, and investigate thoroughly and still fail if, at the end of it, the business cannot get back to work. "The systems are back" and "the business is running" are different claims, and this chapter is about the distance between them.

That is the distinction that anchors the whole chapter, and a lot of organizations blur it until the day it matters. Restoring a system and continuing the business are not the same. A server can come back online while the business is still stopped, because the application on it depends on three other things that are also down. A backup can restore perfectly and still be useless, because it comes back too slowly for a business that measured its tolerance in hours. Recovery is the whole chain, data, systems, dependencies, people, and the business processes riding on top of them, not the single restore job that feels like the finish line but is really just the start. Systems are restored by IT. Services are recovered by the organization.

Three Words That Get Used Interchangeably and Shouldn't

Here they get pulled properly apart, because treating them as one blurry thing is how organizations end up with a "recovery plan" that does not actually let them keep operating. They are usually owned by different teams, written in different documents, tested at different times, and then ransomware hits, or a cloud region fails, and all those separate plans suddenly have to behave like one capability.

Backup is the protected copy of your data, the raw material of recovery. Necessary, and nowhere near sufficient. It looks like it answers one question, can we get the data back?, but even that overstates it: a copy existing does not prove it restores, restores intact, or restores in time. It says nothing about how fast, in what order, or whether the business can function while you do.

Disaster recovery (DR) is the technology side of getting back: restoring systems, applications, and infrastructure after a disruptive event, wherever the disruption came from. DR is what turns a pile of backed-up data into running systems.

Business continuity (BC) is the widest of the three, the capability to keep the business delivering its critical services, or degrading gracefully, while the technology is being restored; the business continuity plan (BCP) is the document that supports it. BCP is the manual workarounds, the alternate processes, the decisions about which services must survive, the people and locations, the customer communication. DR restores the technology; business continuity keeps the organization functioning around it.

The reason the distinction matters is that organizations over-invest in the middle one and neglect the outer one. They build a solid DR capability (a recovery site, tested restores) and never ask what the business actually does during the hours or days that recovery takes. A DR plan without a continuity plan gets the systems back and leaves the business improvising through the outage. The three fit together, and this chapter treats them as one recovery capability with three layers.

It Starts with a Business Impact Analysis

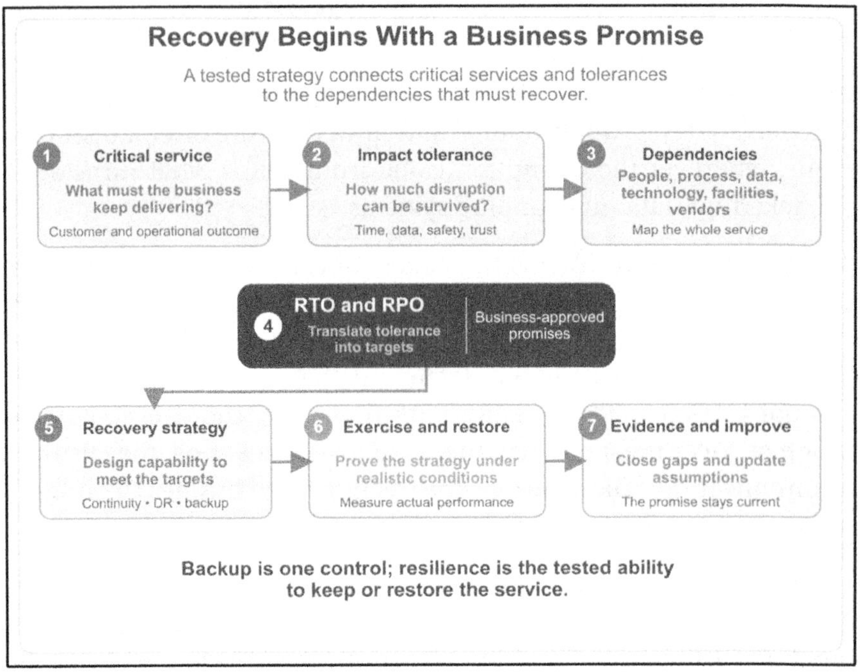

You cannot build a sensible recovery capability without first knowing what you are recovering and in what order, and that knowledge does not come from the technology. It comes from a business impact analysis, the unglamorous, foundational work that most of resilience quietly rests on.

A BIA answers a small set of deceptively hard questions, one service at a time. Which business services actually matter? How long can each one be down before the harm becomes serious, and then unacceptable? How much recent data can each afford to lose? If full service cannot be restored right away, what minimum acceptable level of it must keep running in the meantime? Which come back first, when they cannot all come back at once? And what does "serious harm" even mean for this service, lost revenue, regulatory breach, safety, reputation, a contract penalty?

The reason it is genuinely hard is that the honest answers surprise people. Ask a business owner how long they can tolerate losing a service and the reflexive answer is "not at all" — everything is critical when you ask in the abstract. The BIA's job is to push past the reflex to the real answer, because if everything is top priority, nothing is, and the recovery sequence becomes a fight in the middle of the crisis instead of a decision made calmly in advance.

A good BIA is where the business, not the security team, decides what matters most, which is exactly why it cannot be done by IT alone in a back room. It is a business exercise that security facilitates: business-owned because the business carries the impact, and technically validated because the stated expectations have to be achievable.

Everything downstream in this chapter depends on the BIA. The recovery objectives come from it. The dependency maps are drawn for the services it flags as critical. The DR investment gets pointed at what it says matters. Skip it, and you protect what is technically visible rather than what is genuinely essential, a very expensive way to be unready, where you might spend heavily shielding a system whose outage is merely inconvenient while a smaller service that actually stops revenue sits exposed.

RTO and RPO: Turning Tolerance into Targets

These are promises, not decorations. This is the mechanics.

Recovery Time Objective (RTO) is the target time within which a service should be back, and it is worth being precise, because RTO is easy to conflate with a different number. The maximum tolerable downtime is the outer business limit, the point beyond which the harm becomes unacceptable; the RTO should sit inside it, leaving room for stabilization, reconciliation, and backlog before that outer limit is reached.

Recovery Point Objective (RPO) is how much data you can afford to lose, measured in time, the gap between your last usable recovery point and the moment things went wrong. If your RPO is one hour, you are accepting that up to an hour of data might be gone. If your RTO is four hours, the target is to restore the service within four hours, leaving whatever margin the business has set before maximum tolerable downtime is reached.

The essential thing is that these are business decisions with technical consequences, not technical settings. The business sets the tolerance in the BIA; the technology then has to be built and budgeted to meet it, and the two often do not match on the first pass, which is the useful part. When a business owner says "this must recover in one hour" and the honest engineering answer is "with what we have, it's a day," you have not failed. You have surfaced a gap that was always there and was previously invisible.

Now it is a governed decision: improve the capability, revise the expectation where it is genuinely discretionary, or consciously accept the residual risk, with a named owner and a review date. All three are legitimate, with one boundary: where the tolerance is fixed by a binding legal, safety, or regulatory requirement, you cannot relax it into compliance through internal risk acceptance; that gap has to be met or closed, not accepted. What is not legitimate is quietly leaving the gap inside a plan until an incident exposes it. A written RTO with no tested evidence is aspiration; a tested RTO with a known, accepted gap is governance.

That gap exists because tighter objectives cost more, and the cost curve is steep. Recovering within a day might mean restoring from backup. Recovering within an hour might mean a warm standby environment. Recovering in minutes might mean running two live environments at once. Each step up the speed ladder multiplies the cost, and not every service is worth the top of it. The art is matching the recovery investment to what the BIA says each service is actually worth, expensive fast recovery for the services that genuinely need it, cheaper slower recovery for the ones that do not. Setting one aggressive RTO across everything is how organizations either overspend enormously or, more commonly, quietly fail to hit the number they wrote down.

Dependency Mapping: The Part Everyone Underestimates

Mapping dependencies in detail is this chapter's work, and it is the piece that most often turns a confident recovery plan into a bad afternoon.

The idea is simple: for each critical service the BIA identified, map everything it actually needs to run. Not just the obvious application and its database, but the whole chain, the identity provider it authenticates against, the network paths and DNS and certificates it relies on, the middleware and integrations that feed it, the cloud services underneath it, the third-party APIs it calls, the monitoring and logging it depends on, the specific people who know how it works, and the manual steps nobody wrote down.

The goal is to look at a critical service and know, completely, what has to be alive for it to function. A good recovery map captures, per service, the business owner, the tolerable downtime and data loss, the required systems and data, the identities and access paths, the vendors and people, any manual workaround, the recovery sequence, and the date it was last tested. It does not need to start as an expensive platform, a well-maintained spreadsheet beats a beautiful tool nobody updates. The question is not whether the map is elegant; it is whether it helps someone actually recover the service.

The reason this is hard is that dependencies grow quietly over years and nobody maintains the map. An integration gets added. A vendor becomes load-bearing without anyone reclassifying it. A temporary workaround becomes permanent. A security control quietly becomes part of the critical path. During normal operations these dependencies stay invisible; they only introduce themselves during recovery, usually in the worst way, the database restores fine but the application will not start because a dependent service was not in the runbook; the identity provider is up but an expired certificate blocks everything; the recovery needs a DNS change only one unreachable person is authorized to make.

This is also where single points of failure hide, and the map is what lets you find them before the incident does: the one identity dependency half the environment relies on, the certificate process living in one person's head, the vendor with no tested recovery path of their own. Once you have mapped a critical service, the uncomfortable follow-up writes itself, which of these are single points of failure, undocumented, untested, or outside anyone's recovery plan? That list is your recovery risk register, and it is some of the highest-value work in this whole part. It does not have to be done for the entire enterprise at once; start with the handful of services the BIA flagged as most critical and work outward.

Backup Strategy at Recovery Altitude

Backup is where the raw material of recovery lives, and it is worth being precise about altitude. Volume II, Chapter 19 owns the architecture: storage tiers, immutability, credential separation, and the mechanics of building the backup capability. This chapter owns the strategic layer: what the business needs backups to deliver, and how they fit into recovery. Two different altitudes; this one is about strategy and outcomes.

At the strategy level, three properties matter more than any product choice. Backups have to be recoverable within the window the business needs, which sounds obvious and is the thing most often untrue, because a backup that exists but restores too slowly does not meet the RTO, whatever the dashboard says. They have to be isolated from the thing they are protecting against, the property modern ransomware made non-negotiable, because attackers deliberately target backup systems, knowing an organization that cannot recover is far more likely to pay; backups reachable with the same credentials that run production, or sitting on the network the attacker already owns, are not really a safety net.

And there has to be a recovery point you have real reason to trust, one you assess against the forensic, configuration, and malware evidence you have, and are confident predates the compromise, rather than simply assuming it is clean, recording any residual uncertainty because restoring from an infected backup just reintroduces the problem and starts the incident over. Spacing candidate recovery points far enough apart is what leaves you a trustworthy one to reach for when discovery is delayed.

The strategic tension that always shows up is RPO versus cost: losing no more than a few minutes of data means backing up almost continuously, which is expensive, while tolerating a day of loss is cheap, and the right answer is not uniform; it is what the BIA said each service can tolerate. It is also worth remembering that backups are themselves sensitive data: a full copy of your systems usually contains personal, confidential, and regulated information, so it needs the same access control, encryption, retention discipline, and privacy governance as production, not less. And the strategic reality worth stating plainly, looping back to ransomware readiness: a large part of the value of a trustworthy backup is that it is what lets you recover without paying.

Backups you can reach, trust, and restore inside the window turn "we have no choice" into "we have a choice." That is a real outcome the strategy buys, though not a total one: recovering your systems does not undo stolen-data extortion, regulatory exposure, or customer harm, so a backup strengthens the decision not to pay without, on its own, removing every reason the pressure exists. Which is also why backup deserves to be treated as a security control and an evidence source, not just an operations job. It needs governance, not just a green dashboard.

Restore Testing: The Moment of Truth

Here is the single most important idea in this chapter, and the one organizations most reliably ignore until it is too late: a recovery capability you have never exercised is not a capability. It is a belief.

Backup teams tend to report job-success rates, ninety-eight percent completed, all critical systems covered. Useful, and not sufficient, because the job running is not the same as the service coming back. The metric that actually matters is whether you restored what you needed, to the point you needed, in the time you needed, and the restored service worked, not just that files came back, but that the system booted, users could authenticate, integrations reconnected, data integrity held, and the business owner confirmed the result was usable.

A restore test that recovers files but never validates the application is incomplete. One that recovers the application but not its integrations is incomplete. One that recovers technically but misses the business RTO is a risk finding, not a pass. And one no business owner ever validated is only an IT test. Where a service involves transactions or manual processing, validation also has to cover reconciliation, confirming the recovered data and any work done manually during the outage can actually be squared up cleanly once systems return.

Rehearsal in general — exercises, tabletops, recovery under pressure — is its own discipline. This chapter owns the recovery-specific version of the same truth: you have to actually perform the restore, actually fail over to the DR environment, actually time it against the RTO, and actually check the whole service works end to end. Every layer of recovery has an assumption baked into it, and only doing it for real flushes the assumptions out, the backup that restores slower than anyone measured, the DR site missing a dependency, the recovery that leaned on a person who left, the restore that technically completes but produces a service that does not work because something upstream was not included.

For a smaller organization, start small but real: restore your most important database or file repository into a test environment, time it, document it, and have the business owner confirm it would actually have been usable. The first honest restore test commonly finds embarrassing gaps. Good, better embarrassment on a Tuesday than discovery during ransomware. And it is not a one-time certification; the environment keeps changing underneath the plan, so the most critical services get their recovery validated most often.

Disaster Recovery: Matching the Strategy to the Objective

Disaster recovery is where backups and infrastructure turn back into running systems, and the core decision is how much standing capability you pay to keep ready, which is really the RTO conversation in concrete form. Think of it as a spectrum. At the economical end you recover by restoring from backup onto rebuilt or repurposed infrastructure, cheapest to maintain, slowest to recover, right for services that can tolerate a longer outage. In the middle sit warm-standby approaches, where part of the recovery environment is pre-built and kept partially ready.

At the far end is active-active or fully redundant operation, where the service runs in more than one place at once and a failure is absorbed almost invisibly. Fastest recovery there is, most expensive to run. Cloud widened this spectrum and changed its economics, making warm and even hot standby far more affordable than the old second data center, but the trade-off is unchanged: faster costs more, and you match the tier to what the BIA says the service is worth.

Two things trip people up more than the tier choice itself. The first is recovery sequencing, the order matters enormously, because you cannot restore applications before the identity and network foundations they depend on are back. Recovery has an order of operations, and it is exactly the dependency map turned into a sequence: identity before applications, network and DNS before customer services, databases before the apps that need them, and the security tools themselves (EDR, SIEM, logging, network visibility) back before you reconnect restored systems to production, so you can actually see what is happening as they come online.

Organizations that never worked out the sequence discover it live, restoring things in the wrong order and backtracking while the clock runs, and without an agreed sequence, recovery turns political, with the loudest function or the most senior executive's pain setting priority. A documented sequence does not remove the pressure; it gives the organization a defensible way to handle it. The second is that a DR environment is only real once it has been failed over to. A recovery site that exists on paper, or that has been provisioned but never carried live workload, is an assumption, not a capability, and it fails in the same quiet ways an untested backup does: the failover works but a dependency was not replicated, the capacity is half what production needs, the runbook is out of date.

Recovering from a Cyber Attack Is Different

There is a hard distinction the DR discipline was originally built without, and it matters more every year: recovering from a cyber attack is not the same as recovering from a flood.

In a natural disaster you restore because the old environment failed. In a cyber incident you may not know whether the old environment is safe, whether the attacker is still present, whether privileged credentials are compromised, whether the restore point predates the compromise or contains it, whether restoring fast simply reconnects the attacker to everything. Traditional DR optimizes for speed. Cyber recovery has to optimize for something harder: safe recovery.

That means security checkpoints the flood scenario never needed, compromised accounts disabled and privileged credentials, secrets, keys, and certificates rotated before anything reconnects; persistence removed; the restore point assessed for compromise; restored systems watched more closely than usual; the initial access path understood and closed; and forensic preservation complete enough before anything gets rebuilt over. And it means someone has to own the call that the environment is safe enough to return to production.

This is where disaster recovery and incident response have to work as one. A DR team optimizing only for availability moves too fast; a forensic team optimizing only for investigation moves too slowly; the business pushes to restore, legal needs evidence preserved, and security may not yet know whether the restore point is clean. That tension is normal, and it has to be managed explicitly rather than won by whoever pushes hardest. Often the right answer is phased recovery, bring the most critical service back into a clean, tightly monitored, restricted environment while deeper investigation continues, and sometimes it is delayed recovery, because restoring now would create unacceptable risk. Either way it is a documented decision, not an emotional race back to green.

Continuity: Keeping the Business Alive While the Technology Is Down

Everything so far has been about getting the technology back. Business continuity is the parallel question that is easy to forget in the rush to restore: what does the business actually do during the hours or days recovery takes?

Recovery is never instant, even at the fast end of the spectrum, and for most services there is a real window where the technology is down and the business still has customers, obligations, and revenue on the line. Continuity is the plan for that window: the manual workarounds, the paper process, the phone-based fallback, the degraded mode that keeps the most important thing moving even if slowly; the decision, made in advance, about which services degrade gracefully and which simply stop; the alternate people and locations if the usual ones are unavailable; and the honest recognition that "we'll process it manually" is only a real plan if someone has actually tried to process real volume that way.

A manual fallback nobody has tested at scale is the continuity equivalent of an untested backup. The common failure here is a continuity plan that reads well and collapses under one question: manual processing exists, but no one has practiced it; the alternate contact list lives inside the system that is down; "priority customers first" is agreed until sales, support, and operations discover they each defined priority differently.

Degrading gracefully deserves its own moment, because degraded mode is a decision, not a failure. Running read-only, or priority-customers-only, or taking intake offline for later reconciliation, can preserve trust and cut losses during an outage, but it carries its own risk: manual workarounds introduce errors, reduced controls can open fraud or privacy gaps, temporary access can weaken security. So degraded mode has to be designed, not improvised, which modes are allowed, who can authorize one, what controls stay in force, and how the organization returns to normal.

Crucially, any control that gets relaxed or bypassed in degraded mode has to be logged as a recorded exception, so it connects to the risk-acceptance and audit trail rather than quietly disappearing. During a cyber incident this becomes a genuine business-risk decision: keep the service fully down until clean recovery is complete, or run in limited mode while investigation continues. The CISO articulates the risk; the business owner and executive leadership make the call within agreed authority. And continuity is where the customer-facing reality lands, during a serious outage the business is not just technically down, it has customers wondering what is happening, which is exactly where this connects back to the communication discipline.

When Your Recovery Depends on Someone Else's

One more dependency deserves singling out, because it is the one you control least. For most organizations today, critical services run partly on other companies' infrastructure, cloud platforms, SaaS, payment processors, identity providers, managed services, outsourced support. Which means your recovery may be waiting on their recovery, and their crisis becomes your outage.

Two flavors of this are worth separating. For cloud, the resilience work does not disappear, it moves: can you actually rebuild infrastructure from code, are those repositories and your cloud break-glass credentials protected and available, are backups shielded from a compromised cloud admin, can you restore into another region, and do the network, DNS, certificate, and service-quota dependencies actually hold under a real rebuild? (The deeper cloud control design lives in Volume III, Part 4; here the lens is purely recovery.)

For SaaS, the question is which recovery responsibilities remain yours, can you export critical data, and how often and in what format; can you recover deleted or corrupted records; what logs exist and for how long; what does the vendor's contract actually commit to for RTO and RPO; can you retrieve your data in a usable form if the vendor is unavailable or the contract is ending; and can you operate manually if the platform is simply unavailable? A vendor questionnaire that confirms "they have a BCP and DR plan" is a start and not an answer. The question the business will ask during the incident is sharper: can our service recover if they fail? (The assurance program that answers this at scale (contracts, right to audit, continuous monitoring) is Part 3's; here the point is simply that these dependencies belong in your own recovery map.)

The Frameworks Underneath Continuity and Recovery

Recovery and continuity are another place where several frameworks describe the same capability in different vocabularies, the series' recurring point that you are running one operating model, not adopting separate programs. A few worth knowing, defined briefly and at the same conceptual level:

ISO 22301 is the international standard for a business continuity management system, and it is a continuity standard, not a security one. It frames continuity as a governed, ongoing discipline (understand the business, set objectives, plan, test, improve) rather than a binder written once. If your organization already runs an ISO management system, continuity slots in as a sibling.

ISO/IEC 27031 narrows to ICT readiness for business continuity, the bridge between "the business must keep running" and "here's what technology has to be ready to do." NIST's contingency-planning guidance (the SP 800-34 line) covers the DR and continuity side from the practitioner angle, including the business-impact-analysis and recovery-strategy thinking this chapter is built around. And the CSF's Recover function is the governance-level reminder that recovery is a first-class capability alongside protection and response, not an afterthought bolted on at the end.

The point, as always, is not to adopt all four. It is that when someone drops "we should be 22301-aligned" or "what's our contingency plan?" into a meeting, you recognize it as vocabulary for the capability this chapter builds, and you know it maps to work you are already doing, not a new island to staff.

Industry Pattern — The Backup Was Fine. The Business Was Not.

An organization has genuinely strong backup discipline. Jobs complete, reports get reviewed, storage is healthy, the infrastructure team is confident. On every metric the team tracks, recovery is covered.

Then a major disruption takes a customer-facing service down, and the recovery runs, technically successfully. The database restores. The application starts. From a technical view it worked. But the business service does not come back. The identity integration is missing. A reporting feed is broken. The customer-notification workflow depends on a SaaS platform that is also unavailable. The restored data is from the right backup, but it is further behind than the business can tolerate. Support cannot say which customers were affected, finance cannot reconcile the manual transactions, and the business owner says the service is not usable.

The backup was fine. The business was not. The lesson is simple and uncomfortable: backup success is not service recovery. Recovery is only complete when the business process works again, with acceptable data loss, an acceptable control posture, and the business owner's own validation. Which is why this chapter keeps returning to the same point: systems are restored by IT, but services are recovered by the organization.

What Evidence Should You Expect

A real recovery capability leaves evidence that continuity and recovery are built and validated rather than assumed.

At leadership altitude, a CISO should be able to point to:

- a current business impact analysis naming the critical services and their tolerances, with a review-and-approval date, and recovery objectives signed off by the business owners rather than set by IT alone;
- dependency maps for those services covering the full chain, including monitoring and logging;

- a recovery strategy chosen per critical service and a recovery sequence or runbook that has been approved, not just drafted;
- a backup strategy whose recovery points and recoverability actually match what the BIA requires, with the isolation and known-clean-point properties in place; and
- disaster-recovery and continuity plans that include the cyber-recovery checklist (credential, secret, key, and certificate rotation, plus a named safe-return approver), the degraded-mode procedures with their exception log, and the manual workarounds for the window while technology is down.

The evidence that the capability is real rather than documented is the same kind that ran through the whole part:

- restore-test and failover records showing recovery has actually been performed, timed against the RTO, and validated end to end with the business owner's sign-off — not just that data came back, but that the service worked, including reconciliation where transactions or manual processing were involved;
- a tracked gap analysis between what the business needs and what technology can currently prove, with the accepted gaps carrying a named risk owner and a review date;
- validated escalation and recovery paths for the critical vendors your services depend on;
- evidence that an alternate communication channel and access to the recovery runbook survive even if the usual collaboration tools are down; and
- proof that the plans are re-tested when systems, vendors, or critical services change.

This is also where recovery becomes board-ready. Rather than "backups are green," the useful board message reads like: our top five critical services are mapped; three have tested recovery within target; two have named gaps (one a vendor dependency, one a restore-time gap) with remediation underway and the residual risk accepted by the business owner until closure. That sentence moves the conversation from belief to evidence, which is the language board reporting runs on.

For a small or mid-sized organization, the practical minimum is enough to be genuinely recoverable without an enterprise program:

- Identify your handful of truly critical services and assign each a business owner.
- With those owners, set realistic RTOs and RPOs, and map the major dependencies, including identity, network, monitoring, and the vendors each service relies on.
- Confirm the backups for those services are isolated, include a known-clean recovery point, and can actually be restored in time.
- Perform a real end-to-end restore or failover of your most critical service, time it, and have the business owner confirm the recovered service would have been usable.
- Write a simple continuity plan for the window while technology is down, including one manual workaround for the highest-impact service, and check the workaround actually holds at real volume.
- Confirm you can still reach an alternate communication channel and the recovery runbook if your primary collaboration tools are unavailable.
- Document every gap the tests reveal, decide to fix or formally accept each one, and re-test after significant changes.

That is not a mature continuity program. It is enough to know that when something takes your critical services down, you can actually bring the business back.

Reality Check

> *Pick your single most important business service and answer honestly.*
>
> *Who owns it from the business side, and do they agree with your downtime and data-loss numbers, or have they never been asked? Everything it depends on to run, systems, identity, network, certificates, cloud, SaaS, monitoring, vendors, and the people who know how it works, is that mapped, or would you be discovering it live?*
>
> *When was the last successful restore test behind it, did it meet the RTO and RPO, and did the business owner confirm the recovered service was actually usable? If it went down right now, in what order would things come back, who decides, and which dependency is the least tested? Can it run in degraded mode, who approves that, and what would you tell customers? And which recovery gap is known but not fixed, and who has accepted that risk?*
>
> *If you cannot answer these, the organization may have backups. It does not yet have proven recovery for that service, and that distinction matters on exactly the day everyone wishes it did not. None of it is a reason to panic. It is a reason to schedule the one thing that turns a plan into a capability (an actual, end-to-end recovery) before an incident schedules it for you.*

What This Means for You as a Security Leader

Recovery is the discipline where the security leader has to think hardest like a business leader, because much of it is not really a technology question at all. Which services matter most, how long the business can survive without them, what "acceptable" data loss means, how much to invest in speed. These are business judgments, and your job is to draw them out of the business rather than make them alone in a corner of IT. You may not own business continuity, you may not own disaster recovery, you may not own the backup platform, but you own enough of the risk to care deeply whether they work together, because cyber incidents now routinely trigger all three at once.

Ransomware tests the backups. A cloud failure tests the dependency map. A vendor outage tests third-party resilience. And the business tests every bit of it the moment the service is down. The most common failure in this whole area is a recovery capability designed entirely by technologists to recover technology, which brings the systems back and leaves the business stranded. You are the one positioned to keep the business service, not the server, at the center of the conversation.

Most of the work, as with everything in this part, happens before the incident. You make the business define what matters, make technology prove what it can actually recover, make the gap between them visible, and make a named owner either fund it or accept it. You make recovery testing real rather than assumed, and that is where you will spend your credibility well, insisting calmly and repeatedly that the organization actually perform an end-to-end recovery, because the alternative is finding out during the one event where finding out is catastrophic. And you make the resilience evidence board-ready, so "can the business recover?" is answered with tested fact, not with "we have backups." Those were never the same question.

That is the whole argument in one stance. Assume it happens. Build the plan, rehearse it, communicate honestly through it, and be able to recover, for real, at the end of it. Prevention reduces the odds of the bad day; everything in this part reduces the damage when it comes anyway. And recovery is where that promise gets kept or broken, because it is the part the business and the customer actually feel. A recovery capability you have genuinely built and genuinely tested is, in the end, what lets you say the thing this whole book is pointed at: that even when something goes wrong, the organization can be relied on.

Part 2 Closing Note: Resilience Is Trust Under Pressure

Part 2 was built on a sentence that sounds pessimistic and is actually the most responsible sentence in the series: assume it happens. Not because prevention failed — most of this series is prevention, and good prevention quietly wins every day — but because a program that cannot survive the day prevention loses is not an operating model. It is a wager.

The Part turned that assumption into capability from six connected angles. Threat-informed security operations replaced the inherited SOC — the tool that detects whatever its vendor wrote rules for — with a defensible point of view: who is likely to come for an organization like ours, what would they do, and would we see it? Detection without response authority is observation; response without reliable evidence is improvisation, and the Part built against both. Resilience drew the line between restoring a system and restoring the business, and made RTO and RPO promises rather than decorations. The incident response plan put the answer to the worst hour in writing before the hour arrives — roles, severity, decision rights — because you do not rise to the occasion; you fall to the level of the decisions you already made.

Exercising kept the plan honest: tested capability, not documented intent, with ransomware as the scenario that stresses everything at once. Crisis communication, forensics, and notification handled the part of the incident that decides its lasting cost — what you say, to whom, and when. Saying too little appears evasive; saying too much before the facts are established creates confusion and legal exposure; trust is preserved by stating what is known, what remains uncertain, what is being done, and when the next update comes. And continuity, recovery, and backup answered the question the whole Part had been building toward — because recovery is achieved when the organization can operate acceptably again, not when one technical component restarts.

The connective tissue is evidence under stress. Everywhere else in the series, evidence answers an auditor on a calm Tuesday. Here it answers harder audiences on the worst day — the board mid-incident, the regulator inside an applicable notification window, the customer deciding in real time whether trust was misplaced. The restore test, the exercise report, the incident log, the notification record: this Part's evidence is the kind you cannot manufacture afterward.

For a book called From Risk to Trust, this Part is where the title gets tested most directly. Trust is not what an organization claims before the incident. It is what remains after one, and it is decided by preparation that happened in the quiet.

One dependency kept appearing across every chapter here: many of the systems being defended, investigated, and recovered are not yours. Critical services increasingly run in other people's companies — and you can contract out a service, but you cannot contract out the consequences of depending on it. Part 3 turns that recurring dependency into its own operating discipline.

Bridge to Part 3

When the perimeter is other people's companies, risk management has to work through contracts, evidence, monitoring, and relationships rather than direct control.

VOLUME IV

PART 3

Third-Party, Customer, and Supply Chain Assurance

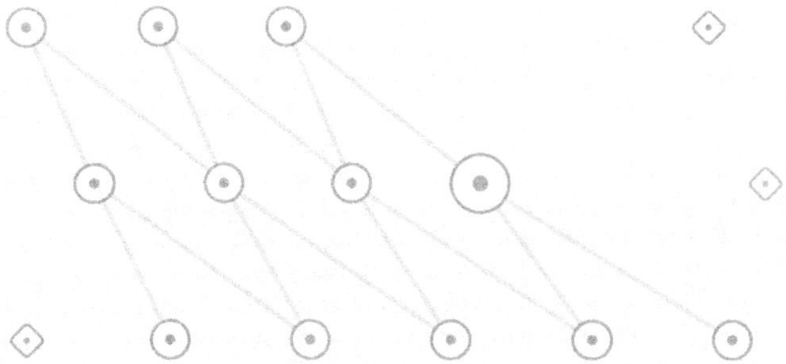

CHAPTER 11

Third-Party Risk — When the Perimeter Is Other People's Companies

You can outsource the work. You cannot outsource the risk.

The familiar picture is an organization defending things it owns: its systems, its data, its people, its network. That picture is dated. The modern organization does not run on infrastructure it controls. It runs on a web of other companies: the cloud platform underneath everything, the SaaS tools the business lives in, the payment processor, the identity provider, the managed service running your security monitoring, the payroll vendor, the analytics platform, the AI service someone connected last week, the sub-processor you have never heard of that one of those vendors quietly relies on.

Your data is scattered across all of them. Your ability to operate depends on all of them. And your security posture, the thing you are accountable for, now extends into companies you do not manage, cannot fully see, and will never control. The modern perimeter is not a wall. It is a relationship map.

That shift changes the shape of the problem. When your risk lived inside your walls, security was about controls you could implement. When your risk lives in other people's companies, security becomes about assurance. Getting confidence about controls you cannot implement yourself, in environments you can only see through a keyhole. It is a genuinely different discipline, and a lot of security programs are stronger at the first than the second, which is a problem, because the second is where more and more of the actual risk now sits.

One sentence anchors the whole part, and it is worth saying plainly because it is the thing organizations most want to forget when a vendor is cheap and convenient: you can outsource the work, but you cannot outsource the risk. When a vendor holding your customers' data gets breached, it is your customers who are affected, your name in the notification, your regulator asking questions, and your trust that erodes.

The vendor may have failed, but the accountability lands on you. A contract can allocate liability, indemnity, and remedies between the parties in meaningful ways; what it cannot do is make the outage disappear, undo the exposed data, or move the consequence. That asymmetry, you carry the risk for things other people do, is the entire reason third-party risk management exists.

Third-Party Risk Is Business Risk Wearing a Vendor Badge

It helps to be precise about the word "vendor," because the narrow version of it hides the risk. A vendor is the commercial counterparty, the company with the contract and the invoice. Third-party risk is the broader thing: the business exposure created whenever the organization depends on an outside entity to deliver a service, process data, access systems, support operations, or otherwise touch your security, privacy, resilience, compliance, or customer trust. Those are not the same set. Some third parties are classic vendors with purchase orders. Some are embedded deep in your technology stack. Some are open-source components nobody signed for. Some are free tools with no contract and enormous data exposure. Some are used by business teams before security ever hears the name.

The risk does not care how procurement classified any of them. If a thing can affect the confidentiality, integrity, or availability of what matters, or your privacy obligations, your regulatory standing, your resilience, or your customers' trust, it belongs in this conversation, whether or not it looks like a "vendor." Which is why the useful question a third-party program asks is not "did the vendor complete the questionnaire?" It is "what risk are we inheriting through this relationship, and are we comfortable with it?" That is a bigger and more honest question, and it is the one everything here is built to answer.

Why This Is Genuinely Hard, Not Just More Work

It is tempting to treat third-party risk as ordinary security with a wider boundary, same controls, just more companies. It is not, and pretending it is produces the kind of program that generates paperwork and no actual assurance. Three things make it a different problem.

The first is visibility. Inside your own environment you can look, run a scan, pull a log, check a config, verify a control actually works. Inside a vendor's environment you cannot do any of that. You are on the outside, and almost everything you learn is reported to you rather than observed by you: a questionnaire they filled out, an audit report they commissioned, a reassurance their salesperson gave. You are reasoning about someone else's security from secondhand evidence, and much of the discipline is about getting trustworthy signal through that keyhole. It is why this discipline leans so hard on independent audit reports and contractual audit rights. They are the mechanisms that turn "they told us they're secure" into something closer to evidence.

The second is scale. A mid-sized organization does not have a handful of vendors; it has hundreds, and the number climbs every quarter because signing up for a new SaaS tool takes a corporate card and five minutes. You cannot deeply assess hundreds of vendors with the rigor you would apply to your own environment. There is not the time, the people, or the access. So third-party risk is unavoidably a prioritization problem before it is an assessment problem. The organizations that do this well are not the ones that assess every vendor equally; they are the ones that figure out which handful could actually hurt them and concentrate their limited scrutiny there.

The third is depth: the risk does not stop at your vendor. Your vendor has vendors. The SaaS platform you rely on runs on a cloud provider, uses its own sub-processors, depends on its own supply chain. Your data may flow three or four companies deep into a chain you can barely see the second link of. One operational consequence is your recovery waiting on a vendor's recovery; Chapter 13 goes deeper on the fourth-party problem itself. The point for now is that the boundary you are accountable for does not stop at the companies you have contracts with; it extends through them.

Not All Vendors Are the Same Risk — and That's the Whole Game

If one idea separates a functioning third-party program from a box-ticking one, it is this: the scrutiny a vendor gets should be driven by how much damage that vendor could actually do to you, not by process fairness, not by contract size, not by how loudly they are pushing to close the deal.

The instinct to treat every vendor with the same process feels responsible and is quietly disastrous. It means the SaaS tool holding your entire customer database gets the same questionnaire as the company that supplies office snacks, and since you cannot do a deep job on all of them, everyone gets the shallow version. The critical vendor gets under-scrutinized, the trivial one gets over-scrutinized, and the total real assurance produced is close to zero. Over-review the harmless ones and you are slow and bureaucratic; under-review the dangerous ones and you are exposed. Usually a program that fails to tier manages both at once.

The alternative is to tier vendors by the risk they actually carry, and the questions that drive the tiering are refreshingly concrete. What data does this vendor touch, none, some internal data, or a pile of your customers' personal information? What access do they have to your systems, and how deep? Are they in the path of a business-critical service, such that their outage stops you operating? Could their compromise become your breach?

A vendor that holds sensitive customer data, has privileged access, or sits in the critical path of a core service is a fundamentally different risk from one that never touches anything that matters, and should get a fundamentally different level of attention. The snack supplier gets a light touch. The vendor running your customer-facing platform gets real scrutiny, real contractual protection, and ongoing attention. That is not unfair; it is the only way limited assurance capacity produces real protection where it counts.

This tiering logic runs underneath the entire third-party program. The lifecycle, fourth-party depth, contract terms, and monitoring all scale to the tier. Get the tiering right and the program has somewhere sensible to point its effort. Get it wrong and no amount of downstream process rescues it.

The Moment That Actually Matters: Before You Sign

Here is a pattern worth internalizing early, because it shapes how much leverage you will ever have over a vendor's security: almost all of your influence exists before the contract is signed, and almost none of it exists afterward.

Before signing, you hold the one thing that concentrates a vendor's mind, the deal is not done yet. You can ask hard questions and expect real answers. You can require security commitments in the contract, insist on the right to audit, demand breach-notification timelines, set data-handling obligations. The vendor wants your business, so the vendor will negotiate. The day after signing, that leverage evaporates. Now you are a customer trying to get a live vendor to do something extra, competing with every other customer's demands, and the honest answer to "will you add this security commitment now?" is usually a polite version of "that's not in the contract."

There is an honest exception worth naming, because you will hit it constantly: for large hyperscalers and dominant SaaS providers, pre-signing leverage may still be limited. They do not rewrite their standard terms for a mid-sized customer. Even then, early review earns its keep, because its value is not only negotiation; it is knowing what those standard terms actually mean, what compensating controls you will need on your side to live with them, and whether the business is consciously accepting the residual risk rather than discovering it later. With a vendor you can negotiate, early review shapes the deal; with one you cannot, it shapes an informed decision. Both beat finding out after signature.

This is where the assurance mechanics first come into play, and where you use them. The security questionnaire, the vendor's SOC 2 report or ISO certificate, the contract clauses on breach notice and data handling and audit rights: these are the tools of the pre-signing moment, and each one has to be used properly. Two things are worth planting now, though, because they separate real programs from performative ones.

A questionnaire is a self-attestation, not assurance: "we use MFA" means little until you know for which users and which systems, and for the vendors that matter you want evidence, not just a checked box. And an assurance report has to be read, not collected, a SOC 2 that covers the vendor's corporate IT but not the product you are buying, or an ISO certificate scoped to one business unit, or a report eighteen months stale, is a green checkmark hiding a gap exactly where your risk lives. Filing the report is not the same as knowing what it says.

All of which is why the single most important organizational fact about a third-party program is whether security gets a look before the deal closes. Being brought in after is one of the most common and most damaging patterns in this area: the business finds a tool, loves it, negotiates it, signs it, deploys it, and then loops security in to "review" a decision that is already made and a contract that is already locked.

At that point security's only moves are to rubber-stamp it or to block something the business already committed to, a fight it usually loses and should not have to have. So the highest-value question is not about questionnaires at all; it is whether there is a step in procurement where security actually gets a look before signature. If there is not, the program is structurally too late no matter how good its paperwork is.

None of this makes security the office of "no." The goal is not to block vendors, the business needs vendors, and a function that reflexively obstructs them just gets routed around, which is worse, because then the risky vendors are the ones you never see. The goal is to be in the room early enough to shape the deal, so the vendor that gets signed is one you can live with.

Shadow Vendors: The Ones You Never Saw

Every organization has official vendors. It also has unofficial ones, and they are often the dangerous ones. A business team buys a SaaS tool on a corporate card. A developer signs up for an API service. Marketing uploads customer data into an analytics platform nobody reviewed. Someone pastes internal documents into a free tool to summarize them. None of this happens because people are reckless. It happens because the tools are easy to buy, the business moves fast, and the formal process feels slow.

From a risk view, these shadow vendors are dangerous precisely because they skip every control that makes third-party risk manageable, no inventory entry, no tiering, no contract review, no data-processing terms, no security due diligence, no offboarding plan, no visibility at all. And the tools most likely to be missed this way are the cheap, self-service ones that never trip a procurement threshold, which are increasingly the ones with real access to real data.

The answer is not "ban everything," which never works. Shadow-vendor risk is mostly a process-design failure wearing a user-behavior costume: if the only sanctioned path is slow and painful, the business will find a faster wrong one.

So the fix is to make the right path easier, a lightweight review for low-risk tools, a few pre-approved options, a clear and fast intake, and to actively discover what is already in use through the signals you have (expense data, single sign-on, SaaS-management and cloud logs, and browser extension and plugin inventories, which is how a growing number of shadow tools quietly enter) rather than assuming the official list is the whole list. A program that only assesses the vendors that come through the front door is blind to exactly the ones most likely to hurt it.

AI Has Made Third-Party Risk More Complicated — and More Urgent

Of all the things reshaping third-party risk right now, AI is the loudest, and for good reason: it is arriving in every organization faster than the vendor process was built to handle, and it usually arrives as third-party risk without anyone labeling it that way.

Here is the thing to see clearly. Most AI tools your organization will adopt are third-party services, someone else's model, running on someone else's infrastructure, processing whatever your people feed it. A business user sees a productivity tool that drafts emails or summarizes documents or answers questions.

The CISO has to see what is actually underneath: a data processor that may be receiving prompts full of confidential or personal information, a supplier that may retain those inputs, a service that may use your data to improve its models, a system that may connect into internal repositories, and a dependency chain (model provider, cloud host, plugins, vector stores) most of which is invisible from the outside. The gap between what the user sees and what the CISO has to assess is wider for AI than for almost any other category of tool, and that gap is exactly where the risk hides.

That means the questions an AI vendor raises are different in emphasis from a conventional one. What data actually gets sent to the service, and does it include customer or personal information? Are prompts and outputs retained, and for how long? Is your data used to train or improve the model, and, a point that trips up a lot of buyers, is training on your data actually disabled by default, or only if you are on a particular enterprise tier or have it written into the contract? Where does the processing physically happen, and does that create a data-residency or cross-border problem? Can data be deleted?

Does the tool reach into internal systems, and with what access? And, the one people forget, do the outputs feed decisions that affect customers, employees, or anything regulated, such that a wrong or biased answer becomes your problem, not the vendor's? AI governance and AI risk are their own subject; the point here is narrower and specifically about third parties: a great deal of your AI risk will enter the organization through the vendor door, and if your third-party program has not adapted to recognize it, AI adoption will simply route around the program, quietly, on corporate cards, one prompt at a time.

There is a cross-country wrinkle worth flagging too, because it is exactly the kind of thing this book's readers hit: where an AI service processes your data, and whose rules apply to it, can differ from your other vendors, and a tool that is fine to use with one customer's data may violate another customer's contractual or jurisdictional terms. AI does not get a pass from the tiering and pre-signing discipline the rest of this chapter argued for. If anything, it needs that discipline more, because it is spreading faster than any vendor category before it, and treating "it's just a chatbot" as a low-risk answer is how a serious data-exposure problem gets onboarded without anyone deciding to accept it.

You're Also Someone Else's Vendor

Third-party risk has a mirror, and it is worth seeing early because it reframes the whole effort. You assess your vendors; your customers assess you. If you provide SaaS, managed services, consulting, data processing, an AI product, or anything hosted, you are sitting inside someone else's third-party risk program, which means their security questionnaire becomes your sales blocker, their audit request becomes your operational burden, and their security addendum becomes your contractual obligation. Plenty of CISOs feel this from both sides in the same week: chasing a vendor's SOC 2 report one day, and the next, answering a customer's questionnaire with 300 rows, a third of them duplicates and a handful asking for things no human should have to answer in a single spreadsheet cell.

The useful realization is that the two sides are the same discipline viewed from opposite ends of the desk, and the maturity you demand of your vendors is the maturity your customers are about to demand of you. Third-party assurance and customer assurance are not two topics. They are one relationship, seen from each side.

The Frameworks Underneath Third-Party Risk

Third-party risk is another place where several frameworks describe the same discipline in different vocabularies, the series' recurring point that you are running one operating model, not adopting separate programs. A couple of orientation points, kept conceptual:

The first is that the major security frameworks already carry a supplier or third-party dimension, which means this is not a separate program bolted onto your security work, it is inside the frameworks you are likely already running. ISO/IEC 27001's control set includes supplier-relationship controls; the CSF treats supply-chain risk management as a first-class governance concern rather than a technical afterthought; SOC 2 and similar attestations consider how an organization manages its own vendors; and privacy regimes bring processor and sub-processor obligations, data-processing agreements, and cross-border transfer considerations. Operational-resilience regimes, particularly in the financial sector, increasingly push third-party technology risk into formal governance as well. If you are aligned to any of these, you already owe some third-party discipline; this part is how you actually do it.

The second is that on the other side of the relationship sit the assurance instruments, chiefly the SOC 2 report and the ISO/IEC 27001 certificate, which are how a vendor demonstrates its security to you, and often the closest thing you will get to inspecting their controls through the keyhole. They have real limits (a certificate shows that a defined scope was certified and sits within an ongoing certification cycle whose current status is worth checking, not that a vendor is invulnerable, or even that the certified scope covers the service you are buying), and reading them properly is a discipline of its own.

The point, as ever, is not to adopt every framework. It is that when a vendor waves a SOC 2 report, or a customer's contract demands "supply-chain risk management," you recognize it as vocabulary for the discipline this part builds, and you know where the real treatment lives. Many frameworks, one third-party operating model.

Industry Pattern — The Small Tool That Grew Teeth

> *A team needs a tool to solve a real problem. It is inexpensive and quick to set up, so it slips under the procurement threshold that would have triggered a security review. Someone signs up on a corporate card, connects it to a system so it can actually do its job, which quietly gives it access to real data, and it becomes part of the environment without ever landing on anyone's vendor list. It is not hidden; it just never crossed the desk of anyone whose job was to ask what data it could reach.*
>
> *Six months later, the small tool is not small. More users have been added, customer data is flowing into it, its reports feed management decisions, an integration has been built, a second team has adopted it, and an administrator account inside it has broad access. The original owner has changed roles. The contract is still the basic one, with no real breach-notification clause; no one has looked at its sub-processors; no one has tested whether you could get your data back out. Then the vendor has an incident, and now it is your incident, in a tool nobody ever assessed.*
>
> *The lesson is not that someone broke a rule, and it is not that every small tool needs enterprise-grade review on day one. That would paralyze the business. It is two things at once. A third-party program is only as good as its ability to see the third parties, and the ones most likely to be missed are the cheap, self-service ones that never trip a threshold. And risk is not fixed at onboarding, a tool reviewed as low-risk can grow critical over time, and a program that never re-checks is blind to exactly the moment a small tool grows teeth.*

What Evidence Should You Expect

A real third-party program leaves evidence that vendors are known, tiered, and scrutinized in proportion to the risk they carry, not that a form was filled out for each one. At leadership altitude, a CISO should be able to point to a vendor inventory that is genuinely reasonably complete, including the self-service and business-signed tools and an AI-tool inventory or AI-vendor flag, rather than only the ones procurement formally handled; a risk-tiering approach that sorts vendors by the data, access, and business-criticality they actually represent, with a named business owner for each of the ones that matter and a record of any tiering override or exception; evidence of a vendor intake trigger that puts security in front of critical vendors before contracting rather than after; sub-processor or fourth-party visibility for the critical vendors; and assurance appropriate to each tier.

Deeper for the vendors that could hurt you, lighter for the ones that cannot, and specifically adapted for AI services where data exposure and retention are the questions that matter most.

The evidence that the program is real rather than performative is about proportionality and follow-through, not volume. A stack of identical completed questionnaires proves activity, not assurance. What proves a working program is that the critical vendors got a pre-sign security review and real contractual protection, that the assurance obtained actually matches each vendor's risk and was read rather than filed, that shadow and SaaS discovery is a running activity rather than a one-time cleanup, that unresolved gaps were named and consciously accepted by a business owner rather than left to drift, and that the inventory reflects reality rather than only the vendors polite enough to come through the official door.

The detailed mechanics — how the lifecycle runs, what the contracts say, how monitoring works — are a separate subject; what a CISO owns at this level is that the program is risk-driven and reasonably complete, rather than a uniform process applied to a partial list.

For a small or mid-sized organization, the practical minimum covers the real exposure without an enterprise program:

- Build and maintain an actual list of your vendors, and make finding the unofficial, self-service ones part of the job, including the AI tools people have quietly started using.
- Sort them into a few tiers by what data they touch, what access they have, and whether they are in the path of a critical service.

- Concentrate your real scrutiny on the handful that could genuinely hurt you; give the rest a light touch.
- Get security a look at critical vendors before the contract is signed, while you still have leverage.
- For the critical ones, get real assurance (an independent audit report or certification, actually read) and real contract terms (breach notification, data handling, audit rights), with depth proportionate to the vendor's actual exposure.
- Periodically review finance and expense data and single sign-on logs for shadow vendors, and re-check critical vendors, because a vendor's risk changes as your use of it grows.

That is not a mature vendor-risk program. It is enough to make sure the vendors who could actually hurt you are not the ones nobody looked at.

Reality Check

> *Two questions, answered honestly.*
>
> *First: could you produce a list, right now, of every third party that holds your customers' data or has meaningful access to your systems, and are you confident it is actually complete, including the tools individual teams signed up for without telling anyone, and the AI services someone connected last month? If the honest answer is "we have a list, but I wouldn't bet it's complete," then you do not yet know your own third-party attack surface, which is the first thing an attacker will map and the last thing you want to be discovering during an incident.*
>
> *Second: for your single most critical vendor, the one whose breach would most clearly become your breach, did security get to look before the contract was signed, and do you have real assurance about their controls rather than a salesperson's reassurance and a report nobody read? If not, you are carrying that vendor's risk on trust alone. Neither answer is a crisis. Both are a reason to start where the exposure is highest: find the vendors you cannot see, and get real assurance on the ones that matter most.*

What This Means for You as a Security Leader

Third-party risk is where the security leader has to be equal parts risk manager and diplomat, because the job runs straight through the business's relationships with the companies it depends on. You are not going to personally assess hundreds of vendors, and you should not try. Your job is to make sure the program exists and points its effort in the right direction: that vendors are actually visible, that they are tiered by real risk rather than treated uniformly, that security gets its look at the point of leverage before signing, and that the scrutiny concentrates where a failure would actually hurt, including on the AI services that are entering faster than any vendor category before them.

Most of the leverage, as this chapter has argued, is organizational and upstream. The single highest-value thing you can do here often is not a better questionnaire. It is getting a security checkpoint wired into procurement so critical vendors cannot get signed without a look, and making sure the self-service tools that never trip a threshold still land on someone's radar. That is a process-design fight worth having, because it determines whether your program sees the risky vendors at all.

And through all of it, hold the posture that keeps the program from being routed around: you are not the office of "no." The business needs vendors, and it will find ways to get them with or without you. A third-party program earns its place by helping the business adopt vendors safely and quickly, shaping the deal, catching the genuinely dangerous ones, and getting out of the way of the ones that do not matter, rather than by making adoption slow and adversarial.

Do it that way and you get brought in early, which is the whole game. Do it the other way and you hear about the important vendors after they are signed, which is no game at all. That is the difference between a third-party program that reduces risk and one that just produces documents, and the rest of this part is about building the first kind.

Bridge to Chapter 12

A vendor is a relationship, not a decision made once at signing; the next chapter follows the vendor risk lifecycle from intake through to offboarding.

CHAPTER 12

The Vendor Risk Lifecycle — Onboarding to Offboarding

A vendor is not a decision you make once. It is a relationship you manage as the risk keeps changing.

Vendor risk is not fixed at onboarding, and that is the idea this whole chapter is built around. It is also the single most common way third-party programs quietly fail. An organization does a genuinely careful job assessing a vendor at the start — questionnaire reviewed, report read, contract negotiated — files the result, and never looks again. Two years later the vendor holds ten times the data, has been acquired, has changed its sub-processors, and had a breach nobody heard about. The assessment on file describes a company that effectively no longer exists.

Here is the way to hold it: if the only serious review happens at onboarding, your program is looking at a photograph of the vendor taken the day the deal closed. But vendor risk is not a photograph. It is a moving object. A low-risk tool becomes business-critical. A vendor that processed no customer data ends up holding sensitive records. A small integration becomes a production dependency. A support-only provider gets handed administrator access. A SaaS product bolts on AI features.

The vendor changes hosting region, sub-processors, ownership, or security posture, and the business quietly expands its use of the tool without telling anyone, while the contract auto-renews without a soul reviewing whether the risk moved. A vendor assessed once and forgotten is not managed; it is just remembered. The fix is not a better one-time assessment. It is recognizing the relationship as a lifecycle (stages, each with its own risks and its own work) and making sure the right question gets asked at the right moment. This chapter walks that arc.

One thing before we start, so the chapter does not read as a demand for enterprise machinery. Every stage scales to the vendor's risk tier. For the handful of vendors that could genuinely hurt you, the full lifecycle is worth running deliberately. For the long tail of low-risk tools, most of it collapses into a light touch — a quick check at intake, a note in the inventory, a glance when something changes. The lifecycle is a way of thinking, not a mandatory gauntlet every vendor has to survive. Applied to everything equally, it becomes the exact box-ticking this risk-based model is meant to prevent.

The Shape of the Arc

A vendor relationship moves through a recognizable sequence: you evaluate and select the vendor, onboard it into your environment, operate alongside it for months or years while watching how the risk evolves, reassess it periodically or when something changes, and eventually offboard it when the relationship ends. A fuller program will name more steps inside those, intake, tiering, due diligence, the risk decision, contracting, access provisioning, go-live, change review, renewal, incident handling, data return, and that longer list is a useful checklist for a mature program. But the five stages are the spine, and the boundaries between them blur in practice anyway.

The thing to notice, and the reason this chapter exists, is where the effort usually goes versus where the risk actually lives. Almost all the attention in most programs lands on the front of the arc: the pre-signing assessment, the onboarding checklist. That is understandable (it is where your leverage lives) and it is also where the least time is spent. The vendor is in evaluation for weeks. It is in live operation for years. Yet the operating years, where the data grows, the vendor changes, and the risk drifts, are exactly the stage most programs never actively manage. The lifecycle view exists to rebalance that: to keep some attention flowing to the long middle, instead of spending it all at the door.

It Starts with Intake — or It Starts with Luck

Before evaluation can happen, something has to trigger it, and that trigger is the intake step, the quiet foundation the whole lifecycle rests on. If the business can buy or connect a vendor without anything prompting a review, then security finds out about vendors by accident: after the contract's signed, after the data's uploaded, after the tool's in production, or after the vendor has an incident. That is not a review process. That is archaeology.

A good intake step is simple enough that business teams actually use it, and it captures just enough to decide the next move, who is asking, what business problem the vendor solves, whether it will touch company or customer or personal data, whether it needs system access or privileged access, whether it connects through APIs or SSO or into production, whether it supports a critical service, whether it uses sub-processors or AI, and whether data leaves the country. That is enough to classify the risk and route the vendor; it is emphatically not a 200-row questionnaire at the front door, which just teaches people to avoid the process.

The single most important property of intake is where it lives. It has to sit in the path the business already walks to buy things, the procurement workflow, the contract or finance approval, the SaaS purchasing step, the IT service request. If security sits outside the buying path, security shows up late, and late security is forced into one of two useless roles: the blocker who arrives after the decision is made, or the rubber stamp who waves it through.

A security checkpoint wired into procurement is the highest-value organizational move in the whole area, and intake is where it lands, seen from the lifecycle's front end. Get intake right and every later stage has something to act on. Get it wrong and the program is running on luck.

Evaluation and Selection: The Stage That Sets the Baseline

Once a vendor is in and tiered, evaluation decides whether to take it on and under what conditions. The work is direct: tier by real risk, get security a look before signing, use the questionnaire and the assurance report and the contract as the tools of the pre-signing moment, and read the report rather than filing it. What the lifecycle adds is a discipline that is easy to miss: the evaluation is not just a gate to pass, it is the baseline you will measure against for years.

The tier you assign, the data the vendor was approved to touch, the access you granted, the commitments it made, the assurance you accepted. All of that becomes the reference point for every reassessment down the line. When you look at this vendor again in eighteen months, the question will not be "is it secure?" in the abstract; it will be "has anything changed from what we approved?" And you can only answer that if you wrote down what you approved. A selection decision that is not captured in a form you can compare against later is not a baseline. It is a memory, and memory is exactly what fails at the two-year mark.

Two beats of this stage deserve naming, because they are where evaluations quietly go soft. The first is that the assessment has to end in an explicit decision, not a vague "approved, with some concerns nobody owns." The honest outcomes are a small set: approve; approve with specific conditions to close before or shortly after go-live; require remediation first; accept the vendor with compensating controls on your side (tighter access, data minimization, extra monitoring) to offset gaps you cannot fix; reject; or consciously accept the residual risk with a named owner and a review date.

Security identifies and explains the risk; legal, privacy, and procurement own their pieces; the business owner owns the need and the residual risk; leadership signs off on material exceptions. The trap to watch is "approved with conditions," which has a way of becoming "approved and forgotten" — a condition without an owner and a due date is a quiet exception, and quiet exceptions are how risk goes invisible.

The second beat is that whatever you agree here has to become enforceable, which means the security, privacy, and breach-notification expectations have to be visible before signature, not discovered after. The actual contract clauses, notification timelines, audit rights, data-handling terms, exit rights, are Chapter 14's to detail; the lifecycle point is only that the risk decision and the contract have to line up before the pen touches paper, because the worst time to learn the vendor only owes you notice "without undue delay" and no real escalation path is when your customer is already asking what happened.

One honest caveat: for large providers with standard terms, alignment may not mean changing the contract at all. It may mean understanding the limits of the standard terms, adding compensating controls on your side, and documenting the residual risk before proceeding, a conscious acceptance rather than a negotiation you were never going to win.

Onboarding: Where Risk Actually Enters

Selection decides whether to trust the vendor. Onboarding is where you actually connect it, and it is a distinct risk stage that programs routinely treat as paperwork. The assessment said the vendor was acceptable in principle. Onboarding is where that principle becomes real access, real data flows, and real integrations, and where the gap between "approved" and "wired in" gets filled, often by people who never saw the assessment. A vendor can pass due diligence cleanly and still fail onboarding.

The failures here are avoidable and grimly familiar. There is over-provisioning: the vendor was approved to touch one dataset and, in the rush to make it work, gets handed far broader access than it needs, because narrow access takes longer to configure and "we'll tighten it later" is a promise the calendar never keeps. There is the integration nobody re-examined, an API token minted, a data feed opened, SSO available but not enabled, MFA optional but not enforced, none of it checked against what the assessment assumed. And there is the ownership vacuum: the vendor goes live and no single person is named as responsible for it, so when it needs attention two years later, there is nobody whose job it is to notice.

So onboarding has real work, and it is mostly about making reality match the approval: provision access to the least the vendor needs, not the most that is convenient; confirm the actual data flows and integrations match what was assessed, because a vendor approved for anonymized analytics and then wired up to receive raw customer records is not the risk you signed off on; enable logging and add the vendor to your access reviews rather than letting it live outside them; and, above all, assign a named business owner. That ownership assignment is the quietly load-bearing part of the entire lifecycle, because every later stage depends on there being a specific person whose job it is to care.

And because vendor access is external, often remote, sometimes privileged, and usually less monitored than your own, it deserves the same discipline you would apply to any privileged access: named rather than shared accounts, MFA enforced, scoped and rotated tokens, and access that actually gets removed when a project or a person's assignment ends. Where a vendor genuinely needs emergency or "break-glass" access for urgent support, that path should be deliberate rather than standing, granted on request, tightly scoped, time-bound, logged, and closed out afterward, not a permanent privileged door left open for the one day a year it is needed. A vendor account that reaches your environment is your access risk, "not our employee" notwithstanding.

The Operating Years: Where the Risk Quietly Grows

Here is the stage the whole chapter points at, and the one most programs simply do not have. A vendor spends the vast majority of its relationship with you in live operation, running, integrated, trusted, and, unless someone makes a point of watching, largely unwatched. And this is precisely the stretch where the risk you assessed at the start slowly stops describing reality.

Think about what changes over a couple of years of a live relationship, none of it announced to you. The vendor's own security posture drifts as key people leave and priorities shift and a control that was solid at assessment quietly decays. The data footprint grows, the "small tool grows teeth" pattern. The vendor gets acquired, and the acquirer's security culture may be nothing like the one you assessed. It changes its sub-processors, so your data ends up somewhere new without a word. It ships features that change what it does with your information. It has an incident you only learn about if the contract obliged them to tell you, and maybe you never learn at all. Every one of those is a change to your risk, produced entirely inside a company you do not control.

The uncomfortable truth is that, without deliberate effort, an organization often has no mechanism to notice any of it. The vendor was assessed, approved, and mentally filed under "handled," and unless it causes a visible problem, it never gets a second look. Closing that gap does not mean watching every vendor constantly, that is impossible and pointless. It means proportionate attention: genuine ongoing awareness for the critical vendors, a lighter periodic glance for the rest.

The mechanics of that awareness, continuous-monitoring services, security ratings, periodic evidence refreshes, the contractual hooks that make a vendor tell you about a breach or a sub-processor change, are the contract's to build. What belongs here is the principle: the operating years are a stage that needs managing, not a void between onboarding and the eventual end. A vendor you approved three years ago and have not thought about since is not low-risk because it has been quiet. It is an unknown risk wearing the costume of a low one.

One operating-stage failure is common enough to name on its own, because it hides in plain sight: silent expansion. The vendor was approved for one use case and gradually becomes part of three more, more teams adopt it, more data flows in, a new integration goes live, an AI feature gets switched on, it quietly becomes the workflow backbone. Nobody calls it onboarding, because the vendor is "already approved." That is the mistake, and the antidote is a principle worth saying flatly and repeating often: approved vendor does not mean approved use.

A vendor cleared for internal project tracking is not thereby cleared to process customer data. One approved for a single region is not approved for cross-border transfer. A productivity tool is not approved to train models on your confidential data. Material expansion, a new data category, a new customer population, a new geography, a new integration, new privileged access, new AI processing, is a fresh risk event, and it should trip the same review a new vendor would. That one sentence, held firmly, prevents a startling share of quiet third-party failures.

Reassessment and Renewal: Catching the Drift on Purpose

If the operating years are where risk drifts, reassessment is the deliberate act of catching that drift before it becomes a problem. It is where you go back to a vendor and ask the lifecycle's central question: has anything changed from what we approved?

Two things should trigger it, and a good program uses both. Time, critical vendors get looked at on a cadence, because enough small changes accumulate over a year or two to be worth a fresh look even with nothing obviously wrong. And the triggering event, the vendor was breached, got acquired, changed sub-processors, started handling a new data category, or your use of it expanded significantly. Time-based reassessment catches slow decay; event-based catches sudden change. Lean only on the calendar and a vendor breached in month three waits until month twelve for anyone to notice; lean only on events and slow drift never gets caught. You want both.

Reassessment works, when it works, because of the baseline from the evaluation stage. It is not starting over; it is comparison. You are not asking "is this vendor secure?" from scratch, you are asking "is this still the vendor we approved, doing what we approved, with the data scope and controls we accepted?" That is fast when you captured the baseline and nearly impossible when you did not. Comparison is not quite the whole job, though: sometimes nothing about the vendor has moved and the baseline itself has gone stale, the threat landscape shifted, a new regulation bites, the assurance lapsed, your own risk appetite changed, so the honest question is both whether the vendor has drifted from what you approved and whether what you approved is still good enough today.

And it has to be allowed to change the answer: a vendor that was tier-three at onboarding but now holds customer data and integrates with a core system is not tier-three anymore, and the program has to be willing to re-tier it upward and apply the scrutiny the new tier demands. A reassessment that can only ever confirm the original decision is not a reassessment; it is a ritual.

Renewal is the same instinct with a bonus: leverage briefly returns. Renewal usually gets treated as a commercial event (price, term, usage) but it is a risk event too, and one of the few moments the vendor wants something from you again. Before you renew a vendor that matters, it is worth asking whether it is still needed, whether its risk tier still fits, whether the assurance is current, whether prior findings were ever closed, and whether the terms still match what the relationship has become. Do not auto-renew risk. A vendor that rolls into a new term unreviewed carries all its stale assumptions with it.

When the Vendor Has a Bad Day

Sooner or later a vendor has an incident, a breach, an outage, a vulnerability disclosure, a sub-processor problem, and your incident response has to be able to absorb it. This is where third-party risk connects straight back to incident response: a third-party incident can become your incident, your customer notification, your regulatory clock, your service outage, and your board update, all triggered by an event inside a company you do not control.

The notice you get may be crisp, or it may be vague, or it may be the maddening "out of an abundance of caution" message that conveys almost nothing while forcing you to determine whether any legal, contractual, or internal clock has started. Either way, your organization still has to decide what it means for you, and that decision is yours, not the vendor's to make for you. Their "security event," "outage," or "no material impact" is a characterization of their environment, not a verdict on your severity, your breach determination, or your reporting obligations; those you assess against your own facts and the rules that apply.

So it is worth settling in advance who receives vendor notices, where they are logged, who assesses the impact on your data and services, and when a vendor's incident trips your own response process, your legal and privacy engagement, and possibly your customer or regulatory notifications. Not every vendor notice deserves a full incident response, many are routine, so the useful discipline is to triage each one against your severity model: most get logged and watched, while the high-impact ones get pulled into your response process with the same seriousness as an internal event.

That preparation is exactly why the contractual notification clauses, the escalation contacts, and the assurance relationships matter before the incident because "we're waiting to hear back from the vendor" is sometimes the honest answer, and it is never a satisfying one to give a customer. The mechanics of investigating and communicating your way through an incident live in Part 2; the lifecycle point here is simply that a vendor's bad day has to be a scenario your program already planned for, not a surprise.

Offboarding: The Stage Everyone Forgets

Every vendor relationship ends eventually, the contract lapses, a better tool replaces it, the business changes direction, or the vendor goes away. And offboarding is, reliably, the most neglected stage of the whole lifecycle, precisely because by the time a vendor is on its way out, nobody is paying attention to it anymore. Which is exactly what makes it dangerous.

The risks cluster around what gets left behind. Access that was never revoked: the vendor's accounts, API tokens, integrations, and remote-access paths quietly stay live, which means a company you no longer have a contract with, and whose security you have entirely stopped monitoring, still has a working door into your environment. Orphaned vendor access is a genuinely common breach vector, and it exists entirely because offboarding got treated as an accounting event rather than a security one.

Data left behind: your data is still sitting in the vendor's systems, and unless someone deliberately confirms it was returned or destroyed, it stays there indefinitely, a privacy and data-protection exposure that outlives the relationship and that a regulator or customer may later ask you about. And the loose ends: the integration still running, the DNS entry still pointing, the scheduled job still calling an API that should not exist.

Done properly, offboarding is a small security project, not a line item, revoke every access path; disable the accounts, rotate any shared credentials, and revoke API tokens; confirm what happens to your data (returned, deleted, and ideally with a written deletion attestation, a hook the contract should have set up back at selection); remove the integrations and clean up the technical remnants, including the certificates, webhooks, DNS entries, and scheduled API calls that outlive most offboardings; and update the inventory so the vendor is genuinely marked as gone rather than lingering as a ghost.

None of it is complicated. It is neglected not because it is hard but because attention has already moved on, which is the whole argument for making it a defined step that someone owns. A vendor that no longer has a contract but still has access is not a former vendor; it is an unmanaged access path. A vendor that no longer provides a service but still holds your data is not offboarded; it is a data exposure waiting for a reason.

Who Actually Owns All This

A quiet reason lifecycles fail is that third-party risk crosses too many functions to be owned informally. The business owner holds the need, the use case, and the residual risk. Procurement runs the sourcing workflow and the renewal calendar. Legal owns the contract language and the breach and termination terms. Privacy owns the personal-data processing, the transfer terms, and retention. Security owns the cyber due diligence, the access and integration risk, and the assurance review. IT or platform teams own the technical integration, the SSO and logging, and the deprovisioning at the end. Each piece has a natural home, which is exactly the problem, because a vendor's risk thread runs through all of them, and it is easy for it to fall into the gaps between.

So the failure mode here usually is not apathy; it is that everyone owns a piece and nobody owns the flow. The CISO does not need to personally perform every step. You cannot, and trying is how the program becomes the bottleneck everyone routes around. What the CISO has to own is that the cybersecurity risk thread does not disappear as the vendor moves from procurement to legal to IT to the business, and that each critical vendor has a named business owner who is accountable for it across the whole arc. That single assignment, a real person responsible for a real vendor, is what turns a set of disconnected functions into a lifecycle that actually runs.

The Frameworks Underneath the Vendor Lifecycle

The vendor lifecycle is another place where the frameworks describe the same discipline in different vocabularies, the series' recurring point that you are running one operating model, not adopting separate programs. Kept conceptual here, since the assurance and contract mechanics come later:

The major frameworks that carry a supplier dimension all describe a lifecycle, not just a gate. ISO/IEC 27001 and 27002's supplier-relationship expectations cover the relationship from agreement through ongoing management and changes in supplier services to termination, the same arc this chapter walks, with explicit weight on monitoring and change, which maps directly onto the operating and reassessment stages. The CSF treats supply-chain risk management as a governance concern you manage continuously across the relationship, not something you certify once, which lines up with the ownership and monitoring this chapter argues for. NIST's supply-chain control catalog is deeper still and shows up most in regulated and high-assurance settings. Privacy regimes add their own lifecycle requirements around processor selection, data-processing terms, sub-processor notice, and data return or deletion at the end.

And the assurance instruments a vendor hands you decay: a SOC 2 describes a specified date or a defined past period, and an ISO certificate covers a scope certified within a cycle whose status can change, which is the frameworks' own quiet admission that assurance ages and must be refreshed. An old SOC 2 describes controls over an old period, which is exactly why the lifecycle needs a reassessment stage. The point, as ever, is not to adopt a framework's lifecycle wholesale. It is that when a framework talks about "supplier relationship management" or "ongoing monitoring," you recognize it as the same arc this chapter describes. Many frameworks, one lifecycle.

Industry Pattern — Approved Once, Forgotten Forever

> *Third-party programs tend to break in the same place, and it is rarely at the start. A vendor is reviewed during onboarding. The questionnaire is completed, the contract is signed, the security folder has the assurance report, the business goes live. Everything about the start is done well.*
>
> *Then the years pass. The vendor adds new features. More teams start using it. Customer data moves into it. An integration is built. The original business owner changes roles. The vendor changes sub-processors. The assurance report ages past any useful coverage. The contract auto-renews. The tool becomes part of a critical workflow. And through all of it, nobody re-tiers it, nobody reviews the new data exposure, nobody updates the contract, nobody tests the escalation path, and nobody checks whether the old findings were ever closed.*
>
> *Then something happens, an outage, a breach, a customer question, a regulator's request, and everyone opens the vendor folder and finds a beautiful, thorough record of what the vendor looked like three years ago. Worse, in some versions of this pattern the relationship had actually ended a while back on paper, and yet a live integration and a copy of the data were still sitting out there, belonging to a company nobody was watching anymore.*
>
> *The lesson is simple and it is the whole chapter: third-party risk is not what you approved. It is what the relationship has become. A lifecycle exists to notice the difference, while there is still time to do something about it.*

What Evidence Should You Expect

A real vendor-risk program leaves evidence that vendors are managed across the whole relationship, not just assessed once at the door. At leadership altitude, a CISO should be able to point to:

- an intake step that catches vendors before signing, with a timestamp that genuinely predates the contract;
- selection assessments that captured a usable baseline, the tier, the approved use case, the approved data and access scope,

the commitments made, and the explicit risk decision with its owner, rather than a one-time yes with unowned concerns;

- evidence that conditional approvals were actually closed;
- onboarding records showing least-privilege access, data flows that matched what was assessed, logging enabled, and a named business owner;
- a material-change and reassessment trigger log;
- evidence that critical vendors are actually reassessed, on a cadence and on triggering events, and re-tiered when their risk changes;
- renewal reviews that reopened the risk question rather than auto-renewing;
- a vendor-incident triage record that connects to your incident-response process; and
- offboarding records, access revocation, a data return or deletion attestation where available, and an orphaned-access review afterward, proving departed vendors are genuinely gone.

The evidence that this is a lifecycle rather than a gate is, above all, whether anything happens after onboarding. A stack of thorough initial assessments with nothing behind them (no reassessments, no ownership, no offboarding records) is the signature of a program that treats vendors as one-time decisions.

What proves a living program is the boring, continuous stuff: conditional approvals that were actually closed or consciously accepted rather than quietly forgotten, reassessments that re-tiered vendors when their risk grew, expansions that were caught and re-reviewed, and exits that were closed out cleanly. The detailed monitoring and contract mechanics sit beneath all of this; what a CISO owns at this level is that the relationship is managed end to end, and that the operating years and the exit are not blind spots.

For a small or mid-sized organization, the practical minimum keeps the lifecycle real without heavy machinery:

- Put a simple intake step in front of contract signature, so security sees vendors before they are signed.
- Capture, for each vendor that matters, a short baseline at selection: its tier, the data and access it was approved for, the key commitments, and an explicit risk decision with an owner.
- At onboarding, give least-privilege access, confirm the data flows match what you assessed, enable logging, and name a business owner.
- Reassess your critical vendors on a simple cadence and whenever something changes, a breach, an acquisition, a sub-processor change, or a big expansion in how you use them, and let a reassessment re-tier a vendor upward.
- Hold the line that approved vendor does not mean approved use: material expansion gets a fresh look.
- Review access for your high and critical vendors periodically, and keep vendor incident contacts current so you know when a vendor's incident becomes yours.
- When a vendor leaves, run a real exit: revoke all access, confirm data return or destruction, remove integrations, and mark it closed in the inventory.

That is not a mature vendor-management program. It is enough to make sure the vendors you are carrying are the ones you think you are carrying, doing what you think they are doing.

Reality Check

> *Pick one high-risk vendor that has been in place for more than two years, and ask honestly: Who is the business owner today? Is the original use case still the only use case, or has more data, more access, a new integration, or an AI feature quietly been added? Has the vendor changed hosting, ownership, or sub-processors? Is the assurance report current, and did anyone actually read it? Were the original findings ever closed? Does the contract still match what the relationship has become, and are the escalation contacts still real people who would answer? When was it last reassessed, and could you offboard it cleanly tomorrow if you had to?*
>
> *If the honest answer to most of those is "I'm not sure," the vendor was onboarded but never managed, and those are very different things. It is not a crisis. It is a prompt to do the one thing this whole chapter argues for: look at the vendor as it is now, not as it was the day you signed it.*

What This Means for You as a Security Leader

The lifecycle view changes what "good" looks like for a third-party program, and the shift is worth naming plainly. A program judged by how thoroughly it assesses new vendors is measuring the easy part, the part with leverage, attention, and a clear moment to act. A program judged by whether it manages vendors over time is measuring the part that actually protects you, because that is where the risk lives and where almost everyone stops looking. Your job is to move the program's center of gravity from the door to the whole house.

In practice that comes down to the two things this chapter keeps returning to: that vendors have named owners, and that something happens after onboarding. The named owner is load-bearing, without a specific person accountable for a vendor, every downstream stage has no one to perform it, and the vendor drifts by default. The "something happens after onboarding" is the cultural shift: getting the organization to treat a signed vendor not as a closed decision but as an open relationship that needs attention proportionate to its risk.

You will not win that by assessing more vendors more thoroughly at the start. You win it by building the modest, unglamorous machinery of the middle and the end, an intake that catches vendors, reassessment triggers, named ownership, a real offboarding step, and by protecting it from the entirely reasonable temptation to declare a vendor "done" the moment it is live.

None of this argues for treating every vendor like a critical one; that way lies box-ticking and a program so heavy the business routes around it. It argues for proportion applied across time as well as across vendors: real, continuing attention on the handful that could hurt you, a light periodic touch on the rest, and, for everyone, a clean exit.

The best vendor programs do not win by asking the most questions. They win by asking the right questions at the right moment, for the vendors that matter most, and making sure someone owns the answer. Do that, and the vendors you are carrying stay the vendors you understand. Skip it, and your risk register slowly fills with companies you assessed once, years ago, and have been trusting on faith ever since.

Bridge to Chapter 13

The lifecycle assumes you can see the vendor; the next chapter takes on the risk you mostly cannot — SaaS concentration, outsourcing, fourth parties, and the supply chain underneath.

CHAPTER 13

SaaS, Outsourcing, and Fourth-Party Risk

You signed one vendor. You inherited their whole supply chain.

This chapter is about the companies you cannot see. Behind every vendor you signed sits a chain of companies you did not: the cloud platform your SaaS tool runs on, the sub-processor it quietly hands your data to, the payment provider buried three screens deep in its architecture, the open-source library nobody chose but everybody depends on. You have a contract with the first link. You have exposure to all of them. And the further down the chain you look, the less you can see, the less leverage you hold, and the more of your risk lives out of sight.

This is where third-party risk stops being about individual vendors and starts being about structure, the shape of the dependency web your organization actually runs on. A modern business is not a fortress with a few supply lines running in. It is one node in a mesh of other companies, most of which it has no relationship with and could not name. That mesh is where some of the largest, least-visible risks now sit, and it is genuinely harder to manage than anything in the last two chapters, because the core tools of the vendor program (assess it, contract it, monitor it) do not work on a company you do not have a contract with.

So the honest goal at this depth is not perfect visibility into every link in every chain. That is not realistic, and a program that claims it is being dishonest with itself. The goal is decision-grade visibility into the chains that matter most. Enough to make an informed call about the dependencies your business genuinely cannot function without. Three structural realities organize the chapter, and they are different shapes of the same theme: SaaS, which changed what "using a vendor" even means; outsourcing, where you hand an entire function to someone else's people and judgment; and fourth parties and the software supply chain, running underneath everything you signed. The risk you are accountable for extends well past the edge of what you directly control.

SaaS Changed the Shape of the Problem

It is worth pausing on how completely SaaS rewired third-party risk, because a lot of vendor thinking is still quietly built for a world that no longer exists. The old model was software you bought and ran:

it sat on your servers, inside your network, under your control, and the vendor's job ended roughly when the license was delivered. SaaS inverted all of that. Now the software runs on the vendor's infrastructure, your data lives in the vendor's environment, the vendor operates the security controls, and the relationship never ends. It is a live, ongoing dependency for as long as you use the tool. You did not buy a product. You moved into someone else's house and put your data in their rooms.

That inversion changes what your security work even is. You cannot patch their servers, harden their configuration, or watch their logs. What you can do is a narrower and different set of things, and getting clear on that boundary is most of the discipline. The vendor secures the platform; you are still responsible for a real slice of the risk that sits on your side of the line. Who you grant access to and how. Whether you actually turned on the security features the platform offers, single sign-on, multi-factor authentication, logging, encryption options, or left them sitting in the box.

Whether those logs ever reach your monitoring, or just accumulate in a console nobody reads. What data you put in, how you configure roles and sharing, which integrations and marketplace plugins you connect, and how you get your data out when you leave. This is the shared-responsibility idea, and the single most expensive SaaS mistake is misreading it. Assuming the vendor covers something that is actually your job, and leaving it undone. Many SaaS incidents are not purely the vendor failing at their half. They involve the customer never doing theirs, because they assumed "it's in the cloud" meant "it's handled."

There is a second shift worth naming: a SaaS tool rarely stays "just a tool." It starts as a convenient way to do one thing, and over months it quietly becomes part of the operating system of the business, the administrators drift into business teams rather than IT, usage expands without procurement noticing, the data inside it grows more sensitive, the vendor adds AI features, and one day a low-cost tool nobody thought hard about is holding data you would very much mind losing.

That is why the useful questions about a SaaS platform are not only "is the vendor secure?" but "what data goes into it, who administers it, is SSO and MFA actually enforced, can we get our data back out, and who owns the business process if it fails?" A cheap tool can carry high risk, not because SaaS is bad, but because SaaS is where the business now lives.

The deeper cloud version of this — how the shared-responsibility model works across the infrastructure, platform, and software layers, and the control design underneath it, is Volume III, Part 4's territory, and I will not re-run it here. The point for this chapter is what SaaS does to the third-party program: "using a vendor" now means an ongoing operational dependency with your data inside it, not a one-time purchase, which is exactly why the vendor lifecycle matters and why the concentration and fourth-party problems below get so sharp.

The Concentration Problem: When Everyone Depends on the Same Few

Here is a risk that only becomes visible when you stop looking at vendors one at a time and start looking at the whole picture: concentration. Individually, each of your vendors might be perfectly sound. Collectively, they may all rest on the same small number of underlying providers, and that shared dependency is a risk no single-vendor assessment will ever show you.

Think about what actually sits underneath a typical mid-sized organization's tool stack. A large fraction of your SaaS vendors run on one of a handful of major cloud platforms. Many of them lean on the same few providers for authentication, email delivery, payments, analytics, or content delivery. So when you picture your resilience, you see a diverse set of independent vendors, but underneath, they converge on a very small number of shared foundations.

If one of those foundations has a bad day, it does not take down one of your vendors; it takes down a dozen at once, in ways your vendor-by-vendor risk register never predicted, because each vendor looked independent on its own line. The outage that stops half your business often is not a failure of one of your suppliers. It is a failure of one of your suppliers' suppliers, felt everywhere at the same moment.

It helps to see that concentration comes in more than one flavor. There is provider concentration, many vendors on one cloud, one identity provider, one payment processor, one delivery network. There is geographic concentration, critical services all leaning on one region, one data center, one jurisdiction, or one offshore support location. There is access concentration, one managed provider or admin platform holding broad reach across many systems.

There is data concentration, one platform quietly accumulating most of your sensitive records. And there is your own concentration, where you have put so much of your critical operation into a single vendor that its failing, being breached, hiking prices, or simply going out of business would be an existential problem, and you have no realistic alternative ready. That last one is a strategic risk hiding inside a procurement decision.

You will not eliminate concentration, and you should not try. Some consolidation onto strong providers is sensible, and often safer than sprawl. Unmanaged concentration is the problem, not concentration itself. The discipline is to know where it exists, decide whether it is acceptable, and build a workaround where the impact would be severe, so a shared-foundation outage is something you anticipated rather than something you discover live.

This is also where third-party risk loops straight back to resilience: a recovery plan that runs on a SaaS tool the same outage just took offline is not a recovery plan, and an incident bridge that depends on the very collaboration platform that is down needs an alternate path decided in advance. Concentration you have named and accepted is a risk decision. Concentration you never mapped is a surprise waiting for a bad morning.

Outsourcing: Handing Over the Function, Not Just the Tool

SaaS hands a vendor your data. Outsourcing hands them a whole function, and that is a different and often deeper dependency, because now someone else's people, processes, and judgment are running a part of your business. Managed IT, an outsourced security operations or managed detection-and-response service, business-process outsourcing, offshore development, a managed help desk, an outsourced payroll or finance operation: in each case you have not just bought a tool, you have delegated an activity, and with it a set of risks that are more human and operational than technical.

The thing that makes outsourcing distinct is the depth of access and trust it usually requires. An outsourced IT provider often has broad administrative access to your environment, sometimes more than most of your own staff. A managed security provider is inside your defenses by design; if they are compromised, so, potentially, are you. An offshore development team writes code that runs in your production systems. A business-process outsourcer handles your customers' data at scale as a matter of routine. You have extended your trust boundary to include their people.

People you did not hire, cannot directly manage, and often cannot even see, and their security culture, their access discipline, their staff turnover, and their own third-party dependencies now sit inside your risk picture. And because the work happens off your floor, the failure modes are easy to miss: a support provider with strong written policies but weak desk discipline, a development partner with clean contracts but developers on unmanaged personal devices, a data-processing vendor with tidy quality checks but far broader access to raw customer data than the job needs.

Managed service providers and outsourced security providers deserve a sharper look, because they combine outsourcing with privileged access, and that combination is one of the most powerful risk paths in the whole environment. A good one genuinely lifts a smaller organization's maturity in ways it could never build alone, that is often exactly the right call. But if the provider is compromised, the attacker may inherit administrative access into your environment; if their remote-management tooling is abused, many systems can be hit at once; and because they serve many clients through the same tooling, an attacker who breaks the provider gets an attack that scales across everyone they support.

That is why the access discipline, least privilege, named accounts rather than shared ones, session logging, time-bound and reviewed access, matters most precisely here, where the vendor's reach is broadest. For any critical managed provider, one blunt question does more than a long questionnaire: if this provider were compromised tonight, how far could an attacker get through the access we have granted them? The discomfort that question produces is usually the useful part.

None of this is an argument against outsourcing. It is an argument for treating an outsourced function as a higher tier of scrutiny than a mere tool, because the access is deeper, the dependency is operational, and the failure modes reach further into the business. It is also worth being honest about where accountability actually sits. Outsourcing transfers execution. It does not transfer accountability.

When the process touches your customers, your employees, or your regulatory obligations, the outcome is still yours to answer for, however the work gets done, which is exactly why the resilience question lands hardest here: if this provider fails or has to be dropped, can you bring the function back in-house or move it elsewhere, or have you outsourced away the very capability you would need to recover?

Fourth Parties: The Risk You Didn't Sign Up For

Now the deepest layer, and the one the whole chapter has been building toward. Your vendor is your third party. Your vendor's vendors are your fourth parties, and your data and your resilience can depend on them just as surely as on the company you actually signed, except you have no contract with them, often cannot name them, and have almost no ability to assess or influence them.

The clearest example is the sub-processor. You sign a SaaS vendor; that vendor uses a cloud provider to host, an email service to send notifications, an analytics tool to understand usage, a support platform to manage tickets, maybe an AI service to power a new feature. Every one of those is now processing, storing, or touching your data, or your customers' data, and you may have no idea any of them exist. Your data has flowed three or four companies deep into a chain whose second link you can barely see. If the sub-processor is breached, it is still your data, your notification, your customers, your regulator. The accountability does not dilute as it travels down the chain, even though your visibility and control evaporate almost immediately.

Modern AI features make this vivid, because a single AI capability is rarely a single vendor. Behind one "AI-powered" feature there may sit a model provider, a cloud host, a vector database, an embedding service, a content-moderation service, and sometimes a human-review team looking at samples, and your prompt, your data, or your customer's data may pass through several of them, each retaining, logging, or transforming it in ways the front-of-house vendor never spelled out. AI is often the clearest modern illustration of a fourth-party chain, where the vendor you contracted is one visible face on a stack of dependencies you did not.

So what can you actually do about a company you have no relationship with? Not nothing, but the tools are indirect, and honesty about their limits matters. You cannot assess a fourth party directly, so instead you manage it through your third party. In practice that means knowing who the important sub-processors are in the first place, many vendors publish a sub-processor list, and for critical vendors you should actually look at it; requiring, in the contract with your vendor, that they tell you when they add or change a significant sub-processor and that they flow their security and privacy obligations down the chain; and watching for concentration again, because your fourth parties so often turn out to be the same handful of major providers everyone else depends on.

The contract mechanics that make sub-processor notice and flow-down enforceable are Chapter 14's to detail, the concept here is that you manage fourth-party risk by making your third party accountable for the chain beneath them, because that is the only lever you actually hold.

There is a privacy dimension running straight through this, and it is worth being precise about the boundary. When a vendor processes personal data on your behalf and hands some of it to another entity, that entity is often a sub-processor in data-protection terms, and the applicable law may give you real rights, to know who they are, where processing happens, and when it changes.

You do not need to become a privacy lawyer to manage this; you need a third-party program that can connect the dots between vendor management, security, and privacy, so you know which vendors process personal data, which sub-processors sit behind them, and how changes reach you. The legal machinery, data-processing agreements, cross-border transfer mechanisms, the statutory definitions, is Volume III, Part 2's territory. The operational reality that belongs here is simpler and just as important: privacy risk travels down the vendor chain, and if the chain is invisible, so is the risk.

The honest bottom line on fourth parties is a posture, not a solution. You will never have full visibility into the chain, and pretending otherwise is its own risk. What you can do is know the chain beneath your most critical vendors well enough that you are not surprised by it, push accountability down through your contracts, and stay alert to the shared dependencies that make the whole web more fragile than it looks.

For a low-risk vendor, you may need almost none of this. For a critical one, opacity itself becomes the finding, a vendor that cannot tell you where your data goes, who supports it, or how sub-processor changes are controlled has not given you a documentation inconvenience; it has given you a governance problem. That is not complete assurance. Complete assurance is not available at this depth. It is informed awareness, concentrated where it matters most.

Exit: Can You Actually Leave?

There is a question that sits underneath every critical dependency in this chapter and rarely gets asked until it is too late: can you leave? A vendor relationship is safer when you know how you would get out of it, and exit is not only a procurement concern, it is a security and resilience one. If a critical provider becomes unaffordable, unreliable, insecure, unable to meet a regulatory requirement, or acquired by an entity you are not comfortable with, the practical question is whether the organization can actually move, or whether it is quietly trapped.

For your genuinely critical SaaS, cloud, outsourcing, and managed-service relationships, the exit questions are worth asking while it is a calm afternoon rather than an incident: can we export our data, and in a usable format? How long would a migration realistically take, and who owns the plan? Is there an alternative provider, or could we bring the function back in-house temporarily? And here is the one that catches people out with outsourced functions especially, what process knowledge does the vendor hold that we would need and do not have written down anywhere?

When you outsource a function, the dependency is not only on the vendor's tooling; it is on the operational muscle memory their people built up running the process, and if none of it ever came back to you, you cannot simply pick the work up again. Exit also runs in the other direction: getting your data out is half the job, and making sure the departing provider actually deletes it, within the agreed retention window, with some confirmation it is done, is the half everyone forgets, right up until an old vendor still holds a copy of data you thought was gone.

Many organizations discover vendor lock-in only at the moment they need to leave, by which point the vendor holds the data, the process knowledge, the configuration, the integrations, and the operational muscle memory, and the exit that looked simple on paper takes months. Exit planning is not pessimism about a vendor you just chose. It is bargaining power, resilience, and plain risk management, and for a load-bearing vendor, "what's our exit?" is a question to answer before the vendor becomes load-bearing, not after.

The Software Supply Chain: Risk That Ships Inside the Product

There is one more link in the chain that behaves differently from all the others, and it has grown from a niche concern into a first-order one: the software supply chain. Modern software, including the software your vendors sell you, and anything your own teams build, is assembled largely from components nobody in the transaction wrote. Open-source libraries, third-party dependencies, build tools, package repositories, container images, and increasingly AI-generated or AI-assisted code all get woven into products that then get shipped to you. You bought a finished product; you inherited everything that went into making it.

The risk here is distinct because it is not a company you can assess. It is code, arriving inside something you trust, from origins you cannot see. A vulnerability in a widely used open-source component becomes, overnight, a vulnerability in thousands of products that quietly depend on it, including ones you run. A compromised build pipeline or a malicious package can plant hostile code inside a legitimate vendor's legitimate product, which then reaches you through the front door, signed and trusted. These are not hypothetical failure modes; the last few years have made the software supply chain one of the most active and consequential areas of risk in the whole field, which is exactly why regulators and customers have started asking pointed questions about it.

For a small or mid-sized organization, the realistic response is not to audit the world's open-source code, that is neither possible nor your job. It is a few proportionate habits: knowing, at least for your critical systems, roughly what they are built on; asking your important software vendors how they manage their own dependencies and build pipeline, a question good vendors increasingly expect; paying attention to the transparency mechanisms that help here, chiefly the software bill of materials that lists what a product is actually made of; and being able to respond quickly when a widely publicized component vulnerability lands, because the question the business will ask that day is "are we exposed through anything?" and you will want to be able to answer it.

It is worth being honest about what that bill of materials actually buys you, though: it is not a security guarantee, and it is not universally adopted yet. It is an inventory, and its value is that it lets you ask and answer the exposure question faster when the bad day comes. The deep technical practice of securing a software pipeline

— dependency scanning, build-system hardening, signing, secrets hygiene — sits outside this chapter. What belongs in this chapter is the third-party framing: when you buy or build software, you are inheriting a supply chain of code, and it deserves a place in how you think about the companies, and components, you depend on.

The Frameworks Underneath SaaS and Fourth-Party Risk

This depth of the third-party problem is, unsurprisingly, where the frameworks have been evolving fastest, because the industry recognized late that the vendor you signed was never the whole story. Kept conceptual here, since the contract and monitoring mechanics come later:

Supply-chain risk management has become its own named discipline across the major frameworks. The CSF treats it as a governance concern, which is the right altitude for fourth-party and concentration questions, because those are accountability and risk-decision problems as much as technical ones, and NIST's broader supply-chain guidance and control catalog (the SP 800-161 line) push explicitly into fourth-party, sub-supplier, and component-integrity territory, the deeper chain this chapter is about. ISO/IEC 27001's supplier controls extend to the ICT supply chain and to a supplier's own suppliers, an acknowledgment that the obligations have to flow downward.

On the privacy side, data-protection regimes carry direct sub-processor requirements, notice, flow-down of obligations, restrictions on where data can go, which is the legal engine behind much of the fourth-party discipline above. Operational-resilience regimes, particularly in financial services, increasingly name critical third-party providers, concentration risk, outsourcing governance, and exit planning as explicit obligations rather than good practice. And for the software supply chain specifically, the industry has moved toward transparency mechanisms, the software bill of materials chief among them, as a practical answer to "what is this product actually made of?", even as adoption is still uneven and no single mechanism is the whole answer.

The point, as always, is not to adopt every framework's supply-chain module. It is that when a customer's contract demands supply-chain risk management, or a regulator asks about your sub-processors, your concentration, and your software provenance, you recognize it as vocabulary for the structural risk this chapter describes, and you know the mechanics live in the chapters and parts alongside it. Different words, same operating reality: know who and what you depend on, understand the chain, govern it proportionately, and be ready when something downstream fails upstream. Many frameworks, one dependency web.

Industry Pattern — The Outage That Came From a Company Nobody Signed

> *An organization has done its vendor work reasonably well. Its critical SaaS tools were assessed, contracted, and onboarded with care, and each one looked solid on its own line in the risk register. Resilience felt reasonable, because no single vendor looked fragile.*
>
> *Then, one morning, several unrelated tools go down at once. The collaboration platform, the customer-support system, and a couple of internal apps are all unavailable, and they are from different vendors, with different contracts, that on paper have nothing to do with each other. It takes a while to even understand what is happening, because the vendor-by-vendor mental model has no way to explain why independent suppliers would fail simultaneously.*
>
> *Eventually the picture resolves: all of those vendors depend on the same underlying cloud region, or the same identity provider, or the same delivery network, and that had the outage. The organization had a diverse-looking vendor list resting on a single shared foundation nobody had mapped, and the failure of a company it had never signed a contract with took out a slice of the business.*
>
> *The lesson is not that anyone assessed the wrong vendors. Each individual assessment may have been fine. It is that risk at this depth does not show up one vendor at a time. It shows up in the shape of the dependency web, in the shared foundations underneath a list that looks diverse on the surface. You can only manage what you can see, and concentration and fourth-party dependencies are precisely the risks that stay invisible until the day they become the whole story.*

What Evidence Should You Expect

At this depth, honest evidence looks different from neat records, because full assurance genuinely is not available and a program that claims it is being dishonest with itself. What a mature program can show is informed awareness concentrated where it matters, not complete coverage.

At leadership altitude, a CISO should be able to point to some real understanding of where the vendor portfolio is concentrated, which underlying platforms and shared services a lot of critical vendors quietly depend on; sub-processor visibility for the critical vendors, drawn from their published lists and their contractual notice obligations rather than a claim to know every fourth party; a genuine answer to the exit and concentration question for the vendors the business cannot function without; some awareness of the software supply chain behind critical systems, and a way to respond when a major component vulnerability is disclosed; and outsourced functions and managed providers treated as a higher tier of scrutiny than ordinary tools, given the depth of their access.

The evidence that the program is realistic rather than performative is, oddly, whether it admits what it cannot see. A third-party register that stops confidently at the vendors you signed, with no acknowledgment of the chain beneath them, is a program that has not looked at this layer. One that can say "here's where we're concentrated, here are the sub-processors behind our critical vendors, here's the exit risk we're carrying on these two, and here's how we'd respond to a supply-chain component vulnerability" is a program that has, even though it cannot claim full coverage, because nobody can.

The contract and monitoring mechanics that make sub-processor notice and flow-down real are detailed separately; what a CISO owns at this level is that the structural risks, concentration, fourth parties, exit, the software supply chain, are seen at all, rather than hidden behind a vendor list that looks reassuringly complete.

For a small or mid-sized organization, the practical minimum keeps this manageable without pretending to omniscience:

- For your most critical vendors, find out what they are built on and who their important sub-processors are, most publish it, and make sure their sub-processor change notices actually reach a person who reads them, not a mailbox nobody checks.

- Look across your critical vendors for shared foundations, so you know where a single outage could hit several tools at once.
- Treat outsourced functions and managed providers (managed IT, managed security service providers, business process outsourcing, offshore development) as higher-scrutiny relationships because of the depth of access they hold, and know how far an attacker could reach if one were compromised.
- For any vendor the business genuinely could not function without, ask the exit questions before the answers matter: What would we do if it failed or disappeared, and would we get our data back and confirm that the old provider deleted its copy?
- Know roughly what your critical systems are built on, and have a simple way to answer "are we exposed?" when a big component vulnerability makes the news.

That is not full supply-chain assurance, which does not exist at this depth. It is enough to stop the deepest risks from being the ones nobody was even looking at.

Reality Check

> *Take a single critical business service and trace the chain behind it, not the tidy vendor line in your register, the actual chain. Which SaaS platform runs it, which cloud region and identity provider sit under that platform, which managed or outsourced team supports it, which payment, email, analytics, or AI providers touch it along the way, and which sub-processors handle the personal data inside it. Now look for the provider that shows up more than once, and ask the two questions that this layer of risk quietly hides.*
>
> *First: if that repeated provider (one cloud region, one identity platform) had a bad day tomorrow, how many of your "independent" vendors would go down together, and do you actually know, or are you assuming your list is as diverse as it looks? If you cannot answer, you have concentration risk you have not measured, which is the kind that surprises you all at once.*
>
> *Second: for the single vendor your business could least afford to lose, do you know who their critical sub-processors are, and do you have any realistic answer to "what would we do if they disappeared"? If the honest answer is "we only ever assessed the direct vendor," then your deepest dependency is also your least examined, which is exactly backwards, and worth fixing while it is a calm afternoon's work rather than an incident.*

What This Means for You as a Security Leader

This chapter asks something harder of a security leader than the previous two did, because it asks you to manage risk you often cannot see and cannot touch, and to be honest, with yourself and with the business, about where that is true. This is where third-party risk stops being a procurement control and becomes ecosystem risk management. The temptation is to let the program stop at the tidy edge of the vendors you signed, because that is where the tools work and the records are clean. The discipline is to keep looking past that edge, to the concentration, the sub-processors, the exit exposure, and the software supply chain, precisely because that is where the risk has quietly migrated and where a vendor-by-vendor program is structurally blind.

Practically, your job here is less about assessing more companies and more about seeing the shape of the dependency web and pointing attention where it matters. You cannot personally control every SaaS provider, sub-processor, cloud dependency, outsourcing partner, managed provider, software component, and AI chain in your environment, and you will lose the business's attention if you try. So start where the impact is highest: critical services, sensitive and regulated data, privileged vendor access, customer-facing dependencies, and the vendors whose failure would become your incident.

For those, push for decision-grade visibility, what they do, what data they touch, what access they hold, who they depend on, what happens if they fail, and what the fallback is, and then put that risk in front of the person who actually owns the decision. Know where you are concentrated. Know the chain beneath your handful of truly critical vendors. Treat an outsourced function as the deep dependency it is, not a tool. Have an answer to the exit question before you need one. None of that requires an enterprise supply-chain team; it requires a leader willing to look one layer deeper than the contract goes.

And through all of it, hold the honesty this layer demands. You cannot fully assess your fourth parties, cannot audit the world's open-source code, cannot eliminate concentration in an interconnected economy, and a program that pretends otherwise is more dangerous than one that names its limits, because false confidence is where the worst surprises breed. The credible posture is not "we have full visibility into our supply chain." Nobody does.

It is "we know where our deepest dependencies are, we've concentrated our limited visibility on the ones that matter most, and we're not pretending to see what we can't." The failure in third-party risk was never accepting a dependency you could not fully control. The failure is accepting it unknowingly. That honesty (informed, proportionate, and candid about its own edges) is what managing risk actually looks like once you are past the companies you can see.

Bridge to Chapter 14

Promises become enforceable through the contract, and remain credible through usable audit rights and continuous monitoring.

CHAPTER 14

Contracts, Right to Audit, and Continuous Monitoring

Before the contract, everything a vendor tells you is a promise. The contract makes some of those promises enforceable.

Let me be clear about the boundary up front, because this is a contracts chapter and it matters. I am not a lawyer, and nothing here is legal advice. The drafting, the negotiating, the liability language, that belongs to counsel, and you should involve them early rather than playing lawyer yourself. What belongs to you, the security leader, is different and just as important: knowing which clauses carry security weight and why, so that when legal and procurement sit down to negotiate, they fight for the right things.

Legal knows liability. Procurement knows price. You are the only person in the room who knows that a breach-notification clause with no timeframe in it is worth almost nothing, or that a SOC 2 report can run to sixty pages and still not cover the thing you are actually worried about. That knowledge is the contribution only you can make.

The Contract Is Where Trust Becomes Enforceable

Here is the shift worth internalizing. Before a contract is signed, every reassuring thing a vendor told you during the sales cycle: "we take security seriously," "we're SOC 2 compliant," "your data is encrypted and safe" — is exactly that: something they told you. It might be true. It might even be mostly true. But it is not yet anything you can act on if it turns out not to be.

The contract is where a subset of those statements stops being sales language and becomes an obligation: the vendor will maintain a defined security standard, will notify you of an incident within a stated window, will let you see evidence, will use your data only for what you agreed, will return and delete your data when you leave, will tell you when the chain beneath them changes.

Most security people find contracts tedious and quietly leave them to legal and procurement. That instinct is understandable and it is a mistake, not because you should be redlining paragraphs, but because the security-relevant terms are the ones nobody else in the process knows to insist on. A lawyer optimizing for liability and a procurement lead optimizing for cost can produce a perfectly signed contract that gives your security program nothing it can use.

The clauses that matter to you rarely matter to them until you say so. And the timing is unforgiving: the right moment to care about all of this is before signature, because afterward everything is harder, not impossible, but harder, and from a much weaker position. Reading the security-relevant parts of a vendor contract, and knowing what "good" looks like in them, is one of those unglamorous skills that quietly separates a real third-party program from a folder full of signed PDFs.

The Security Clauses That Actually Matter

You do not need to win every clause in every contract, that is a fast way to stall the business and burn your credibility. You need to know which clauses carry security weight, and then apply them proportionately to the vendor's tier. A vendor that waters the office plants does not need the security schedule you would put on the one hosting your customer data. A handful of topics come up again and again.

The first is a real security requirement, not a vague one. There is a meaningful difference between a contract that says the vendor will maintain "reasonable and appropriate security" — language whose meaning may be disputed later — and one that commits the vendor to something defined: a named framework, a control baseline, a security schedule appropriate to the service, or maintenance of a recognized certification for the life of the agreement. The right level depends on the vendor; the point is that vague is easy to sign and hard to enforce, while defined gives you something concrete to hold to. The second is data use, the limitation that the vendor uses your data only for the purpose you agreed, and not for their own analytics, benchmarking, product improvement, or model training unless you have explicitly allowed it.

This one has quietly become one of the most important clauses in the book, because you cannot infer a platform's data use from its label, some retain, review, or train on what flows through them and some do not, and it varies by service tier and configuration, and an AI feature bolted onto a tool you already use can turn "our data" into "their training set" without anyone signing anything new. It is worth knowing that vendors often draw fine distinctions here, between your actual customer content, the telemetry and metadata generated as you use the service, and the derived data built from both, and a limitation that covers only "customer content" can quietly leave the rest fair game.

The third is breach and incident notification, important enough that it gets its own section below, because the single word that makes or breaks it is a number. The fourth is the cluster around data lifecycle: where it lives, whether it moves across borders, that you get it back in a usable form when you leave, and that the vendor actually deletes their copy on exit, the loose thread left hanging by the fourth-party chain.

Where GDPR applies to a controller-processor relationship, Article 28 is the legal anchor for those processing terms, including return or deletion at the end and equivalent data-protection obligations for sub-processors. The fifth is the right to audit and to evidence, which gets its own treatment below because how you use it in practice is not how it reads on paper. The sixth is sub-processor notice and flow-down, the enforceable engine behind the fourth-party discipline, which closes out this chapter.

A few more sit at the edges and are worth understanding even where legal owns them. Termination and suspension rights, the ability to cut off access or exit the agreement when a vendor has a serious security failure, rather than being locked in with a provider you no longer trust. Liability and indemnification, and in particular the liability cap, which is often where the real allocation of risk quietly happens: a vendor whose liability is capped at the last twelve months of fees has, in practical terms, limited how much financial responsibility it is willing to carry, and that ceiling is usually far below what a serious breach would actually cost you.

You will not negotiate that language, but you should read it, because it tells you how much residual risk is landing back on you regardless of what the security clauses say. And insurance comes up for some vendors, useful, occasionally worth requiring, but never a substitute for the controls themselves; a cyber policy pays out after the damage, it does not prevent it.

None of these clauses are magic. A vendor can sign strong language and still fail operationally; a large provider may refuse every change; a small one may cheerfully accept terms it has no real ability to meet. That is why the contract cannot stand alone. It has to connect to the due diligence that checks whether the vendor can actually do what they have signed, and to the monitoring that watches whether they keep doing it. Where the contract and reality do not line up, that gap does not disappear; it becomes a risk decision someone has to own.

Breach Notification: The Clause Your Incident Response Depends On

If you fight hard for one clause, make it this one, because your entire incident-response capability rests on an assumption that this clause either honors or quietly breaks: the assumption that you will find out. Your incident plan starts its clock the moment you learn something is wrong. If a vendor is breached and your data is in it, everything you would do depends on them telling you, and telling you fast enough and clearly enough to act.

This is where a phrase that lawyers are comfortable with and incident responders dread shows up: "without undue delay." It is genuine legal language with a legitimate place in many agreements, and in some contexts it is perfectly workable. But on its own it commits to almost nothing you can plan a response around. Undue delay according to whom, measured from when, confirmed by what?

Where the relationship is critical and your own notification clocks are tight, it needs to be supplemented with a concrete operational expectation: notification within a defined number of hours or days of the vendor becoming aware, covering suspected incidents and not only fully confirmed breaches, with enough detail in that first notice to understand whether your data is involved, a commitment to keep updating you as facts firm up, and, this is the part people forget until it fails, a contact path that actually works outside business hours. Incidents do not wait for Monday, and a notification clause that routes to a general inbox nobody watches on a weekend is a clause that fails at the exact moment you need it.

It is worth going one small step further and confirming, at least for your critical vendors, that the contact the clause names is real and current, a notification path that has never once been tested is another form of hope, not a control. You are not being difficult by pushing for a number and a working channel here. You are making sure that the promise, if it is ever called upon, is one you can build a response on rather than one you will be arguing about while the clock runs. The mechanics of what you do once that notice arrives belong to Part 2; the point here is that the clause is the tripwire, and a vague tripwire is one you may never feel go off.

The Right to Audit — and Why You'll Almost Never Use It

Almost every mature vendor contract includes a right to audit, and almost no small or mid-sized organization ever exercises it. That sounds like a contradiction worth resolving, and the resolution tells you something real about how this actually works.

You rarely use the right to audit directly because a genuine audit is expensive, slow, and something most vendors resist for anyone but their largest customers, and honestly, most organizations do not have the capacity to send auditors into a vendor's environment even if the vendor agreed. So why fight for a right you will not use? Two reasons. It is leverage, a right you hold in reserve changes the conversation, especially if something goes wrong and you need cooperation. And it is a fallback for the case where the normal mechanism fails.

Because in practice, the right to audit is almost always satisfied a different way: the vendor offers you their independent assurance report instead of an on-site audit, and you accept it. That trade: "you don't audit us, we give you our SOC 2" — is the everyday reality of third-party assurance for the vast majority of relationships, and for a global platform serving thousands of customers it is genuinely the more scalable and reliable path; nobody wants ten thousand customers each running their own audit. Which means the skill that actually matters is not conducting audits. It is reading the reports you get in lieu of one.

Reading an Assurance Report Properly

You will recognize the pattern, because almost everyone does it at first: a SOC 2 report lands in your inbox, you glance at the cover, you see the words "unqualified opinion," you feel reassured, and you file it. The relationship is now "assured." Except that a report you filed without reading is a document, not assurance, and reading one properly is a learnable skill that pays for itself the first time it saves you from a false sense of security. A few things are worth knowing how to look for.

Start with the type. A Type I report describes whether the controls were suitably designed at a single point in time; a Type II tells you whether they actually operated effectively across a period, usually several months, often six to twelve. Type II is the one that tells you something durable; a Type I is a point-in-time view of design, not proof that the controls actually operated over time.

Then check the scope, which is where a lot of quiet disappointment lives, a report often covers one product or service, not the whole company, and it is entirely possible to receive a clean report that simply does not cover the system you are buying. Check which criteria are actually in it: security is always there, but availability, confidentiality, processing integrity, and privacy are only included if the vendor chose to be assessed against them. If your real worry is uptime and the report only covers security, it does not speak to your concern.

Then read the parts most people skip. The opinion itself can be clean (unqualified) or qualified, and a qualified opinion means the auditor found something they could not sign off on cleanly, that is not a page to skim past. The exceptions are where the truth of the report lives. Zero exceptions across a full-year Type II can genuinely reflect a mature control environment, it is not a red flag by itself, but it should not stop you reading the scope, the testing, and the criteria carefully, and where there are exceptions, it is worth reading what they were and whether any of them touch something you care about.

And then there is the section almost nobody reads and everybody should: the complementary user entity controls, the controls the report explicitly assumes that you, the customer, are performing. The vendor's assurance is conditional on your half. The report might state, in effect, "we secure the platform on the assumption that the customer enforces strong authentication and manages their own user access" — and if you are not doing those things, the assurance you are leaning on is partly hollow. This ties straight back to the shared-responsibility idea: the report itself is telling you where your responsibilities begin, and filing it unread means missing the one section that spells out your own homework.

Two more that catch people. Assurance reports have their own fourth parties, sub-service organizations, the providers the vendor themselves relies on, most notably their cloud host. A report can treat these two ways: the inclusive method folds their controls in, while the carve-out method explicitly excludes them. A carve-out report can therefore have a clean opinion and a quiet hole exactly where the cloud provider sits, and you are expected to go get that provider's own report separately. And finally, check the date. A report covering a period that ended eighteen months ago is telling you about a version of the vendor that may no longer exist. Assurance ages.

An ISO/IEC 27001 certificate works differently but rewards the same skepticism. It shows that an independent certification body audited an information security management system and certified it for a defined scope within a certification cycle whose current status is worth checking. Accreditation is separate: it is not compulsory, but it independently confirms the certification body's competence and is therefore worth verifying. If you can obtain it, the Statement of Applicability identifies the controls the organization deemed necessary, their implementation status, and the justifications for inclusion or exclusion; the certificate alone tells you far less.

A narrowly scoped certificate covering, say, the corporate headquarters' management system tells you almost nothing about the product you are actually buying. And SOC 2 and ISO are not the only artifacts you will be handed, a Payment Card Industry (PCI)

Attestation of Compliance speaks only to a cardholder data environment and may say nothing about the rest of the vendor, a penetration-test summary is worth little if it does not state scope, methodology, and whether findings were actually remediated, and an entry in the Cloud Security Alliance's STAR registry rewards checking its level.

Level 1 is a self-assessment and carries about as much independent weight as a whitepaper, while Level 2 is built on third-party certification or attestation and is a good deal stronger, and a vendor's own security whitepaper, being self-authored, is the weakest form of the set. The lesson across all of them is the same: these are real evidence, but evidence about a defined thing at a defined time, and they reward the person who reads the scope, the exceptions, and the fine print over the person who reads the cover page.

From Point-in-time to Continuous

Notice what every one of those reports has in common: it describes the past. Even a good Type II covering a full year is a rear-view mirror by the time it reaches you. And vendors are not static, between one annual report and the next, a vendor can add sub-processors, be acquired, lose the security leader who built their program, suffer a breach, or quietly let a control slip. If your entire assurance model is an annual report, you are flying on information that is stale the day it lands and staler every month after.

Assurance has a shelf life, which is why the evidence behind your critical vendors needs refreshing on a cadence, and that cadence is the reassessment discipline built into the lifecycle, triggered both by time and by change: a breach, an acquisition, a move to new hosting, a new sub-processor, a new AI feature, or the business quietly expanding what it runs through the tool. An old assurance file means old confidence.

Closing the gap between reports is what continuous monitoring is meant to do: the shift from assessing a vendor once to keeping half an eye on it over time. For a large enterprise that can mean a whole tooling category; for a small or mid-sized organization it needs to be more modest and honest. In practice it looks like a few proportionate habits. Security-ratings and external-scanning services can watch the outside of a vendor, exposed services, certificate hygiene, whether the vendor is turning up in breach data, and surface a signal when something changes.

A reassessment cadence tied to the vendor's tier keeps your critical vendors from going years between real looks. Watching for vendor incidents in the news and in breach notifications, and actually routing the contractual notices (the sub-processor changes, the material-change alerts) to a person who reads them rather than an unread mailbox, closes the loop between what the contract entitles you to and what you actually notice.

Two honesties keep this useful. First, external monitoring sees the outside, not the inside. A strong security rating is a reassuring signal, not proof of a healthy internal security culture, a ratings service cannot see a vendor's access discipline, their staff turnover, or how they would actually handle an incident; it can flag an exposed asset that turns out to be a forgotten marketing site while missing weak access governance on the service you actually use. Treat a rating as one input that tells you where to look harder, not a verdict that lets you stop looking.

Second, monitoring only earns its keep if something happens when it fires. A finding that lands in a dashboard nobody acts on is not a control, it is noise, so a signal about a critical vendor has to enter the same risk workflow as anything else: security explains the risk, the business owner who owns the dependency weighs in, and someone decides whether to press the vendor, add a compensating control, or accept it. Continuous monitoring done well does not give you certainty about your vendors. It gives you a better chance of noticing when something changed before it becomes your incident.

Sub-Processor Notice and Flow-Down: The Enforceable Engine

Fourth-party risk is managed indirectly, by making your third party accountable for the chain beneath them. The mechanics live almost entirely in the contract.

There are really three moving parts. The first is notice: a term requiring the vendor to tell you before, or at least promptly when, they add or materially change a significant sub-processor, ideally against a maintained sub-processor list you can actually see rather than a static appendix that was accurate on the day of signing and never again. The second is a right to object to a material change, limited, honestly, because your practical leverage to block a large vendor's choice of sub-processor is usually small, but it exists, and it at least forces the change into the open rather than letting it happen silently.

The third, and the one that actually does the work, is flow-down: a term requiring the vendor to impose security and privacy obligations on their sub-processors that are substantially equivalent to the ones they have committed to you. Flow-down is the mechanism by which your requirements travel down a chain you have no direct contract with, the vendor becomes contractually responsible for making the companies beneath them meet a comparable bar, and remains accountable to you for the whole chain rather than being able to shrug and point downstream when something breaks. One honest limit worth holding onto: flow-down does not hand you direct control over the sub-processor.

It gives you a contractual path that runs through your vendor, a real lever, but a mediated one, only ever as strong as your vendor's willingness and ability to enforce it downstream. The legal machinery underneath all of this, the data-processing agreements, the cross-border transfer mechanisms, the statutory definitions of processor and sub-processor, is Volume III, Part 2's to detail. What belongs here is the recognition that fourth-party accountability is not a technical control you deploy; it is a set of contract terms you insist on, and without them the whole "manage through your third party" posture has nothing holding it up.

The Reality of Leverage

There is an uncomfortable truth running under this entire chapter, and it is better to name it than to pretend otherwise: a small or mid-sized organization has limited leverage, and everything above assumes a negotiation you often will not actually get to have. You will not redline a major cloud platform's contract. You will not extract a custom breach-notification window from a dominant SaaS vendor. For the giants, the contract is take-it-or-leave-it, and your choice is to accept the standard terms or walk away from a tool the business wants.

So the practical question is not "how do I win every clause" — it is "where do I spend the leverage I actually have." And you have real leverage in specific places: with smaller vendors who want your business, with any vendor before signature rather than after, and with the critical relationships where you are prepared to make security terms a genuine condition of the deal. That is where the clauses in this chapter earn their keep. For the large vendors you cannot negotiate, the move is not negotiation at all.

It is informed acceptance: read their published terms and their assurance, understand precisely what you are signing up for, and where the terms fall short of what you would want, do something on your own side of the line about it, limit the data you put in, tokenize or encrypt what you can, tighten your own configuration, lean harder on monitoring, keep a manual workaround, and then decide, with open eyes, that the value is worth the residual risk. Write that decision down as a documented risk acceptance rather than a shrug.

There is no shame in accepting a large vendor's standard terms. The failure, the one that echoes the whole series' theme about honesty, is accepting them without knowing what they say, and telling the business "approved" because the deal matters while hoping the gap never surfaces. Hope is not a contract term. A contracts program that insists on winning everything from everyone grinds the business to a halt and loses the room; one that spends its leverage where it counts and accepts the rest knowingly is one the business will actually work with.

The Frameworks Underneath Contracts and Monitoring

The frameworks show up in this chapter less as things to implement and more as the currency the whole assurance economy is denominated in. Kept conceptual, as always:

The independent assurance report, the SOC 2 and the standards that govern how it is produced, is the industry's answer to "how do I get evidence about a vendor I can't audit myself," and understanding its structure, its scope, its exceptions, and its assumptions about your own controls is most of what makes it useful. The trust services criteria give the SOC 2 its vocabulary, security as the common baseline, with availability, confidentiality, processing integrity, and privacy as the categories a vendor may or may not have chosen to be measured against.

ISO 27001 certification plays a parallel role: an accredited certification body attests that a management system was audited and certified for a defined scope. The attestation carries more weight where that body is properly accredited, and the Statement of Applicability provides the detail behind the badge.

The major cybersecurity frameworks now treat supplier and supply-chain risk as a governed area in its own right, defining security expectations with suppliers, monitoring their services, and making a risk decision when third-party obligations sit outside your direct control. The higher-assurance control catalogs extend that to external service providers and acquisition. Operational-resilience regimes, particularly in financial services, push it furthest, naming critical third-party dependencies, outsourcing governance, audit and access rights, and exit planning as explicit obligations. And the privacy regimes carry the contractual requirements — processor terms, sub-processor controls, breach-notification support, and data return and deletion — that turn much of the discussion above from good practice into legal obligation.

The point is not to master every report format and clause library. It is that when a vendor hands you a certification, or a customer's contract demands specific security terms, or a regulator asks how you assure your third parties, you can read what you are being given, ask for what is missing, and know which clauses to hold out for. The frameworks supply the vocabulary; the contract supplies the leverage. Many frameworks, one set of obligations you can actually hold someone to.

Industry Pattern — The Report on the Shelf

> *Vendor assurance fails in a particular way, and it looks like this. An organization does the responsible-looking thing: it requires a SOC 2 report from its important vendors, collects them dutifully at onboarding, notes the clean opinions, and files them. On paper, the vendors are assured. The folder is full. Everyone feels covered.*
>
> *Then something goes wrong at one of those vendors (an outage, or an incident touching customer data) and the report comes off the shelf for the first time since it was filed. And it turns out to say less than everyone assumed. The scope covered a different product line than the one in use.*
>
> *Or the report's complementary user entity controls listed several things the customer was assumed to be doing, enforcing strong authentication, managing user access, reviewing configurations, that nobody on the customer side had ever read, let alone implemented. Or the report was simply old, covering a period that ended long before the current arrangement even began. The assurance everyone had been relying on had been sitting in a folder, unread, describing a narrower and older reality than anyone realized.*
>
> *The lesson is not that assurance reports are worthless. They are genuinely valuable, and requiring them was the right instinct. It is that a report is only assurance if someone reads it, checks that its scope matches what you actually use, notices what it assumes about your own controls, and confirms it still describes the present. Collected and filed, it is a document. Read and understood, it is evidence. The difference is entirely in whether anyone opened it past the cover page before the day they needed it.*

What Evidence Should You Expect

Evidence at this layer is about whether the contract turned promises into obligations, and whether the assurance you collect is actually read rather than merely held. At leadership altitude, a CISO should be able to point to security terms in the contracts for critical vendors, a defined security standard, a data-use limitation, a breach-notification clause with a real timeframe, data return and deletion on exit, and sub-processor notice and flow-down, rather than a set of relationships resting on vague "reasonable security" language.

Just as important is evidence that assurance reports are reviewed and not just filed: a record that someone read the report, confirmed its scope matched the service in use, checked the exceptions, and, the part that most often reveals a gap, mapped the complementary user entity controls against what the organization is actually doing. For the critical vendors, some form of ongoing signal rather than a single point-in-time check, a validated escalation contact so a notice reaches someone who acts on it, and a documented risk acceptance wherever standard terms were taken as-is because negotiation was not available. The tell of a mature program here is subtle: it is not the thickness of the vendor folder, it is whether anyone can show they understood what was in it.

For a small or mid-sized organization, the practical minimum keeps this achievable:

- For your critical vendors, make sure the contract carries a defined security standard, a data-use limitation, a breach-notification clause with an actual timeframe, and data-return-and-deletion-on-exit terms, and involve legal in the wording rather than drafting it yourself.
- When you receive a SOC 2 or equivalent, actually read it: confirm the scope covers the service you use, glance at the exceptions, and check the date so you are not relying on something stale, and note when the next report is due, so a critical vendor's assurance does not quietly lapse.

- Read the complementary user entity controls in every critical vendor's report and check whether you are doing your half, that section is where the shared-responsibility gaps hide.
- Put sub-processor notice and flow-down terms in your critical vendor contracts, route the resulting notices to a person who reads them, and confirm your incident-notification contact for each critical vendor is real and current.
- Where you had to accept a big vendor's standard terms, write down that you accepted them knowingly, with whatever you did on your own side to reduce the exposure, so it is a documented decision rather than an unexamined default.

That is not an enterprise contracts-and-monitoring function. It is enough to make sure the promises you are relying on are ones you could actually enforce, and the assurance you are holding is assurance you have actually read.

Reality Check

Two quick tests that reveal whether this layer is real in your program or just paperwork.

First, pull the last assurance report you accepted from an important vendor, the most recent SOC 2 or ISO certificate that came in, and ask whether anyone actually read past the opinion letter. Did someone confirm the scope covered the service you are using, look at the exceptions, and check the complementary user entity controls against what you are doing on your side? Or did it get filed the day it arrived, assurance assumed? If it is the latter, you do not yet know what that report says. You only know it exists, which is a different and much weaker thing.

Second, take your single most critical vendor and find the breach-notification clause in the contract. Does it commit them to a real timeframe, a number of hours or days, and does it cover suspected incidents, not just fully confirmed breaches? Or does it hide behind "without undue delay" or something equally soft? And if that notice went out tonight, do you know who on your side would receive it, and whether they would recognize it for what it was? If the clause is vague and the recipient is a mystery, then the one tripwire your entire incident response depends on may not actually be wired to anything.

What This Means for You as a Security Leader

The contract is the security leader's quietest and most underused tool. You do not draft it, you are not the lawyer, and you should not try to be, but you are the only person in the process who knows which clauses carry security weight, and if you stay out of it entirely, those clauses simply will not be there when you need them.

The whole of this chapter is really one move made in three places: turn the vendor's promises into obligations you could enforce (the contract), turn the assurance you are handed into something you have actually read and understood (the reports), and turn a one-time check into an ongoing awareness (continuous monitoring). None of it requires deep legal or audit expertise. It requires you to know enough to ask for the right terms, read the reports past the cover page, and keep half an eye open after the deal is done.

Practically, that means picking your battles honestly. Insist on the clauses that matter, a real security standard, a data-use limitation, a breach-notification window with a number in it, data return and deletion, sub-processor notice and flow-down, and insist on them proportionately, hardest for the vendors whose failure would hurt most.

Learn to read an assurance report properly, because that single skill quietly upgrades your entire program from collecting paper to understanding risk, and the complementary user entity controls section in particular will tell you where your own homework is hiding. Accept that your leverage is finite, spend it where you have it, and where you do not, accept standard terms with your eyes open, a compensating move on your own side where you can make one, and a note in the file rather than a shrug.

And hold the honesty this chapter runs on, because it is the same honesty the last few chapters have asked for. A contract does not make a vendor secure; it makes some of their obligations enforceable, which is a smaller and more useful thing to be clear-eyed about. An assurance report does not prove a vendor is safe; it is evidence about a defined scope at a defined time, and it is only worth anything if you read what it actually says.

Continuous monitoring does not give you certainty; it gives you a better chance of noticing a change before it becomes a problem. The credible posture here is not "our vendors are locked down by ironclad contracts and clean audit reports." It is "we've made the obligations that matter enforceable where we could, we read the assurance we rely on, we watch the relationships that matter, and where we had to accept terms as-is, we did it knowingly." That is not a weaker position than false confidence. It is the only honest version of a strong one.

Bridge to Chapter 15

The desk has another side; the next chapter walks around to it — customer due diligence and the questionnaires that land in your inbox.

CHAPTER 15

The Other Side of the Desk — Customer Due Diligence & Security Questionnaires

For four chapters, you asked the questions. Now someone is asking them of you — and your answer can win or lose the deal.

Everything in this part so far has put you in the same chair: the buyer, the assessor, the one sending the questionnaire and reading the SOC 2 and deciding whether a vendor was good enough. This chapter walks around to the other side of that desk, because your organization is not only a consumer of other people's services. To someone out there, you are the third party. You are the vendor sitting in another company's risk register, on another security leader's tier list, being run through the exact process the last four chapters described. Their questionnaire is in your inbox. Their contract wants your security addendum signed. Their team wants to see your assurance report. The desk has two sides, and you sit on both.

That turns out to be a genuinely useful place to stand, because the four chapters you just spent learning to assess vendors are the same four chapters that teach you how to be assessed well. You know what the person on the other side is really trying to learn, because you have been that person.

But it is also a place a lot of small and mid-sized organizations handle badly, treating each incoming questionnaire as a surprise, a scramble, a fire drill owned by whoever happens to be free that week, and handling it badly has a cost that shows up not in a breach report but in a sales pipeline. This chapter is about handling it well: answering honestly, answering efficiently, and understanding that being on the answering side is not a chore bolted onto the security role but a real and increasingly strategic part of it.

Security Has Quietly Become a Condition of Doing Business

Start with the shift that makes this chapter matter, because it has changed faster than a lot of security thinking has caught up with. Not long ago, a customer's security due diligence was often a formality, a questionnaire someone filled in near the end of a deal, filed, and forgot. That is over.

For anyone selling business-to-business, running a SaaS product, handling another company's data, or sitting anywhere in a customer's critical path, security posture has become a gate the deal has to pass through. A prospect's security team can now stop a purchase their own business badly wants, and increasingly they do. The questionnaire is not a formality at the end of the sale. It is a checkpoint in the middle of it, and sometimes it is the checkpoint the whole thing hinges on.

That reframes what security is to the business, and it is worth saying plainly to yourself and to your leadership: on the answering side, security is not only a cost center. It is also a revenue enabler. A security program that can pass due diligence quickly and credibly accelerates deals; one that cannot becomes the reason a deal stalls for six weeks or dies in procurement.

That is a very different story to tell the board than "security is overhead we tolerate," and it is true, the same controls you justify as risk reduction are the controls that unlock the enterprise customer who will not sign until you can prove them. For a small or mid-sized organization trying to win larger customers, this is often the moment security stops being a cost the CEO grudgingly funds and starts being a capability the sales team actively needs. Use that. It is one of the few places where doing the security work and growing the business point in exactly the same direction.

There is a cross-border dimension here too, and it sharpens as you sell into more markets. A customer in one country will ask about the data-protection regime that binds them, and expect you to speak it, a European customer will want to understand your posture under their privacy law, a customer in a regulated sector will push their sector's rules onto you, a customer in another region will care about where their data physically lives.

You do not need jurisdiction-by-jurisdiction legal expertise, but you do have to recognize that the questionnaire landing from a new market is partly a test of whether you understand the compliance world your customer lives in. Volume III, Parts 2 and 3 are what let you answer those without flinching; here the point is just that "customer due diligence" increasingly means "customer's-country due diligence," and the organizations that sell across borders feel it first.

What Actually Lands in Your Inbox

The requests come in a few recognizable shapes, and knowing the shapes helps you stop treating each one as unprecedented. Some are standardized industry questionnaires. Long, structured spreadsheets built by shared-assessment bodies and cloud-security groups, designed so that one well-maintained set of answers can serve many customers. Some are the customer's own custom questionnaire, which might be twenty sensible questions or three hundred exhausting ones, often clearly assembled by copying an older one nobody has pruned. Some arrive as a portal you are asked to log into and complete. And the largest customers may send their own security addendum, their own audit request, and an expectation that you will bend your program to their template rather than the other way around.

Underneath the different formats, though, the content converges hard. Strip away the branding and the row counts, and most questionnaires are asking the same few dozen things in different clothes: do you encrypt data in transit and at rest, do you enforce multi-factor authentication, how do you manage access and offboard people, do you patch and scan, do you log and monitor, do you have an incident response plan and will you tell us if you are breached, who are your sub-processors, where does our data live, can we get it back, do you have a recognized certification.

More and more, there is a newer cluster too, do you use AI in the service, do you train models on our data, which model providers sit behind it, can we opt out, the customer-facing edge of AI governance, and one you will increasingly be expected to answer plainly. But if the core list feels familiar, it should: it is the mirror image of what you were asking your own vendors. Once you see that the hundredth question is usually the tenth question rephrased, the volume stops looking like a thousand unique problems and starts looking like one answerable set of facts about your organization, asked over and over in slightly different words. That realization is the difference between drowning and building a machine, which is most of what the rest of this chapter is about.

Answer Honestly — Because Your Answers Are Representations, Not Marketing

Before any efficiency, the hardest and most important discipline: tell the truth. And the reason is not only that honesty is right. It is that a security questionnaire is not a marketing document, however much it feels like one when a deal is on the line. Your answers are representations. They frequently get referenced in the contract, sometimes formally incorporated into it, and they become part of the permanent, evidentiary record of what you told a customer was true.

Which means the questionnaire you fill in optimistically today is the document that gets pulled off the shelf and read line by line on the worst day you will ever have, the day something goes wrong and a customer, or their lawyer, or a regulator, wants to know whether what happened contradicts what you claimed.

The temptation runs exactly the wrong way. A deal is close, the questionnaire asks whether you encrypt everything, do full background checks, run annual penetration tests, notify within a fixed window, never train AI on customer data, and the honest answer to some of those is "not quite" or "partly," and saying so feels like handing the prospect a reason to walk. So the optimistic "yes" creeps in. Do not let it.

An overstated "yes" does not disappear when the deal closes; it sits in the file as a promise you have now made and may not be keeping, and if an incident ever exposes the gap between what you claimed and what you did, that gap is no longer just a maturity shortfall. It can harden into a misrepresentation, and that is worse than the shortfall would ever have been on its own. The classic version is the blanket "yes, all customer data is encrypted at rest" when the production database and file stores are covered but some quiet legacy export is not, technically almost true, materially a landmine, and the difference only surfaces on the day it hurts most.

The good news is that honest answers are far more survivable than people fear, because sophisticated customers are not expecting perfection. They are expecting truth and self-awareness. There is a clean way to answer that is not a naked "no." You can answer yes where it is genuinely true; answer no plainly where it is not; and for the large middle, answer with precision and a boundary, the specific scope it is true within ("yes, for the production platform"), the compensating control ("we don't do X, but we address that risk through Y"), or the roadmap ("that's planned for this quarter, here's where it stands").

A confident, specific "no, and here's what we do instead, and here's what we're building" reads as a mature program that knows itself. A wall of unqualified "yes" answers, ironically, reads as the opposite to anyone experienced because nobody's program is perfect, and a questionnaire with no "no" in it anywhere is either untruthful or unexamined. Honesty is not just the ethical answer here. It is the one that ages well, survives the incident, and tends to earn more trust than the polished lie would have won.

Build the Machine, Not a Fire Drill

Once you accept that the questions repeat, the operational answer is obvious: stop answering from scratch. The organizations that handle this well have quietly built a small machine; the ones that suffer answer every questionnaire as if it were the first they had ever seen, pulling a different person off their real job each time, reconstructing the same answers from memory, and (the part that quietly damages trust) giving subtly different answers to different customers because there is no single source of truth. Inconsistent answers across customers are their own red flag; a customer who compares notes, or who assesses you twice a year and gets two different stories, learns something about you that you did not mean to tell them.

The machine has a few parts, and none of them are exotic. The core is a maintained answer library, a single, owned, current set of the organization's standard answers to the questions that keep recurring, written once, reviewed periodically, and reused so every questionnaire starts eighty percent complete and consistent rather than at zero. To be worth anything, each entry needs three things attached to it: the scope it is actually true for (which product, which environment), a named owner who keeps it honest, and a link to the piece of evidence that backs it, so an answer is never just a claim floating free of the thing that proves it.

And it has to be maintained like controlled content, not tribal knowledge in an inbox: when a policy changes, an architecture shifts, the assurance report's period rolls over, or an AI feature launches, the answers change with them, because an out-of-date answer library is not efficiency. It is a way to answer incorrectly at scale. Around it sits an evidence pack: the documents you can hand over instead of re-explaining, your assurance report, your certification, a penetration-test summary you are comfortable sharing, the policies you are willing to show.

Evidence is where a second discipline comes in, because not everything should be shared freely. Some security evidence is itself a risk in the wrong hands. A raw penetration-test report with exploitable detail, a full vulnerability list, an internal network diagram, an internal incident report, another customer's data: handing these out to prove your security can quietly undermine it.

The mature move is not to refuse everything or share everything, but to decide in advance what sits at each tier, what is public, what goes out only under a non-disclosure agreement, or NDA (the assurance report, the certification, summaries), and what you do not share at all, and to have graceful language ready for the "not shared" tier: "we don't release raw penetration-test reports, but we can provide an executive summary, a remediation attestation, and walk through scope under NDA." It is worth keeping a simple record of what you released to whom and when, too, so that if a report is later superseded or an access needs pulling, you know where it went. That is not evasive. It is controlled transparency, and an experienced customer reads it as a sign you know what you are doing.

Many organizations put a public face on the whole thing in the form of a trust page or trust center, a single place where a prospect can self-serve your certifications, your posture, and your basic security facts, which deflects a real fraction of questionnaires before they are ever sent and signals maturity to the ones that still come.

And the whole machine needs an owner and a light process: someone who receives incoming requests, knows where the answers and evidence live, and routes the genuinely new or risky questions to the right person, legal for a contractual term, privacy for a data-processing question, product for a roadmap or AI claim, so that responding is a defined workflow rather than a recurring emergency in which sales, legal, privacy, and security each answer separately and the customer receives fragments that do not line up.

The single highest-leverage move in the whole machine, though, is getting your own independent assurance, a SOC 2, an ISO 27001 certification, whatever fits your market, proactively, before customers force it. This is the exact mirror of vendor assurance, where a vendor handed you their SOC 2 instead of submitting to your audit and answered most of your questions in one document. Now you are the vendor doing precisely that: a current, well-scoped assurance report answers a large share of any questionnaire at a stroke, replaces dozens of individual "do you…" questions with "yes, and here's the independent evidence," and turns the exhausting many-questions problem into a point-at-the-report problem.

It costs real money and effort, and it is not something every small company needs on day one, let the market you sell into tell you when it is time, but for an organization selling to security-conscious customers it is almost always worth it, because it does not just reduce questionnaire pain; it is frequently the thing that makes you eligible for the deal at all. Scope it to cover the service customers actually buy (the scope lesson cuts both ways), keep it current, and it becomes the most valuable single artifact in your evidence pack.

Knowing What They're Really Asking

Here is where having sat on the other side of the desk pays off directly. Because you spent four chapters learning to assess vendors, you can read an incoming questionnaire the way its author intended rather than answering it literally and mechanically. When a customer asks who your sub-processors are, you know they are not collecting trivia. They are trying to see the chain beneath you, and a helpful, transparent answer builds more trust than a grudging minimal one.

When they ask about breach notification, you know they are wiring a tripwire into their own incident response, and that a clear commitment to a real timeframe is worth more to them than vague reassurance. When they ask about data return and deletion, you know they are thinking about their own exit and their own regulators. Understanding the intent behind a question lets you answer the concern rather than just the words, which is both more useful to the customer and more persuasive on your behalf.

It also lets you read the customer. Some questionnaires are thoughtful, risk-based, and clearly written by someone who knows what matters; others are a bloated, un-pruned checklist where a third of the questions were copied from another industry entirely and do not apply to what you do. You can tell the difference now, and it tells you something about the relationship you are entering. With the good ones, engage seriously, a sharp customer security team is worth impressing, and often becomes an ally inside their organization for the deal.

With the checkbox ones, answer accurately and efficiently without contorting your program to fit questions that were never meant for a company like yours, and do not mistake a long questionnaire for a rigorous one. Reading the asker is a skill you earned by being the asker, and it turns questionnaire response from rote form-filling into something closer to a conversation you already understand.

When the Customer Wants More Than Answers

Sometimes a customer, usually a large or heavily regulated one, wants more than a completed questionnaire and a report. They want their own right to audit you, their own security terms flowed onto you, their own addendum layered over your standard contract, the demanding end of vendor assurance, now pointed in your direction. The leverage is reversed, and it deserves clear eyes.

The first trap is quiet: a questionnaire answer and a contract term are not the same object, and the gap between them can bite. You may have answered, truthfully, “we notify customers promptly after confirming an incident affecting their data” — and then the customer’s security addendum arrives demanding “notification within twenty-four hours of any suspected incident.” Those are very different obligations, and the second one may be one your incident process genuinely cannot meet.

The questionnaire was a description; the addendum is a commitment, and every clause you accept becomes a future test. When something goes wrong, the customer will not ask what you intended. They will ask what you agreed. So the security addenda, the audit clauses, the residency and deletion and penetration-testing terms all have to be read against what you actually do, and the ones that do not fit have to be negotiated rather than signed under deal pressure.

There is a second, slower trap. A big customer’s security demands can be entirely reasonable, and meeting them can be exactly the right call when the deal is worth it, sometimes their requirements even push your program somewhere it should have gone anyway. But say yes to enough of them, one deal at a time, and you accumulate a hidden library of customer-specific commitments: this customer gets twenty-four-hour notification, that one gets data in a particular country, another has approval rights over your sub-processors, a fourth gets a custom recovery objective. Individually each is manageable.

Collectively, if nobody tracks them, they become obligations you can breach without even knowing they exist because the promise is buried in a contract nobody reads after signature, while the team that would have to honor it never heard about it. And these are not just contract trivia: each one is an obligation that has to map to a control that delivers it, an owner who runs it, and evidence that it is actually happening, the same discipline every other requirement in your program demands, which is exactly the tangle a unified operating model exists to untangle.

The move is to negotiate here the way you would want a vendor to negotiate with you, meet what is reasonable and strengthens you generally, push back honestly on what does not fit, and be willing to say "we can't truthfully commit to that, but here's what we can do" — and then to record every non-standard commitment you do make, note who approved it, and route it to the function that has to operate it. Saying no honestly is the same posture as the questionnaire itself, and it is far better than agreeing to a term you will quietly breach.

The Mirror Makes You Better on Both Sides

There is a deeper payoff to sitting on both sides of this desk, and it is the quiet thesis of the whole part. Answering questionnaires honestly forces you to actually have the things you claim. A question you cannot answer "yes" to without lying is, right there in the row of a spreadsheet, a gap in your own program made visible, the customer's questionnaire has just done a piece of your gap analysis for you, for free. Organizations that take the answering side seriously often find their own security maturing faster than they expected, because nothing motivates finally turning on a control quite like needing to answer for its absence in front of a customer who might walk.

And it runs the other way too. Having been assessed makes you a fairer and sharper assessor of your own vendors, because you know from the inside what a good answer looks like, what a reasonable "no" sounds like, which questions genuinely matter and which are checklist filler, and how it feels to be on the receiving end of a bloated, thoughtless questionnaire.

The best third-party programs are run by people who have been the third party, who ask what they would be willing to answer, demand what they could themselves prove, and extend the professionalism they would want extended to them. What you require of your vendors and what you can credibly answer for yourself should be the same standard, held from both directions. When they are, the whole thing stops being adversarial paperwork and becomes what it always should have been: two organizations doing honest diligence on each other, each better at it for having sat where the other one sits.

From the Real World

> *At one organization I worked with, the third-party onboarding program did not exist, and management had not been persuaded that a formal security program and certification were worth paying for. The cost showed up somewhere management was not looking: new customer onboarding. Every prospect's risk team sent its own questionnaire, sales expected a response in a day or two, and the answers had to be assembled from scratch each time. For one healthcare customer it took almost five months. Their risk analyst kept coming back with follow-up questions, and although we neither held nor processed their data, our users had access to the records and the customer was regulated under HIPAA, so the scrutiny was legitimate and it was not going to stop. What changed management's mind was not another argument about security maturity. It was a presentation that put a number on the delay: the revenue sitting in deals that could not close because we could not answer questions about ourselves. Once the organization had a real security program and a certification from a recognized audit firm, assessment time fell sharply and the deals moved. That is what it looks like when a security program is aligned with the business rather than argued for beside it.*

The Frameworks Underneath Customer Due Diligence

On the answering side, the frameworks show up as the shared language that lets one organization's diligence talk to another's, and as the artifacts you produce rather than consume. Kept conceptual, as always:

The standardized questionnaires themselves are the most visible frameworks here: Shared Assessments' Standardized Information Gathering (SIG) questionnaire and the Cloud Security Alliance's Consensus Assessments Initiative Questionnaire (CAIQ) v4.1 exist precisely so that a common set of questions and a common set of maintained answers can serve many relationships at once, which is why building your library against them pays off across every customer.

An independent assurance report such as SOC 2, written in the Trust Services Criteria vocabulary, is an artifact you commission and hand over — the same instrument you learned to read, now produced from the other side. An ISO/IEC 27001 certification plays a similar role as a portable management-system credential, with stronger assurance when the certification body is properly accredited. Depending on what you sell and to whom, a payment-card attestation, a health-sector assurance, or a cloud-assurance registry entry may be the artifact a given customer expects.

And running under all of it, the privacy and regional regimes that a customer's own obligations force onto you, their data-protection law, their sector rules, their residency expectations, are the frameworks you have to be conversant in to answer a cross-border customer credibly. The point is not to implement a new framework for the answering side. It is that the same frameworks you have met throughout the series now face you from the customer's direction, and fluency in them is what lets you turn due diligence from an ordeal into a demonstration. Many frameworks, one set of answers you can stand behind.

Industry Pattern — The Yes That Came Back Around

A growing company is chasing a large, important customer, the kind of deal that changes the year. Late in the process the customer's security questionnaire arrives, long and detailed, and the sales deadline is tight. Security is busy. Someone pulls the answers from a prior questionnaire, adjusts a few words, and sends it back. One of the answers reads, cleanly and confidently, "yes, all customer data is encrypted at rest." The main production database is encrypted, and so are the file stores, so it feels true. But a legacy reporting export is not, and it holds a limited slice of customer data. The person answering did not know it existed. The customer is satisfied, the deal closes, everyone moves on.

Then, some time later, there is an incident, not a catastrophic one, but enough to trigger notifications and questions, and in the course of it that legacy export comes to light. Now the problem is not only the unencrypted export. It is the statement. The customer pulls the original questionnaire and asks: you told us all customer data was encrypted at rest, so why was this one not encrypted? The answer had never been malicious. It was rushed, copied, and broader than the evidence supported. And that is exactly the point: a manageable security event handled between partners has become a trust problem and a contractual one, because the record shows the company claimed something that was not true.

The lesson is not that the company should have had every control in place before chasing the deal, maturity takes time, and no growing organization has everything. It is that an honest, scoped answer: "customer data in the production platform is encrypted at rest; a legacy export is being remediated under restricted access and compensating controls" — would have cost, at most, a slightly harder conversation during the sale, and would have left nothing on the shelf to contradict later. The optimistic "yes" felt like it saved the deal. What it actually did was convert a temporary gap into a permanent liability. On the answering side of the desk, the truth is not only the right answer. It is the cheaper one.

What Evidence Should You Expect

Evidence on the answering side is about whether the organization can respond to customer due diligence credibly, consistently, and honestly, and whether the answers it gives are backed by controls that actually exist. At leadership altitude, a CISO should be able to point to a maintained, owned answer library (each answer scoped, owned, and linked to its evidence) rather than a history of ad-hoc responses reconstructed from memory; current independent assurance scoped to what customers actually buy, offered proactively rather than extracted under pressure; an evidence pack with defined sharing tiers and, increasingly, a trust page that lets a prospect self-serve the basics; and a defined owner and intake process for incoming questionnaires so that responding is a workflow, not a recurring emergency.

Just as important, and harder, is evidence of integrity in the answers: consistency across customers, alignment between what the questionnaires claim and what the controls actually do, a register of the non-standard commitments made to individual customers, with who approved each one, so none of them quietly go un-honored, and some mechanism for tracking the forward-looking "planned for this quarter" answers so they are actually delivered rather than forgotten until a customer asks again. The tell of a mature program here is not a fast turnaround time. It is that a customer's auditor, arriving unannounced, would find the reality matching the answers.

For a small or mid-sized organization, the practical minimum keeps this achievable:

- Build and maintain a single answer library for the questions that keep recurring, owned by one person and scoped and dated, with each answer linked to the evidence that backs it, so every questionnaire starts from a consistent, current base rather than from scratch.
- Get independent assurance appropriate to your market (SOC 2, ISO 27001, or equivalent) when the market you sell into calls for it, scope it to the service customers actually buy, keep

it current, and lead with it. It answers most of any questionnaire at once.

- Answer honestly: yes where it is true, a plain no with a compensating control or roadmap where it is not, scoped where it is only partly true, and never an optimistic "yes" you could not prove to an auditor tomorrow.
- Keep an evidence pack ready to hand over, assurance report, certification, shareable pen-test summary, key policies, with clear rules for what is public, what is NDA-only, and what you do not share; and consider a simple trust page so prospects can self-serve the basics.
- Track the non-standard commitments you make to individual customers, recording who approved each one, and the forward-looking promises in your questionnaires, so a tight notification window is not something sales agreed to alone under deal pressure, and a "planned for next quarter" answer becomes something you actually deliver rather than a promise that ages into a misrepresentation.

That is not an enterprise trust-and-assurance function. It is enough to turn customer due diligence from a repeated fire drill into a credible, honest demonstration that helps win business instead of stalling it.

Reality Check

> *Two quick tests for whether your answering side is real or improvised.*
>
> *First, pull the last security questionnaire your organization returned to a customer and read your own "yes" answers as if you were their auditor arriving tomorrow to verify them. Could you prove each one, with a control, a log, a document, a report? If there is a "yes" in there you would struggle to stand behind, you do not have a completed questionnaire, you have a liability with a due date you do not control, sitting in a customer's file waiting for the day someone checks.*
>
> *Second, ask how the last three questionnaires actually got answered. Was it the same owned library and evidence pack each time, producing consistent answers, or was it three different people, three separate scrambles, and quite possibly three subtly different versions of the truth sent to three different customers? And of the commitments those three responses made, a tighter notification window here, a data-residency promise there, does anyone actually know they were made, and is anyone tracking them? If it was the scramble, the cost is not only the wasted hours. It is that somewhere out there, two of your customers may be holding answers that do not quite match, and a third may be holding a promise nobody inside your walls remembers making.*

What This Means for You as a Security Leader

The answering side of the desk asks you to hold two things at once that a lot of security leaders never quite reconcile: that security is now part of how the business wins, and that the way it wins is by being honest rather than impressive. Both matter, and they pull in the same direction more often than you would expect.

The instinct to treat customer questionnaires as a nuisance to be dispatched by whoever's free misses that this is one of the few moments where your program is visible to people who can hand you revenue, and the instinct to make your program look as good as possible in that moment is precisely the instinct that plants a liability in a customer's file. The leaders who do this well treat the answering side as a genuine capability: they build the machine so it is efficient, they get the assurance so it is credible, and they answer honestly so it is durable.

Practically, that means a few things you can start on regardless of your size. Build the answer library and get the independent assurance when your market calls for it, because those two moves together convert the recurring pain into a repeatable strength and make you eligible for customers you cannot win otherwise. Decide your evidence-sharing tiers before you are under pressure, so "prove it" has a controlled answer rather than an improvised one.

Tell your leadership the true story, that security is now a revenue enabler, that a credible posture accelerates deals and a weak one stalls them because it reframes the whole function in terms the business actually values, and it happens to be accurate. And hold the honesty line under deal pressure, every time, because that is where it is hardest and where it matters most; the overstated "yes" that saves a deal today is the misrepresentation that costs you far more the day an incident reads it back to you.

And keep sight of the mirror, because it is the quiet gift of this whole part. What you demand of your vendors and what you can honestly answer for yourself should be one standard, held from both sides. Being assessed makes you a fairer assessor; assessing makes you a sharper respondent. The credible posture on the answering side is not "we can pass any questionnaire" — it is "we answer honestly, we back every answer with something real, and we'd be comfortable if any customer checked." That is not a weaker position than a polished one. Held consistently, it is the strongest position there is, because it is the only one that is still standing on the day someone reads it back to you.

Part 3 Closing Note: You Can Outsource the Work. You Cannot Outsource the Risk.

Part 3 began by retiring the picture the rest of the series quietly leaned on — the organization defending things it owns — and replaced it with the real one: a business that runs on other people's companies. When the risk lived inside your walls, security was controls you could implement. When it lives in vendors, platforms, and chains of sub-processors, security becomes assurance: earning justified confidence about controls you will never touch.

The unit that matters is not the supplier's name. It is the relationship — the service delivered, the data and access involved, the dependency created, the countries and fourth parties underneath it, the consequence of failure, and the organization's ability to exit. One supplier can create several very different risks; several apparently different suppliers can depend on the same hidden provider and create one concentration risk. So the Part followed the problem outward, ring by ring. First the discipline itself, made manageable by the only two levers that scale: visibility of the population, and tiering that concentrates real attention where consequence lives.

Then the lifecycle, because a vendor is not a decision made at signing but a relationship that drifts — the photograph taken at onboarding versus the moving object the vendor actually is, all the way to the offboarding everyone forgets. And offboarding is itself a security control: access removed, keys rotated, integrations disconnected, data returned or disposed of, continuity held — a relationship that cannot be exited safely is more concentrated than its risk rating suggests.

Then the layer you cannot see: SaaS concentration, outsourced functions, fourth parties you never signed, the software supply chain shipping risk inside the product — and the honesty this layer demands, because a program that pretends to control the invisible is more dangerous than one that names its limits. Then the contract, where a vendor's promises become obligations — with the discipline that a notification clause nobody can route, an audit right nobody intends to use, or an exit obligation unsupported by architecture is not a control. It is reassurance in legal language.

And finally the other side of the desk, where you are the vendor — answering the questionnaires you spent four chapters learning to send, with answers that are representations, not marketing. That mirror is the Part's real teaching. What you demand of your vendors and what you can honestly answer for yourself are one standard held from both sides. Being assessed makes you a fairer assessor; assessing makes you a sharper respondent. Honest assurance is not weaker assurance. It is the only kind that survives verification.

By now a repetition has become impossible to ignore. The same few ideas — scope, ownership, evidence, honest limits — have surfaced in every Part from every angle, described in every framework's dialect. That repetition is not redundancy. It is convergence, and the next Part finally gives it a home: one control universe, every applicable framework mapped onto it, the common control core built once, and scope-specific proof preserved where it genuinely differs.

Bridge to Part 4: The Unified Framework

Controls and obligations now have to resolve into one operating model, mapped honestly by intent, scope, ownership, and evidence.

VOLUME IV

PART 4

Unified Cybersecurity Framework

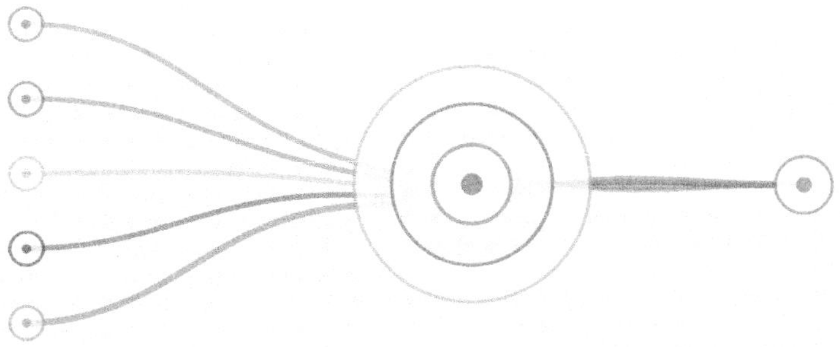

CHAPTER 16

The Case for One Control Universe

Nobody sells you one framework. They arrive in a crowd, and separate programs make you spend more time proving security than doing it.

Here is the situation almost every security leader walks into, usually without anyone warning them it is coming. You do not get to pick a framework, implement it cleanly, and be done. Instead they show up one at a time, from different directions, each with its own vocabulary and its own demands. A big customer wants to see a SOC 2. A regulator points you at a national standard.

Your industry expects you to speak a particular framework's language. Your cyber-insurer hands you a questionnaire built around yet another one. Someone on the board read about a well-known framework and wants to know if you "have it." Take a payment and PCI is suddenly in the room. Expand into a new country and its regime joins the pile. None of them asked whether you had room for one more.

Faced with that, the natural instinct, and the one that quietly wrecks small and mid-sized security teams, is to treat each framework as its own project. A program for this one, a separate program for that one, a third effort for the customer's requirements, each with its own policies, its own control list, its own evidence folder, its own audit, its own spreadsheet. It feels responsible. It looks thorough.

And it is a trap, because it multiplies your work by the number of frameworks you are subject to while barely improving your actual security, and it scales in exactly the wrong direction: every new framework, every new market, every new customer demand adds another parallel program to run, until the team spends more of its week reconciling frameworks than defending the organization.

This part of the book is about the way out, and this chapter makes the case for it before the rest of it shows you how. The way out rests on a single observation that, once you see it, you cannot unsee: the frameworks are mostly asking for the same things. Not identically, not with the same words, not in the same order, but underneath the vocabulary, they converge on a shared core.

And if that is true, then you do not need a dozen programs. You need one. One coherent set of controls, built as your own operating model, that each framework then maps onto. That is the control universe, and it is the difference between a program that buckles under every new requirement and one that absorbs them.

One thing to be clear about from the outset, because it is the most common misunderstanding: the answer is not another framework. The industry has no shortage of those. Some weeks it can feel like every standards body, regulator, cloud provider, and consultancy woke up convinced the world needed one more control taxonomy. It does not, and the control universe is not one. It is not a new standard to adopt on top of the others; it is your own organized picture of what you actually do, that the existing frameworks map into. You are not adding a voice to the crowd. You are building the one place all the other voices can point.

The Framework Sprawl Problem

Start by naming the pain honestly, because if you have lived it you will recognize every part of it, and if you have not yet, you will. The root of it is that frameworks tend to get handled as separate projects rather than as different views of one program. A SOC 2 effort spins up because a customer asked. A certification effort starts because leadership wants the badge. A payment-standard effort begins because payments came into scope. A privacy effort starts because legal needs it. Each arrives with its own consultant, its own spreadsheet, its own control language, its own evidence requests, and its own deadline, and the same underlying reality ends up described, documented, and proven over and over in slightly different clothes.

You write an access-control policy for one framework, then a subtly different one for the next, and now you have two policies that say almost the same thing and will slowly drift apart until they contradict each other. You enforce multi-factor authentication once, in reality, on your actual systems, but you get asked to prove it four separate times, in four formats, for four audits, and each one wants the screenshot arranged its own way. An auditor for one framework asks for your access reviews; six weeks later an assessor for another asks for the same reviews, and nobody connects the two, so your team pulls the same evidence twice.

Your policies use one term, your risk register uses another, your customer answers use a third, and a careful reader notices they do not quite line up. And the quiet tragedy underneath all of it: your best security people, the ones who should be hardening systems and hunting for weaknesses, are instead spending their days as translators, mapping this framework's requirement to that framework's control to the other framework's evidence, in a full-time job of reconciliation that produces almost no additional safety.

That is framework sprawl, and its cost is not just wasted hours. It is audit fatigue that burns out the team. It is inconsistency that makes you look less mature than you are, because the same fact told four slightly different ways reads as four uncertain answers rather than one confident one. It is fragility, because a program held together by parallel spreadsheets breaks the moment the person who understood the mapping leaves.

And it is a ceiling on growth, because if adding your fifth framework means standing up a fifth program, at some point the business's ambition outruns your capacity to keep up. For a small or mid-sized organization with a lean team, sprawl is not an inconvenience. It is the thing that stops the security function from scaling with the company, and the real problem was never the frameworks themselves, but that each one was being run as its own operating model.

The Insight: They're Mostly Asking for the Same Things

Now the observation that changes everything. Line the major frameworks up next to each other and read them not for their differences but for their common ground, and a striking amount of overlap comes into view. They are, to a real degree, dialects of the same language.

Take one concrete control to see it. Access review, the discipline of periodically checking who has access to what and removing what is no longer warranted, shows up in essentially every framework you will meet, wearing a different name each time. The broad information-security standard expects user access to be governed and reviewed. The service-provider assurance criteria expect logical access to be controlled in support of the commitments in scope. The payment-card standard expects access to the cardholder environment to be limited and reviewed. The prioritized-controls list expects disciplined account and access management.

A privacy regime expects access to personal data to be restricted to those who need it. A customer questionnaire simply asks, "do you review user permissions periodically?" These are not six different controls to build. They are one control. Access is authorized, appropriate, reviewed, and removed when no longer needed, seen through six lenses. You perform the review once, as a real operating discipline; the frameworks become six different questions the single control already answers. (Doing that lens-by-lens mapping systematically, across the major frameworks at once, is the work of Chapter 18; here it is just the clearest possible illustration of the point.)

Widen the aperture and the same thing holds across the board. Nearly every serious framework wants you to know what you have and who can touch it, to authenticate strongly and grant least privilege, to encrypt sensitive data, to patch and manage vulnerabilities, to log and monitor, to have an incident response capability, to manage your vendors, to train your people, and to govern the whole thing with policies and clear accountability.

One framework calls a requirement by a control number, another by a category name, a third by a trust criterion, a fourth by a regulatory article, but the underlying thing being asked for is, again and again, the same underlying thing. This is not coincidence or sloppiness. It is because they are all describing good security, and good security has a real shape that does not change just because the document describing it does.

A fair caution before we go further, because I do not want to oversell it: the overlap is large but it is not total. Frameworks genuinely differ in places, and some of those differences matter, a payment standard carries specific requirements a general framework does not, a national regime may demand something no international standard mentions, a sector rule may impose a hard timeline that a voluntary framework leaves open. The unified approach does not pretend those differences away. It handles the large common core efficiently so you have the time and clarity to give the genuine differences the specific attention they need. That balance — one core, honestly acknowledged edges — is the whole art of it.

One Control Universe, Many Frameworks

So here is the model, stated plainly. Instead of a program per framework, you build a single, organized set of controls that represents everything your organization actually does to manage security, your control universe. It is yours, structured your way, in your language. Then, rather than implementing each framework separately, you map each framework onto that universe: this framework's requirements point to these controls of yours, that framework's requirements point to those. You maintain one set of controls and one set of evidence, and the frameworks become lenses you look at your program through, not separate programs you run.

The whole shift lives in the direction of that mapping. The weak version of a security program says, "we have ISO controls, and SOC 2 controls, and PCI controls, and privacy controls" — as if they were separate collections of things to do. The strong version says, "we have one access-management control family, and ISO, SOC 2, PCI, our privacy obligations, our customer questionnaires, and our own policy all map onto it."

Same reality, inverted: the weak version organizes around the frameworks and ends up owning many overlapping copies of the same control; the strong version organizes around the control and lets the frameworks be the many things that single control happens to satisfy. Get that inversion right and the mountain of overlapping requirements collapses into something much smaller, a finite set of things you actually do, each of which answers to several frameworks at once.

The payoff of that inversion is the quiet promise this whole book has been making since its early chapters, and it is worth saying in its canonical form: many frameworks, one operating model. You govern once and satisfy many. When a new customer wants a framework you already mapped, you are not starting a project. You are pointing at controls you already run and evidence you already have. When a regulator asks about a requirement, you trace it to the control that already addresses it. When you improve a control, you improve it everywhere at once, across every framework it maps to, instead of patching the same fix into a dozen parallel programs. The mountain of separate obligations becomes a single well-run program viewed from several angles.

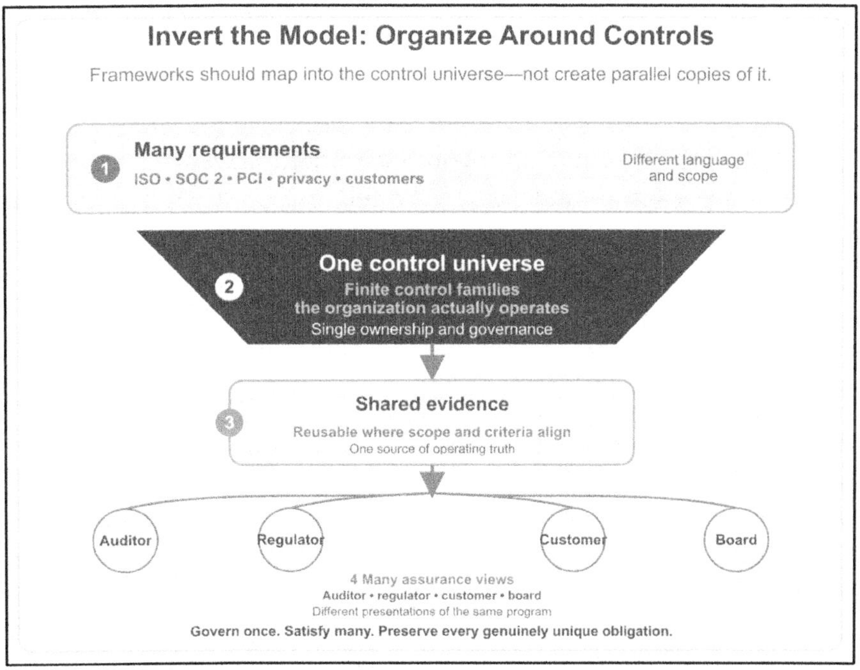

This is also, and this matters for the readers this book is written for, the thing that finally lets a small security function scale. A lean team cannot run twelve programs. It can run one program that answers to twelve frameworks. The unified control universe is what converts "we're subject to more and more requirements every year" from a crisis into a manageable, additive exercise because each new framework is no longer a new program to build, but a new set of pointers into a universe that mostly already covers it.

What It Actually Buys You

It is worth being concrete about the returns, because they compound. The first and most obvious is the end of avoidable duplicated effort: one authoritative policy set instead of near-duplicates that drift, governed evidence sources reused when control, scope, period, and assertion match instead of the same screenshots gathered four ways, and one control improvement flowing through every mapping it affects. That alone gives a stretched team back a meaningful slice of its week.

The second is coherence, which quietly raises how mature you look to everyone assessing you. When your policies, your risk register, your control descriptions, and your customer answers all trace back to the same control universe, they tell one consistent story. An auditor, a customer, a regulator, and your own board all hear the same account of how your security works, because there is only one account. Consistency reads as competence, and it is the natural byproduct of a single source of truth rather than something you have to manufacture.

The third, and this is where the series' cross-border theme comes home, is how gracefully a unified universe absorbs a new market. When you expand into another country, or land a customer bound by their own nation's regime, you are not rebuilding your program to that regime's shape. You are mapping the new regime onto controls you already run, finding the genuine gaps where it demands something your universe does not yet cover, and closing just those.

Entering a new compliance world becomes a mapping-and-gap exercise measured in the specific deltas, not a from-scratch rebuild. For anyone whose organization is growing across borders, or who is personally moving toward markets with unfamiliar regimes, that is the difference between expansion being a security bottleneck and security being ready before the business arrives.

And the fourth is resilience of the program itself. A single, documented control universe with clear framework mappings does not live in one person's head or one fragile spreadsheet. It survives turnover, it onboards new team members faster, and it makes the whole security function legible, to auditors, to leadership, and to the next person who inherits it. A program you can hand over cleanly is worth far more than a heroic one that only works while its author is in the room.

And a control universe only becomes an operating model, rather than a tidy library, when every control in it has an accountable owner, usually not the CISO, but the team that actually runs it. A control nobody owns is a control that quietly stops happening; the universe makes that ownership explicit, which is half of what makes it real.

What It Doesn't Do — and Where It Can Go Wrong

Honesty demands the other side of this, because a unified control universe done badly can create its own problems, and I would rather you see them coming than discover them the hard way.

The first and most important: mapping is not compliance. Drawing a line from a framework's requirement to one of your controls says the control is relevant to that requirement. It does not, by itself, prove the control is adequate or operating. A tidy crosswalk with every requirement neatly pointed at a control can create a dangerous illusion of coverage, where the map looks complete but the underlying controls are weak or half-implemented. Worse is the false equivalence that hides in a hasty mapping: two requirements that sound alike but differ in scope, so the map claims coverage the control does not actually provide.

This is where audit surprises are born: "we thought our access review covered the payment standard, but it excluded the admin portal for the payment system," or "we thought our vendor review covered our privacy obligations, but it never looked at sub-processors," or "we thought our AI policy covered all our AI use, but employees quietly using public AI tools were never in the inventory." The map is a navigation aid, not the territory, and a beautiful map over shaky ground is arguably worse than no map, because it hides the shakiness. Mapping intelligently, by obligation and scope rather than by matching words, is enough of a discipline that it is a subject of its own; the point here is simply that the unified model organizes your work and never substitutes for actually doing it well.

The second failure mode is over-abstraction. In the effort to make one control serve many frameworks, it is tempting to describe controls so generically that they technically map to everything and specifically satisfy nothing. When a framework requires something precise and your unified control is written vaguely enough to "cover" it on paper, you have mapped the requirement without meeting it. The discipline is to keep controls concrete enough to be real while common enough to be shared, and that tension never fully resolves; it is something you manage rather than solve.

The third is losing the genuine differences in the noise of the common core. The overlap is large, but the edges are where the specific, sometimes non-negotiable requirements live, the payment standard's particular demands, the regulation's hard deadline, the sector rule's specific obligation. A unified approach that smooths everything into one comfortable average will quietly drop exactly those sharp edges, and the sharp edges are often the ones with legal or contractual teeth. The universe has to hold the common core efficiently and preserve the genuine differences explicitly, not blur them together.

And the fourth is subtler: the unified model can become a bureaucracy of its own. If maintaining the mapping becomes a heavier job than the security work it was meant to streamline, you have reinvented the sprawl you were trying to escape, just in a single spreadsheet instead of many. The point of the control universe is to reduce total effort, and if a given piece of it is not doing that, it does not belong. Right-sizing is not a footnote to this approach; it is central to it.

Right-Sizing It for a Smaller Organization

That last point deserves its own breath, because the biggest way this idea goes wrong for the readers this book is written for is over-engineering it. The full-blown enterprise version of a control universe, a five-hundred-control master catalog, a dedicated platform, a team of people maintaining mappings across twenty frameworks, is real, and for a large regulated enterprise it earns its keep. It is also almost certainly not what your organization needs, and trying to build it at a small or mid-sized company is a fast way to spend a year on infrastructure instead of security.

The right-sized version is far humbler and far more useful. You need a sensible, organized set of the controls you actually run, not five hundred, but the manageable set that reflects your real environment. You need it mapped to the two or three frameworks that genuinely apply to you over the next year or so (the ones you actually need, not every framework you admire) rather than to every framework that exists. You need it in one place, with an owner against each control, and you need it maintained lightly, updated as your controls and obligations change rather than lovingly gold-plated.

And a word on tools, because the question always comes up: the control universe is a model, not a piece of software. A good platform can help once you have outgrown a spreadsheet, but it can only ever automate the model you give it, and if the model is messy, the tool will faithfully automate the mess, producing impressive dashboards that say very little.

A clear model in a well-structured spreadsheet beats a muddled one in an expensive platform every time. Do not buy a tool to avoid thinking; get the model right first, and let the tool come later, if and when your obligations actually warrant it. The unified control universe is a direction of travel and a discipline, not a mandatory megaproject, and the smaller you are, the more the value comes from the discipline and the less from the tooling.

The Frameworks Underneath One Control Universe

One control universe has to accommodate several kinds of instrument without pretending they all ask the same thing, so it is worth naming the cast before the build begins:

The recognizable control frameworks are the ones that get mapped into the universe: the broad international information-security control set, the government control catalog, the high-level functional framework used to communicate security outcomes, the service-provider assurance criteria, the payment-card standard, the widely used prioritized control list, and the cloud-specific control matrix. Each describes good security at a different altitude and for a different audience, which is exactly why they overlap so heavily and why one universe can serve them all.

Alongside them sit the overlays that are not classic control frameworks but still land requirements in the same universe: privacy and data-protection regimes, AI governance, and sector-specific regulation. They fold into the same operating model rather than standing apart as disconnected islands. And threading through everything is the traceability that turns the model from a static map into a living assurance system. The point of naming them is not to master any of them; it is to see that, collectively, they are the reason the unified build exists.

Industry Pattern — The Same Control, Audited Four Times Over

A growing organization picks up its security obligations the way most do, one at a time, as they arrive. First a customer requires an assurance report, so a project spins up to get one. Then the industry expects a recognized standard, so a second project starts, with its own policies and its own control list. Then a regulator's expectations land, and a third effort begins. Each is run by whoever was available, each builds its own documentation, each collects its own evidence, and none of them talk to each other. On paper, the organization is admirably diligent: three security programs, three sets of controls, three evidence folders.

Then comes the year the audits stack up, and the cost of running them as separate worlds becomes undeniable. The same multi-factor authentication is demonstrated three times to three assessors in three formats. The same access reviews are pulled from the same system and re-formatted for each. The team, already stretched, spends weeks not improving security but re-proving the security it already has, in triplicate, and along the way someone notices that the three policy sets have quietly drifted, saying subtly different things about the same practices, so that a careful auditor could find the organization contradicting itself. Nothing is actually insecure. Everything is exhausting, and slightly incoherent, and impossible to scale.

Eventually someone does the obvious thing that nobody had time to do: they lay the three programs side by side and map them against each other. And the finding is the one this chapter has been promising, the overlap is enormous. The great majority of the controls are the same controls, described three ways. The three programs could have been one program viewed through three lenses all along, and the years of duplicated effort bought almost no additional safety. The lesson is not that any of the individual programs was wrong. It is that running them as separate universes, rather than as one universe with three mappings, turned a manageable job into a punishing one, and the punishment scaled with every new framework the business took on.

What Evidence Should You Expect

At this level, the evidence is less about any single control and more about whether the organization has a coherent, single source of truth for its controls at all, and whether the frameworks it answers to are mapped onto that source rather than run as separate worlds. At leadership altitude, a CISO should be able to point to an organized set of the controls the organization actually operates, expressed once in the organization's own terms, each with a named owner; a mapping from each framework the organization is subject to onto that control set, so that any given requirement can be traced to the control that addresses it; and evidence that improvements and updates are made once, at the control, and flow through to every framework that control serves, rather than being patched separately into parallel programs.

Just as telling is the absence of the sprawl symptoms: no near-duplicate policies quietly contradicting each other, no team spending the bulk of its time reconciling frameworks by hand, no scramble to build a fresh program every time a new requirement arrives. The mature signal here is not a thick binder per framework. It is a single, legible control universe that several frameworks all point into.

A caution belongs in the evidence discussion itself, because this is exactly where the mapping-is-not-compliance risk bites: a clean crosswalk is evidence that you have organized your obligations, not that you have met them. The mapping shows coverage of a requirement by a control; it is the underlying control's own evidence, that it is implemented and operating in the right scope, that shows the requirement is actually satisfied. A mature program can produce both and never confuses the one for the other.

For a small or mid-sized organization, the practical minimum keeps this achievable:

- Write down the set of controls you actually operate, once, in your own language, not a five-hundred-control catalog, just an honest, organized list of what you really do, grouped by theme (governance, access, assets, vulnerabilities, logging, incident response, backup, vendor risk, and so on).

- Assign a real owner to every control, so each one has someone accountable for operating it, a control with no owner is a control that quietly stops happening.
- Map the two or three frameworks that genuinely apply to you today onto that list, so each requirement points to the control that addresses it, and keep a short register of the genuine gaps, the requirements nothing yet covers, so honest mapping surfaces what to build next rather than papering over it.
- Keep it in one place that everyone works from, a single well-structured document is enough to start; a platform can wait until your obligations actually warrant it, and it will only ever automate the model you give it.
- Remember that the map shows coverage, not adequacy, keep the underlying control's own evidence of operation and its scope, and do not let a tidy crosswalk stand in for controls that actually work.

That is not an enterprise governance-and-assurance function. It is enough to stop the frameworks from multiplying your work, and to make each new one an additive mapping rather than a fresh program.

Reality Check

> *Two questions that reveal whether you have a control universe or just a pile of frameworks.*
>
> *First, pick a single control you know you operate well (say, multi-factor authentication, or your access reviews) and ask how many separate places in your organization describe it, document it, and hold evidence for it. If the honest answer is that the same control lives in three policies, four evidence folders, and however many audit spreadsheets, each maintained separately, then you do not yet have a control universe; you have the sprawl, and you are paying for it in duplicated effort every time any of those frameworks comes up. One control should have one authoritative description and governed evidence sources, then be pointed at from wherever it is needed; reuse a given artifact only when its scope, period, and assertion match the question.*
>
> *Second, imagine a new customer arrives tomorrow requiring a framework you are not currently mapped to. Is your honest reaction "we'll trace their requirements onto controls we already run and find the real gaps," or is it "we'll need to stand up another program"? If it is the latter, then every new framework is a fresh mountain rather than a mapping, and your security function will keep hitting a wall the moment the business's ambitions outrun your capacity to build parallel programs. The whole point of a control universe is to make that second reaction impossible.*

What This Means for You as a Security Leader

The shift this part asks of you is more mental than technical, and it starts with refusing the instinct that feels most responsible: the instinct to treat each framework as its own project. That instinct is how diligent, well-meaning security leaders bury their own teams. The move is to stop organizing your program around the frameworks and start organizing it around your controls, to build one coherent universe of what you actually do, and let the frameworks be the many lenses that look into it.

You stop being a framework implementer and start being an architect of assurance, whose job is to keep one control story straight rather than to keep a dozen framework stories running in parallel. Everything else is machinery in service of that single reframe.

Practically, and especially if you are leading a small or mid-sized function, that means starting modestly and honestly. Write down what you actually do, once. Give every control an owner. Map the frameworks that truly apply, not the ones that merely exist. Keep it in one place, keep it light, and let it grow only as your real obligations grow. Resist both failure modes with equal care, the sprawl of running everything separately, and the over-engineering of building an enterprise mapping apparatus a company your size does not need.

And hold onto the honesty this approach lives or dies by: the map is not the territory, mapping a requirement is not meeting it, and the whole exercise is worthless if it becomes a beautiful crosswalk laid over controls that do not actually work. The unified control universe earns its keep only when it makes real security easier to run, not when it makes your paperwork prettier.

Done right, though, this is one of the highest-leverage moves a modern security leader can make. It is the thing that turns "we're subject to more requirements every year" from a source of dread into a routine, additive exercise. It is what lets a lean team answer to a growing crowd of frameworks without growing in proportion. It is what makes expanding into a new market a mapping problem rather than a rebuild. And it is the concrete form of the promise this series has been making all along, that the goal was never to collect frameworks, but to run one good program that satisfies them all. This part is where you build it.

Bridge to Chapter 17

Agreement now has to become a working method: a unified taxonomy mapped honestly by intent and scope.

CHAPTER 17

Building the Unified Control Taxonomy and Mapping Methodology

The case for one control universe is easy to agree with and easy to get wrong.

Agreement is the cheap part. The moment you sit down to build one control universe, two questions arrive. What should the universe look like? How do you organize a pile of controls into something navigable rather than shapeless, and rich enough to be useful without becoming an unmaintainable catalog? And how do you map a framework full of requirements to those controls honestly, rather than producing a spreadsheet of hopeful guesses that looks complete and means nothing?

Those are the two halves of this chapter: the taxonomy, which is the structure, and the mapping methodology, which is the method that populates it. Neither is hard in the way that a technical problem is hard. They are hard in the way that organizing anything well is hard, the trap is not complexity, it is the quiet ways a reasonable-looking structure turns out to be wrong once you lean on it. Most control universes that fail do not fail because the idea was bad.

They fail because the taxonomy was built framework-first instead of intent-first, or because the mapping matched words instead of meaning, and nobody noticed until an auditor or an incident leaned on the weak spot. That is the thing to hold onto through everything that follows: a bad mapping can be worse than no mapping. No mapping at least tells you there is work to do. A bad mapping tells you the work is done when it is not, and that is how organizations walk into audits, customer reviews, and incidents carrying confidence they never actually earned.

A word before we start, aimed especially at the smaller organizations this book is written for: everything here scales down. The full enterprise version of this, a formal control ontology, a dedicated team maintaining it, mapping software with its own administrators, is real, and if that is your world, the principles still apply. But you do not need any of that to do this well. You need a clear head about intent, a sensible structure, an honest method, and the discipline to keep it current. A good taxonomy in a well-built spreadsheet beats a muddled one in an expensive platform, every single time. Hold onto that as we go, because the biggest way this chapter's advice gets misused is by treating it as a mandate to over-build.

Start with Control Intent, Not Framework Language

Here is the single most important decision in the whole build, and almost everything else follows from getting it right: define each control by its intent, what it is actually trying to achieve, expressed in your own plain words, before any framework's language touches it.

This sounds abstract until you see what it prevents. If you build your control universe by starting from a framework and lifting its wording, you inherit that framework's structure, its granularity, and its blind spots, and then every other framework has to be awkwardly bent to fit the shape of the first one you happened to start with. You end up with a universe that is secretly just one framework wearing a coat, and the mappings from the others never sit quite right. Every other framework becomes a guest in someone else's house, and you find yourself arguing about why one framework's language is "primary" and another's is "secondary."

Intent is what breaks that trap. When you write a control as "access to systems and data is granted deliberately, kept to what the role needs, reviewed on a schedule, and removed promptly when it's no longer warranted," you have described a real thing your organization does, in language that belongs to no framework and therefore welcomes all of them. The broad information-security standard's access requirement points at it. The assurance criteria's logical-access requirement points at it. The payment standard's access requirement points at it. The privacy regime's access-limitation requirement points at it. They all point at the same clearly-stated intent because the intent is the real thing and they are all describing it.

Intent is, in effect, your translation layer, the thing that turns a dozen dialects into one language. Frameworks phrase requirements as control numbers, category names, trust criteria, and regulatory articles; intent phrases them as the plain operating question underneath: can we show that this actually happens, for the things it needs to happen to? Build your controls as answers to those plain questions and the mapping becomes a matter of recognizing which framework requirement is asking which question, which is far easier, and far more honest, than trying to reconcile one framework's wording against another's.

Organizing the Universe: Domains, Then Controls

With intent as the building block, the structure almost designs itself. You group your controls into a manageable set of domains, the natural territories of security work, and place the individual controls within them. If you have built out a control set before, this will feel familiar, because it is the same organizing logic: access management, asset and configuration management, vulnerability and patch management, logging and monitoring, incident response, backup and recovery, secure development, cryptography, vendor and third-party management, awareness and training, physical security, change management, AI governance, customer assurance, and governance over the top of it all.

The exact list is yours to shape around your environment, a bank, a SaaS provider, a healthcare processor, and a manufacturer will each organize a little differently, and that is correct, because the taxonomy should mirror how you actually run security. What matters is that it is a set a human can hold in their head, not an alphabetized sprawl of two hundred entries with no shape. The domain structurc is not sacred scripture; it is a navigation system, and its only job is to help people find controls, assign ownership, and produce evidence without getting lost.

The structure should be shallow enough to navigate and deep enough to be precise, which in practice means two or three levels, not seven. Domains at the top, controls within them, and at most a light grouping in between where a domain is genuinely large. A single control, in turn, often decomposes into a handful of concrete activities, an access-review control quietly contains "new access is approved before it's granted," "privileged access is reviewed periodically," "leavers' access is removed on time," "exceptions are tracked to closure" — and that is useful to see, because different frameworks map at different levels: a broad requirement lands on the whole control, a specific one lands on a single activity.

But resist the pull toward an elaborate hierarchy for its own sake, because every extra layer is something you have to maintain and something a control owner has to navigate to find their own control. For a smaller organization, domain and control with an owner, a scope, and evidence attached is very often enough; the extra layers earn their place only when a domain is genuinely too large to hold otherwise. The goal of the structure is simply that anyone in the organization can find the control they are responsible for, see what it is for, and know it is the only place that control lives.

That last point is the load-bearing discipline: one canonical home per control. A given control has exactly one place in the taxonomy, one authoritative description, clear accountable ownership, and pointers to its governed evidence sources; every framework and every other domain that needs it points to that home rather than copying it. Evidence can remain scope- and period-specific without creating duplicate controls. That single rule is what makes the whole "map, don't duplicate" promise structurally true rather than merely aspirational. The moment a control exists in two places, the two copies begin to drift, and you are back to reconciling near-duplicates.

One more thing that matters more than people expect: name your controls for the humans who will use them, not for the frameworks or the tool. A control called "AC-02.04 Logical User Recertification" satisfies a governance, risk, and compliance (GRC) platform and baffles the system owner who actually has to run it; "Do access stuff" helps nobody. Plain, stable, recognizable names: "Periodic Access Review," "Privileged Access Management," "Backup and Restore Testing," "Vendor Risk Assessment" — let the people who operate controls recognize their own work at a glance, and the detail can live in the description.

And avoid naming a control after a framework unless it genuinely exists only for that framework: "Payment Environment Access Control" (mapped to the payment standard and whatever else applies) travels; "PCI Requirement 8 Control" locks the control to one external vocabulary and quietly makes that framework the spine again. The taxonomy should speak your organization's language first, and let the frameworks speak through the mappings.

Getting the Granularity Right

The question that trips up almost everyone building a taxonomy for the first time is how big a control should be, and it is a real tension with no clean formula, only a workable judgment. Make your controls too coarse, a single monolithic "access control" that swallows authentication, authorization, privileged access, reviews, and deprovisioning all at once, and you cannot map to it precisely (a framework requirement about privileged access specifically now points at a blob), you cannot assign it cleanly (who owns "access control" in its entirety?), and you cannot evidence it (what one artifact proves that whole thing?).

Make them too fine (a hundred micro-controls, each a single sentence) and you drown in maintenance, the mappings multiply beyond anyone's ability to keep them current, and control owners lose the forest in the trees. And there is a related failure worth naming: the control written so narrowly that it is actually a procedure: "on the first Monday after quarter-end, the app owner exports users from System X, emails the sheet to GRC, and files the signed PDF in Folder Y" is not a control, it is a workflow, and it becomes obsolete the moment the workflow tool changes. The control is the intent that outlives the procedure.

The workable grain sits where a control is a thing one owner can operate and evidence as a unit. That is the practical test: if a single accountable person can be responsible for it, and a recognizable body of evidence can show it is happening, it is about the right size. "Privileged access is restricted, approved, and reviewed" is a control, one owner, one evidence set. "Access control" is a domain.

"Privileged accounts have their session idle-timeout set to fifteen minutes" is a configuration detail, not a control in its own right. The grain that survives contact with reality is the one that maps to an owner and an evidence story, and it is worth repeating the phrase because it is exactly the balance you are managing: concrete enough to be real, common enough to be shared.

Each control, at this grain, carries a small set of attributes that make it operable and mappable, and it is worth naming the ones that matter most here even though some get their full treatment later. Every control has an owner, and getting ownership right is its own small discipline. It helps to separate two roles that people blur: the accountable owner, the function leader answerable for the control existing and working, and the operating owner, the team or platform that actually performs it day to day. The operating owner is almost never security by default: security may govern, advise, and test, but the access review is run by the system owner, the patching by infrastructure, the secure-code review by engineering.

Defaulting every control to "security" because it appears in a security framework is exactly how controls get orphaned, everyone assumes someone else owns it, and it quietly stops happening. For genuinely cross-functional controls like incident response or vendor risk, a light RACI chart, naming who is responsible, accountable, consulted, and informed, can help clarify who does what; for everything else, do not build wallpaper, a single clear accountable owner that everyone respects beats a beautiful matrix nobody reads. Beyond the owner, every control has a scope, which systems, data, environments, or services it actually applies to, and scope turns out to be the quiet hero of honest mapping, for reasons we are about to see.

Every control has the frameworks it maps to, and every control has a pointer to where its evidence lives. A larger organization will want more attributes than these; a lean team should start with owner, scope, frameworks, evidence, and status, and add fields only when someone will actually use them. Unused attributes are just governance dust.

Mapping by Intent and Scope, Not by Matching Words

Now the second half: the method for actually connecting a framework's requirements to your controls. And the method is defined mostly by the failure it exists to prevent, because there is an obvious wrong way to do this that feels productive and produces garbage. The wrong way is word-matching, reading a framework requirement, finding one of your controls whose name shares some vocabulary with it, drawing a line between them, and moving on.

Do that across a whole framework and you get a spreadsheet where every requirement has a line to a control, everything looks covered, and a meaningful fraction of those lines are false. Two requirements that share words can mean genuinely different things, and two that use entirely different words can be asking for exactly the same thing. Matching on vocabulary catches neither case correctly.

The honest method maps on two things instead: intent and scope. For each framework requirement, you ask first what is this actually asking us to achieve, its intent, and find the control whose intent genuinely covers it, regardless of whether the words line up. That handles the meaning. Then you ask the question that word-matching never thinks to ask: does my control's scope actually cover the scope this requirement demands? This is where the real work is, and where most false mappings die.

Your access-review control might genuinely, correctly address a payment standard's access-review requirement in intent, but if your control's scope is "production systems" and the payment requirement means "everything in the cardholder data environment," and your cardholder environment includes an administrative system your access review has never touched, then the intent matches and the scope does not, and the honest mapping says so. Word-matching would have drawn a confident green line straight over that gap. Intent-and-scope mapping finds it. That difference (checking scope, not just meaning) is most of what separates a mapping you can trust from one that will ambush you at audit.

Coverage Isn't Binary: Full, Partial, and Not Covered

Which leads directly to the most important correction the method makes to how people instinctively map: coverage is not yes-or-no. The instinct is to mark each requirement "covered" or "not covered," a green box or a red one. Reality has more states than that, and the extra ones are where the truth lives. A control can fully cover a requirement, same intent, and its scope reaches everything the requirement needs. A control can partially cover a requirement, right intent, but its scope falls short, or it addresses part of what is asked and not all of it. There is the genuine not covered, where nothing you do actually addresses this requirement at all.

And one more honest state earns its place: not applicable, where the requirement genuinely does not apply to your business, environment, or data. That is a legitimate answer as long as you record why, because an unexplained "N/A" is just a not-covered in disguise. A compensating control is different. It is not a fifth coverage state to apply freely; it is a documented alternative to use only when the governing framework or obligation permits one and the alternative meets its criteria. It cannot turn a hard legal, regulatory, or contractual requirement into "covered" merely because another control reduces the risk. So the working coverage set is four: full, partial, not covered, and not applicable. Partial and not covered flow into the gap register; any permitted compensating-control treatment should be recorded alongside the mapping, with its rationale and approval.

The partial case is the one that hides in binary thinking, and it is precisely where the earlier false-equivalence trap lives. A partial coverage recorded as "covered" is a lie your own spreadsheet is telling you, and it is a lie you will believe right up until the day it is tested. So the method insists on recording the state honestly, and on partial coverage carrying a note of what is missing, the scope it does not reach, the frequency it does not meet, the piece of the requirement it does not address.

That note is not bureaucratic overhead; it is the exact thing that tells you what work remains. A mapping that only ever says "covered" is decoration. A mapping that says "fully covered here, partially covered there and here's the specific shortfall, not applicable there and here's why, and these three requirements aren't covered at all" is a map you can actually navigate by, and, not incidentally, one that will not embarrass you when someone checks. Partial is not failure. Partial is honesty, and honesty is the whole point.

It is also worth being clear that the relationships between controls and requirements are not tidy one-to-one lines, and the method has to hold that. Most of the time, one of your controls satisfies many requirements across many frameworks at once, that is the entire point, the leverage that makes the universe worth building. But it also runs the other way: a single framework requirement sometimes needs several of your controls working together to be fully met, and mapping it to just one of them records a partial coverage dressed up as a full one. Good mapping expects both shapes, one control to many requirements, and one requirement to many controls, and does not force the messy reality into clean single lines just because clean lines are easier to draw.

The Over-Broad Control Trap

There is a second way mappings go quietly false, and it is the mirror image of word-matching. Word-matching maps too loosely. This one builds a control too broad, and then hides real work behind it. Some controls genuinely map to many requirements; access management, incident response, logging, vendor risk, and governance are legitimately broad, and there is nothing wrong with that. But when a single control like "Information Security Governance" or "Security Policy" starts mapping to a hundred or two hundred requirements, be suspicious, because a control that covers everything usually operates against almost nothing. It has become a hiding place, a way to mark requirements "covered" without ever building the specific controls those requirements actually need.

The tell is the difference between a control and a claim. A policy that says something should happen is not a control that makes it happen. A governance meeting that discusses a risk is not a control that reduces it. A process that exists for one environment is not a control that covers all of them. When a mapping points a requirement at a policy document: "our security policy mentions encryption, so the encryption requirement is covered" — it has mapped to an intention, not an operating control, and the requirement is not actually met by anything real.

The distinction between the layers matters here: policy defines the expectation, the control is the mechanism that satisfies it, and evidence proves the mechanism ran. Mapping a requirement to a policy statement, or to a control so broad it means nothing, satisfies the spreadsheet and leaves the risk exactly where it was. So when a control maps to a great many requirements, interrogate it: is it actually operating against each one, with evidence and the right scope, or is it a vague umbrella you reached for to avoid creating the specific controls the requirements really demand? A control universe is supposed to reduce duplication, not become a place for real work to hide.

The Gap Register: Where Mapping Earns Its Keep

Here is the reframe that changes what mapping is for. It is tempting to think the purpose of mapping is to prove coverage, to generate the satisfying spreadsheet full of green that you can show an auditor or a customer. That is a use, but it is the smaller one, and treating it as the main event is how mappings drift toward dishonesty, because a map whose job is to look complete will quietly find ways to look complete.

The higher purpose of mapping is the opposite: to honestly surface what you do not cover. Every partial and every not-covered the mapping records is an item of real security work the exercise has just discovered for you, a place where a framework you are subject to expects something your program does not yet do, or does not do widely enough.

Gather those partials and not-covered items into one place and you have a gap register: the genuine to-do list that the mapping produces as its most valuable output. A partial marked without a description is nearly useless, it tells you something is incomplete but not what to do, so each entry earns its keep by carrying enough to act on: the requirement, the control it partly maps to, what specifically is missing, the scope affected, who owns the fix, and roughly when.

It also needs a sense of priority, because not every gap deserves the same urgency, a missing control on a system full of customer data is not the same as a minor documentation shortfall, and a gap register that is not risk-rated will have you fixing the easy things while the dangerous ones wait. Rate them, and work the dangerous ones first. Done that way, the register turns vague compliance pressure into concrete, prioritized, assignable tasks: not "we're weak on privileged access" but "privileged access reviews cover infrastructure but not SaaS administrator roles; that's high risk because those platforms hold customer data; the identity and access management team and the platform owners will add quarterly SaaS admin reviews by the third quarter; this touches the assurance criteria, the broad standard, and two customer commitments."

This is where mapping stops being a compliance chore and becomes a security tool, because the gap register is a prioritized picture of where your actual coverage falls short of your actual obligations, sourced not from someone's opinion but from a systematic pass across every requirement you are bound by. For obligations already mapped, later customer, regulator, or audit questions should bring fewer surprises, but they can still introduce a new obligation, interpretation, or operating failure the mapping did not contain. The organizations that get real value from a control universe are the ones that treat the gap register as the point and the green coverage as the byproduct, not the other way around.

Keeping the Mapping Alive: Owned, Not Copy-Pasted

A mapping spreadsheet ages into fragile uselessness, and the method has to answer that directly, because a mapping is not a thing you build once and file. It is a living connection between two things that both change underneath it. Frameworks get revised. Your controls get added, retired, re-scoped, and reorganized. Your obligations shift as you take on new customers and new markets. A mapping built once and abandoned goes stale the moment the frameworks or your controls move underneath it, and grows actively misleading as those changes accumulate, because it now confidently asserts connections that no longer hold, and a stale control universe is dangerous precisely because it still looks authoritative. Outdated confidence is worse than visible uncertainty.

What keeps a mapping alive is unglamorous and non-negotiable: an owner and a cadence. Someone has to be accountable for the mapping as an artifact, not for every control in it, but for the mapping itself staying true, and there has to be a rhythm on which it is revisited, plus a trigger discipline so that certain events force a check rather than waiting for the next scheduled pass. The triggers worth wiring in are the obvious ones once you name them: a framework releases a new version, a new product or service launches, you take on a customer commitment that adds an obligation, you enter a new market or country whose regime brings its own requirements, a control is materially re-scoped or retired, or an audit finding exposes something the mapping missed.

Any of those should send you back to the affected mappings deliberately. A light change log does most of the supporting work here: what was added, what was retired, what got re-scoped, whose ownership moved, and when. Enough that anyone can tell at a glance whether the mapping is current. That is the difference between mapping, which is fine, and unowned mapping, which is the actual problem. The deeper machinery of evidence freshness, testing, and the full assurance rhythm is a subject of its own; the structural point here is simpler and load-bearing: a mapping without an owner is a mapping that has already started to rot, and the rot is invisible until you rely on it.

Right-Sizing the Method for a Smaller Organization

Everything above can be read as a lot, so let me bring it back to earth for a lean team, because the method genuinely does scale down without losing its integrity. You do not need an ontology, a mapping platform, or a dedicated GRC function to do this honestly. You need a spreadsheet with the right columns and the discipline to fill them in truthfully.

Concretely, that looks like this. List your controls, grouped by a dozen or so sensible domains, each with an owner and a scope. Take the two or three frameworks that actually apply to you and, requirement by requirement, ask the two honest questions, does a control's intent cover this, and does its scope reach far enough, and record full, partial, not covered, or not applicable, with a note on anything partial. Collect the partials and not-covered items into a gap list. Give one person responsibility for keeping the whole thing current, and look at it on a sensible rhythm rather than never. That is the entire method, and it fits in a well-structured spreadsheet a small team can actually maintain.

And here is the most freeing part, the thing that stops this from becoming the year-long design project that sinks so many good intentions: build the first version quickly, and let real use shape it. Do not disappear for six months to craft the perfect taxonomy in isolation and unveil it fully-formed, that version almost always turns out not to match how the organization really works, because it was designed away from the work. Build a rough, honest first version from what you already have: the frameworks you already need, the controls you already run, the evidence you already collect, the owners you already know, and the gaps you already suspect.

Then use it, run one real audit or one real customer questionnaire through it and watch where it breaks, because it will, and the breakages are the design feedback you cannot get any other way. Fix those, then expand. A working first version that improves through contact with reality beats a beautiful design nobody has stress-tested, every time. The sophistication is not in the tooling or the completeness; it is in the honesty of the two questions and the refusal to let "mentioned" masquerade as "met." A small organization that does this truthfully has a better handle on its real coverage than a large one with an expensive platform full of word-matched green.

The Frameworks Underneath Control Mapping

This chapter is deliberately framework-agnostic: it teaches the method rather than presenting the completed mapping. The recognizable control frameworks — the broad international information-security control set, the government control catalog, the functional cybersecurity framework, the service-provider assurance criteria, the payment-card standard, the prioritized control list, and the cloud control matrix — are the instruments you run the intent-

and-scope method against, requirement by requirement. Each brings a wrinkle the method has to respect rather than smooth away.

The payment standard demands scope discipline above all: a control can be enterprise-wide and still owe evidence specific to the cardholder environment. The assurance criteria distinguish design from operation: a Type II examination speaks to operating effectiveness over a period, a Type I only to design at a date, and the mapping has to preserve which one you actually have. The functional framework is more useful for high-level coverage and executive communication than for line-by-line mapping.

The overlays that are not classic control frameworks (privacy regimes, AI governance, sector regulation) map by the same method but carry obligations that reach past security controls into lawful processing, data-subject rights, model governance, and hard regulatory deadlines. Those nonsecurity obligations must remain explicit rather than being flattened into controls. One control universe does not mean one level of detail for everything; it means one model that can hold different levels of detail honestly. The method is uniform even though the frameworks differ, and that uniformity is exactly what makes many frameworks resolve into one operating model.

Industry Pattern — Mapped, Not Met

An organization sets out to do the right thing and build a proper framework-to-control mapping. Someone capable is handed the job, and they work through it the fastest way that feels productive: they read each framework requirement, find a control whose name looks like a match, and draw the line. Requirement about access, meet the access control.

Requirement about logging, meet the logging control. Requirement about vendors, meet the vendor control. It goes quickly, because word-matching always does, and at the end there is a clean, satisfying spreadsheet where nearly every requirement has a control beside it and almost everything is green. The dashboard says high coverage. Leadership feels reassured. The organization believes, reasonably, that it has finally gotten its arms around its obligations.

Then the mapping meets its first real test, an audit. The assessor picks a mapped requirement for privileged access review; the mapping points at the enterprise access-review control, and the evidence shows solid quarterly reviews for the key corporate systems. Good control, real evidence, nothing fabricated. Then the assessor asks whether the payment administration portal was included, and it was not. The requirement was not wrong, the control was not fake, the evidence was not false.

The mapping was too broad: it had treated "an access review exists" as equivalent to "the access review covers the required in-scope environment." It matched the words and missed the scope. The dashboard said covered; the audit said partial. And the same thing was quietly true elsewhere, the vendor control mapped to a privacy requirement addressed direct vendors but never sub-processors; the incident control mapped to a notification requirement covered the internal process but not the specific customer-notification timing the requirement demanded.

> *None of the controls were bad. The mapping was, because it had recorded that a control was relevant to a requirement and let everyone read that as the control meeting the requirement. The gaps were not security disasters; they were fixable. But the organization had spent months believing it had coverage it did not actually have. The lesson is not that the mapping was a waste; it is that it was done at the wrong depth.*
>
> *A mapping built on intent and scope, recording full, partial, and not covered honestly, would have found every one of those shortfalls calmly, in advance, as entries on a gap register to work through, instead of surfacing them all at once, under pressure, in front of someone whose job was to find them. Mapped is not met. A beautiful map is useful only if it tells the truth about the territory, and where scope is concerned, the scope is the mapping.*

What Evidence Should You Expect

The evidence at this stage is about whether a real, usable structure exists underneath the good intentions, whether there is an actual taxonomy and an actual method, rather than a slogan about one control universe and a spreadsheet that word-matches.

At leadership altitude, a CISO should be able to point to a control taxonomy organized by domain, controls named in the organization's own language, each with an owner and a scope and a single home; a mapping performed by intent and scope rather than vocabulary, recording full, partial, not covered, and not applicable rather than a wall of undifferentiated "covered"; a gap register that falls out of that mapping as its most useful product, risk-rated so the dangerous shortfalls surface first; and a named owner, a change log, and a review rhythm for the mapping itself, so it is a living artifact rather than a snapshot rotting quietly in a shared drive.

The subtle tell of maturity here is the presence of honest partials and not-covered items at all, a mapping that claims total green coverage is almost always one that word-matched, because real programs subject to real frameworks always have shortfalls, and the ability to name them is the sign the work was done properly.

For a small or mid-sized organization, the practical minimum keeps this achievable:

- Organize your controls into a handful of sensible domains, each control named plainly, in one home, with an owner and a scope written down. Scope especially, because it is what makes honest mapping possible.
- Define each control by its intent in your own words, not by any framework's wording, so every framework can point at it cleanly.
- Map the frameworks that apply to you by asking the two honest questions, does a control's intent cover this requirement, and does its scope reach far enough, and record full, partial, not covered, or not applicable, never a bare "covered," and never a policy statement standing in for an operating control.
- Pull every partial and not-covered item into a single gap register, each with what is missing, who owns the fix, and a rough priority, and treat it as the real to-do list the mapping exists to produce.
- Give one person responsibility for keeping the mapping current with a simple change log, and revisit it on a rhythm and whenever a framework, a control, a product, a customer commitment, or a new market changes, and build a rough first version fast rather than perfecting one in isolation.

That is not an enterprise mapping function. It is enough to make the control universe real rather than notional, and to make sure the mapping tells you the truth about your coverage instead of a comfortable story.

Reality Check

> *Two tests for whether your taxonomy and mapping are honest or decorative.*
>
> *First, open your framework mapping, if you have one, and look for the partials and the not-covered items. If every requirement is marked covered, with no partials and no gaps anywhere, be suspicious of your own spreadsheet, not reassured by it. Full coverage is possible for a narrow, mature scope — but only when every line can show its intent, scope, evidence, and applicability, and has been challenged recently. Far more often, a mapping with no shortfalls word-matched its way to a comforting picture, and the shortfalls it failed to record are still there, just invisible until something tests them. A trustworthy mapping looks a little uncomfortable, because it is telling you the truth.*
>
> *Second, pick any single requirement marked "covered" and interrogate the scope. Does the control that covers it actually reach every system, environment, and dataset the requirement demands, or does it cover the intent on the main systems and quietly stop at the edge of some environment nobody checked? And while you are there, check what it is mapped to: is it an operating control with evidence, or a policy that merely says the thing should happen?*
>
> *If you cannot answer confidently, then "covered" in your mapping means "we have a control shaped like this somewhere," which is a very different and much weaker claim than "this requirement is met everywhere it applies." The whole method exists to turn the first claim into the second, and the check is simply whether you recorded scope, and reality, honestly.*

What This Means for You as a Security Leader

This chapter is where the control universe stops being a good idea and becomes an actual thing you can build, and the two moves that make or break it are both about honesty more than cleverness. Build the taxonomy intent-first, describe what your controls actually achieve, in your own words, named for the people who run them, at a grain where one owner can operate and evidence each one, in a structure shallow enough that people can navigate it and strict enough that each control has exactly one home.

And map intent-and-scope-first, connect requirements to controls by what they mean and how far they reach, not by what words they share, and record full, partial, not covered, and not applicable truthfully rather than painting everything green. Everything else is refinement on those two foundations. This is architecture, not clerical work: the model you build is what determines whether leadership receives truth or theater.

The failure modes are worth holding in view because they are the common ones and they masquerade as diligence. Building framework-first gives you a universe that is secretly one framework in disguise, and it fights every other framework you try to map. Word-matching gives you a mapping that looks complete and lies. An over-broad control gives real work a place to hide behind a reassuring green cell.

Over-engineering gives you a taxonomy so elaborate that maintaining it costs more than the sprawl it replaced. Each of these looks, in the moment, like doing a thorough job, which is exactly why they catch careful people. The antidote to all of them is the same discipline of honesty: intent over wording, scope checked not assumed, operating controls not policy statements, gaps written down not glossed, and structure kept only as heavy as it earns.

And the payoff, done right, is considerable and compounding. A taxonomy built on intent absorbs each new framework as a mapping exercise rather than a rebuild, including a new country's regime, which becomes simply another set of requirements run through the same two honest questions, its genuine novelties surfacing as gaps to close rather than a program to stand up from scratch.

A mapping built on intent and scope produces, as its natural output, a gap register that is one of the most useful documents a security leader can own: a truthful, prioritized picture of where your real coverage falls short of your real obligations. That register is the quiet reward for doing this properly. It is the thing that lets you walk into any audit, customer assessment, or regulator's question already knowing the gaps your own work has found, because you found them first, on purpose, and have been working the list ever since. It cannot predict every testing result or interpretation, but it replaces avoidable surprise with clarity. The goal was never perfection. It was clarity.

Bridge to Chapter 18

A method only earns its keep on contact with real frameworks; the next chapter lays the major control sets into the universe side by side.

CHAPTER 18

The Control Universe: Mapping ISO 27002, NIST 800-53, SOC 2, PCI DSS, CIS, CSA CCM

Different frameworks ask different questions. Good controls answer many at once.

The frameworks are largely asking for the same things, and the method for proving it is already in hand: intent and scope, full and partial and not-covered, honestly recorded, never confusing "mapped" with "met." This chapter is where the claim and the method meet the actual frameworks, all at once, and you get to watch the correlation happen instead of taking my word for it.

Let me set expectations, because there is a wrong way to read a chapter like this. The wrong way is to expect (or worse, to build) a giant master table with every control ID from every framework cross-referenced in a grid of thousands of cells. Those tables have their place, and an appendix is where a detailed crosswalk belongs. But the chapter itself has a different job: to show how these frameworks behave when you bring them into one control universe.

Where they converge. Where they diverge. Where one control satisfies several expectations at once. Where scope quietly changes the answer. And where a clean-looking mapping can still be wrong because it ignored the actual obligation. Once you have seen that happen on a real domain or two, you can do it yourself on the rest, and that recognition is worth far more than any table.

Six Frameworks, Six Altitudes

The single most useful thing to understand before mapping anything is that these frameworks are not competitors describing the same thing at the same level. They are different kinds of document, sitting at different altitudes, built for different audiences and different jobs. Treat them as identical and the mapping will lie; treat them as entirely separate and the operating model drowns. The useful middle is to treat them as different lenses on one shared control universe, and the lens metaphor only works if you know each lens's focal length. Each is named below with the edition this chapter maps against, verified in July 2026; if any of them moves, the mapping needs rechecking.

ISO/IEC 27002:2022 is the broad international reference, 93 controls across four themes: organizational (clause 5), people (clause 6), physical (clause 7), and technological (clause 8). It is the control companion to ISO/IEC 27001's certifiable management system, and its altitude is mid-level and comprehensive: broad enough to cover the whole field, specific enough to implement against, and phrased as good practice rather than hard mandate. Its great value in a unified model is breadth. It reminds you that security is governance and people and suppliers and physical, not just technology. Just do not copy its structure wholesale and call it your taxonomy; that is framework-first design creeping back in. Use ISO to inform your universe, not to be it.

NIST SP 800-53 Revision 5 is the deep government catalog, 20 control families, each a two-letter code (AC for access control, AU for audit, IR for incident response, SC for system and communications protection, SR for supply chain, and so on), with a very large number of controls and enhancements beneath them. Its altitude is low and detailed: it goes deeper than anything else here, which is exactly why it anchors high-assurance and government-adjacent environments and is usually more granularity than a lean team needs. You rarely adopt it wholesale; you reach into it when a specific control needs depth, and you document why the parts you skipped do not apply.

One framework in this lineup is not named in the chapter's title, and that is deliberate. The CSF 2.0 is the outlier of the set, not a control catalog at all, but six functions describing outcomes: Govern, Identify, Protect, Detect, Respond, and Recover. Its altitude is the highest here, built for organizing and communicating a program at the level a board can follow, with the 2.0 revision adding Govern as its own function.

You do not implement CSF the way you implement a control; you use it to structure and talk about the program your controls sit inside, which is why it maps to many of your controls loosely and to none of them one-for-one. I include it throughout as a reference lens rather than a seventh catalog to crosswalk, because you cannot explain the other six to an executive without it, but you do not map to it the way you map to them. Think of it as the altitude from which the whole universe is viewed, not another set of requirements to satisfy.

SOC 2, built on the Trust Services Criteria of the American Institute of Certified Public Accountants (AICPA), is an assurance instrument rather than a control list, the thing you met from both sides of the desk. Its criteria fall into five categories: Security, Availability, Processing Integrity, Confidentiality, and Privacy. Security is the always-present baseline, expressed as the Common Criteria (CC1 through CC9, covering the control environment, communication, risk, monitoring, control activities, logical and physical access, operations, change, and risk mitigation); the other four are included only if the service commits to them. Its altitude is assurance-shaped, and it makes a demand the pure control frameworks do not: it cares not just that a control is designed but, in a Type II examination, that it operated effectively over a period.

PCI DSS v4.0.1, the Payment Card Industry Data Security Standard, is the specialist, 12 requirements under six goals, narrow and deep and mandatory where it applies, all aimed at protecting payment-card data. Its altitude is deep within a tight scope: little about the whole enterprise, a great deal about the cardholder data environment, in prescriptive detail, with real consequences. It is the clearest example of a framework whose sharp edges you cannot sand off.

CIS Controls v8.1 is the practical, prioritized one, 18 controls, each broken into safeguards, organized into three Implementation Groups (IG1, IG2, IG3) that tell a smaller organization what to do first. Its altitude is implementation-first and opinionated about sequence, which makes it the friendliest starting anchor for a lean team that needs to know where to begin. It will not satisfy every regulatory or customer obligation by itself, but it is often the best bridge between abstract control language and operational reality.

And the CSA Cloud Controls Matrix v4.1 is the cloud specialist, organizing cloud-security controls across the shared-responsibility line between provider and customer. It spans domains you will recognize from the rest of this series, cloud governance, identity and access, data security, logging and monitoring, business continuity, infrastructure security, and interoperability and portability, but frames each around who owns the control on which side of the provider-customer line. It is the natural reference when much of your risk lives in cloud services; you will see its access controls in the worked example just ahead, but its full domain-by-domain cloud detail belongs with the cloud material in Volume III, Part 4, where getting it exactly right is the whole job.

Hold that altitude picture, because it explains how the mapping behaves. High-altitude frameworks such as the CSF map broadly across clusters of your controls. Mid-altitude catalogs such as ISO/IEC 27002 and the CIS Controls sit closer to operational controls but still map many-to-many. Detailed catalogs such as NIST SP 800-53 may require several of their controls and enhancements to map to one of yours, or several of yours to satisfy one requirement. Scoped standards such as PCI DSS may align cleanly in intent but demand a scope check every single time. Same universe underneath; very different lenses looking in.

The Same Control, Six Ways

Enough setup, let us watch it happen. Take the one control every framework has an opinion about, the running example since the case was first made: managing who has access to what. Here is that single control in your universe. Access to systems and data is granted deliberately, kept to least privilege, authenticated strongly, reviewed on a schedule, and removed when no longer warranted, and here is where each framework's version of it lands.

ISO 27002:2022 spreads it across several controls: 5.15 (access control) sets the policy, 5.16 (identity management) and 5.17 (authentication information) handle identities and credentials, 5.18 (access rights) governs granting and review, and in the technological theme 8.2 (privileged access rights), 8.3 (information access restriction), and 8.5 (secure authentication) carry the enforcement. NIST 800-53 puts it in two families: AC (access control), with account management (AC-2) and least privilege (AC-6) among its controls, and IA (identification and authentication) for proving who someone is (IA-2). NIST CSF 2.0 rolls the whole thing into a single outcome category under Protect, PR.AA, "Identity

Management, Authentication, and Access Control" — the result without the mechanism.

SOC 2 addresses it through the Common Criteria, principally the CC6 series on logical and physical access. PCI DSS splits it into two of its twelve requirements: Requirement 7, restricting access by business need to know, and Requirement 8, identifying and authenticating users. And CIS Controls covers it in two of its eighteen: Control 5 (account management) and Control 6 (access control management). And the CSA Cloud Controls Matrix carries it in its Identity & Access Management domain, IAM-05 (least privilege), IAM-06 (access provisioning), IAM-08 (access review), and IAM-13 (strong authentication) among its controls. Framed, as CCM always is, around who owns each control across the provider-customer line.

Look at what just happened. Six frameworks, six vocabularies, as many levels of granularity, one clause here, a whole family there, a handful of criteria, two requirements, two controls, a cloud domain, and a single outcome category framing them all from above, and every one of them is describing the same thing you do. You do not run six access-management programs. You run one, and six frameworks each recognize it in their own dialect.

That is the thesis made concrete: implement the control once, maintain governed evidence sources for the scopes in which it operates, and point all six framework references at it. Reuse an artifact where control, scope, period, and assertion match; collect scope-specific evidence where they do not. Improve your access reviews and you improve your standing against ISO, 800-53, SOC 2, PCI, CIS, and CSA CCM simultaneously, and against the CSF outcome they all sit beneath, because their core intent overlaps even where scope and proof differ.

The one thing you must not do is build six access controls (one for ISO, another for PCI, another for SOC 2, and so on) which is precisely the sprawl this whole part exists to kill. One access-management family, with real controls beneath it (provisioning and approval, access review, privileged access, multi-factor authentication, deprovisioning on termination, service-account management, and so on), and every framework points into it. The control statement is shared. What differs, and this is the hinge the rest of the chapter turns on, is the evidence, because evidence is where scope lives.

Scope Tags: The Trick That Keeps Mapping Honest

Here is a small, practical technique that does an outsized amount of work, and it is the thing that turns “check the scope” from good advice into something you can actually operate. Give each control a set of scope tags, plain labels for where it actually reaches: enterprise-wide, production, cloud, SaaS, payment environment (the cardholder data environment, or CDE), personal data, customer data, critical service, AI system, privileged access, third-party, sub-processor, region-specific, customer-specific. Then, when you map a requirement, you do not just ask whether a control’s intent covers it; you check whether the control’s tags cover the scope the requirement demands.

The payoff is that overclaiming becomes visible instead of invisible. An access-review control tagged production but not SaaS is honestly partial against a cloud-assurance requirement that means the SaaS admin consoles. A vulnerability control tagged infrastructure but not application does not fully satisfy an application-security requirement. A vendor control tagged direct vendors but not sub-processors is partial against a privacy requirement that reaches down the chain. A backup control tagged systems but not business service is partial against a resilience obligation.

An access control tagged enterprise but not CDE is partial against PCI. The tags turn the vague instinct “does the scope match?” into a mechanical check anyone can run, and they pay off beyond audits, because now you can ask your own universe useful questions: which controls touch payment? which touch customer data? which touch AI? which support this specific customer commitment? That last capability is when the control universe stops being a compliance artifact and starts being a management tool.

And it directly answers the evidence problem, because one control statement can be shared while its evidence must be scope-specific.

The enterprise access review may satisfy ISO broadly; the SOC 2 version must cover the system in the report's scope; the PCI version must cover the cardholder data environment; the cloud version must reach tenant admins and federated identities. One control, several evidence sets, each proving a different scope. Share the control freely; never share a single evidence file across scopes without checking that it actually covers each one. That check is the entire difference between mapping and wishful thinking.

The Common Core, and Why It's So Large

Step back from individual controls and the shape of the whole comes clear: the great majority of what these frameworks require is shared. Strip them to intent and a common core emerges that any of them would recognize, know your assets, control access, authenticate strongly, protect data, manage vulnerabilities, log and monitor, respond to incidents, recover from disruption, manage your vendors, train your people, govern it all with policy and accountability. Your whole control universe is really about fifteen domains like these, and the six frameworks are, to a striking degree, the same territory surveyed by different mapmakers: ISO's 93 controls, 800-53's twenty families, CIS's eighteen controls, PCI's twelve requirements, SOC 2's common criteria, and CSF's six functions.

This is why the leverage is real and not theoretical. When most of six frameworks collapses onto one shared core, a control you build in that core satisfies the corresponding requirement in every framework at once, the multiplier that makes the whole approach worth the effort. It is also why the published crosswalks between these frameworks exist and largely agree: they are all tracing the same underlying shape. (Those official crosswalks are a genuine head start, treat them as a first draft to verify against your own controls, not gospel to paste in, for reasons the honesty section will make clear.)

Where They Genuinely Diverge — the Sharp Edges

If the story were only convergence, this chapter could be one page. The reason it is not is that the divergences are real, and they are exactly the parts you cannot afford to smooth away. Four kinds of difference matter.

The first is scope, and PCI DSS is the standing example. Its intent overlaps almost entirely with the others, access, logging, encryption, vulnerability management, nothing unfamiliar, but it demands all of it specifically within the cardholder data environment, in prescriptive detail, with defined testing. A control that satisfies ISO and SOC 2 enterprise-wide can still fall short of PCI if it does not reach every system in payment scope.

This is why PCI mapping has to start with scope, where card data is stored, processed, or transmitted, and what connects to it before any control claim means anything. Enterprise MFA exists, yes; does it cover every access path into the payment environment? Same intent, non-negotiable scope. Map PCI by intent alone and you will overclaim; map it by scope and it stays honest.

The second is depth, and 800-53 is the example. It goes deeper by design. Its controls carry enhancements specifying things the mid-altitude frameworks leave general. A single control of yours might fully satisfy ISO's version of a requirement and only partially satisfy 800-53's, because 800-53 asked for three specific things and your control does two. That is not a flaw in your mapping; it is the depth difference showing up honestly, and it is why a program built for ISO or SOC 2 often carries genuine partials against 800-53.

The third is the assurance dimension, which a SOC 2 Type II report makes explicit. Frameworks and standards define control expectations at different altitudes, and their associated assessments can also require evidence of design, implementation, and operation. A SOC 2 Type II examination specifically addresses whether controls operated effectively over a defined period for the system described in the report. A control can map cleanly to a Trust Services criterion in intent and still fail that test if you cannot show it operated across the review window for the in-scope system. The criterion is not necessarily harder in what it asks; the report is more explicit about what must be proved over time.

The fourth is altitude mismatch, which is CSF's contribution. Because CSF describes outcomes, it does not map one-to-one with anything, a single category like "Identity Management, Authentication, and Access Control" sits above a whole cluster of your actual controls. That is not a problem to fix; it is the nature of an outcome framework, and it makes CSF excellent for organizing and communicating coverage at the top and a poor choice for line-by-line mapping.

The right way to hold these sharp edges is not to blunt them into a lowest-common-denominator control, but to keep one base control and hang scope-specific overlays off it. One incident-notification control. Notification decisions are made per legal, privacy, contractual, and regulatory obligations, with an overlay for the customer contract that demands notification within 24 hours of confirmed impact, an overlay for PCI-specific payment escalation, an overlay for the privacy breach-assessment path. The base stays single; the sharp edges live as explicit obligations attached to scope. That is how a unified model stays unified without dissolving into the mush of the average. Unity, not dilution.

Reading a Crosswalk Honestly

Which brings us back to the warning that governs this whole part, now that you have seen a real crosswalk: mapping is not compliance. A line from a requirement to one of your controls records that the control is relevant, not that it is adequate or operating. A chapter full of clean correlations is exactly the kind of thing that lulls people into believing the coverage is done. It is not. The crosswalk tells you which control should answer a requirement; it is the control's own evidence, at the right scope, that tells you it actually does.

Two practical cautions follow. First, the published crosswalks are a real gift and a real trap. Use them. They save enormous time and they are made by people who know the frameworks intimately. But they map framework-to-framework in the abstract, not framework-to-your-controls, and they cannot know your scope. A published mapping saying ISO 5.15 corresponds to a particular 800-53 control is true in general and silent on whether your access implementation covers your payment environment. Treat the crosswalk as the first draft of your mapping, then run each line through the two honest questions against your actual controls.

Second, watch your evidence assertions, because vague evidence makes vague mappings. "We back up our systems" is not the same claim as "we tested that we can restore them" — a backup-success report proves the jobs ran, not that a restore works, and a framework asking for recovery capability is not satisfied by proof that backups completed. Name what each piece of evidence actually asserts, and the partials reveal themselves honestly; at this stage, it is enough to know that scope-vague evidence is how a green cell lies.

The Frameworks Underneath the Control Universe

The cast of this chapter is, unusually, the whole point of it, so rather than reintroduce them, it is worth closing on their distinct roles and on what this part still owes you. ISO gives breadth and management-system alignment; 800-53 gives depth on demand; SOC 2 gives service-organization assurance with its operating-effectiveness bar; PCI gives payment-environment scope discipline; CIS gives prioritized, practical safeguards and a place for a lean team to start; and the CSA Cloud Controls Matrix gives cloud-specific, shared-responsibility structure. Together they do not create six programs. They create one control universe seen through six lenses, and the CISO's job is to keep the common core shared, the sharp edges preserved, and the evidence honest.

Two things sit deliberately just outside this chapter. Cloud is one: the CSA matrix belongs to the same exercise, but the shared-responsibility split it forces is a discipline of its own. Cloud logging is the clean illustration of that split. Platform logging may be covered by the provider's own assurance, while enabling, configuring, exporting, and retaining tenant logs is your evidence to produce; the provider is certified for their half of the line, and you still owe proof of yours. "The provider is certified" is evidence for their side, never a substitute for yours.

And the overlays that are not classic control frameworks at all, privacy and data-protection regimes, AI governance, sector regulation, map by the same intent-and-scope method but carry obligations that reach past security controls into lawful processing, individual rights, model governance, and hard regulatory deadlines. Folding those in honestly, without letting a security control pretend to satisfy a privacy or AI obligation it only half touches, deserves its own chapter, which is exactly where we go next.

Industry Pattern — Six Frameworks, One Weak Control

An organization finds itself preparing for several assurance needs at once, an ISO surveillance audit, SOC 2 readiness, a PCI review, a large customer's security assessment, and an internal audit, and each one has its own tracker, its own owner, its own deadline. Then the same topic shows up on all of them. Vulnerability management.

The ISO tracker asks whether technical vulnerabilities are managed. The SOC 2 tracker wants evidence that vulnerabilities affecting the service are found and remediated. The PCI tracker wants scan and remediation evidence for the payment environment. The customer asks whether critical vulnerabilities are fixed within a defined timeframe. Internal audit asks whether remediation tickets close on time. Five requests, five formats, five owners chasing them separately, and underneath, one control. When someone finally lays the five side by side, the real picture appears: scanning exists, tickets exist, some remediation happens, but asset coverage is incomplete, exceptions are informal, and the timeliness reporting is inconsistent. Each framework was asking a slightly different question, and all five were pointing at the same weak control.

That discovery changes the whole conversation. Instead of answering five audit requests as five separate scrambles, the organization improves the vulnerability-management control itself, asset coverage, scan scope, remediation timelines, exception approval, reporting, evidence, and the single improvement satisfies all five obligations at once. The lesson is not only that a unified mapping reduces duplicate work, real as that saving is. It is that the mapping tells you which controls matter most, the ones a whole crowd of obligations quietly depend on. A weak control that carries six frameworks and three customer commitments is worth more of your attention than ten strong controls that each carry one. That is where the mapping stops being compliance overhead and starts directing where a stretched security leader should actually spend.

What Evidence Should You Expect

The evidence at this stage is about whether the frameworks the organization is subject to have actually been related to its own controls, mapped into the single control universe, rather than run as separate worlds or declared covered from a downloaded table. At leadership altitude, a CISO should be able to show each in-scope framework mapped to internal controls by intent and scope, with full, partial, not-covered, and not-applicable recorded honestly rather than a wall of borrowed green; scope tags that make overclaiming visible; and evidence that the divergences were seen and handled, PCI's scope checked rather than assumed, 800-53's depth allowed to produce honest partials, SOC 2's operating-effectiveness demand distinguished from mere design, CSF used at its outcome altitude, and CSA's provider-versus-customer responsibility split made explicit.

Where published crosswalks were used, there should be evidence they were verified against the organization's actual controls, not simply adopted. The strongest warning sign is a mapping across six frameworks showing no partials and no scope-driven gaps; it almost certainly mapped framework-to-framework from a table rather than framework-to-reality against the controls.

For a small or mid-sized organization, the practical minimum keeps this achievable:

- Build one internal control universe and map only the frameworks you are actually subject to now, do not map a framework you are not using yet unless there is a clear business need for it in the next twelve to eighteen months. Map using intent and scope, and let one control legitimately satisfy the corresponding requirement across all of them at once.
- Keep scope tags (payment/CDE, cloud, customer data, personal data, critical service, AI, sub-processor) on your controls, and check the tag against the requirement's scope before you call anything covered.
- Record full, partial, not covered, and not applicable honestly; where an alternative is permitted, record the compensating control as a separate approved treatment rather than as

ordinary coverage, and reuse an evidence file across scopes only when it actually covers each one.

- Treat PCI (and anything similarly scoped) as a scope check every time, and use published crosswalks as a head start you then verify line by line against your own controls.
- Identify the few controls that carry the most obligations, and fix those first, that is where a stretched team gets the most assurance per unit of effort.

That is not an enterprise crosswalk function. It is enough to make the frameworks resolve into one program you actually run, with the sharp edges flagged rather than lost.

Reality Check

Pick one control family, access management, vulnerability management, logging, incident response, vendor risk, or backup and recovery, and interrogate it from the control side out.

Which frameworks map to it, and which requirements are fully covered, which partial, which not applicable? Which scope tags does it carry, and which does it lack, is it tagged for production but not SaaS, for infrastructure but not applications, for direct vendors but not sub-processors, for the enterprise but not the CDE? Which evidence proves it, and does that evidence actually cover each scope you are claiming, or is one file quietly standing in for several? Which framework has the sharpest requirement on it, and which customer commitment depends on it?

And the question that turns this from an audit into a strategy: if this one control is weak, how many obligations does its weakness touch? If you can trace one real control out to its several framework homes and answer those honestly, you are reading your coverage from the control side, which is the honest direction. If you can only go the other way, from a framework requirement to a control you are not sure operates at the right scope, then the frameworks are mapped somewhere, but not yet operating through one control universe.

What This Means for You as a Security Leader

This is where the promise stops being an argument and becomes something you can see: six frameworks, genuinely different in altitude and audience and detail, resolving onto one set of controls you actually run. The move it asks of you is a change of direction more than a change of effort. Stop thinking framework-out: "what does ISO want, what does PCI want, what does SOC 2 want," as three questions with three answers, and start thinking control-out: "here is what we do about access, and here is every framework that recognizes it." The first direction multiplies your work by the number of frameworks. The second divides it, because one good control answers all of them at once.

Hold two truths in balance, because the whole chapter lives in the tension between them. The convergence is real and it is your leverage: most of what these frameworks ask for is the same shared core, and building that core well pays out across every framework simultaneously. But the divergences are real too, and they are where the danger hides: PCI's scope, 800-53's depth, SOC 2's demand for operating evidence, CSF's outcome altitude, cloud's shared-responsibility split. A leader who sees only the convergence overclaims and gets caught; one who sees only the divergence rebuilds the same program six times and burns out the team. The skill is holding both, mapping the common core efficiently and flagging the sharp edges explicitly, which is exactly what honest intent-and-scope mapping produces.

And here is the real prize, the thing that lifts this above compliance housekeeping. A good unified mapping does not show everything green; it shows the truth clearly, and the truth is control intelligence. It tells you which handful of controls carry most of your assurance burden, which gaps block SOC 2 or fail PCI, which controls a customer commitment leans on, which weak control, if you fixed it, would strengthen your standing against six frameworks and three contracts at once.

A weak security leader reports, “we mapped ISO, SOC 2, PCI, CIS, NIST, and cloud.” A strong one says, “these ten control families carry most of our assurance; these four are solid, these three are partial by scope, these two gaps affect multiple obligations, and here’s the investment that fixes the most at once.” The first is spreadsheet compliance. The second is a CISO conversation, and it is the one this whole part was built to let you have.

Bridge to Chapter 19

The operating model now has to absorb obligations that are not security controls: privacy, AI governance, and sector regulation.

CHAPTER 19

Integrating Privacy, AI Governance, and Sector Regulation

The security frameworks fold in cleanly. These do not, because they are not only asking for security.

The unified model works cleanly for security frameworks because, despite their differences in altitude and detail, they are all describing security controls. Access is access whether ISO or PCI or CIS is asking. Privacy, AI governance, and sector regulation do not resolve so neatly, because they ask for more than security.

This chapter is about the obligations that do not play so nicely, and it is important precisely because they are the ones most likely to trip a modern CISO, since they have arrived fastest and they behave least like the security frameworks you already know. Three of them dominate the title of this chapter: privacy and data-protection regimes, AI governance, and sector-specific regulation. Two more travel with them, operational resilience and the commitments in your customer contracts, and they fold in by the very same logic, so they belong in the conversation too.

Every one of these maps into the control universe by the same intent-and-scope method as everything else, and a good chunk of each genuinely is security controls you have already built. But each also carries obligations that are not security controls at all, legal duties, process obligations, governance requirements, hard regulatory deadlines with named owners, and no security control, however well built, satisfies those. The whole discipline of this chapter is folding these overlays into your one operating model honestly: mapping the parts that are genuinely controls, and refusing to let a security control pretend to satisfy an obligation it only half touches.

Get that discipline right and these overlays become a manageable extension of the universe you have already built. Get it wrong, usually by mapping a legal or process obligation onto a security control that sounds similar, and you build exactly the false confidence this whole part has been warning against, except now the false green cell has a regulator or a data-protection authority behind it rather than an auditor. The stakes on these particular sharp edges are higher, which is the reason they get their own chapter.

Why These Overlays Don't Fold in Cleanly

Start with the thing that makes privacy, AI, and sector regulation different in kind from the security frameworks, because it is the insight the whole chapter rests on. A security framework asks: is this control in place and operating? Access control, encryption, logging. These are things you do, and a control either exists and works or it does not. Privacy, AI governance, and sector regulation ask that question too, for their security-shaped parts, but they also ask questions that no control can answer, because they are not about controls at all.

They ask whether you have a lawful basis to process personal data, a legal question, not a security one. Whether a person can exercise their right to see, correct, or delete their data, a process obligation, not a control. Whether a human meaningfully oversees an AI system's decisions, a governance requirement. Whether you reported an incident to a regulator within a defined number of hours, a deadline with legal force. Whether the right named person is accountable, with the right independence, an organizational-structure requirement. You can have flawless security controls and still fail every one of these, because they are asking about lawfulness, rights, oversight, timeliness, and accountability, not about whether your controls are switched on.

This is why the trap here is so easy to fall into and so costly. A security control can support these obligations, encryption supports privacy, access control supports data-subject rights, your incident process supports regulatory reporting, but supporting is not satisfying.

The honest model keeps two things clearly separate: the parts of these overlays that are genuinely security controls, which map into your control universe like every other control, and the parts that are legal, process, or governance obligations, which have to be tracked as obligations in their own right, with their own owners and their own evidence, sitting alongside the controls rather than hiding inside them. Blur those two and you will report a privacy program that is really just a security program wearing a privacy label, which is fine until the day someone asks for the thing security never covered.

Privacy: Where It Maps, and Where It Doesn't

Privacy is the clearest illustration because so much of it genuinely is security, which is exactly what makes the non-security parts so easy to lose. Data-protection regimes, the European GDPR, India's emerging Digital Personal Data Protection (DPDP) regime, and the many others Volume III's privacy Part covers in depth, lean heavily on security controls you already run, and those parts fold into the control universe with no trouble at all.

The requirement to protect personal data with appropriate security maps straight onto your access, encryption, and monitoring controls. The requirement to delete data you no longer need maps onto your retention and disposal control. The requirement to manage the processors and sub-processors who handle personal data maps onto your vendor and third-party controls. The breach-security parts map onto your incident response. If privacy were only these, it would fold in as cleanly as PCI.

But privacy carries a second category of obligation that no security control touches, and this is the part that gets lost when people treat privacy as "security for personal data." You can encrypt personal data you had no lawful basis to collect, restrict access beautifully to data you should never have retained, and securely transfer data across a border you had no legal mechanism to cross, strong security sitting on top of a privacy failure it does nothing to fix.

You need a lawful basis to process personal data in the first place — GDPR Article 6 sets out the grounds — and no encryption or access control supplies one; lawfulness is a legal determination made before a single security control is relevant. You have to honor data-subject rights: a person's ability to request access to their data, correct it, delete it, or have it ported elsewhere, each of which is a process you must be able to run on demand, not a control you switch on. You have to maintain records of processing, documentation of what personal data you hold, why, and where it goes.

You need data-processing agreements with your processors, and lawful cross-border transfer mechanisms when personal data crosses jurisdictions. You may need a data protection impact assessment before a risky processing activity and, under GDPR Article 37 in defined circumstances, a data protection officer. And breach handling carries a legal obligation stacked on the security one: GDPR's requirement to notify the supervisory authority without undue delay and, where feasible, not later than 72 hours after becoming aware of a personal-data breach. Your incident-response control detects and contains the breach; it does not, by itself, discharge the legal duty to assess and report it on that clock.

There is a tell in the evidence, too, that reveals whether privacy was really integrated or just relabeled: privacy evidence looks different from security evidence. Security evidence is logs, tickets, scans, access reviews, incident records. Privacy evidence is records of processing, privacy notices, consent records, data maps, data-processing agreements, sub-processor lists, data-subject-request logs, retention schedules, transfer assessments, breach-assessment memos. If your "privacy program" produces only security-shaped evidence, it is not holding the privacy-native obligations, the shape of the evidence gives it away.

So the discipline for privacy is to fold it in as two connected pieces, not one: the security-shaped requirements map onto controls you already run (full reuse, exactly the leverage this part promised), and the legal-and-process obligations, lawful basis, rights handling, records of processing, DPAs, transfer mechanisms, DPIAs, the reporting clock, the accountable role, become tracked obligations with owners who are usually not you: legal, the privacy office, the DPO. Both live in the same operating model, connected where they touch, but never collapsed into each other. What belongs here is the folding-in discipline: map the controls, track the obligations, and never let the first stand in for the second.

AI Governance: The Newest Overlay, and the Easiest to Fake

AI governance is the youngest of these overlays and the one where the map-a-control-and-call-it-done trap is most tempting, because "we secured the AI system" sounds so much like "we governed the AI system" that the two are easy to conflate, and they are not the same thing at all.

The security-shaped parts map in cleanly, as you would expect by now. The AI system needs access control, logging, data protection, and secure configuration like any other system; the model providers and AI vendors behind it need third-party management like any other vendor chain; the training and prompt data need data governance; model pipelines need change control. All of that folds into your control universe with no special handling. If AI governance were only "secure the AI like you'd secure anything else," it would need no chapter.

But AI governance asks for a set of things that are governance, not security, and that your best security controls do nothing to provide. It starts with a question security never asks: do you even know where AI is used? An AI inventory, every system and model in use, including the ones a business team quietly switched on inside a SaaS tool, is the foundation, because you cannot govern what you have not found, and shadow AI is now what shadow IT was a decade ago.

From there it asks for human oversight of consequential automated decisions rather than a model deciding unchecked; transparency and explainability, can you explain, to a person affected or a regulator asking, how a decision was reached; impact assessment, have you evaluated what this system could do to the people subject to it, including bias and fairness, before deploying it; and in some regimes, rights for people subject to automated decisions.

The emerging frameworks organize exactly this territory: the NIST AI Risk Management Framework structures it into four functions, Govern, Map, Measure, and Manage; ISO/IEC 42001 defines an AI management system, the governance wrapper around AI much as an ISMS wraps security; and the EU AI Act takes a risk-tiered approach, sorting AI uses into prohibited (unacceptable-risk) practices, high-risk systems that carry substantial obligations, limited-risk uses that mainly owe transparency, and minimal-risk uses that mostly fall outside the heavy obligation set, with the weight of the requirements landing on the high-risk tier. Here they matter as the sources of obligations that fold in alongside your AI security controls.

The honest test for AI governance is a single blunt question: could you secure an AI system perfectly and still be governing it terribly? Absolutely, a model can be locked down, encrypted, access-controlled, and beautifully logged while making biased, unexplainable, unsupervised decisions that no one inventoried and no human reviews. Security is necessary and nowhere near sufficient. And this is the overlay where ownership scatters most, which is exactly why it fails most: the business owns the use case and its outcome, product owns the feature's behavior, the data owners own whether the data was suitable and permitted, engineering or data science owns model implementation and monitoring, security owns access and threat and secure integration, privacy and legal own personal-data impact and regulatory interpretation, and risk owns the assessment method and evidence.

That looks complicated because AI is complicated; the answer is not to pretend it is simple by assigning it all to security, it is to make the ownership explicit. AI folds in the same two-piece way privacy does, security-shaped parts onto controls, governance obligations into the register, but with the added discipline that the obligations have owners scattered across the business, and the control universe's job is to make that scatter visible rather than to absorb it into security.

Sector Regulation: The Sharpest Edges of All

Sector regulation, the rules that bind financial services, insurance, healthcare, critical infrastructure, and other regulated industries, produces the least control-shaped obligations of the three, and therefore the ones most dangerous to map casually onto security controls. Where a voluntary framework says "have an incident response process," a sector regulator says "report this type of incident to this authority within this timeframe, using this channel, with this information, and inform the board."

Where a framework says "manage third-party risk," a regulator says "classify your critical providers, keep an outsourcing register, secure audit and access rights, test your exit plans, and notify us of material arrangements." The regulator's version has hard edges the framework's does not: a named accountable role, a specific deadline, a mandatory report, a board approval, an independent assessment, a defined cadence.

Consider the shapes these take, because they are genuinely different from a control. They set hard reporting deadlines: guidelines from the Insurance Regulatory and Development Authority of India (IRDAI) require insurers to report cyber incidents to the national computer emergency response team, CERT-In, within six hours of noticing the incident or being brought to notice about it, and the EU's DORA regime requires reporting major ICT-related incidents to competent authorities on defined, phased timelines. A six-hour reporting clock is not a security control. It is a legal deadline your incident process must be built to meet, and missing it is a compliance failure even if your security handled the incident flawlessly.

They mandate named accountabilities and independence: that a CISO exist, sit at a defined level, and have structural independence from the functions they oversee, an organizational-structure obligation no control satisfies. They prescribe specific cadences: vulnerability assessments and penetration tests at defined frequencies, risk-committee meetings on a set rhythm, board-level reporting. They demand resilience testing of particular kinds. DORA, for example, requires digital operational resilience testing, including threat-led penetration testing for the more significant financial entities that meet its criteria. And they extend oversight to critical third parties, DORA's regime for critical ICT third-party providers reaches past your walls into your providers' governance.

These fold into the operating model, but mostly as obligations with dates and owners rather than as controls. Your vulnerability assessment and penetration testing (VAPT) control might already run penetration tests, but the sector obligation adds a required frequency and scope the control must meet — and that the organization must evidence. Your incident process might already notify people, but the obligation adds a specific regulator, a specific clock, and a specific report format. Your governance already has a security leader, but the obligation adds independence and reporting-line requirements about structure, not control operation.

Mapping these means recording the obligation, attaching it to the control or process that must satisfy it, noting the deadline and cadence and named owner, and holding the evidence that you actually met the timeline, not just that the underlying capability exists. The specific regimes, DORA in Europe, India's SEBI, RBI, and IRDAI frameworks across securities, banking, and insurance, Saudi Arabia's SAMA framework, and the rest, are Volume III, Part 3's subject in depth; here they are the archetype of the obligation that has a date attached, and the reason your operating model needs somewhere to put dates.

The Other Overlays Fold in the Same Way

Two more obligation sources travel with the title's three, and naming them matters because they fold in by the identical logic and are just as easily flattened. The first is operational resilience, which overlaps security but is not the same thing, and the classic mistake is mapping it to backup. Backup and disaster recovery answer "can we restore systems and data?" Resilience answers a harder question: "can the organization keep delivering an important service through disruption?"

A database restore can pass while the business service still fails because the payment provider is down, the identity provider is offline, or the manual workaround was never trained. Resilience carries obligations a backup control never touches, identifying your critical services, mapping their dependencies, setting impact tolerances, testing severe-but-plausible scenarios, planning around third-party outages, running crisis communication, and those fold in as tracked obligations, connected to your security and vendor and continuity controls but not satisfied by any of them. Here, resilience is another overlay that a control-shaped mind will quietly shrink to "we have backups."

The second is customer commitments, which are obligations that behave like regulation without being law. A customer contract can require breach notification within a defined window, quarterly security reporting, data residency in a named region, sub-processor approval rights, a specific vulnerability-remediation timeline, or restrictions on AI use, and these accumulate, one deal at a time, into a hidden library of promises nobody tracks.

They belong in the same place every other obligation does: recorded with their source (which customer, which contract), their scope, their owner, the control or process that satisfies them, and their deadline. A commitment that lives only in a signed contract and a sales email is a commitment you will breach without knowing it existed. Fold it into the operating model, or it is not in the operating model at all.

The Obligation Register: How Overlays Actually Fold In

By now the mechanism has revealed itself, and it is a natural extension of the overlay idea. Your control universe holds the controls, the things you do, mapped to every framework that recognizes them. Alongside it, connected to it, you need a second structure that holds the obligations that are not controls: an obligation register.

Think of every law, regulation, contract, customer requirement, and internal policy as an obligation source. Something that creates a thing you must do. The register is the honest home for everything those sources demand that a control cannot satisfy. Each entry is an obligation, maintain a lawful basis for this processing; run a data-subject access request within the legal timeframe; report a major incident to this regulator within this many hours; keep a model inventory; ensure human oversight of this automated decision; run threat-led resilience testing at this cadence; meet this customer's 24-hour notification clause.

And each entry carries what makes it real: the scope it applies to (this jurisdiction, this personal-data processing, this AI system, this regulated entity, this customer), the owner accountable for it, very often legal, privacy, or compliance rather than security, the deadline or cadence where one exists, the control or process it connects to, and the evidence that it is actually being met. The obligation register is not a silo standing apart from the control universe; it is connected to it, by the mapped controls that support each obligation, the shared evidence, the owners, and the gaps, so the two read as one model: your breach-response control links to your breach-reporting obligation; your access control links to your data-subject-access obligation; your penetration-testing control links to your sector-mandated testing-cadence obligation.

The reason this matters is that it is the only structure that keeps the non-control obligations from vanishing. Controls have owners and get tested; obligations, if they are not tracked somewhere deliberate, quietly become nobody's job, and a lawful-basis gap or a missed reporting deadline surfaces not at an audit but at a data-protection authority or a sector regulator, which is a far more expensive place to discover it.

The obligation register is where "we fold privacy, AI, and sector regulation into one operating model" stops being a slogan and becomes a thing you can point at. (How obligations, controls, and evidence chain together into a single traceable line of assurance is the next chapter's subject; here the point is simply that the obligations need a home of their own, distinct from the controls but connected to them, or they get lost.)

The Trap: When a Control Pretends to Be an Obligation

It is worth naming the specific failure this chapter exists to prevent, sharply, because it is the false-equivalence trap wearing its most dangerous clothes. The trap is mapping a legal, process, or governance obligation onto a security control that merely sounds related, marking it covered, and moving on, and it is dangerous here precisely because the security control is often genuinely excellent, which makes the false claim feel true. Four bad mappings recur so reliably they are worth naming as a set.

Privacy equals encryption. Encryption supports privacy, but privacy is lawful basis, notice, rights, retention, transfer, and purpose, and none of those is satisfied by a cipher, however strong. AI equals secure development. Secure development supports AI, but AI governance is use-case approval, data suitability, model monitoring, human oversight, transparency, and decision accountability, a secured model with no inventory and no oversight is governed by nothing. Resilience equals backup. Backup supports resilience, but resilience is critical-service continuity, dependency mapping, third-party-outage planning, and crisis response, a passing restore test is not a service that survives disruption.

And regulatory reporting equals incident response. Detecting and containing an incident supports the reporting obligation, but assessing reportability and notifying a regulator within a legal window is a separate duty on a separate clock, a program that stops at the security response sails past the deadline while feeling fully covered. In every case a real, working, well-built control is quietly asked to stand in for an obligation it structurally cannot satisfy, and the green cell that results is a lie with legal consequences.

These bad mappings happen for an understandable reason: security teams map what they know. That is not a character flaw, it is a default, which is why the defense has to be deliberate. When you map an overlay requirement, ask not just “does a control’s intent cover this?” but “is this even a control-shaped requirement at all — or is it a legal, process, or governance obligation that a control can support but never satisfy?” If it is the latter, it does not belong marked covered by a control; it belongs in the obligation register, with its own owner and evidence, and with links to any controls that support it without pretending to satisfy it. The skill this chapter teaches is, more than anything, the ability to tell a control from an obligation, and to route each to the place that can actually hold it.

Crossing Borders: The Same Overlay, a Different Country

This is where the whole discipline pays off in the way that matters most to a security leader whose organization is growing across borders, or who is looking to work in a new market, or who simply has customers bound by their own countries' laws, and it is the moment the unified model earns its keep for anyone whose compliance world is not confined to one jurisdiction.

Here is the thing that makes it manageable. When you expand into a new country, or take on a customer governed by an unfamiliar regime, you are not starting over. The security-shaped core of that country's privacy law, its sector regulation, its AI rules is largely the same core you already run, access control, encryption, breach response, vendor management, the whole common core, which is why it is so heavily shared across jurisdictions. What changes, and what you actually have to work through, is the delta: the specific obligations that country's regimes add on top of the shared core.

A different privacy regime grants a different set of data-subject rights, sets a different breach-reporting clock, imposes different cross-border-transfer rules, and names accountability differently, India's DPDP regime and Europe's GDPR share an enormous amount of security substance while differing in exactly these specific obligations. A different financial regulator sets its own reporting deadlines, its own testing cadences, its own governance requirements, DORA, SAMA, and India's sector regulators all want operational resilience, and each wants it reported and tested and governed on its own terms. The names change; the themes repeat.

Entering a new compliance world is a mapping exercise. Do not stand up an isolated "Country X compliance program" unless the scope genuinely demands it. Confirm applicability with legal (the one step a CISO must not decide alone, because whether a regime applies is a legal call), extract the obligations, map the security-shaped ones onto controls you already run (most will already be covered; record the genuine deltas as gaps), and add the non-control obligations to your register, each with its jurisdiction as its scope, its deadline, and its owner.

What could feel like a terrifying wall of foreign regulation resolves into a manageable set of specific additions to a model you already operate. This is the concrete form of one of this book's central promises: the CISO who has built a real control universe and a real obligation register can walk into a new country's requirements and see, quickly, what they already cover and what they genuinely need to add, rather than facing every new jurisdiction as a program to build from scratch. Many frameworks, many jurisdictions, one operating model.

The Frameworks Underneath Privacy, AI, and Sector Regulation

Because this chapter deliberately points outward to the parts that teach these regimes in depth, the frameworks appear here as the overlays that fold in rather than as subjects to master; source-dependent details are pinned to the versions verified for this book, while the treatment remains conceptual where the depth belongs elsewhere.

On privacy, the European GDPR is the reference model for much of the world, with its lawful-basis requirement, its data-subject rights, its records-of-processing and DPIA obligations, its data protection officer role where circumstances require one, and its 72-hour supervisory-authority breach-notification clock; India's DPDP regime is the fast-emerging example of a major new market's data-protection law; and ISO/IEC 27701:2025 specifies requirements and provides guidance for a privacy information management system that can stand alone or align with ISO/IEC 27001, a useful example of integration without making privacy merely an extension of security. On AI, the NIST AI Risk Management Framework (Govern, Map, Measure, Manage) gives a voluntary structure for AI risk, ISO/IEC 42001 defines a certifiable AI management system, and the EU AI Act brings risk-tiered legal obligations from prohibited practices through high-risk systems to transparency and minimal-risk uses.

On sector regulation and resilience, Europe's DORA sets ICT risk, incident-reporting, resilience-testing, and critical-third-party obligations for financial entities; India's SEBI, RBI, and IRDAI frameworks bind securities, banking, and insurance respectively, IRDAI's six-hour incident-reporting requirement being a sharp example of the deadline-shaped obligation; and Saudi Arabia's

SAMA framework governs its financial sector. What this chapter adds is the discipline that lets all of them — including the ones that were never only about security — fold into the one operating model without any of them pretending to be a security control it is not.

Industry Pattern — The Privacy Program That Was Really a Security Program

An organization decides, sensibly, that it needs a privacy program, and hands the job to a capable security team because privacy is about protecting personal data, and protecting data is what security does. The team does genuinely good work: personal data is encrypted, access to it is tightly controlled, it is included in the monitoring, retention rules are set, and the vendors who touch it are assessed. On a security questionnaire, the privacy posture looks strong, and everyone reasonably concludes the privacy program is in good shape.

Then a real privacy demand arrives that is not a security question. A person exercises their right and asks for a copy of all the personal data the organization holds about them, and there is no process to find it, assemble it, and provide it within the legal timeframe, because the program was built to keep data safe, not to hand it over on request. Or a regulator asks on what lawful basis a particular processing activity rests, and the honest answer is that nobody ever established one, because the security team was never asked to and it is not a security question.

Or a personal-data breach occurs and the security response is textbook (contained fast, cleaned up well) but the separate legal duty to assess and notify the authority within the required window slips, because the incident process was built around security recovery, not regulatory reporting. The controls were all there. The obligations were nowhere, because the program had quietly mapped every privacy requirement onto a security control and never noticed that the most important privacy requirements are not security controls at all.

The lesson is not that the security work was wrong. It was excellent, and privacy genuinely needs it. It is that privacy is two connected things, and the organization built only one of them. The security-shaped half was strong; the legal-and-process half (lawful basis, rights handling, records, the reporting clock) had no owner because it had been invisibly folded into controls that could not hold it.

> *A privacy program is not a security program with a privacy label. It is a security program and an obligation program, and the second half is exactly the part a control-shaped mind forgets to build. The same story, with different nouns, waits for any organization that treats AI governance as "secure the model," resilience as "we have backups," or sector compliance as "we have the controls." The controls are necessary. They were never the whole obligation.*

What Evidence Should You Expect

The evidence at this stage is about whether the overlays have been folded in honestly, the security-shaped parts mapped to controls, and the legal, process, and governance obligations tracked as obligations in their own right rather than quietly absorbed into controls that cannot satisfy them.

At leadership altitude, a CISO should be able to show that privacy, AI governance, sector regulation, resilience, and customer commitments each fold into the one operating model with that separation intact: the control-shaped requirements reusing the control universe, and a distinct obligation register holding what the controls cannot, lawful basis and data-subject-rights processes and reporting clocks for privacy, model inventory and human oversight and impact assessments for AI, named accountabilities and reporting deadlines and testing cadences for sector regulation, critical-service and dependency work for resilience, and the tracked commitments from customer contracts. Just as telling is who owns what: obligations correctly assigned to legal, privacy, compliance, product, or the business where they belong, rather than dumped on security because security happened to build the adjacent control.

And for anything with a deadline, a breach-reporting clock, a testing cadence, a contractual window, there should be evidence the timeline was met, not merely that the underlying capability exists. The mature tell here is an organization that can point to the seam clearly: here are our controls, here are our obligations, here is where they connect, and here is the owner of each, rather than one that shows a wall of green and, asked about lawful basis or the reporting clock or the model inventory, discovers those questions were never really answered.

For a small or mid-sized organization, the practical minimum keeps this achievable:

- Fold the security-shaped parts of privacy, AI, sector regulation, resilience, and customer commitments onto controls you already run, do not rebuild; reuse.
- Keep one simple obligation register for the parts that are not controls, lawful basis, data-subject rights, breach-reporting clocks, model inventory, human oversight, named accountabilities, mandated testing cadences, customer commitments, each with a scope, an owner, and a deadline where one exists, connected back to the controls that support it.
- Put obligations with the right owner, legal, privacy, or compliance for the legal and process ones; product and the business for AI use-case accountability, rather than assuming security owns everything it built a control near.
- For every obligation with a deadline, hold evidence you actually met the clock, not just that the capability exists.
- When you enter a new country or take on a customer under a new regime, treat it as a delta exercise, record who determined applicability and on what basis, map the security-shaped parts to existing controls, add the new obligations to the register, not a program to rebuild.

That is not an enterprise privacy-and-compliance function. It is enough to make sure the obligations a security control cannot satisfy actually have a home, an owner, and a due date before a regulator asks about the one nobody was watching.

Reality Check

> *Two questions that reveal whether your overlays are folded in honestly or hidden inside your controls.*
>
> *First, take your privacy program (or your AI governance, or your sector-compliance posture) and ask which of its requirements are actually satisfied by a security control, and which are legal, process, or governance obligations that no control can satisfy. Then ask, for that second category, who owns each one and where it is written down.*
>
> *If the honest answer is that your privacy program is mostly your security controls, and lawful basis and data-subject rights and the reporting clock do not have clear owners outside security, then you have a security program wearing a privacy label, and the requirements that are not security-shaped are quietly unowned, which is exactly the set a regulator asks about. And be doubly careful of two answers: "we mapped it to policy" (policy defines the expectation; it does not prove the obligation is met) and "security owns it" (security may own part; it rarely owns all).*
>
> *Second, pick the single obligation in your world with the tightest deadline, a breach-reporting clock, most likely; six hours, or seventy-two, depending on your regime and jurisdiction. Now ask: if a reportable incident happened tonight, is there a person who knows that clock is running, a process that assesses reportability against it, and evidence you would meet it, or does your incident response effectively end at "contained and recovered," with the legal report as an afterthought nobody rehearsed? If it is the latter, your security response is fine and your obligation is exposed, and the gap between the two is precisely what this chapter is about.*

What This Means for You as a Security Leader

This chapter asks you to hold a distinction that a security-shaped mind finds genuinely hard, because it cuts against the instinct that made you good at the job: not everything that lands on your desk is a control, and some of the most consequential obligations you are now accountable for cannot be satisfied by building a better control.

Privacy, AI governance, sector regulation, resilience, and customer commitments each arrive looking like security problems, and each is partly a security problem, which is the trap, because the security-shaped part is the part you will instinctively solve well, and the legal-process-governance part is the part you will instinctively map onto a control and forget. The whole skill this chapter teaches is telling those two apart, reliably, and routing each to the place that can actually hold it: the control universe for the controls, the obligation register for the obligations.

Practically, that means resisting the reflex to own everything because a unified control universe does not mean the CISO owns every obligation, and when everything gets assigned to security, the model is not mature, it is overloaded. When a privacy obligation is really a legal question (lawful basis, transfer mechanisms) it belongs with legal, and your job is to connect your controls to it, not to pretend a control answers it. When an AI obligation is really governance (oversight, transparency, inventory) it is shared with data science and the business, and securing the model is your slice, not the whole. When a sector obligation is really a deadline, six hours to the regulator, your job is to build the process that meets the clock and hold the evidence that you did, not to point at the incident capability and call it done.

You are the person who sees how all of it connects to the security controls underneath; you are not, and should not try to be, the sole owner of every legal and governance duty that touches data. One of the quiet benefits of the control universe is that it makes non-security ownership visible. It lets you say, precisely, "this obligation needs security controls, but legal owns the interpretation, privacy owns the rights process, product owns the feature behavior, and the business owns the risk decision." That sentence is governance. Security connecting everything is the mature posture; security owning everything is the overloaded one.

And hold onto the cross-border payoff, because it is the reward for doing all of this properly and the one that matters most for where this book's readers are heading. An operating model that cleanly separates controls from obligations is one that can absorb a new country's regime as a set of specific additions rather than a wall of foreign law, map the shared security core to what you already run, add the new jurisdiction's distinct obligations to the register, and expansion becomes a delta exercise instead of a rebuild.

That capability, to walk into an unfamiliar regulatory world and quickly see what you already cover and what you genuinely need to add, is one of the most valuable things a modern CISO can offer a growing business, and it exists only if you did the honest work of keeping controls and obligations distinct. Many frameworks, many jurisdictions, one operating model. That is the whole of it.

Bridge to Chapter 20

A control mapped to a framework is still a claim until you can trace it; the last chapter of this part builds the traceability chain from policy down to the evidence that proves it runs.

CHAPTER 20

Policy → Control → Evidence Traceability and the Integrated Assurance Model

The control universe tells you what should exist. Traceability is how you prove it actually does.

A unified control universe is a structure of claims. It says one set of controls can satisfy multiple frameworks, maps obligations to owners, and distinguishes what is covered from what is not. But structure alone does not prove that any control exists or operates, and that is the final problem this operating model has to solve.

If you stopped here, you would already be ahead of most organizations your size. But there is a quiet problem sitting underneath all of it, and you feel it the first time someone with authority looks at you and says, "Show me."

A control mapped to a framework is a claim. An obligation logged in a register is a claim. A neat crosswalk showing that one access control satisfies six requirements at once is, until proven otherwise, a very well-organized claim. None of it is wrong. But none of it is yet *provable,* and the distance between organized and provable is exactly where a lot of security leaders get caught out. The map looks finished. The moment of the check reveals it was not.

This chapter closes that distance. It is about the thread that runs from the top of your operating model to the bottom and back, the one that lets you follow any single requirement down to the rule that demands it and up to the artifact that proves it is real and running. That thread is traceability, and once you have it, something changes in how the job feels. The audit stops being a scramble. The customer questionnaire stops being an ordeal. The board question stops being a moment of quiet panic. You just follow the line.

The Gap Between Organized and Provable

Here is a scene you will recognize. A team has evidence, lots of it. Screenshots, policies, tickets, scan reports, meeting minutes, log exports, training records, access reviews, vendor assessments, SOC reports, certificates. The shared drive is full. The audit folder is full. The GRC tool, if there is one, is full.

Then an assessor asks a simple question: "Which control does this evidence support?" There is a pause. Or: "Does this access review include your privileged SaaS administrators?" Another pause. Or: "The incident process is documented — show me that the customer-notification decision was made inside the required window." Longer pause.

The evidence exists. The traceability does not. The team can show files; it cannot always show what the files prove. And that is the whole problem in one moment, because it turns every check into an excavation. You are not demonstrating a system that works. You are reconstructing, after the fact, a story about a system and hoping the pieces still line up. Do that four times a year for four frameworks and you understand why so many small security teams feel permanently behind. It is not the security that is exhausting. It is proving the security, over and over, from scratch.

The way out is not more evidence. It is connected evidence.

The Traceability Chain, Link by Link

The whole thing rests on one simple chain, and it is worth walking slowly, because each link does a specific job and each one fails in a specific way when it is weak.

Policy says what must happen, the organization's stated intent, that access is granted on least privilege and reviewed regularly. Underneath it, a *standard* sets the measurable floor: reviewed how often, covering which roles, within what tolerance. Policy is the promise; the standard is the promise made checkable. When both are missing, controls float. They exist because someone once configured them, not because the organization decided they mattered, and that is a fragile footing the first time someone senior asks whether a control can be dropped.

Controls define how the intent is met, the access-management capability the policy calls for. This is where your framework crosswalk attaches: one control, mapped to many requirements. But a control named in a mapping is still just a name until the next links prove it operates.

Procedures make the control repeatable. This is the link people skip, and it is the one that quietly decides whether a control survives the person who built it. A control that only works because one engineer remembers to run it every Friday is not a control; it is a habit with good intentions. The procedure is what turns "we do this" into "this is done, the same way, regardless of who's on shift."

Evidence proves it happened, not that it *could,* or is *supposed to,* but that it *did,* on real systems, during the period in question. This is the link most often faked without anyone meaning to fake it, because it is where people reach for the wrong artifact. A policy says privileged access must be reviewed quarterly; someone asked for proof uploads the policy. But the policy is the promise, not the proof. The evidence has to show the review actually ran: the population that was reviewed, who reviewed it, when, what inappropriate access turned up, and how it was resolved. Policy and evidence are both necessary, and they are not interchangeable. Treat one as the other and the whole universe becomes theater.

Testing checks it actually worked. Evidence tells you the control ran; testing tells you it ran *correctly,* that the access review did not just happen but caught the dormant accounts it was meant to catch. Plenty of controls generate flawless evidence of doing nothing useful.

Risk acceptance records who chose to live with the gap. Sometimes the honest answer is that the control is not fully there, an exception is standing, or a requirement genuinely does not apply. The chain does not demand perfection; it demands honesty about where perfection stops, a named owner, a documented decision, a review date. An accepted risk, properly authorized and time-bound, is a functioning end to the chain, though acceptance governs residual risk and never turns an unmet legal or contractual obligation into a satisfied one. A silent gap is a broken one, and the only difference is whether someone chose it on purpose.

Read those as a sentence and you have the shape of assurance: *this policy requires it, this standard sets the bar, this control delivers it, this procedure repeats it, this evidence shows it happened, this test confirms it worked, and where it did not, the gap becomes a tracked issue with an owner and a fix, and this decision records what we chose to accept.* When the links are present and connected, you can stand at any requirement in any framework and walk the line to proof. When one is missing, you have a claim, and you usually learn which link failed at the worst possible moment.

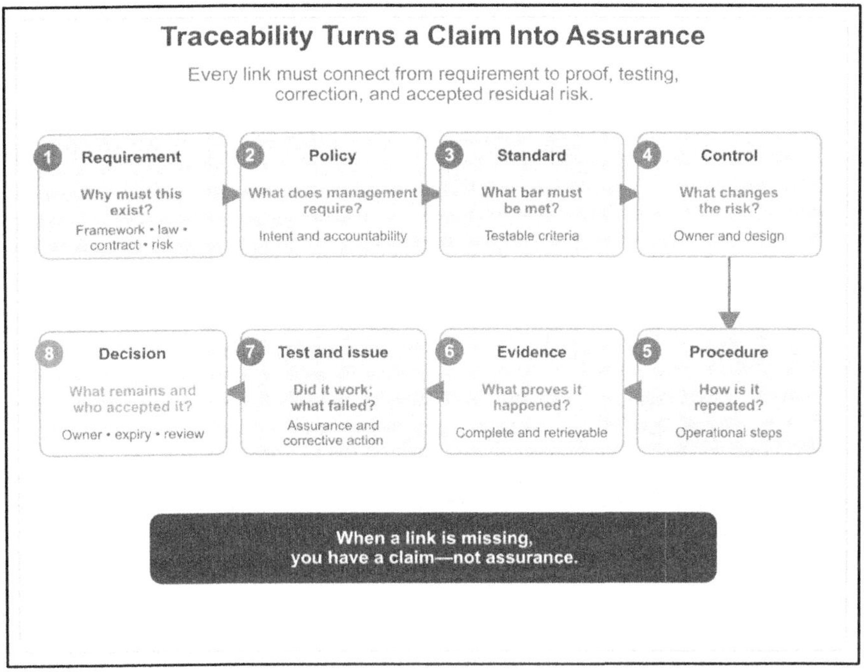

Evidence That Earns Its Keep

Not all evidence is worth the folder it sits in, and one of the more useful instincts you develop in this role is the feel for the difference. Evidence earns its keep when it points at a specific assertion, comes with a date and an owner, and would survive a follow-up question.

The assertion is the part people forget. A screenshot of a dashboard proves nothing until you can say what claim it backs. So it helps, for any real piece of evidence, to attach a plain-language assertion to it, what it proves, for which control, over which scope and period, and, just as importantly, what it does *not* prove. Take a quarterly privileged-access review for production. The assertion might be: system owners reviewed privileged access for production systems A through D in Q2, and inappropriate access was found and tracked to remediation. Scope: those four systems. Period: Q2. Limitation: excludes SaaS administrator roles and cloud root accounts, which sit under separate controls.

That last line is what keeps you honest. A backup-success report proves jobs ran; it does not prove a restore works. A vulnerability scan proves scanning happened for the assets in scope; it does not prove anything got remediated. A training-completion report proves people clicked through the module; it does not prove they understood it. A penetration test proves the scope that was tested; it says nothing about the APIs and cloud configurations that were not.

Evidence has boundaries, and integrated assurance depends on those boundaries being visible. The best evidence, by the way, is the kind a control produces on its own as it operates, rather than the kind a human assembles specially for the check because a control that only generates evidence when an audit looms is telling you something uncomfortable about whether it runs the rest of the year.

Testing: The Two Questions

Testing asks whether what happened was good enough, and it really asks two separate questions that people tend to blur together. Is the control *designed* properly, would it address the risk if performed correctly? And did it *operate*, did it actually run as designed during the period?

An access review can be beautifully designed (right systems, right reviewers, right cadence, exceptions handled) and simply not have happened on time. It can also run like clockwork every quarter while covering the wrong population, in which case it is operating faithfully and protecting nothing. Both questions matter, and a mature assurance model answers both rather than assuming that a control which exists on paper is a control that works in practice. You do not need to test everything this hard; you do need to test your *key* controls this hard, the ones carrying many obligations at once, where a failure ripples across SOC 2, ISO, PCI, a customer commitment, and a regulator simultaneously. Testing priority follows control importance.

The Integrated Assurance Model

Here is the payoff, and it is the reason the last several chapters were worth the effort.

Because you built a *unified* control universe, one control satisfying many requirements, the evidence for that control is unified too. A single well-run access review does not prove one framework's requirement; it proves the access-management assertion, and that assertion is what a whole cluster of requirements across every framework was pointing at all along. One piece of evidence, collected once, answers many masters at the same time.

That is the practical inverse of the exhausting alternative. The old way runs the assurance chain once per framework: gather access evidence for the security audit, gather it again for the customer questionnaire, gather it again for the sector regulator, each in a different vocabulary, each on its own clock, each from scratch. The integrated way runs the chain once per *control* and lets the crosswalk you already built do the translation. You collect the evidence a single time; when three different audiences ask in three different dialects, you point all three at the same artifact through the same mapping.

But this is exactly where discipline matters most, because evidence reuse and evidence abuse look identical from a distance. Reuse is honest only when the control, the scope, the period, and the assertion all genuinely match the new requirement. Using an enterprise access review to answer a PCI requirement when the cardholder data environment was excluded from that review is not reuse. It is overclaiming.

So is using a vendor risk assessment to satisfy a privacy obligation when sub-processors were never in scope, or using a security tabletop to satisfy resilience testing when business-service continuity was never exercised, or leaning on a cloud provider's certification to prove your own tenant configuration. The test before you reuse anything is boringly simple: same control, same scope, same period, same assertion? If yes, reuse it and save everyone the duplication. If not, collect the extra evidence, mark the coverage as partial, or record the gap. Reuse should cut duplication. It should never cut truth.

The Machinery Around the Chain: Issues, Exceptions, and Accepted Risk

Testing will find problems. So will audits, incidents, and customer reviews. The value of the chain is precisely that it surfaces those breaks before someone else does, but only if the findings go somewhere structured, linked back to the control and obligation they touch. A finding that says "access review incomplete" is mildly useful. The same finding tied to the access-review control, the SOC 2 criteria and PCI scope it supports, and the privileged-access risk it exposes, is something leadership can actually prioritize. It also blocks closure theater: an issue closes when the gap is genuinely remediated, the evidence exists, and someone validated the closure, not when a spreadsheet cell turns green.

Exceptions are the next piece, and they are necessary. There will always be a legacy application that cannot support modern authentication, a vulnerability that cannot be patched inside the window, a vendor that cannot produce every artifact. An exception is a *controlled* deviation from an approved requirement: scoped, reasoned, backed by a compensating control, owned, approved, and given an expiry and a review date. That last part is what separates the discipline from the drawer.

A good exception is visible, time-bound, owned, and risk-informed. A bad exception is an excuse with no expiry. And when an exception touches something that matters, an access-control gap on a system in PCI scope, a vulnerability exception on an internet-facing app handling personal data, it should not sit quietly in a ticket queue. Someone with the standing to care should know it is there.

Risk acceptance is where the chain honestly ends when a gap cannot be closed. It is not a security-team shrug. It is an accountable business decision to live with a defined exposure, for a defined period, under defined conditions. The distinction that trips up new CISOs is ownership: you can recommend, explain, challenge, and document, but the business owner accepts the business risk, because they are the one who can weigh it against the budget, the deadline, or the strategy that created it.

If the accepted risk touches a legal or regulatory obligation, legal and compliance belong in the decision. If it touches a customer commitment, so do account leadership and legal. And if it is material, it belongs in front of senior management or the board. Risk acceptance is where the control universe, the risk register, and the governance model meet, and without that connection it becomes a drawer full of uncomfortable truths nobody reads.

From Activity to Meaning

One reporting habit undercuts all of this: reporting activity instead of assurance. Policies updated, controls mapped, evidence files collected, questionnaires answered, audits passed. These are real operational metrics, and they tell leadership almost nothing about whether the organization is actually protected. Leadership needs the control story: which key controls are working, which are weak, which obligations are not fully covered, which gaps carry material risk, which evidence has gone stale, which exceptions are overdue, which accepted risks are about to expire.

The difference is the difference between "access-review evidence collected" and something like: *privileged access management is partially effective. Reviews are operating for production systems, but SaaS administrator roles and cloud break-glass accounts are not yet fully in scope. That affects SOC 2, ISO, customer assurance, and internal policy. Remediation is underway with the IAM and SaaS owners, and the residual risk is accepted by the COO through Q3 with compensating monitoring.* One is a count. The other is assurance. Push your reporting toward the second, always.

Making It Real Without a Platform

If you are at a small or mid-sized organization, you might be bracing for the part where this requires an expensive governance platform. It does not. Tooling helps at scale, but the discipline is the thing, and the discipline fits in a workbook.

At its most basic, the integrated assurance model is a control library with a row per control and columns for the links in the chain: the policy and standard that require it, the frameworks and obligations it maps to, the owner, the scope, the procedure that runs it, where the evidence lives and when it was last refreshed, when it was last tested, any open issue, any standing exception, and any accepted residual risk.

Alongside it sit an obligation register, a simple evidence index that records what each artifact proves and for what scope, and a combined gap-and-exception log. That may sound like several registers; at the start it is one workbook. The point is not tool sophistication. It is connection, controls to evidence, evidence to assertions, findings to controls, exceptions to risks, obligations to owners, accepted risks to the people who accepted them.

The reason to start with the register and not the platform is that a platform will happily automate a broken chain. If controls do not produce their own evidence, if procedures live in people's heads, if half the artifacts are undated, a tool does not fix that. It just makes the gaps searchable and produces wrong dashboards faster. Get the chain honest first. A spreadsheet with honest traceability beats a platform full of false links every time. Automate after the model is clear; do not automate confusion.

Industry Pattern — The Obligation No One Could Trace

An organization preparing for a customer assessment is asked to prove that privileged access is reviewed regularly, a requirement it has genuinely met for years. The policy exists. The quarterly access-review control exists and runs. The evidence sits in the folder: signed review records, current and tidy. On paper the obligation is covered, and the team walks in confident.

Then the assessor asks one question the folder cannot answer: does that review include the privileged administrators of the SaaS platforms, the ones provisioned outside the core identity system? A pause. The review had been built years earlier around the on-premises directory, and the SaaS admin accounts were added to the business later, by teams who never looped in the review. The control was real and the evidence was real, but the population it covered had quietly drifted from the population the obligation required. The green cell was true about the systems it named and silent about the ones it did not.

Nothing here was negligence. Policy, control, procedure, evidence all existed, the chain simply had a broken link nobody could see until someone pulled on it, because no one had traced the obligation down to the population the review actually covered and back up to what it claimed. Once they did, the fix was small: widen the review's scope, add the SaaS admins, re-evidence it, and record the gap that had stood in the interim. The lesson was not that the team was careless. It was that evidence you cannot trace to a scope is evidence you cannot fully trust, and you find out which link is broken the moment someone checks, unless you have walked the line yourself first.

What Evidence Should You Expect

The evidence you are after here is evidence *about the assurance system itself*: proof that your line of assurance is real and maintained, not just claimed. At a practical minimum for a small or mid-sized organization, expect to be able to produce:

- A control library or traceability matrix, one row per control, carrying the policy and standard behind it, the requirements and obligations it maps to, its owner and scope, where the evidence lives and how fresh it is, when it was last tested, and any accepted risk. That single artifact *is* your integrated assurance model.

- End-to-end walkthroughs for a handful of high-stakes controls (access management, change, logging, incident notification) each traced from policy down to a dated artifact and back, showing the chain holds without a scramble to reconstruct it.
- Dated, self-produced evidence for those controls, recent enough to show they are running now, each carrying a plain assertion of what it proves and, just as clearly, what it does not.
- An issue-and-exception log and a risk-acceptance register, every item owned, dated, and tied back to the control and obligation it affects, issues carrying a remediation status and a validated closure, and standing exceptions and accepted risks carrying a review date.
- A cross-framework coverage view with at least one worked case where a single piece of evidence answers requirements in two or more frameworks. Proof the integrated model is actually running, not just drawn.

Reality Check

> *Pick one control that matters, privileged access review, critical-vulnerability remediation, incident notification, backup-restore testing, an AI human-oversight step. Now trace it end to end, out loud: which policy or obligation requires it, who owns it, what procedure runs it, what is in scope, what evidence proves it operated, what that evidence asserts and what it deliberately does not, whether it was tested, what issues or exceptions are open, and which frameworks and customer commitments lean on it.*

> *If you can narrate that in one clean paragraph, you have the foundation for assurance, the trace itself; the assurance still rests on reliable evidence and an honest conclusion. If you cannot, you have activity. And watch for the link where you hesitate, nine times out of ten it is the procedure, the one everybody skips, the one that turns out to have a resignation-shaped hole in it.*

What This Means for You as a Security Leader

This is the chapter where your whole operating model stops being a design and becomes something you can stand behind. The universe, mapping method, crosswalk, and overlays lead to a single practical capability: when asked about any requirement, from any framework, by anyone with the standing to ask, you can answer by following a line rather than launching an excavation.

That capability changes your posture in the room. Compliance activity says *we have policies, we mapped the controls, we collected the evidence, we passed the audit.* Assurance says something sharper: *this obligation maps to this control, this owner operates it, this evidence proves it for this scope and period, this test found these gaps, this remediation is due by this date, and this residual risk is accepted by this business owner.* One is a stack of well-organized claims. The other is a line of proof.

The shift is what turns the CISO from a collector of frameworks into an architect of trust, and it is the reason the unified framework was never about a prettier spreadsheet. It was about making security, privacy, AI governance, resilience, regulation, audit, and customer trust all traceable to the same operating truth — one line of proof. It scales in the one direction that matters, too: the more frameworks the world throws at you, the more it pays off, because you are collecting evidence through one governed model, reusing it when control, scope, period, and assertion match, and letting the mapping translate.

Part 4 Closing Note: One Operating Model, One Line of Proof

Part 4 resolved the tension the whole series has been building. Frameworks arrive in a crowd — the anchor you chose, the certification a market demands, the regulation a country imposes, the questionnaire a customer sends — and the instinct that feels most responsible, a separate program for each, is precisely the one that buries lean teams. The alternative this Part built is the series' central promise made operational: implement once, describe many, and preserve what each one uniquely demands.

The construction ran in five moves. The case: they are mostly asking for the same things, so build one control universe and let the frameworks point at it. The method: a taxonomy organized by control intent rather than any framework's language, mapped by intent and scope rather than word-matching, with coverage recorded honestly — full, partial, not covered, or not applicable — and permitted compensating controls recorded separately as approved treatments. The crosswalk: six instruments at six altitudes — ISO 27002, NIST 800-53, SOC 2, PCI DSS, CIS, CSA CCM — resolving onto one set of controls you actually run, with the sharp edges preserved where they genuinely diverge.

The overlays: privacy, AI governance, and sector regulation folded in without flattening, because not everything that lands on your desk is a control — some of it is an obligation with a deadline, a legal decision, a reporting duty, and pretending otherwise overloads the model and the CISO alike. And traceability: policy to control to scoped implementation to evidence to testing, link by link — a line that must also run in reverse, so that when a control changes or fails, the organization can name which frameworks, obligations, customers, and assurance claims are affected.

Two honesty rules carry the whole structure. Mapped is not met — the line between two reference numbers is where the work starts, not where it finishes. And the universe must describe what your controls actually achieve, in your words, because a taxonomy built framework-first is secretly one framework in disguise, and it fights every other one you try to map.

That line of proof changes the quality of the leader's answer. Compliance activity says: we have policies, we mapped the frameworks, we passed the audit. Assurance says something sharper: this obligation maps to this control, this owner operates it in this scope, this evidence proves it ran, this test challenged it, this exception is known, and this person accepted what remains. The answer becomes more precise — and therefore more credible. Efficiency comes from truth organized well, not from making broader claims.

The payoff compounds precisely where this book's readers are heading: the next framework, the next customer, the next country stops being a rebuild and becomes a mapping exercise. That is "many frameworks, one operating model" — not a slogan about paperwork, but the difference between a program that scales and one that multiplies.

The operating model is now complete: built, governed, proven, unified. What remains is different in kind — the toolkit that turns all of it into things you can pick up on a Monday morning. That is the final Part.

Bridge to Part 5

Part 5 turns the operating model into things you can pick up on a Monday morning: playbooks, reporting templates, libraries, metrics, and interview readiness.

VOLUME IV

PART 5

CISO Playbooks, Metrics, Templates, and Interview Readiness

CHAPTER 21

How to Use the Playbooks

The thinking is done. What follows is the toolkit.

Something changes here, and it is worth naming before you turn another page. Everything up to this point has been about understanding the work. How risk becomes trust, how frameworks relate, how a control universe holds them together, how you prove any of it is real. That is the hard part, and it is largely behind you. What is left is different in character.

This is the part you actually reach for on a Monday morning, when there is a board deck due, an auditor booked, a control set to rationalize, a new role to step into, or a client waiting. It is the operating model built across this series, turned into things you can pick up and use, reporting formats, a control library and policy index, readiness checklists, a first-ninety-days plan, interview preparation, patterns for doing this work as an outside advisor, a cyber-insurance claim-readiness playbook, and an M&A security due-diligence playbook.

But a toolkit is deceptively dangerous, and this short chapter exists to keep you from the two ways people misuse one. The first is treating a template as an answer instead of a starting point, filling in the blanks and mistaking that for having done the work. The second is treating it as a script that must be followed exactly, and either forcing your organization to match the template or abandoning the template because your organization does not. Both misunderstand what these tools are for. So before you use any of them, it is worth a few minutes on what a playbook actually is, why the structure earns its place, when to reach for which one, and how to make it yours.

What a Playbook Is — and What It Isn't

A playbook, in the sense this part means it, is scaffolding. It is the shape of a piece of work, the sections a board report needs, the fields a control library carries, the questions an audit-readiness check asks. Captured so you do not have to rediscover the structure from scratch every time. The value is in the shape, not the contents. The contents are yours to supply, from your organization, your risks, your obligations, your operating model.

What a playbook is *not* is a substitute for judgment. A template is not evidence. A checklist is not maturity. A filled-in dashboard is not governance. Each of those can *look* like the thing it stands in for, which is exactly the danger. A playbook can tell you that a board report should connect risk to a decision the board can actually make; it cannot tell you which risk your board needs to hear about this quarter. It can give you a control-library structure; it cannot decide which controls your organization runs. Everywhere in this part, the template carries the structure and you carry the substance, and the moment you forget which is which, the tool stops helping and starts hiding the gap where the thinking should have been.

That is the mental model to hold: these are starting points that save you the blank page, not finished products that save you the work.

Why the Structure Earns Its Place

If the tools cannot do the thinking for you, it is fair to ask what they are actually for. Here is the honest answer, and it comes from watching where security leaders come undone. Most CISOs do not fail because they lack frameworks. They fail because they cannot turn frameworks into operating decisions fast enough. The board is in the room asking whether you are exposed, and the answer is somewhere in your head in the language of controls, and the translation has to happen live, under pressure, without omissions.

That is what the structure buys you. When the shape of the work is already in front of you, you are not composing it from nothing while everyone waits. A reporting format reminds you to connect risk to control health to investment to the decision you actually need. A readiness check reminds you to look at scope and evidence freshness and open findings before the auditor does.

A first-ninety-days plan reminds you not to spend month one buying tools before you understand the business. None of that is the answer, the answer is still yours, but the structure keeps you from panicking, keeps you from forgetting the obvious thing, and, most usefully, helps you ask the right question before everyone is waiting on you for it. In a role that runs on constant pressure, that is not a small gift.

The Template Trap

There is a specific failure these tools are built to help you avoid: the false green cell, a control marked "covered" because a downloaded crosswalk said so, not because anyone checked it against reality. The template trap is the same failure wearing different clothes. You find a policy template, a risk register, a board deck, a control matrix; you fill in the obvious blanks; and you walk away with a document that looks complete and proves almost nothing.

The danger is not that the template is bad. It is that a half-adapted template creates confidence out of proportion to the work behind it. A policy you downloaded and lightly edited reads exactly like a policy you built from your actual environment, right up until someone asks whether it reflects how your organization really operates, and it turns out to describe a company that is not yours. An untouched risk register looks like risk management. A generic control library looks like a control program. The polish is the problem, because polish is what everyone reads as diligence.

So before you rely on any template, it is worth asking a few plain questions of it: what decision is this meant to support, who is the audience, what must come out because it does not apply here, what must go in because this organization is different, and, the one that saves you most, what would be dangerous to claim in here if we could not actually prove it? Answer those and you are adapting. Skip them and you are populating, and a populated template is a liability with good formatting. The way out is never to avoid templates; it is to take the structure, throw away the assumptions baked into it, and refill it from your own operating model.

How to Actually Use Them

There is a rhythm to using these well, and it is the same for every tool in the part.

Start by reading the intent, not the fields. Every playbook here comes with the reason it is shaped the way it is. Why a board report leads with the decision, why a control library needs an owner column, why a readiness checklist asks what it asks. Understand the intent first, because the intent is what survives when your situation does not match the template exactly. When you know *why* the structure exists, you can adapt it confidently. When you only know the fields, you can only copy them.

Then fill it from your own context and operating model, not from imagination. This is where the whole earlier book pays off. You already built a control universe, an obligation register, and the traceability that connects them; the tools in this part are just different views onto that same underlying truth. A board report is your risk picture, summarized for a specific audience. A control library is your control universe, written down. An audit-readiness checklist is your assurance line, stress-tested before someone else stress-tests it. You are not inventing content for these templates.

You are drawing it from the model you have already built, filtered through what this particular organization actually is: what it does, what its crown jewels are, which obligations bind it, what its real maturity is, and where the known weaknesses already sit, in the open findings and standing exceptions. A playbook applied without that context is a ritual. Applied with it, it is a leadership tool. And if you find yourself making things up to fill a template, that is not a template problem. It is a signal that the underlying work is not there yet.

Then make sure the thing produces a decision, not just a meeting. This is the failure that catches even diligent people: you run the playbook, you have the conversation, everyone nods, and nothing is actually decided, owned, or written down. A good playbook always ends in something durable, a decision, an accepted risk with an owner, an action with a date, an artifact that goes back into your risk register or control library. A meeting that produces no artifact depends on memory, and memory is not governance.

Which is the deeper point about all of these tools: their job is not to make you sound polished, it is to help you *ask the better question*, the one everyone else skipped. When did we last restore, not just back up? Are we about to promise a customer something the control owner cannot support? Who is the business owner accepting this risk, and when does that acceptance expire? A playbook used well is a question engine, and the questions are worth more than the formatting.

And once it is adapted, keep it living (dated, owned, and revisited) because a tool that was accurate the day you filled it in and never touched again slowly becomes another form of fiction. The best playbooks get sharper every time you use them; the worst become stale monuments to a company you used to be.

When to Reach for Which

The rest of this toolkit is a set of tools for specific moments, and part of using them well is knowing which one the moment calls for. It is worth a quick orientation so you can navigate straight to what you need rather than reading the part as one undifferentiated block.

When you need to talk to leadership — the board, the risk committee, an executive who controls the budget — reach for the reporting templates. When you are building, rationalizing, or documenting your control set and the policies behind it, use the control library and policy index to create structure without drowning. When a check is coming — an audit, a customer assessment, a certification — the audit, evidence, and readiness checklists help you walk in prepared instead of scrambling. When you are stepping into a new role, or into the interview for one, use the 30/60/90 plan and interview-readiness material for that transition.

And if you are doing this work for other organizations rather than inside one (as a fractional or virtual CISO, or an advisor) the consulting and advisory use cases show how the same toolkit adapts when you are the outside expert brought in to move a client from confusion to clarity. When a cyber incident may become an insurance claim, the claim-readiness playbook connects incident command to notice, consent, approved providers, expense tracking, and proof of loss before those requirements become a second crisis. And when the organization is buying, integrating, separating, or selling a business, the M&A playbook carries cyber risk from diligence through Day 1, integration, and divestiture.

One thing to notice as you go: the same tool changes behavior depending on *why* you picked it up. Your control library is a diagnostic when you are hunting for gaps, an operating record when you are running the program day to day, and an assurance artifact when an auditor is sitting across the table, one document, three different jobs. Knowing which job you are doing tells you how much detail, which audience, and what evidence the moment actually needs. You do not read a toolbox cover to cover before you use a screwdriver; treat this part the same way.

Your Organization Is Not the Template

One more thing, because it is the mistake small and mid-sized organizations make most often, and it runs in the opposite direction from what you would expect. Most templates are built by, and for, large enterprises because that is who tends to publish them. So the default shape usually assumes more team, more tooling, more process, and more layers than you have. Faced with that, the wrong instinct is to pad: to keep every row, stand up every process, and produce a control program sized for a company ten times yours, most of it aspirational and none of it real.

The right instinct is almost always to strip, deliberately, cutting duplication and aspiration rather than anything a real risk, law, contract, or control dependency requires. A tool sized correctly for your organization. Fewer controls, run properly, with real evidence behind them, beats a comprehensive one that mostly describes work nobody is doing.

Cutting a template down to what you can actually operate is not a compromise or a sign you are behind; it is the more mature move, because it produces something true. Right-sized and real beats comprehensive and aspirational, every time. Adapt down without apology, and when a sector regulation or a major customer genuinely demands something the default does not carry, add it deliberately, because a real obligation requires it, not because the template happened to include it. Adaptation runs both ways.

The other axis to tune is the audience. The same underlying model has to become very different things depending on who is reading it: a board wants risk, trade-offs, and the decisions it is being asked to make, not a tour of your tooling; an auditor wants scope, control design, and evidence of operation; a customer wants assurance and clear boundaries; a regulator wants obligation-specific proof against a clock; an engineer wants the control's intent and the exception path; an interview panel wants to see your judgment, not your program. Same truth underneath, six different presentations on top. A CISO who gives every audience the same answer is either burying some of them or under-informing the rest.

Where the Playbook Meets the Real Organization

Here is the part no template prints on itself: none of them survive contact with your organization's culture unchanged, and pretending otherwise is how good plans quietly fail. The written playbook is the clean version. The actual place you work is messier, and the messiness is usually political, not technical.

The formal process says risk acceptance requires a named business owner; the culture may expect security to "just approve it" and move on. The policy says no production change without review; engineering may experience that review as pure delivery friction and route around it. The board says it wants honest risk transparency and then reacts badly to bad news. Sales may commit to a customer's security demands before anyone in security has seen them. Procurement may wave through an urgent tool without a vendor review.

So when you pick up any of these tools, do not only ask what the process *should* be. Ask the quieter questions: where will this get bypassed, and by whom? Who has informal authority that the org chart does not show? Which step creates enough friction that people will avoid it? Which decision is one nobody actually wants to own? And which control is holding only because one particular person happens to care, and what happens the week they are on leave?

That instinct, reading the organization as it really behaves, not as its documents describe it, is a lot of what separates an experienced security leader from a competent checklist operator. The playbook is the map. The territory is politics. Your job is to make the tool work in the mess, not to pretend the mess is not there.

Industry Pattern — The Template That Described Someone Else's Company

> *A small team, under pressure to show a security program quickly, downloads a well-regarded policy set and control library, the kind a large, mature enterprise publishes. They change the obvious fields: company name, a few role titles, the logo. The result is genuinely impressive: dozens of polished policies, a control library hundreds of rows deep, a program that reads, on the page, like a company ten times their size.*
>
> *It holds right up until someone reads it closely. An auditor, or a demanding customer, asks a plain question: your policy says a security operations center monitors your systems around the clock, so walk me through last month's coverage. There is no security operations center. The policy described one because the template did. The library lists controls for network segments the company does not run, data-loss tooling it never bought, and a change-advisory board that has never met. Row after row describes an organization the reader is slowly realizing is not this one. Nothing was false on purpose; the document simply described the company it was built for, and no one had walked through it asking which lines were actually true here.*
>
> *The fix was not more polish. It was less. The team went back through the policies and the library and cut everything that described work nobody was doing, leaving a smaller set that was entirely real: fewer controls, honestly owned, with evidence behind each one. It looked less impressive and was worth far more, because now every line could survive a question. The lesson was not that templates are dangerous. It was that a template describes the company it was built for until you make it describe yours, and adapting it down to what you actually operate is not falling short of the template, it is the whole point of using one.*

What Evidence Should You Expect

The evidence at this stage is not about any single control. It is about whether your toolkit is a living part of how you operate or a set of documents that were filled in once and quietly went stale. At a practical minimum for a small or mid-sized organization, expect to be able to show:

- Tools that are demonstrably adapted, not adopted, a control library, policy set, or board report that plainly reflects your actual environment (your systems, your sector, your size) rather than a generic structure with the blanks filled in.
- An owner and a date on every living tool, each playbook you rely on assigned to someone accountable and carrying a last-reviewed date, with a light version history that shows it was actually revisited after the moments that should change it: a board meeting, an audit, a customer assessment, an incident. That is how you tell a tool that still describes reality from one that describes whenever it was created.
- A visible line back to the operating model, the content in these tools traceable to your control universe, obligation register, and assurance line from earlier in this volume, so the board report and the control library and the readiness checklist are all telling the same story.
- Right-sizing you can defend, where a template was cut down, a clear reason it was cut, so an assessor sees deliberate scoping rather than an accidental gap.
- Evidence the tools actually get used and produce decisions. Board reports that were presented, checklists run before a real audit, a 30/60/90 that was followed, each leaving behind a decision, an action, or an artifact rather than just a meeting. A pristine, never-opened playbook is itself a tell.

Reality Check

> *Take the last template, report, checklist, or dashboard you actually used. Before worrying about whether it looked polished, ask what came of it: what decision did it support, who was the audience, what did they need to understand, and what changed after it was used? Then the harder one, if someone read it back to you, would it describe* **your** *organization, or a generic one, and could you trace every meaningful line in it to something real: a control you run, an obligation you carry, a risk that is actually yours?*
>
> *If the honest answer is "we produced the document," that is activity. If it is "it helped someone make a better decision," that is the point. And if you were filling rows because the template* **had** *rows, stop. You had slipped from adapting to populating, which is exactly the polished fiction that fails the first real question.*

What This Means for You as a Security Leader

This part is where the series stops being something you read and becomes something you use, and that shift asks a small but real change in posture. Up to now the work was understanding; from here it is applying, and applying well means resisting the pull of the finished-looking artifact. The tools that follow will save you real time, the blank page is one of the genuinely hard parts of this job, but they only help if you bring the substance, and the substance is everything you have built across this series: the risk judgment, the framework fluency, the control universe, the obligations, the assurance line.

The difference between a weaker and a stronger leader shows up right here. A weaker one copies a template and hopes it looks mature. A stronger one adapts it to context, audience, evidence, and the decision at hand, and reads the room it has to survive. The same board template can bury directors in security noise or hand them the three decisions they actually need to make.

The same audit checklist can collect files or prove control operation. The same 30/60/90 can list meetings or build trust and surface real risk. Your job was never to fill templates. It is to use tools to create clarity, for a board, an auditor, a new team, or a client. That is what turns a folder of documents into a leadership kit.

Bridge to Chapter 22

The moment that tests whether the operating model really holds is usually the board meeting; the next chapter turns it into a reporting structure.

CHAPTER 22

Board and Risk Reporting Templates

The board does not need more security data. It needs a clearer security decision.

Sooner or later, everything you have built gets compressed into twenty minutes and a handful of slides, in front of people who do not live in security but are accountable for it and control your budget. That room is where a lot of otherwise strong security leaders come undone, not because their program is weak, but because they walk in speaking the wrong language. Inside the security team, everything matters: vulnerabilities, incidents, tool coverage, phishing results, audit findings, cloud config, identity exceptions, backups. Then you get thirty minutes with a board, and if you try to carry the whole program into that room, the room politely suffocates.

This is worth taking seriously, because board reporting is not a side task you do after the real work. For many CISOs it *is* a large part of the real work, and it is the single most visible thing you do. Much of the board's impression of whether the organization is well-protected forms in that room, from what you show them and how you frame it. Get it right and you build the standing that gets you budget, air cover, and a seat at the table when it matters. Get it wrong and you can be running an excellent program and still lose the room, and a CISO who has lost the board's confidence has a much harder job than one who has not.

So this chapter is about doing it well: what the board actually needs, a reporting structure you can adapt, the metrics and honesty that make it work, and the traps that catch people. Not prettier slides. Better conversations.

Report for a Decision, Not a Display

Here is the mental shift that fixes most bad board reporting in one move: you are not there to display activity. You are there to enable a decision.

Most weak security reports are activity dumps, a proud tour of everything the team did last quarter. Patches applied, alerts triaged, tools deployed, projects underway. It feels like accountability; it reads like noise. The board cannot do anything with it, because none of it is framed as a choice they need to make. They sit through thirty operational charts and leave knowing the team was busy but not knowing whether the organization is safe, whether it is safer than last quarter, or what they are being asked to do about it.

Flip it. Walk into the room knowing the two or three things you actually need from these people, a funding decision, a risk they need to formally accept, an awareness they need to carry, and build the report backward from that. Every slide should earn its place by moving toward a decision or informing one. If a chart does not help someone in that room decide, fund, escalate, or accept something, it belongs in an appendix or nowhere.

Operational Reporting Isn't Board Reporting

The most common version of this mistake is sending operational reporting upward unchanged, the security team's own dashboard with fewer rows. A SOC dashboard is useful for the SOC; a vulnerability report is useful for remediation owners; a project tracker is useful for your leadership team. None of them is automatically useful for a board, because they answer the wrong question. Operational reporting asks *how much work is happening?* Board reporting asks *what risk does this create or reduce?* The whole skill is the translation between those two, and it is easiest to see in the swap:

"We identified 1,426 vulnerabilities this month" becomes "how many *critical* vulnerabilities remain overdue on our internet-facing and business-critical systems, and what exposure does that leave open?" "EDR coverage is 92%" becomes "which critical assets are *outside* endpoint detection, why, and what's the risk?" "We assessed twenty vendors" becomes "are our critical third parties understood and within acceptable risk?" "Backups completed successfully" becomes "have we tested *restoring* critical services, and can we recover from ransomware inside business tolerance?" Same facts underneath, entirely different question on top. Skip that translation and you can report a great deal and still leave leadership under-informed, which is worse than saying less, because it looks like diligence.

What the Board Actually Needs to Know

Strip away the security detail and a board is asking the same small set of questions every time, no matter the quarter. Answer these and you have reported well; miss them and no amount of polish saves you.

Are we exposed, and where? The top risks in business terms, not "unpatched CVEs on twelve hosts" but "our customer-facing platform has a weakness an attacker could use to reach customer data, and here's what that would mean for us." Name the handful that matter, not the hundred that do not.

Is that better or worse than last time? Boards think in trend. A single snapshot tells them nothing; the direction tells them everything. A risk that is stable, one that is shrinking, and one quietly getting worse are three different conversations, and the board needs to know which is which.

Are we inside the risk we agreed to carry? This is where risk appetite earns its keep, we will come back to it, but the board can only judge exposure against a line they have agreed to. "We have this risk" is incomplete. "We have this risk, and it's above the level we agreed was acceptable" is a decision waiting to happen.

What do you need from us? The ask. Money, a formal risk acceptance, a policy blessing, top-cover for a hard call. If you need nothing, say so plainly, but most quarters you need something, and burying it is the most common self-inflicted wound in board reporting.

What happened, and what did we learn? Incidents at decision altitude, not the packet captures, but what happened, how bad it was, what it exposed, and what changed as a result. Boards forgive incidents. They do not forgive being surprised by them, and they do not forgive an incident that taught the organization nothing.

Are we meeting our obligations? The regulatory and contractual exposure, deadlines coming, commitments made to customers, anything you are at risk of missing. This is where the obligation register from earlier becomes a board slide: the deadlines with a regulator or a major customer behind them, and whether you are on track.

Everything else is detail. These six are the report.

A Structure You Can Adapt

Underneath those questions is a reporting structure that works across most organizations, and, in the spirit of everything here, it is a starting shape to adapt, not a script to copy. Strip what does not apply, add what your sector or your board demands, and size it to the twenty minutes you will actually get.

- The headline. One honest sentence up top: are we okay, what changed, and what do we need from you today. Executives read the first slide and skim the rest, so make the first slide carry the whole story, if nothing else lands, the essential message did.
- Top risks, in business terms. The three-to-five that matter, each with a plain-language description, a trend arrow, an owner, and where it sits against appetite. Not the whole risk register.
- Decisions requested. The ask, stated explicitly and separated so it cannot be missed, what you need decided, by whom, and what happens if it is not.
- Investment and resourcing. What you are spending and asking for, and, crucially, what that spend buys in risk terms. Not "we need two more headcount" but "here's the exposure that stays open until we have them."
- Incidents and lessons. What happened this period, at board altitude, and what the program changed because of it. Empty is fine when it is true; honest is mandatory.
- Obligations and compliance exposure. Upcoming deadlines, customer commitments, and anything at risk of being missed, the obligations with real consequences, not a compliance checklist.

- Progress against the plan. Are we doing what we said we would do, on the roadmap the board already agreed to. This is where credibility compounds: a CISO who delivers against a stated plan quarter after quarter earns a trust no single impressive deck can buy.

To see the difference a headline makes, compare two openings. The weak one: “Security program is progressing. EDR coverage is 92%, MFA is 98%, vulnerability SLA compliance is 81%, phishing failure rate is 7%.” All true, and it means nothing yet.

The strong one: “Cyber risk remains elevated but stable. Our real exposure isn’t detection — endpoint and network controls are solid — it’s privileged access governance on our critical SaaS platforms, where admin-role reviews are incomplete. That affects SOC 2 readiness, customer assurance, and ransomware response. Remediation is underway, but we need executive support to make the business application owners actually complete their reviews.” That second paragraph tells a story, names the risk, ties it to obligations, and ends in an ask. That is a headline. The first is a status bar.

Risk Appetite: The Yardstick That Makes the Rest Legible

Here is a quiet problem that undermines more board reports than any presentation flaw: the organization has never actually defined how much risk it is willing to carry, so every risk you present floats without a reference point. You call a risk “high,” and a director privately wonders, high compared to what? High and acceptable, or high and alarming? Without an agreed line, they cannot tell, and honestly neither can you.

Risk appetite is that line, the board’s own statement of how much exposure the organization will tolerate before it must act. It changes everything about how your report reads, because now every risk lands as either *inside the line* (managed, informational) or *over it* (a decision is required). A risk that is over appetite is not a status update; it is a prompt. Either the board funds bringing it down, formally accepts it within its authority, or revisits the appetite itself through the proper governance process, a change that should reflect strategy, not the wish to make a red indicator disappear. All three are legitimate choices, which is exactly what you want the board making.

If your organization has never set an appetite, and many small and mid-sized ones have not, helping the board articulate one is genuine leadership, not a compliance exercise. You do not need a heavy framework. You need a few plain statements the board will stand behind, usually phrased as bright lines: no critical internet-facing vulnerability left past its deadline; no privileged access without a named owner and a review; no material customer security commitment made without the control owner seeing it first; no critical service without a tested recovery plan; no reportable incident without a legal and regulatory notification assessment; no AI use touching personal data without approval.

It does not have to be perfect at first. It has to be usable. Once that line exists, your reporting has a spine, and metrics stop floating. Until it does, you are presenting weather with no sense of what counts as a storm.

Metrics the Board Can Actually Use

Metrics are where good intentions go to die in a board deck, because the instinct is to show numbers that prove effort, and the board does not need proof of effort. The test for any board metric is simple and unforgiving: does this number change what someone in the room decides? If it does not, it is decoration, and decoration costs you the attention you needed for the things that matter.

The metrics that fail this test are usually the ones that feel most impressive, attacks blocked, alerts generated, emails filtered, training completed, vulnerabilities found. Big, satisfying, and inert, because "we blocked forty thousand attacks" prompts no decision at all. Fine as context for your own team; filler in front of a board. The ones that earn their place connect to a risk and point at an action, the kind where a bad reading makes a director lean forward and ask *should we do something about that?* The share of critical systems still missing a key control. Critical, internet-facing weaknesses sitting open past their deadline.

High-risk vendors overdue for reassessment. Accepted risks about to expire with nobody revisiting them. The freshness of evidence on the controls you most rely on. Whether your critical SaaS platforms are actually inside the access review, or quietly excluded. Each of those, read badly, forces a choice: fund it, escalate it, accept it, reprioritize. A board metric is a question in numeric form, and the question is always some version of *do we need to act?* Pick a small number of those and hold the line against adding more. Five metrics that each drive a decision beat twenty that merely reassure.

Red, Amber, Green — Without Lying

A word on the status colors every board deck uses, because they are useful and dangerous in equal measure. Useful, because executives need a fast signal. Dangerous, because a color hides everything underneath it, and "green" is the worst offender, since it can mean fully implemented, or partially implemented but improving, or implemented on *some* systems, or designed but never tested, or tested a year ago, or owned by someone who left, or simply "we haven't looked closely." Seven very different truths, one reassuring color.

The fix is to never let a color travel alone. Every status carries a one-line reason, a scope, and a trend, so the board reads meaning rather than mood. "PAM: Amber" tells them nothing. "Privileged access: amber and worsening — we have it covering infrastructure and cloud admin accounts, but our critical SaaS admin roles aren't onboarded yet, and SaaS keeps growing; we're assigning application owners and pulling the top ten platforms into the quarterly review by Q3" tells them exactly what is true and what is being done.

And be strictest with green: it should mean implemented, in scope, evidenced, reasonably tested, no overdue exceptions, operating within appetite, and if it does not mean that, say what it does mean, or the board will believe more than the evidence supports. This is the wall-of-green trap from the other side: honest amber beats decorative green every time.

What Usually Goes Wrong

A few failure modes catch nearly everyone at least once, and naming them helps you feel them coming.

The *fear deck*, leaning on threat drama and worst-case scenarios to manufacture urgency. It works once. After that the board either tunes out the alarm or starts seeing you as the person who is always frightened, and neither builds standing. Report real risk soberly; the sobriety is what makes it credible.

The *activity dump*, busyness mistaken for accountability. If your report could be summarized as "here's everything we did," it is the wrong report.

The *comfort deck*, the all-clear where every indicator reassures. It feels like good news to present, but a board that sees only green either stops paying attention or gets blindsided the first time something breaks, and then wonders what else the green was hiding.

And the worst, the *surprise*. Never let a board learn something serious for the first time in the room, especially bad news. Pre-wire it, walk the chair or the relevant director through it beforehand, so the meeting is a discussion and not an ambush. Boards forgive a great deal, but being surprised in front of their peers is the thing that ends the relationship. Board reporting is a standing relationship built on the board never being caught off guard, and that relationship is worth more than any single quarter's slides.

Same Truth, Different Forum

One practical note, because you will rarely report to just one audience. The board, the risk committee, the audit committee, and the executive committee overlap but are not the same room, and reusing one deck unchanged for all of them serves none of them well. Reuse the *truth*, change the *view*. The board wants material risk, oversight, and decisions. The risk committee wants the deeper posture, the indicators outside appetite, the treatment plans, the standing exceptions. The audit committee wants control effectiveness, findings, evidence, and remediation status.

The executive committee wants the operational decision, who has to do what, by when. One privileged-access problem becomes, for the board, "elevated risk, executive support needed"; for the risk committee, "this indicator is outside appetite, here's the treatment plan and acceptance status"; for the audit committee, "this control is operating only partially, and the evidence gap affects SOC 2"; for the exec committee, "application owners must complete reviews by this date or we escalate." Same issue, four legitimate views. That is not spin. It is meeting each forum where its accountability actually sits.

Reporting After an Incident

Incident reporting to the board is its own case, and the instinct to over-share detail is exactly wrong. The board does not want the blow-by-blow; it wants to exercise oversight. What happened, when did we know, what was affected, was customer or regulated data involved, which controls worked and which failed, what decisions were made, were the legal and regulatory and customer notification clocks assessed, what is contained, what is still uncertain, and what we are doing next.

One discipline matters more than any of these during a live or recent incident: be careful with early certainty. Facts change mid-incident, so the honest language is "based on current evidence," "confirmed so far," "still under investigation," "not yet determined." That is not hedging. It is accuracy, and it protects your credibility when the picture shifts. Boards handle uncertainty fine. They handle *false* certainty very badly, and a CISO who stated something as fact that later unravels spends the next several meetings rebuilding trust.

Industry Pattern — The Board Deck Nobody Could Act On

> *A capable security team builds a board deck it is proud of. Thirty-odd slides, dense with real work: coverage percentages, alert volumes, patch rates, training completion, a control heat map, a threat-landscape section with the quarter's headlines. Every number is true and every slide is polished. The team walks in expecting the board to be reassured by how much is under control.*
>
> *The board is not reassured; it is lost. Twenty minutes in, a director asks the only question that matters to them: are we exposed on anything that could actually hurt the business, and is there something you need us to decide? The deck has no clean answer, because it was built to show activity, not to surface a decision. The risks are buried inside operational metrics; the one funding request the team genuinely needed sits on slide 26, unmarked; the status is a wall of green that says nothing about direction. The meeting ends with polite thanks and no decision, so the team leaves with none of what it came for, and the board leaves unable to tell whether it should be worried.*
>
> *Nothing in the deck was wrong. It was answering questions the board had not asked while missing the handful it had. The rebuild was mostly subtraction: one honest headline up front, three or four risks in business terms with a trend and a named owner, the ask stated plainly on its own slide, and everything operational moved to an appendix nobody had to read.*
>
> *It was a fraction of the length and did far more, because now a director could act on it. The lesson was not that the team reported too little. It was that a board deck measured by how much it contains is measuring the wrong thing, the board does not need to see the work; it needs to make a decision, and a report that does not help it do that has failed no matter how complete it looks.*

What Evidence Should You Expect

The evidence here is not a control artifact. It is whether your reporting actually functions as a decision-making instrument rather than a quarterly ritual. At a practical minimum for a small or mid-sized organization, expect to be able to show:

- A board report built around decisions, where the ask is explicit and every section traces to a risk, an obligation, or a choice the board needs to make, not a tour of team activity.
- A defined risk appetite the board has actually agreed to, even a lightweight set of bright lines, so reported risks land as inside-the-line or over-it rather than floating without a reference point.
- Trend, not just snapshot. Reporting that shows direction over time on the key risks, with a short reason behind every status color rather than a bare red-amber-green.
- A short set of decision-driving metrics, each connected to an action a bad reading would force, with the operational noise kept out of the boardroom.
- A traceable line back to the operating model, the risks, control health, and obligations in the board report drawn from your control universe, obligation register, and assurance line, so the summary the board sees and the detail underneath tell the same story.
- Evidence the report is pre-wired, not sprung, a pre-read distributed ahead of the meeting, and, for anything material or bad, a note that the chair or the relevant committee lead was briefed beforehand. The no-surprise rule is only real if there is a trail showing you actually did it.
- A record that reporting drove decisions, minutes or a decision log showing risks accepted (each with an owner and an expiry, because an acceptance with no expiry is risk storage, not risk governance), investments approved, and actions owned as a result. A report that never changes anything is theater.

Reality Check

> *Pull up your last board report and read it as a director would, someone smart but not technical, with fifteen other things to worry about. Can they tell from the first slide whether the organization is okay and what you need from them? Can they find the ask without hunting for it? Does every risk come with a direction and a sense of whether it is inside the line the board agreed to, and if there is no agreed line, is that not the first thing to fix?*
>
> *Do the metrics show risk, or only activity? Does the report separate what you know from what you are still figuring out? Now the hardest question: when the meeting ended, did anything actually get* ***decided****, or did you inform them and move on? If your honest answer is that you presented and they nodded, you produced a status update, not a board report. The report's job is to send people out of the room having made a choice.*

What This Means for You as a Security Leader

Board reporting is a translation skill, and it is a different skill from the security itself, which is exactly why so many technically strong leaders struggle with it, and why getting good at it sets you apart. The work is taking everything you have built, the risk picture, the control universe, the obligations, the assurance line, and rendering it in the only three currencies a board deals in: risk, money, and decisions.

Not dumbing it down, which boards can smell, but distilling it up, to the altitude where they can actually act. It takes translation to turn cyber facts into business risk, judgment to decide what is important enough for scarce board time, and a bit of courage, because honest reporting sometimes means showing weakness, incomplete coverage, overdue remediation, an accepted risk, an investment you cannot avoid asking for.

Do that consistently and something compounds. Each honest, decision-focused report builds a little more trust, and trust is the currency that gets you the budget, the authority, and the standing to do the rest of the job well. The CISO who reports in security language stays the technical person who is occasionally summoned to explain things. The one who reports in the board's language becomes a leader the board relies on, and that difference, more than any tool or certification, is what turns a security manager into a CISO. This is the room where trust stops being an idea and becomes something you either earn or do not, one quarter at a time.

Bridge to Chapter 23

Beneath the board's summary must sit a governed record; Chapter 23 builds that control library and its policy index.

CHAPTER 23

The Control Library and Policy Index

The board sees one reassuring line for control health. Underneath it sits the working record you run the program from.

The board report shows control health at a comfortable altitude: a color, a trend, a sentence. That summary is only ever as honest as what sits beneath it, and the moment a sharp director asks the obvious follow-up — *which* controls, covering *what,* owned by *whom,* and how do we know they work? — you need somewhere real to point. If the answer lives only in your head, you do not have a control library. You have personal heroics, and personal heroics do not scale, do not survive an audit, and do not survive the day you resign.

A single control universe is one organized set of controls that many frameworks resolve onto. The control library is that universe made real and populated. The universe is the map; the library is your actual territory, filled in: every control you genuinely run, what it covers, who owns it, which frameworks it answers, which policy requires it, and what evidence proves it is operating.

It is the backbone the whole program hangs on, and almost everything else you produce, the board summary, the audit evidence pack, the customer questionnaire answer, is really just a different view drawn from this one record. Get the library right and those tasks get dramatically easier, because you are reading from a source of truth instead of reconstructing one every time.

This chapter builds two connected records: the control library (what we actually do, and whether it is working) and the policy index behind it, what we have said must happen. It does so at a scale a small or mid-sized organization can actually maintain, because a control library you cannot keep current is worse than none at all.

What the Control Library Actually Is

Strip away the tooling and a control library is a simple thing: the single, authoritative list of the controls your organization runs, with enough detail attached to each that you can stand behind it. Not the controls you aspire to. Not the controls a framework describes. The ones that are real, operating, and yours.

That distinction matters more than it sounds, because the most common failure here is not a missing library. It is a library that describes a fantasy. Someone downloads a control set from a framework or a template, drops it into a spreadsheet, and now the organization "has a control library." It lists a hundred and eighty controls, most of which nobody runs, half of which have no owner, and none of which carry evidence. It looks comprehensive. It is fiction with columns. The first time an auditor or a serious customer walks a few rows, the gap between the list and the reality is exposed, and every other claim you make inherits the doubt.

A real control library is the opposite instinct: fewer entries, each one true. It is the operational instance of the traceability chain from earlier in this volume, policy, control, procedure, evidence, testing, accepted risk, turned from a concept into a table you can actually query. A small organization can run it in a spreadsheet; a larger one may reach for a platform. The tool matters far less than the discipline, because a control library is not useful for being large. It is useful for being *trusted*, for being the one place that answers the questions everyone eventually asks, the same way every time, no matter who is asking or in which framework's dialect.

The Columns That Earn Their Place

You do not need many columns. You need the few that carry weight, and you need them filled in truthfully, and the test for any field is simple: if nobody uses it to operate, evidence, test, report, or improve the control, do not add it yet.

Every control carries an *ID and a plain-language name*, so it can be referenced without ambiguity. A short statement of *what it actually does*, the intent, in a sentence, because a control nobody can describe in a sentence usually is not one. A *scope*: which systems, data, or environments it covers, and, just as important, which it does not. An *owner*, a named human accountable for it operating, because a control owned by "the team" is owned by no one.

The *frameworks and obligations it answers*, drawn from the crosswalk you built earlier rather than re-derived here, the column that turns one control into many answers. The *policy that requires it*, linking down into the policy index. *Where the evidence lives and how fresh it is*, so proof is a click away rather than an excavation. And its *current state*: last tested, any open issue, any standing exception or accepted risk with a review date.

Two of those columns deserve extra care, because they are where libraries quietly lie without meaning to. The first is *scope*. A control that says "enterprise-wide" but means corporate IT, or "all systems" but excludes SaaS, or "production" without anyone knowing whether the dev admin consoles count, that is false assurance waiting to be exposed. Write scope so someone else can verify it: "in-scope production systems flagged business-critical in the asset inventory," "privileged accounts for infrastructure, cloud, and critical SaaS platforms," "vendors that process personal data or support critical services." Be especially wary of the word *all*. It is dangerous unless you can actually prove the population.

The second is the *control statement* itself. "Access is secure" is untestable and therefore useless; "access to in-scope systems is approved before provisioning, granted on least privilege, reviewed periodically, and removed when no longer needed" is plain, scoped, observable, and testable. Write statements the control owner can run and an assurance reviewer can check, not ones only an auditor could love.

Read as a single row, those columns are the whole traceability chain for one control on one line. Take access management, because it is the control nearly every organization runs and nearly every framework asks about. The row might read: name, *access management and periodic access review*; intent, *access is granted on least privilege and reviewed on a set cadence so inappropriate access is found and removed*; scope, *production systems and cloud infrastructure, SaaS admin roles not yet fully in scope*; owner, *named identity lead, with business application owners for their own systems*; frameworks answered, *ISO's access-control and identity clauses, SOC 2's logical-access criteria, PCI's access requirements, CIS's account and access-control controls, per the earlier crosswalk*; policy, *the access control policy in the index*; evidence, *the quarterly review records, refreshed this quarter*; state, *operating, with an accepted risk covering the SaaS gap and a review date set.*

One row, and you can already answer the board, the auditor, the customer, and the control owner, because the honest scope note tells the truth instead of hiding it, and the frameworks column shows this single control quietly satisfying four masters at once. That last part is the whole efficiency dividend of the series arriving in a spreadsheet cell.

Give Your Controls Your Own IDs

A small but consequential decision sits inside that ID column, and it is worth getting right early because it is painful to unwind later: use your own stable control IDs, not a framework's numbering.

The temptation is obvious. ISO has numbers, NIST has numbers, PCI and CIS have numbers, and it feels efficient to just adopt one set. But the moment your internal controls are named after one framework's scheme, that framework quietly becomes your master structure, and the next framework that arrives does not fit its numbering, so everything gets awkward, and you have undercut the whole point of a neutral control universe that many frameworks map *onto* rather than one framework everything bends *to*.

Give controls their own stable identifiers instead, something like GOV-01 for governance, ACC-04 for periodic access review, VLN-02 for vulnerability remediation, INC-01 for incident classification. The exact scheme does not matter; stability does. Framework numbers change with every revision. Your control IDs should not have to panic every time they do, the frameworks column absorbs the change while your backbone stays put. This is the same principle expressed as a naming convention: your structure is yours, and the frameworks hang off it.

The Policy Index: The Other Half

A control library answers *what we do and whether it is working*. It does not answer *why we are required to do it*, and that is the policy index, the catalog of your governance documents with each one mapped to the controls it demands.

To build it well, you have to be clear about document *types*, because mixing them is where policy sets turn to mush. A *policy* states what the organization expects and why. A *standard* sets the minimum mandatory requirement, the policy made checkable. A *procedure* explains how it is actually performed, repeatably. A *guideline* offers recommended practice. Access control runs cleanly through all four: the *policy* says access is on least privilege and business need; the *standard* says privileged access uses MFA, is approved before provisioning, and is reviewed quarterly; the *procedure* says system owners export the access lists, certify them in the review workflow, and raise removal tickets; the *guideline* suggests naming conventions for privileged roles.

Keep them distinct, because they do different jobs, a standard can be violated and trigger an exception, a procedure can be tested for operation, a policy gets approved by leadership. If a "policy" is ten pages of configuration steps, it is really a standard or procedure; if a "guideline" is actually mandatory, it is a standard wearing the wrong label.

The library and index are two halves of one machine, and you feel the seam most clearly in the two ways it breaks. A *policy with no control beneath it* is a promise the organization is making and not keeping, the access policy says privileged access is reviewed quarterly, but no control does the reviewing, so it is a liability the day someone quotes it back.

A *control with no policy above it* is a control nobody decided to keep. It exists because an engineer once configured it, not because the organization committed to it, which makes it fragile and unexplainable. The index sitting alongside the library makes both failures visible: run your eye down the index and see which policies have real controls under them, down the library and see which controls have a policy behind them. The gaps that surface are exactly the work.

Small and mid-sized organizations tend to fail this in one of two directions, and a third worth naming. Some have *too many policies*, a thick binder of downloaded templates, professionally worded, describing a company that is not theirs, with no controls under most of them. Others have *too few real ones*, the controls operate, but nothing writes down that the organization requires them, so they live entirely on the goodwill of whoever set them up.

And many suffer *policy sprawl*: an Information Security Policy and an IT Security Policy and a Cybersecurity Policy that overlap; an Access Control Policy, a Privileged Access Policy, a Password Policy, and an MFA Standard that repeat and occasionally contradict each other, none reviewed in years. Sprawl makes an organization look more governed than it is, and the index is what exposes it, so you can retire the duplicates, merge the overlaps, push technical detail down into standards, and assign the owners. The honest middle is the same discipline this whole part keeps returning to: fewer, real, and connected beats comprehensive and hollow.

One Control, Many Frameworks

It is worth pausing on the frameworks column, because it is where the central promise of this book becomes something you can point at.

The old, exhausting way to run compliance is one library per framework: an ISO control set, a separate SOC 2 set, a PCI set, each maintained on its own, each re-describing the same access and logging and backup controls in that framework's dialect. You end up maintaining the same control three or four times, and when it changes you have to remember to change it everywhere. The control library inverts that. You maintain one entry for access management, and the frameworks column records every framework that entry answers. Change the control once, and every framework it serves updates at the same moment because they were never separate things, just different questions pointed at the same underlying control.

That mapping should never be a wall of green, though. A single control can answer a framework and still only *partially* cover it, and the library's job is to show that honestly, using explicit coverage grades — full, partial, not covered, not applicable, compensating — rather than painting everything satisfied.

This is what “many frameworks, one operating model” looks like once it stops being a slogan and becomes a working record: one well-run control, entered once, mapped through the crosswalk, honestly answering ISO and SOC 2 and PCI and CIS and whatever your customers’ countries add on top, full where it is full, partial where it is partial. That is the correlation the series has been building toward, sitting in rows you can actually maintain, and it is the reason the library is worth the discipline: not tidiness, but the collapse of four parallel programs into one.

Status That Doesn’t Hide the Truth

One green cell can conceal a great deal, so it helps to hold a control’s status as three separate questions rather than one color. *Design*: is the control defined properly, would it address the risk if performed correctly? *Operation*: is it actually being performed? *Assurance*: has it been evidenced or tested recently? These come apart in practice all the time. An access review can be beautifully designed and simply overdue (good design, poor operation).

It can run like clockwork while excluding privileged accounts (operating, badly designed). It can genuinely happen while nobody retains a shred of proof (operating, no assurance). A single overall status that blends those into one amber tells you almost nothing; keeping them distinct is what stops the library from manufacturing false comfort. If you must roll them into one status for a board line, derive it from the three underneath and be ready to say which one is dragging.

Right-Sizing: A Workbook, Not a Platform

If you are picturing an expensive governance platform, put it down. A control library is a discipline, not a product, and for most small and mid-sized organizations it starts, and often stays, as a single well-structured workbook: one tab for the library, one for the policy index, a link out to wherever the evidence actually lives. That is a real, defensible control library, and it will carry you a long way before you need anything heavier.

The instinct to resist is padding. Faced with a framework's full catalog, the temptation is to enter all of it so the library looks complete. Do not. Start with the controls that actually matter, the ones protecting your crown jewels, the handful every framework and every customer asks about: access, identity and MFA, logging, vulnerability management, backup and recovery, incident response, vendor risk. Get the grain right, too: "access control" is too broad to own or evidence, "review Salesforce admins on the third Thursday of the quarter" is too narrow to be a control, and "periodic access review for critical systems and privileged roles" is about right, big enough to own, small enough to test.

Enter those truthfully, with real owners and real evidence, and you have something worth far more than a two-hundred-row library that is mostly aspiration. You can always add rows as the program grows; what you cannot do is fake your way through controls you do not run, that is just the false green cell moved into a new spreadsheet. A platform earns its place later, when manual upkeep genuinely outgrows the workbook, but a tool automates whatever model you feed it, and if the library is dishonest or unowned, the platform just makes the dishonesty searchable and the wrong dashboards faster. Get the library true first; the tooling question comes after.

Keeping It Alive

The last thing to understand about a control library is that it decays. One that was accurate the day you built it and never touched again drifts from reality, a control gets retired, a new system comes online outside the scope notes, an owner leaves, a framework updates, evidence goes stale, and a library that is quietly wrong is more dangerous than none, because people trust it. The whole point is that it is the source of truth; a source of truth nobody maintains stops being either.

So it needs an owner of its own, and here is a distinction worth holding: the *library owner* is not the same as the *control owners*. Someone in governance, or the CISO's office, keeps the record's structure, mappings, and review cycles honest; the individual controls are still owned by the people accountable for them operating. If every control ends up "owned" by whoever maintains the spreadsheet, the library is quietly wrong. It is meant to make accountability clearer, not absorb it.

Beyond an owner, the library needs a rhythm: it updates when a control changes, when a new obligation lands, when an audit or incident reveals something it did not capture, and on a light periodic sweep to catch the drift nobody flagged. Set a review cadence you can actually meet, a missed review date on every entry just teaches people that governance dates are decorative. Version it lightly, so you can see it was genuinely revisited rather than filled in once and abandoned. The organizations that stay ready all year are the ones whose library is a working document they touch often, not one they rebuild in a panic whenever someone asks to see it.

Industry Pattern — The Two-Hundred-Row Library Nobody Ran

An organization, wanting to look mature, builds a control library the thorough way: it takes a framework's full catalog and enters every control as a row. Two hundred rows, neatly formatted, every cell filled. On a screen it is genuinely impressive, a complete-looking control program, mapped to the framework, ready to show an auditor or a customer.

Then someone tries to use it. A row claims quarterly access reviews across all systems; in reality the reviews cover one directory and have not run since spring. Another lists a formal threat-intelligence program that amounts to one analyst reading a newsletter. Dozens of entries describe controls the organization aspired to, or lifted straight from the catalog, but never actually operates. The library was not a record of what the company does. It was a record of what the framework lists, and the two had quietly drifted apart. Worse, nobody owned it, so the drift had no one to catch it. When an auditor finally pulled three rows at random and asked for evidence, two of the three had none.

The fix was the uncomfortable one: cut it. The team went row by row and kept only the controls the organization actually runs, each with a real owner and real evidence, and the library dropped from two hundred rows to a few dozen. It looked far less impressive and was worth immeasurably more, because now every row was true and someone could stand behind it. The lesson was not that the library was too big. It was that a control library is a record of what you do, not a wish list of what a framework contains, and a shorter library that is real beats a comprehensive one that is fiction every single time.

What Evidence Should You Expect

The evidence here is the library and index themselves, and whether they are honest and alive rather than aspirational and abandoned. At a practical minimum for a small or mid-sized organization, expect to be able to show:

- A control library that describes controls you actually run, each entry with its own stable ID, an owner, a plain-language statement, a scope note honest about what it does not cover, and a link to real evidence, rather than a downloaded catalog of controls nobody operates.

- A policy index mapped to controls, governance documents sorted by type (policy, standard, procedure, guideline), each with an owner and a review date, and each connected to the controls that make it true, so policy-without-control and control-without-policy gaps are visible rather than hidden.
- A frameworks-answered view, at least the key controls showing which frameworks and obligations they satisfy and at what coverage grade (full, partial, not covered, not applicable, compensating), drawn from the crosswalk, so one control demonstrably answers many masters without a wall of false green.
- Separated design, operating, and assurance status on key controls, so a green line traces to a control that is defined, performed, *and* evidenced, not just one of the three.
- A live walkthrough of a few real rows, the ability to take two or three key controls and trace each one end to end in front of someone: the policy that requires it, the control that delivers it, the evidence that proves it operated, and the honest status of any open issue or accepted risk. This is the traceability chain proven on your own library rather than described.
- Clear ownership on both the controls and the library, control owners distinct from the library owner, with light version history showing the record was updated after the moments that should change it: a new control, an audit, an incident, a framework revision.
- Right-sizing you can defend, a library scoped to the controls that matter, with a clear reason it stops where it does, rather than an accidental gap dressed up as completeness.

Reality Check

> *Open your control library, or the spreadsheet standing in for one, and pick a single row at random. Can you name its owner, describe in one sentence what it does, say honestly what it covers and what it does not, point to the policy that requires it, and put your hand on dated evidence that it operated? Can you tell whether it is designed, operating,* **and** *assured, or only some of those?*
>
> *Then the harder test: pick a control you* **know** *you run (access review, say) and check that it is actually in the library, under your own ID, mapped to every framework it answers, not sitting only in someone's head. And the real one: could another capable person find that same answer without calling you? If the answer depends on who you ask, the library is not yet your source of truth. It is a partial sketch that will let you down at exactly the wrong moment. The goal is a record where every row is true and every real control has a row.*

What This Means for You as a Security Leader

The control library and policy index are not glamorous. Nobody joins cybersecurity dreaming of maintaining a control library. But the library is, quietly, the most important document you own (more than any policy, any board deck, any certificate) because it is where the whole operating model becomes concrete and maintainable, and it is the single artifact everything else draws from. The board summary is a view of it. The audit evidence pack is a slice of it. The customer questionnaire is a translation of it. Build it honestly and you stop living in permanent reconstruction, where every request sends you assembling the same answers from scratch; instead you read them off a record you already trust.

The deeper thing it does is turn personal memory into organizational memory. A program that works only because a few people remember where everything lives will function for a while, but it is not mature, and it is one resignation away from a crisis. A mature program can be handed to another capable person and still make sense, and the control library is a large part of what makes that possible: it is where scattered knowledge becomes shared structure, where policy promises become control expectations, where framework requirements become mapped controls, and where recurring questions become reusable answers.

It is also where the series' central argument stops being philosophy and becomes something you operate: the frameworks column makes that argument part of daily work rather than a slogan. This is simply how the program works. The discipline is real — honesty over comprehensiveness, ownership over aspiration, and maintenance over one-time effort — but the payoff is that you run one program instead of four, answer many masters from one record, and walk into any room able to point at something true. Not because the library is beautiful. Because it is findable, owned, current, and true.

Bridge to Chapter 24

Chapter 24 asks the library's practical test: when an examiner arrives, can the organization prove what it claims?

CHAPTER 24

Audit, Evidence, and Readiness Checklists

The control library is the record. Readiness is proving, on demand, that the record holds.

The control library tells you what you run and points at where the evidence lives. What it does not tell you, on its own, is whether you are *ready*, whether the evidence is fresh enough, the scope tight enough, the gaps closed or at least owned, so the whole thing survives someone examining it in earnest. That is a different question, and it almost always arrives with a date attached: an audit booked, a customer assessment scheduled, a SOC 2 window opening, a certification due, a cyber-insurance renewal, a regulator asking. Every one of them, underneath the different vocabulary, asks the same thing: *can you prove it?*

Here is the uncomfortable truth this chapter is built around: you can be running a genuinely good program and still have a bad audit. The two are not the same skill. Security is doing the work; readiness is being able to *show* the work, on demand, in a form someone else will accept. Plenty of organizations that are actually well-protected walk into a check and stumble, not because the controls are not there, but because the evidence is scattered, the scope was never pinned down, half the artifacts are undated, and the person who could speak to the key control is on leave. Readiness is not pretending everything is perfect. It is knowing what is true before someone else finds out for you.

So this chapter is about walking in prepared: the discipline of doing the examiner's job to yourself first, honestly, so that by the time the real one shows up, you already know where you would pass and where you would not, and you have done something about it.

Preparation, Not Panic

Most organizations do not prepare for audits. They panic for them, and you can spot the pattern from a distance. The date lands on the calendar. Someone opens last year's evidence folder. Somebody else starts chasing screenshots. Control owners get asked for "the latest evidence," usually without a clear scope, and upload whatever looks related. File names multiply, evidence gets duplicated, old policies surface, missing approvals appear, access reviews get reconstructed from memory, and everyone works late. Then the audit begins and the team spends weeks explaining the distance between what the document says, what the process actually does, and what the evidence only partly proves. That is the screenshot sprint, and it is exhausting and unnecessary.

Preparation is the opposite instinct, and it starts from the control library rather than the evidence folder. Panic asks, *what can we find?* Preparation asks, *what should exist, does it exist, and what does it prove?* That single change of question is most of the difference between a calm audit and a bad one because it turns the check from something that happens *to* you into something you rehearsed.

The mental shift is to treat the audit as a thing you run on yourself first. An examiner is going to pick some of your controls, ask you to prove they operated, check the proof covers the right scope and period, and probe whether it is real or theater. Nothing stops you from doing all of that to yourself weeks earlier, sampling your own controls, pulling your own evidence, finding your own findings on your own calendar, where a finding is a to-do item instead of a black mark. The organizations that stay calm through audits are not the ones with nothing to hide. They are the ones with no surprises. Surprise is the enemy, the same lesson as board reporting, in a different room.

The Four Questions Behind Every Check

Strip away the framework-specific language and an examiner is really asking four things about any control they land on. These are also the lens you run readiness through, so it is worth knowing them cold.

Does the evidence exist? Not the policy that says the control should happen, the artifact that shows it did. A dated record, a log, a signed review, a ticket. If the only thing you can produce is the policy, you are pointing at the promise instead of the proof. This is the design-versus-operation trap, and it catches people constantly: a policy, a standard, a configuration baseline are *design* evidence. They show the control exists.

A completed access review, a vulnerability closure report, a backup-restore record, an incident ticket with escalation and resolution are *operating* evidence. They show it ran. Examiners usually ask both in sequence: "do you have a process?" then "show me you followed it." Do not answer the second question with the first artifact. If the check is about operating effectiveness, design evidence alone will not carry you.

Does it cover the right scope? Evidence for the wrong systems is not evidence. If the check is about the systems supporting a specific customer, or the cardholder data environment, or the SOC 2 boundary, the proof has to cover *that* population, not "access reviews in general" but access reviews for the systems actually in scope. And it has to cover the *population*, not just a comfortable sample: the moment you show one access review, the examiner asks how the system list was selected; show one vulnerability report and they ask whether every critical asset was included. A sample without a defined population is just an anecdote. If you cannot say what the population is and how you know it is complete, you cannot prove scope.

Is it current? Evidence has a shelf life. Proof that a control operated eighteen months ago says little about whether it is operating now, and most checks care about a specific recent period. Stale evidence is one of the most common readiness failures, because controls that only produce evidence when an audit looms leave long gaps the rest of the year.

Can someone stand behind it? There has to be a human who owns the control, understands it, and can speak to it credibly, not read a definition off a slide, but explain how it actually runs, what it covers, and where it does not. A control with perfect paperwork and no one who can talk about it wobbles the moment the examiner asks a follow-up. There is a deeper tell here too: a control owner who cannot explain the control may not really own it. Before a real check, walk your key control owners through their own controls, requirement to control to evidence, and if they cannot make that walk, fix it before the assessor is the one asking.

Exist, cover, current, owned. Run any control through those four and you know, honestly, whether it is ready, and if it fails one, you know exactly which one to fix.

The Readiness Checklist

A readiness check is that four-question lens run across the controls in scope for whatever's coming, and it is most useful as an actual checklist you work through, control by control, against the library you built. The library is the source; the readiness checklist is you interrogating it before the auditor does.

It starts with scope, always, because skipping scope is the fastest way to collect the wrong evidence very efficiently. Every examination has a boundary, a SOC 2 system boundary and period, an ISO management-system scope, a PCI cardholder data environment, the single service a customer actually buys, and if that boundary is unclear, stop and clarify it before anyone attaches a file. Good evidence in the wrong scope is still the wrong evidence.

Then, for each in-scope control, you confirm a short honest set of things: is the evidence identified and can you actually put your hand on it, or is it "somewhere in a shared drive"? Does it cover this check's scope and period? Is it fresh, or aged past proving anything current? Does it prove operation, not just design? Is there a named owner who can speak to it? Are the known gaps documented honestly, and is there anything in the library claiming more than the evidence supports?

You do not give every row equal attention. You start with the controls most likely to matter: the key ones, the ones carrying several frameworks and customers at once, the ones with prior findings, the ones you already suspect are weak. Work that down your in-scope controls and the output is an unglamorous, honest map: here is where we are solid, here is where the evidence is thin, here is the honest gap, here is who is fixing what before the date. That map is the entire point. It converts a vague dread of the coming audit into a specific, ownable list, and a specific list is something a small team can actually work through, where vague dread just produces the screenshot sprint.

Evidence Readiness: Having It Isn't the Same as Having It Ready

Most readiness failures are not a missing control. They are evidence that exists but is not *ready*, and the distance between those two is where a lot of audit pain lives.

Ready evidence is organized, dated, mapped to the specific thing it proves, and retrievable without a treasure hunt. Unready evidence is a screenshot someone took once, filed somewhere, that nobody can date with confidence or tie to a particular assertion. Both technically exist; only one survives "show me." This is where the evidence-to-assertion discipline earns its keep: every artifact should come with a plain statement of what it proves, for which control, over which scope and period. Good evidence tells the story of the control operating, not a story invented for the audit, but the real one: for an access review, the population it was drawn from, who reviewed it, what exceptions turned up, and how they were resolved, not just a signed spreadsheet.

The strongest position is evidence a control produces as a byproduct of simply operating: a review that generates its own dated record every time it runs, a system that logs the change through the approved path automatically. That makes freshness visible and reduces dependence on someone remembering to capture proof before the audit, but it is not self-validating: you still need to know that the evidence generation, retention, population, and scope are working. Where you can, build controls so that operating them *is* producing the evidence. Where you cannot, at least keep a living evidence index — what proves what, where it lives, when it was last refreshed — so assembling an evidence pack is a morning's collection, not a fortnight of archaeology.

Honest Gaps, and the Readiness Decision

Readiness is emphatically not about a flawless picture. No real organization has one, and pretending to is the fastest way to lose credibility. What readiness gives you is the power to choose how a gap shows up: as something you already knew, owned, and were addressing, or as something the auditor discovered that you did not.

Those two are worlds apart. Compare "we don't know" with: "this is a known partial — the payment admin platform wasn't in the Q2 access review; the risk is accepted by the payment operations owner until Q3, with remediation scheduled alongside the IAM onboarding." The second answer is not perfect. It is *credible*. It is a program that knows itself.

The same gap, hidden and then uncovered, reads as ignorance or concealment and makes the examiner wonder what else you did not disclose. So when readiness surfaces gaps you cannot close in time, do not paper over them: fix what you can, and for the rest do the honest thing: document them as exceptions or accepted risks with owners and review dates, and walk in able to speak to them plainly.

That honesty is also what lets you make readiness an actual decision rather than a hope. Before any check, put the whole thing in one of three states. *Ready:* scope clear, controls operating, evidence current and complete, owners prepared, no material unmanaged gaps. *Ready with gaps:* you can proceed, but known limitations must be managed, disclosed where appropriate, or accepted, and that is often a perfectly legitimate business call, as long as the risk is visible.

Not ready: material evidence, scope, or owner readiness is missing, and proceeding would do more harm than delay. Naming which of the three you are in, and, if it is the middle one, saying exactly which gaps and who accepts the risk of proceeding, is a leadership decision, and a far better one than declaring yourself ready and hoping the assessor does not ask.

Two things that quietly protect you here. First, review prior findings before every check. They are not history, they are open credibility tests. A repeat finding changes the question from "why is this control weak?" to "why did management not fix what it already knew?", which is a much worse conversation, so walk in knowing what was promised last time and whether it is closed. Second, and this needs saying plainly, do not manufacture evidence.

Do not backdate an approval, do not create a record for a review that did not happen, do not rename old evidence to look current, do not claim scope the evidence does not cover. The short-term pressure to just get through the audit is real; so is the lasting damage when the credibility of your evidence is questioned, because once an examiner doubts one artifact, they doubt all of them. If a control did not operate, record the gap. Evidence integrity is not negotiable. It is the one thing you cannot rebuild once it is gone.

The Dry Run — Find Your Findings First

The single highest-value readiness activity is also the simplest: do a mock version of the check before the real one. Sample a handful of your own in-scope controls exactly the way an auditor would, pick them, demand the evidence, check the scope and period, ask the owner to walk you through it, and see what breaks.

It feels slightly artificial to audit yourself, and it is worth pushing past that, because everything the dry run surfaces is a finding you get to fix quietly instead of one an examiner writes up. The review that excludes the SaaS admins. The evidence that is six months stale. The control whose only owner left in the spring. The scope statement that says "all" and means "most." Far better to meet those on your own calendar than in the room with the examiner watching. It need not be heavy, for a small organization, a single focused day of a colleague playing skeptical auditor against your key controls does the job. The value is not formality; it is that you meet your own findings first.

One Readiness, Many Checks

It is tempting to treat each type of check as its own project, a SOC 2 effort, a separate ISO effort, a PCI effort, a customer scramble, an insurance questionnaire, each on its own timeline. That is the parallel-programs trap the whole series argues against, and readiness is where consolidating pays off most visibly, because underneath they are all asking the same four questions of the same controls.

A SOC 2 audit, a big customer's assessment, and a cyber-insurance renewal will each want to see that access is reviewed, changes are controlled, logs are kept, backups are tested, incidents are handled, just in their own dialects and scopes. Prepare the evidence once, organized and current and mapped through the library, and each new check becomes a matter of pointing that ready evidence at this examiner's questions, in the scope they care about. The collection work is done once and carries across, the assurance model from earlier arriving at the audit door: one ready control base answering many masters, not a fresh fire drill each time.

The reuse caution from before still applies: ready evidence carries across only where the control, scope, and period genuinely line up, a pack built for one customer's systems does not automatically satisfy a certification with a wider boundary. And a couple of check types have their own edge worth knowing. A customer assessment is often tied to revenue and renewal, so its real risk is consistency: your answers have to line up with your control library, your contracts, and your obligation register, because if sales, legal, and security are answering from different truths, the customer eventually notices, a questionnaire answer is a representation, not a brochure, which ties straight back to the customer-assurance work earlier in this volume.

It is also worth knowing, before a customer assessment, which of your evidence is actually cleared to share externally. Plenty of genuine, current proof is internal-only until someone approves it for release, and "the evidence exists but I can't hand it over" is its own kind of unreadiness. A cyber-insurance questionnaire looks deceptively simple (short yes/no questions about MFA, EDR, backups, patching) which is exactly the trap, because those answers can become material representations that decide whether a future claim is paid.

Before you answer "yes" to MFA, know whether it really covers privileged, remote, admin, SaaS, and virtual private network (VPN) access; before "yes" to tested backups, know they are actually tested. Do not round up, and do not let a rushed yes become a coverage dispute. In every one of these, the answer should come from the evidence, not from optimism, which is, again, why the control library exists.

Industry Pattern — The Audit You Could Have Passed

An organization with a genuinely solid security program walks into an audit and has a hard time, not because the controls are weak, but because it cannot prove them cleanly. The access reviews happen, but the records are scattered across three people's inboxes and a shared drive nobody has tidied. The backups run and restore, but nobody has actually documented a restore test this year. The controls are real. The proof is a scramble.

So the audit becomes an excavation. The examiner asks for evidence of quarterly access reviews, and the team spends two days assembling screenshots from different systems, some undated, some for the wrong quarter. A request for the scope of the last penetration test turns up a report, but no one can quickly show which systems it covered or whether the ones in scope for this audit were included.

Every answer takes a day to produce, and each delay makes a capable team look disorganized. The findings that land are not about broken controls. They are about evidence that could not be produced on demand, scope that could not be shown, owners who could not speak to their own controls under questioning. It was, in the end, an audit the organization could have passed comfortably, if it had done the examiner's job on itself first.

The fix cost almost nothing but a change of habit. Before the next check, the team ran a dry run: they sampled their own key controls, asked their own owners to produce evidence on demand, and met their own findings first, the undated screenshots, the restore test nobody had recorded, the scope no one could draw. Everything the dry run surfaced was something they got to fix in advance instead of explain live. The next audit was calm. The lesson was not that the program needed to be better. It was that a good program and a good audit are two different achievements, and the second one is mostly about proving, on your own schedule, what you were already doing.

What Evidence Should You Expect

The evidence here is about the readiness discipline itself, whether the organization proves things on its own schedule or scrambles on someone else's. At a practical minimum for a small or mid-sized organization, expect to be able to show:

- A readiness tracker run before a real check, your in-scope controls worked through the exist/scope/current/owned lens ahead of the audit, with scope pinned and results recorded, rather than a scramble that started when the auditor's email arrived.
- An organized, dated evidence pack, proof for your key controls collected, mapped to the assertion each supports, proving operation (not just design), and current for the period in question, retrievable in a morning rather than a fortnight.
- Provable scope and population, a clear boundary for each check and evidence you can demonstrate the population for, not just assert, so "all" and "critical" mean something you can stand up.
- A mock-audit or dry-run record, evidence you sampled your own controls, walked your own owners through them, and found your own findings first, with what surfaced and what you did about it.
- An honest gap list and a readiness decision, known limitations documented as exceptions or accepted risks with owners and review dates, plus a clear ready / ready-with-gaps / not-ready call for the check, and a prior-findings review showing last time's commitments are closed.
- Evidence that readiness is standing, not seasonal, controls that produce their own dated proof as they operate, and an evidence index kept current year-round, so readiness is not rebuilt from zero every cycle.

Reality Check

> *Imagine an examiner books a check for three weeks from now and picks one of your key controls at random. Access review, backup restore, change management, whichever. Right now, today, could you produce dated evidence that it operated, covering the exact scope the check cares about, for the period it will examine, evidence that proves it* **ran***, not just that a policy exists? Could you name the person who would walk them through it, and would that account hold up under a follow-up question?*
>
> *Do you already know where that control is thin, and are last time's findings closed? If your honest answer is that you would need to scramble to assemble the proof, you have a readiness gap independent of how good the control itself is, and the fix is not more security, it is the discipline of proving what you already do, on your own schedule, before someone else asks. The goal is simple: nothing the examiner finds should be news to you.*

What This Means for You as a Security Leader

Readiness is where a lot of otherwise strong security leaders learn a hard lesson: doing the work and proving the work are two different jobs, and the second is what the outside world actually judges you on. A check (an audit, a customer's assessment, a regulator's question) is the moment your program meets an outside standard of proof, and it is unforgiving of the gap between what you do and what you can show.

The leaders who handle it well are not the ones with perfect programs; they are the ones who have internalized that surprise is the enemy and built a standing habit of auditing themselves before anyone else does. That habit is not about letting auditors run your program. It is about using audit pressure to sharpen your own discipline: scope, evidence, ownership, gaps, follow-up.

The payoff is a changed relationship to every check that lands on your calendar. Instead of dread and a month of manufactured paperwork, you have a tracker, an evidence pack that is already current, and a short honest list of gaps you are already on top of.

You walk in calm because you already know the answer to the only question the examiner is really asking, *can you prove what you claim?*, and where you cannot fully, you are the one who found it first.

That calm is not a personality trait; it is the compounding return on an honest control library, ready evidence, and the discipline to look at your own program skeptically before the world does. And every check, used well, should leave the operating model sharper than it found it, a control description improved, an evidence gap closed, a readiness step added, so you are getting the value of the scrutiny, not just paying its cost. That is readiness: not perfection, but prepared truth, and prepared truth, on demand, is a large part of how an organization earns the trust that is the whole point of the job.

Bridge to Chapter 25

The focus now moves from the program to the leader; Chapter 25 covers entering a role through a 30/60/90 plan and preparing for the interview that comes first.

CHAPTER 25

The CISO 30/60/90 Plan and Interview Readiness

Everything so far has been about proving the program.

This chapter is about proving you, in the first ninety days of a new role, and in the room where someone decides to give you the keys.

Every tool in this part until now has been about the program: reporting it, documenting it, proving it holds. This chapter turns the lens around, because sooner or later the readiness question stops being about your controls and becomes about you. There are two moments in a security leader's life where you are judged as a leader from a standing start, with limited information, in an organization that is not yet yours: the first ninety days of a new role, and the interview that got you there. Both come down to the same thing. Earning trust fast, before you have had time to prove yourself the slow way. And trust, as this whole book has argued, is the job.

We will build the ninety-day approach first, because it is the substance of stepping into the role well, and because, as you will see, it is also your strongest material in the interview that comes before it. A good answer to "how would you approach your first ninety days" is really an answer to "do you know how this job actually works," and that is the thing an interview is trying to find out.

The First Ninety Days: The Trap and the Opportunity

The first ninety days in a security leadership role set your reputation, faster and more durably than you would like. The people around you form their read of you early, is this someone who understands the business, or a security person here to say no; someone who listens, or someone who arrived with answers to questions they have not asked. That early read is hard to change later, which makes the entry disproportionately worth getting right. The plan for it is not really an interview artifact you prepare to sound organized; it is a controlled entry into accountability, the way you take on the role without either moving too slowly or breaking something because you moved too fast.

The trap is the instinct to act fast. You are new, you want to demonstrate value, and security has a bias toward action, so the temptation is to arrive and immediately start changing things: buy the tool you liked at your last place, rewrite the policies, flag everything that looks wrong, announce a transformation. It feels like leadership. It is usually a mistake, because you are acting on an understanding you do not have yet.

Every organization has reasons its security looks the way it does, budget constraints, historical decisions, business pressure, staffing gaps, prior leadership choices, some good, some bad, most invisible from outside. The leader who charges in changing things before understanding them tends to break something that was load-bearing, alienate the people whose help they will need, and spend political capital they have not earned. The fastest way to fail in the first ninety days is to treat them like the ninety-first.

The opportunity is the opposite. The first ninety days are the one time you have permission to ask basic questions, to not know things, to listen without being expected to have already fixed anything. That permission expires. Spend it well, on understanding before acting, and you build the foundation for everything after. Your job in that window is not to prove how much you know, or to have changed the organization. It is to find the truth without burning the relationships you will need to fix it, and to understand the place well enough that the changes you make next are the right ones, in the right order, with the right people behind them.

The 30/60/90 Shape

The plan that structures those ninety days is simple, and like every tool in this part it is a starting shape to adapt, not a script. It moves through three phases (roughly listen, assess, then plan) and the phases matter more than the exact day counts.

The first thirty days are for listening and learning. Resist the urge to conclude anything. Meet people, not just your own team, but the CIO, the CTO, the heads of product and engineering and sales and legal, and whoever owns the money, because security touches all of them and you need to know how each one sees it. Learn the business before you learn the security: how the organization actually makes money, who its most important customers are, which deals and renewals and deadlines are coming, what would genuinely hurt it, where the crown jewels really live because security priorities should follow business reality, and a plan that does not is generic, and generic plans are easy to write and hard to fund.

Find out what security has already promised, the frameworks committed to, the customers assured, the regulators answered to, the obligations on the books. And approach it with curiosity rather than judgment; the questions that get you closer to truth are the open ones. What is working well? What worries you? Where do things slow down? Which risks got accepted because there was no better option? Which control only works because one person remembers to run it? What do people route around? Ask for evidence later, first understand the system you have joined. You are building a map, not rendering a verdict.

The next thirty days are for assessing and validating. The first month tells you what people believe; the second tests whether it is true. Now you turn what you heard into an honest picture of reality. Sampling the controls that matter, checking claims against evidence, separating real strength from assumed strength. This is where the operating model becomes your assessment lens: you are effectively building, or inheriting and correcting, a control library and a risk picture.

And it is where you prioritize by leverage, not just severity, asking not only "what's broken?" but "what fix improves the most things that matter?" Fixing privileged access, for instance, can improve ransomware resistance, SOC 2 readiness, audit posture, and customer assurance all at once. That leverage question is the framework-correlation idea arriving in your entry plan. A couple of well-chosen quick wins belong here too, something visible and genuinely useful that builds credibility while you are still forming the bigger plan. Not theater; a real, small improvement that shows you can execute.

The last thirty days are for committing and aligning. Now you turn the assessment into a prioritized roadmap, the handful of things that matter most, in the order that makes sense, sized to what the organization can actually absorb and fund, and grouped into themes rather than a shopping list of tools (an "identity and access uplift," a "ransomware resilience" theme) so leadership can follow it.

Just as importantly, you get buy-in: you walk leadership through what you found and what you propose, in risk-and-business language, and you pre-wire it. No one should be surprised by the roadmap in the room. A plan presented without stakeholder alignment can be technically right and organizationally dead. The endorsement is what turns your ninety days from a personal exercise into an organizational mandate.

The structure holds across roles; the emphasis shifts with the job, a turnaround leans on urgent stabilization, a scale-up on operating model and customer assurance, a regulated entity on governance and evidence, a product company on secure development and data and AI. Adapt the emphasis, keep the shape. And for a small or mid-sized organization, keep all of it light: you may be a team of one wearing several hats, and a hundred-page assessment is neither realistic nor useful. A focused stakeholder map, an honest read of the top risks and the real control picture, one or two quick wins, and a short prioritized plan leadership has agreed to, that is a genuinely strong ninety days, achievable even while you are doing the actual security work at the same time.

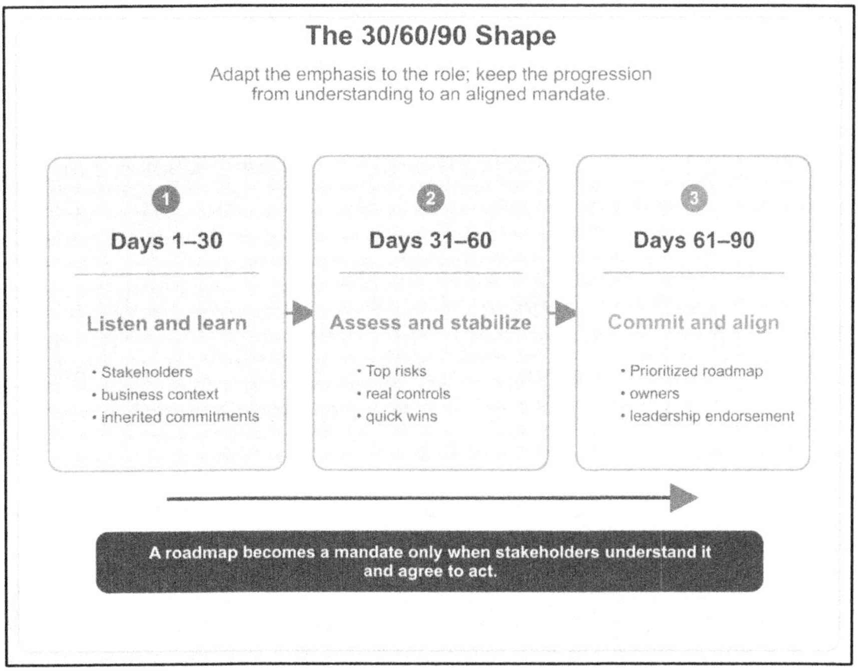

Don't Walk in Like an Auditor — but Don't Sit on a Fire Either

There is a specific way new security leaders sabotage themselves, and it is worth naming because it is so tempting: arriving as an auditor. You have got fresh eyes, you can see the gaps everyone inside stopped noticing, and the instinct is to catalog them and present the findings, to establish credibility by showing how much is wrong.

"Show me the policy. Where's the evidence. Why isn't this done. Who approved this exception." The questions may be valid; the timing is not. Interrogate people before you understand context and you will get answers, but not truth. They will manage you, show you the clean folders and the safe explanations, and you will learn the program's brochure before you learn the program. A CISO needs audit discipline, but not an audit personality.

It backfires the other way too: the people who built the current state hear a list of their failures from someone who has been there three weeks, and you make enemies of exactly the people whose cooperation you will need. The move is to find the risk without making it personal, frame what you find as the organization's shared challenge, not individual failure ("here's where we're exposed and what I'd propose we do," not "here's what you've all been doing wrong"), credit what is working before you name what is not, and assume the current state has reasons before you assume incompetence.

This is the playbook lesson in its most sensitive form: the written plan meets a messier, political reality. You are building trust *while* finding risk, and those goals only feel like they are in tension: the leaders who do it well are trusted *because* they surface hard truths in a way that helps rather than blames.

One caution in the other direction, though, because listening can curdle into paralysis. The ninety-day discipline is not a reason to sit on something material. If the first weeks turn up open heat, an active incident, a critical internet-facing exposure, a regulatory deadline already slipping, a backup that will not restore, escalate it now.

Separate urgent stabilization from broad transformation: the burning platform gets acted on immediately; the ninety-day process builds the plan for everything else. A leader who "listens" past a live exposure is not being patient, they are being negligent, and everyone will remember which it was.

The First Ninety Days Should Leave Something Behind

Like every readiness discipline in this part, entering a role well produces artifacts, not just impressions. By the end you should be able to point to something real: a stakeholder map, an honest baseline of the top risks and the actual control picture, one or two delivered quick wins, and a prioritized plan leadership has seen and endorsed. Those artifacts separate a professional entry from a vibes-based one, and they let you, and the people who hired you, actually judge whether the ninety days worked.

They also connect straight into the operating model you will run from here. The baseline becomes the seed of the control library. The risks feed the reporting you will take to the board. The obligations you inventory become the register you will manage. And every finding needs an owner, a decision, or a risk acceptance attached, a beautiful ninety-day assessment that nobody owns is a consulting artifact, not a leadership plan.

The first ninety days are not a separate onboarding exercise you file away; they are you building the first version of the operating model this whole book describes, for this specific organization, from a standing start. Do them as owned artifacts and you have begun the real work. Do them as impressions and you have just had ninety days of meetings.

Interview Readiness: Showing Judgment Before You Have the Job

Everything above is also, conveniently, the best thing you can bring into an interview because an interview for a security leadership role is not really testing what you know. It is testing your judgment, and those are different things.

Here is the reframe that changes how aspiring CISOs interview: nobody hiring a security leader is trying to find out whether you can recite ISO's control families or list the PCI requirements. They can get that from a certification. What they cannot get from a certificate, and what they are actually probing for, is judgment: can you walk into ambiguity and figure out what matters, prioritize under constraint, handle the CIO who sees security as friction and the board that wants comfort and the sales team making commitments you have not seen, translate risk into business terms, be trusted with the keys.

The candidates who struggle are often the technically strongest ones, who answer every question by demonstrating knowledge when the interviewer was trying to assess thinking. A weak answer is "I'll implement ISO, NIST, SOC 2, and best practices." A strong one shows *how* you would think: "I'd start by understanding the business model, the critical services, the regulatory and customer obligations, the current control maturity, the recent incidents and open findings — then validate the key controls and build a risk-based roadmap. I wouldn't start with a framework checklist; I'd use frameworks to structure the assessment and translate what I find into business risk."

Your single strongest piece of interview material is the ninety-day approach we just built. Asked "what would you do in your first ninety days," do not recite a generic list, and do not give the same answer to every company; the *structure* stays 30/60/90 while the *emphasis* shifts to the business in front of you, and interviewers can hear the difference between a memorized template and role-specific judgment. Scenario questions work the same way. "A customer is demanding SOC 2 in three months." "Engineering says security is slowing delivery." "A regulator raised a finding." Do not reach for a framework; walk a structure: clarify the real scope, name the material risk, stabilize anything urgent, identify the stakeholders and obligations, weigh the options, recommend a path with an owner and a timeline, and communicate upward.

On the SOC 2 one, a mature answer sounds like: "First I'd clarify the actual scope — which service, Type I or II, which criteria, the real customer deadline, what evidence already exists. Then a readiness assessment against the control library, focused on access, change, vendor risk, incident response, logging, and availability. I'd separate must-fix control gaps from evidence gaps, align leadership on what we tell the customer, and bring back a remediation plan with owners and dates — and I wouldn't promise a report date until evidence readiness is confirmed." That answer understands scope, connects customer pressure to control readiness, and does not overpromise. It sounds like a CISO, not because it names more frameworks, but because it shows how decisions get made.

A few more things worth carrying into the room. Connect everything to business impact, because a leader who only speaks in threats and controls signals they will be hard to put in front of a board. Be honest about what you have not done. No one has personally led every framework, regulator, sector, and cloud, and "I haven't run that end to end; here's the method I'd apply, leaning on local expertise for interpretation" reads as judgment, where inflated claims read as risk.

This matters most when you are moving across borders or sectors. Asked about a regulation you have not personally implemented, say an EU resilience regime like DORA when your background is elsewhere, the strong answer is not a bluff; it is the method: "I'd confirm applicability with legal, map the ICT-risk, incident-reporting, resilience-testing, and third-party obligations into the control-and-obligation model I already run, and build the remediation plan with local regulatory expertise." That shows a leader who can absorb a new regime, which is exactly what a cross-border hire is being tested for.

Tell your examples with a little structure (context, challenge, action, result, and what you learned) rather than rambling through your résumé, and choose the ones that show judgment and trade-offs, not just activity. Come with questions of your own, too, because good questions show maturity and let you judge the role: what does the board actually worry about; which external pressure is strongest right now; where does security currently create friction; what authority will this role have over business-owned risk.

And know the series' through-lines cold, because they are increasingly what a modern security leader is hired for: how the frameworks relate rather than any one in isolation, how compliance shifts when your customers sit in other countries, how data protection and privacy sit alongside security. An interviewer who hears you talk fluently about *correlation*, one operating model answering many frameworks, is hearing someone who thinks like a leader, not a checklist operator.

Industry Pattern — The Candidate With the Perfect Framework Answer

> *Two people interview for the same security leadership role. The first has the credentials and the vocabulary: asked about any framework, they recite its structure cleanly, name the controls, quote the clauses. On paper they are the obvious hire, and for the first twenty minutes they sound like it.*
>
> *Then the panel asks a real question: you arrive Monday and know nothing about the environment yet, what do you actually do first? The polished candidate reaches for the framework again: they would run a gap assessment against a standard, score the controls, produce a maturity rating. It is a fine answer to a different question. What the panel wanted was judgment, who they would talk to, what they would learn before concluding anything, how they would tell a real risk from a documented one, how they would avoid walking in like an auditor and torching their credibility by week three. The framework answer was correct and told the panel almost nothing about whether this person could lead.*
>
> *The candidate who got the offer was not more certified. Asked the same question, they described a ninety-day approach: listen first, map the stakeholders, check the claimed controls against real evidence, find one or two quick wins to build trust, then commit to a short, funded roadmap tied to the business. The same knowledge sat underneath, shaped as judgment rather than recitation. The lesson was not that frameworks do not matter; they plainly do. It was that nobody hires a security leader to recite a catalog. They hire the person who can walk into ambiguity and show, calmly, how they would think their way through it.*

What Evidence Should You Expect

The evidence here is a little different, because it is about *your entry as a leader* rather than a control, proof that you stepped into the role as a professional rather than improvised it. At a practical minimum, whether you are entering a small or mid-sized organization or preparing to, expect to be able to produce:

- A stakeholder map from the first phase, who owns technology, product, data, legal, procurement, risk, and the money, how each sees security, and where the real influence and friction sit, so your read of the organization is written down, not just felt.
- An honest baseline of the top risks and the actual control picture, claims checked against evidence, that becomes the seed of your control library and risk reporting rather than an onboarding document you file away.
- One or two delivered quick wins, small, real, useful improvements made early, evidence you can execute while still forming the bigger plan. Kept distinct from the structural work that takes longer.
- A prioritized roadmap leadership has endorsed, the handful of things that matter most, grouped into themes, sized to what the organization can fund and absorb, each with an owner, agreed rather than imposed, and delivered as a first board or executive update, so the entry closes the loop from assessment into an ongoing governance rhythm rather than ending as a document.
- A repeatable way to show judgment, for interviews and for the role itself, the ability to walk through *how* you would approach an unfamiliar problem (clarify, find the material risk, weigh, sequence, involve, own) rather than reciting what a framework says, because judgment is what you are actually hired and trusted for.

Reality Check

Picture yourself three weeks into a new security leadership role, or three weeks from now in the interview for one. Could you name the handful of people whose view of security actually determines whether you succeed, and do you know how each of them sees it? Could you describe how you would spend the first ninety days without defaulting to "I'd assess the tooling and buy what's missing" — who you would meet, what you would validate first, what you would report by day thirty, what you would deliberately ***not*** *do too early?*

If someone asked how you would handle a hard situation, a CIO who treats security as friction, a customer commitment sales made without you, a board that wants only good news, could you walk through your ***thinking*** *rather than reaching for a framework? And the honest one: would your instinct in a new role be to charge in and fix what is visibly wrong, or to spend your scarce, expiring permission to not-know on understanding why it is that way first, while still escalating anything genuinely on fire? A CISO who cannot explain the first ninety days clearly is asking the organization to trust improvisation, and improvisation has its place, but not as an entry strategy.*

What This Means for You as a Security Leader

This chapter sits close to the heart of what this book is for, because most of its readers are aspiring CISOs or leaders stepping into bigger roles, and this is the moment the whole thing gets tested, not in a quiet office running a mature program, but in the exposed first weeks of an unfamiliar organization, or in a room full of people deciding whether to trust you.

That is where everything the series has built has to become something you *are*, not just something you know. The first ninety days are not about proving you are the smartest security person in the room; they are about proving you can lead the room, listening before judging, understanding before prescribing, validating before promising, aligning before announcing, and acting fast where risk genuinely demands it.

The through-line holds all the way down. The interview and the first ninety days are both readiness problems, the same shape as every other chapter in this part: know what matters, be able to show it, walk in prepared rather than hoping to improvise. They are both trust problems, too. You are earning confidence from a standing start, from people who do not yet know you, and you earn it the same way the series has argued you earn it everywhere: by understanding before acting, being honest about what you do not know, translating security into the business's language, and surfacing hard truths in a way that helps rather than blames.

A good CISO enters with humility to learn what came before, structure to make sense of it, urgency to act where exposure is real, and patience not to break trust before change is possible. That balance is the work. Do it in the room and you get the job. Do it in the first ninety days and you keep the standing to do the job well. It is the whole series, aimed at you instead of the program. Trust is the thing you arrive without, and this is where you first have to earn it.

Bridge to Chapter 26

Everything so far assumes you are inside one organization; the final chapter is about doing this work from outside it, as a fractional CISO, consultant, or advisor.

CHAPTER 26

Consulting and Advisory Use Cases

The same operating model, delivered from the outside, with authority, context, time, and accountability defined by the engagement.

Everything in this book so far has assumed you are inside one organization, running its program and sitting in its rooms. But a growing number of security leaders do this work from the outside, as fractional or virtual CISOs, as consultants, as board advisors, as the experienced second set of eyes an organization brings in before the real auditor, customer, or regulator arrives.

There is a real and growing need there, because most small and mid-sized organizations sit in exactly that position: they have real security obligations, real customer demands, maybe a failed audit or a frightening contract clause, and no one senior enough to make sense of it, but not enough work, or budget, to hire a full-time CISO. The person who can walk into that and bring order is genuinely valuable, and increasingly in demand.

It is also one of the best paths into this career and one of the most flexible ways to stay in it. For an aspiring CISO, fractional and advisory work is an accessible on-ramp. You get to be the security leader for several small organizations before anyone hands you a single big one, and you learn faster from five different messes than from one tidy program.

For an experienced leader, it is a way to do the work on your own terms, across more organizations, without the weight of a single seat. Either way, this chapter is about how the toolkit you have built across the series changes when you deliver it as an outsider because it does change, and the leaders who do not adjust for that struggle in ways that have nothing to do with their security knowledge.

What Actually Changes When You're Outside

The security is the same. What changes around it depends on the role: an independent advisor, a readiness reviewer, a board advisor, and a fractional CISO may all sit outside the payroll or org chart, but they do not carry the same authority, access, or accountability. Across those roles, four dimensions need to be made explicit before the work begins: authority, context, time, and ownership of the outcome.

You usually have *less embedded authority*. A point-in-time advisor may be able only to recommend. A fractional or virtual CISO may be delegated decision rights, direct a team, influence budget, or carry executive accountability under the engagement, but even then the authority is narrower and less assumed than it is for a fully embedded leader. Do not infer it from the title. Define what you may decide, direct, approve, and escalate, and write those boundaries down.

You have *less context*. An internal CISO builds understanding over months and years; you often get days or weeks. You are always working with a partial picture, and a lot of the skill is being useful anyway, finding the material risk fast, being honest about what you cannot yet see, and not pretending to a completeness you do not have.

You have *less time*. Engagements are bounded, so ruthless prioritization is not a nice-to-have; it is the whole game. The client is not paying you to catalog every gap. They are paying you to find the ones that matter and say what to do about them.

And the last of the four is *ownership of the outcome*. You do not own the client's enterprise risk merely because you advise on it. Management retains the organization's decisions and risk acceptance. But your accountability for the work itself can be real, and a fractional CISO may own specified program outcomes if the engagement grants that authority. The safe boundary is precise rather than absolute: name what you advise, what you operate, what you may decide, what management retains, and what happens when the client rejects a recommendation. The worst place to stand in advisory work is with responsibility everyone assumes and authority nobody granted.

Which is why the first question of any engagement is not technical at all. It is *what role am I actually playing here?* Advisor, fractional CISO, readiness reviewer, board advisor, independent reviewer: they overlap, but they are not the same, and the client often will not know the difference. You have to. Because if the role is vague, expectations expand quietly until the client expects you to be advisor, implementer, auditor, risk owner, and accountable executive all at once. Define it early, write it down, and return to it whenever scope pressure begins.

Scope Is a Control

If there is one place advisory work goes wrong, it is scope, and the reframe that fixes it is to stop thinking of scope as an administrative section in a proposal and start treating it as a *control*. It does exactly what a good control does: it prevents overclaiming, protects the client from assuming more was reviewed than actually was, protects you from being blamed for areas you never examined, and keeps the engagement focused enough to deliver value. When advisory work sours, the security was usually fine; the *agreement* was the problem.

So be explicit, before you start, about what the engagement covers and what it does not, what you will deliver and in what form, and, most importantly, where your responsibility stops and the client's decision-making begins. "This assesses SOC 2 readiness for the described platform, based on interviews and sampled evidence; it is not an audit, an attestation, or a certification" is not timid throat-clearing. It is the sentence that keeps the client from believing you certified something you only reviewed, and keeps you from being held to an outcome you never owned.

That same honesty extends to your assumptions, which every advisory output rests on whether you name them or not: that management's information is complete unless noted, that evidence review is sample-based, that legal applicability needs confirmation by counsel. Stating assumptions is not hedging. They are truth labels, the difference between a recommendation that is honestly bounded and one that sounds more certain than the work behind it, which is why the assumptions belong in the final deliverable itself, not just the engagement letter, so the report can never read as more definitive than the work allowed.

Right-sizing belongs here too, as it has all through this part. A fixed engagement cannot fix everything, and a small, stretched client cannot absorb a fifty-item remediation plan. Scope to what matters and what they can actually do, the handful of things that move the risk most, in an order they can follow after you are gone. The instinct to prove your worth by finding *everything* is the one to resist; the value is in finding the *right* things and making them actionable.

The Main Ways This Work Shows Up

"Consulting and advisory" spans quite different engagements, and knowing which you are in shapes everything, but the discipline underneath stays constant, and each type draws on a different part of the operating toolkit.

The *fractional or virtual CISO* is the most common: you are the security leader on a fraction of your time, running the reporting, guiding the roadmap, sitting in on the decisions that need you, representing security to the board and to customers. It is not "CISO work, just fewer days" — the needs are full-time and your hours are not, so the whole skill is deciding what genuinely needs you and letting the rest go. One thing to settle before you sign: what happens during an incident. Are you available for emergency advisory support, at what response time, and who owns the legal, customer, and regulator communication? Sort it out before the incident, because it will be painfully unclear during one.

The *point-in-time assessment* is the 30/60/90 entry, compressed and aimed at a deliverable, listen fast, validate against evidence, prioritize by leverage, hand back a plan. The *readiness engagement* is Chapter 24 delivered as a service: get them through a specific SOC 2, certification, customer assessment, or insurance requirement, with an honest ready / ready-with-gaps / not-ready verdict.

Do not blur readiness support with the independent examination. You may help a client identify and remediate gaps, but a formal audit opinion, attestation report, or certificate must come from the appropriately qualified independent practitioner or certification body when the applicable scheme requires it. The *board-advisor* role is Chapter 22's translation skill sold on its own. You run nothing; you are the trusted outside voice that turns "the SIEM coverage is incomplete" into "we may lack the visibility to detect a material incident in time," and clarity from someone with no agenda is rare enough to be worth a lot.

And one engagement type is this book's entire thesis sold as a service: *framework consolidation*, or control rationalization. A staggering number of small and mid-sized organizations are drowning in exactly that mess: a separate scramble for every framework, overlapping questionnaires, a control set nobody can map, a growing pile of customers in different countries each demanding something. Untangling that into one operating model (one control universe, many frameworks answered from it) is enormously valuable, and it is work the internal team often cannot do because they are too close to it.

It also carries a boundary worth stating plainly: when a client's questions cross into other countries' regulation, you can map the *operational* implications, but you are not giving legal advice unless you are qualified and engaged to. Say what is known, flag what legal must confirm, and then build the operating plan. If there is a single advisory offering this book equips you for above all others, it is bringing "many frameworks, one operating model" to an organization that has only ever known the many.

Entering as an Outsider, with Even Less Permission

The entry problem is the same here, only harder: less time, less accumulated context, and only the internal standing the engagement and the client's leaders have actually granted. You still cannot walk in as an auditor cataloging failures; it lands even worse from a stranger, and you will get the brochure instead of the truth just as fast. And there is an extra dynamic internal CISOs do not face: the client's own team may see you as a threat. Here to tell the boss they are doing it wrong, to recommend replacing them, to take over. Until you defuse that, they will give you the polished version and quietly work against you.

The move is to make yourself obviously an ally of the people already there, not a judge of them. Credit what is working and mean it. Frame the engagement as helping the team get where they are trying to go, and be clear you are there to make them look good to their leadership and their customers, not to make them look bad to you. The advisors who thrive are the ones the client's team is glad to see arrive, because they have learned the fastest route to the truth, and to work that actually gets implemented after they leave, runs through the people who will still be there when they are gone.

Independence Is the Whole Product

Here is the tension at the center of advisory work: you are paid by the client, and there is a constant, subtle pull to tell them what they want to hear, or to scope the problem in a way that sells more of your own time. Resisting that pull is not an ethical extra. It is the entire reason your advice is worth anything. The advisor who flatters, who confirms whatever the founder already believed, who never delivers uncomfortable news, is worthless, and clients eventually work that out. The one who tells hard truths clearly and kindly: "this is genuinely a problem and here's what I'd do," even when it is not what the room hoped to hear, is the one who gets called back and referred on.

It shows up in concrete disciplines. Do not manufacture urgency to sell more work. Do not recommend the tool you have a relationship with over the one that is right for them. Do not scope a two-day problem as a two-month engagement. Resist the overpromise, too, because it is the same failure wearing a confident face: "we'll make you compliant," "SOC 2 in three months," "we'll ensure regulatory compliance" are broad promises about outcomes you do not control; the honest version is "we'll assess readiness and identify the gaps against the agreed scope, and the outcome depends on evidence, operating effectiveness, and the auditor's judgment."

A promise you cannot control is not confidence, it is risk you have quietly taken on. And be willing to tell a client they *do not* need what they came asking for, or that the cheaper path is better because the times you talk a client out of spending are the times they learn your advice is genuinely theirs-first. In a market full of consultants selling fear and complexity, honest clarity is rare enough to be a real differentiator. It is the same thing that makes a CISO trustworthy inside an organization, just more exposed, because trust is what you are actually selling.

One practical corner of that trust is the boring, unglamorous handling of the client's material. As an advisor you will be handed network diagrams, vulnerability reports, incident records, contracts, sometimes personal data, and a consultant advising on security should never become the client's data-leakage event. Agree up front how sensitive material is shared, stored, and returned, and do not casually move client evidence into personal drives, unmanaged tools, or AI systems without explicit approval, and yes, that includes running their material through an AI assistant; get the client's sign-off first. It sounds obvious. It still happens, and it ends engagements.

Leave Them Better, Not More Dependent

The measure of good advisory work is uncomfortable for the business model but right: the client should be *more capable* after you leave, not more reliant on you. It is tempting to make yourself indispensable, to hold the knowledge, keep the model in your head, ensure they cannot function without your monthly days. Resist it. The engagements that build a real reputation are the ones where you left the client genuinely stronger: an operating model they can run, a control library that is *theirs* and maintainable by their own people, a roadmap they own, a team that learned something from working with you.

This is the artifact discipline from across this part, sharpened by distance, a beautiful assessment the client cannot execute is worthless, and worse from a consultant, because you are not there to execute it for them. Which is also why every engagement should have explicit exit criteria: a clear picture of what "done" looks like, whether that is a control library built and handed over, a readiness verdict delivered, or a vCISO role transitioned to an internal owner.

Sometimes the right outcome is continued support and sometimes it is a clean handover. Both are fine, but the client should know which one they are buying. Paradoxically, the advisor who works to make themselves unnecessary is the one who gets the most repeat work and the warmest referrals, because they have proven the rarest thing an outsider can prove: that they were there to help, not to embed.

Industry Pattern — The Consultant Who Became the Risk Owner

> *A fractional security advisor is brought into a small company to help it mature. The advisor is good, and generous with their time. They do not just advise, they do. They write the policies themselves, run the risk assessments themselves, sit in the vendor calls, make the security decisions the client is not sure how to make. The client is delighted: security is handled, and handled well.*
>
> *Two years in, something has quietly gone wrong. The client has no security capability of its own, no owner who understands the program, no one who could run the reporting or answer an auditor without the advisor on the call. Every decision still routes through the outsider. When a real incident hits on a weekend and the advisor is unreachable, the client discovers it has been renting judgment it never learned to produce, and nobody inside is sure who decides whether to notify a customer.*
>
> *Without ever choosing to, the advisor has become the de facto owner of risks that were never theirs to own, accountable in practice for a program the business had stopped engaging with. The engagement was a success by every invoice and a failure by the only measure that matters.*
>
> *The advisor who does this well works in the opposite direction from the start. They make the client's own people do the work, with guidance, so the capability stays behind. They put a named client owner on every risk and every decision, and refuse to be that owner themselves. They build a control library and a reporting rhythm the client's team can run without them, and they measure the engagement not by how indispensable they have become but by how unnecessary. The lesson is not that generous advisors are the problem. It is that the job is to leave a client more capable, not more dependent, and an advisor the client cannot function without has, however unintentionally, sold dependence instead of maturity.*

What Evidence Should You Expect

The evidence here is about the *engagement* being run professionally, scoped, role-clear, independent, and leaving the client able to act. Whether you are advising a small or mid-sized organization or engaging one, expect to be able to point to:

- A scope-and-role agreement, what the engagement covers and does not, which role you are playing, the deliverables and their form, the assumptions behind the work, and an explicit line where your responsibility ends and the client's decision-making begins.
- A prioritized, right-sized deliverable, a focused picture of the risk and the handful of things that matter most, in an order the client can follow, rather than an exhaustive catalog they will never work through, with each finding scoped, owned, and timelined enough to act on.
- Recommendations the client owns, every finding attached to a client owner, a decision, or an accepted risk, and a management-approval trail behind any external representation you helped draft (a customer questionnaire, an audit response, an insurance form, a regulator reply), since the sign-off must be management's, not yours, so the work continues after you leave rather than sitting in a document nobody actions.
- An operating model the client can run without you, a control library, a reporting rhythm, a roadmap that belong to their people and are maintainable by them, plus clear exit criteria for what "done" means.
- Evidence of independence and care, advice that reflects the client's interest over your own utilization (including the times you scoped *down* or talked them out of spending), and disciplined handling of their confidential material so you never become their data-leakage event.

Reality Check

If you were dropped into an unfamiliar organization for a bounded engagement, could you answer the questions that keep advisory work honest before you started? What role am I playing, and what am I ***not*** *doing? Who owns the risks I find, and who approves the answers I help draft for customers or auditors? What have I actually reviewed, versus what am I relying on management to have told me truthfully? What does "done" look like?*

Then the harder one: when the client wants to hear they are fine, or wants to buy the expensive tool, or wants you to bless the decision they had already made, could you tell them the honest thing instead, even at the cost of the easier engagement? If those role and scope answers are unclear, the engagement is already carrying risk, not cyber risk, ***advisory*** *risk, the kind that becomes real when accountability and expectations quietly drift apart. And if your instinct is to please the person paying you, that is the reflex to unlearn, because your independence is the only thing you are really selling.*

What This Means for You as a Security Leader

Advisory and fractional work deliver the whole series under constrained conditions: authority may be narrow or merely advisory, time is bounded, context is partial, and management retains the enterprise risk. Everything you have built — the operating model, the framework correlation, the reporting, the readiness, the entry discipline — has to work within the role the engagement actually grants. For a point-in-time advisor, that may mean influence alone. For a fractional CISO, it may include delegated leadership and decision rights. The boundary has to be explicit either way.

Which is exactly why it is such a good test of whether you have actually internalized this material or just learned it: an engagement letter or borrowed title can create access, but only judgment and trust make the work useful. And the tools do not do the work for you here any more than they did inside; a board format, a control library, and a readiness checklist are only as good as the judgment you bring to using them. From the outside, the limits of that judgment become visible quickly because neither familiarity nor organizational position can carry it for long.

It closes a loop the series has been drawing from the start. The reason this work is possible at all, the reason a small organization can bring in a security leader for two days a month and be genuinely better for it, is that the job was never really about running tools or holding a title. It was about bringing clarity to risk and earning the trust to act on it, and that travels: across organizations, across sectors, across borders, into rooms where you have no standing but your judgment.

If you can walk into a stranger's chaos, find what matters, tell them the truth kindly, and leave them more capable than you found them, then you have understood what this whole series has been about because that is the job in its purest form, stripped of the org chart and the tooling and the title, down to the two things that were always the point: risk, and the trust to do something about it.

Bridge to the Cyber Insurance and Claim Readiness Playbook

Two operating moments move faster than normal governance can absorb; the first is the insured cyber incident, and whether the organization can actually use the transfer it bought.

PLAYBOOK

Cyber Insurance and Claim Readiness

Making the transfer work when the incident is real

The ransomware note is on the screen. A customer-facing service is down, legal is pulling the response team together, finance wants an estimate, the CEO wants to know whether insurance will cover it, and somebody asks a question that should have had an answer six months ago: *who has the policy?*

The policy gets found. Then the harder questions start. Who is authorized to notify the insurer? Does notice go to the carrier directly, or through the broker? Can the team use its usual forensics firm, or does the policy expect a panel provider? Does the insurer have to consent before serious money is spent? Which costs should be recorded separately? When does the business-interruption clock start? And who is keeping the claim record while everyone else is trying to contain the incident?

None of those is the first priority in a cyber emergency. Containment, safety, continuity, legal duties, and honest communication do not wait for an insurance discussion. But treating the claim as paperwork to reconstruct later is how a valid transfer becomes a disputed, delayed, or poorly evidenced recovery. Claim readiness is the discipline of making the policy usable under pressure, connecting the incident-response plan to the insurance contract without letting the insurer run the incident, and without letting the incident team ignore the conditions attached to getting paid.

The goal is not to guarantee a claim gets paid; no playbook can promise that. The goal is narrower and entirely within your control: to prevent avoidable damage to your position because notice was late, consent was assumed, the wrong provider was engaged, costs were mixed together, decisions went undocumented, or the loss could no longer be reconstructed.

Start After the Policy Is Bound

Volume II, Chapter 4 made the core point: insurance finances specified parts of a loss. It does not transfer accountability, restore customer trust, or replace a control. That earlier chapter also owns the design decisions, the limits, retentions, exclusions, the application and clarifications submitted about your control posture, the renewal, and the risk you chose to retain. This playbook starts the day *after* that policy is bound, and its first meeting should not happen during a claim. Hold it when the policy is placed or renewed, while people can read slowly and ask inconvenient questions.

Bring together the policy owner, finance, legal, security, incident response, business continuity, the broker, and whatever specialist adviser you rely on. The job is not for security to interpret policy wording alone; it is to translate the policy's operating conditions into actions the response team will recognize and execute.

Work a handful of realistic scenarios, a ransomware or destructive attack on operations; theft of personal or confidential data; a fraudulent funds transfer; an outage or compromise at a critical cloud or technology provider; a security defect affecting customers; and an event involving an acquired entity or a country near the edge of policy scope. For each, ask how a potential claim would be activated, which policy might respond, who must be notified, which providers can be used, which approvals may be required, what records will prove the loss, and what stays your responsibility regardless of coverage.

This is not a coverage prediction. It is a rehearsal of the handoffs, and its output is a response card and a short set of claim procedures, not a second copy of the policy written by people who are not coverage specialists.

Keep the Promises Visible After Binding

The application does not stop mattering when the policy is issued. Depending on the wording, the insurer may have relied on statements about the organization's controls, operations, entities, systems, revenue, data, suppliers, or prior incidents. The policy may also contain conditions, change-notification duties, or response requirements that remain relevant during the policy period.

Do not assume that every application answer is a continuing warranty, and do not assume that none of them matters after binding. Have the policy owner, broker, and legal or insurance adviser identify the statements and conditions the organization must continue to monitor, and translate them into an operational record that names:

- the representation or condition;
- the applicable scope;
- the control or business owner;
- the evidence supporting it at placement;
- what change could make it inaccurate;
- who must be told when that change occurs;
- and who decides whether the insurer or broker needs to be notified.

This is where insurance governance connects to change management, acquisitions, control exceptions, major technology changes, and the risk register. If the application said a control covered the whole organization and an acquisition introduces an uncovered environment, the security team should not wait until the next claim to discover that the operating reality has moved away from the placement record. The CISO should not interpret the legal effect of a changed fact; the CISO should make sure material changes in control reality become visible to the people who own that interpretation and the insurance relationship.

Build the Claim-Response Card

During an incident the team needs a summary it can read in minutes, not a contract it has to parse. Build a controlled claim-response card that captures:

- the policy period, policy numbers, insurers, and any primary and excess layers;
- the internal policy owner and an alternate;
- broker, insurer, claim, and emergency-contact details;
- who is authorized to give notice, and how notice must be submitted;

- the notice triggers and time requirements as the actual wording states them;
- any material consent-before-spend or pre-approval requirements;
- the approved or panel providers for legal, forensics, restoration, notification, communications, and negotiation;
- the process for requesting an alternative provider when you have a justified preference;
- the retentions, waiting periods, sublimits, and expense categories the incident team needs to recognize operationally;
- where the policy, endorsements, application, submitted clarifications, and prior insurer correspondence live;
- the other policies that may need review, crime, technology errors and omissions, property, directors and officers, kidnap and ransom;
- the claim-log owner and the finance cost code; and
- the internal escalation route when a policy requirement is unclear.

The card is a navigation aid, not a substitute for the policy, and it should say so. Date it, version it, protect it, and, this matters more than it sounds, keep a copy reachable when your normal systems are not. A response card stored only inside the environment the incident just took down is an elegant way to make it useless. Review it at renewal and whenever the insurer, broker, panel firms, business structure, critical providers, or incident leadership change, and actually test the contacts: an emergency number nobody has dialed since binding is an assumption, not a capability.

Put a Claim Lead Beside the Incident Commander

The incident commander runs the incident. The claim lead runs the insurance workstream. Combining the two is fine in a small event and risky in a serious one, because the claim work is quiet, continuous, and easy to drop when everyone is fighting the fire. The claim lead can sit in finance, risk, or legal — the role matters more than the department — and coordinates notice, insurer and broker communication, provider approvals, cost capture, documentation, deadlines, and open coverage questions. The claim lead does not decide technical containment and must never slow an urgent action needed to protect people, systems, evidence, or legal obligations.

Role	Primary responsibility during a potential claim
Incident commander	Containment, eradication, recovery, workstream coordination, operational decisions
Claim lead	Notice, consent, insurer coordination, the claim calendar, documentation, cost and loss workstreams
Legal lead	Legal obligations, privilege strategy, regulatory and contractual advice, legal-provider coordination
Finance lead	Cost codes, invoices, payroll records, revenue and extra-expense analysis, proof-of-loss support
Business owner	Operational impact, workarounds, customer effects, recovery priorities, decision authority
Broker	Placement knowledge, notice support, insurer coordination, policy and market guidance
Insurer / claim representative	Coverage process, approvals, information requests, panel coordination, claim evaluation
Security and forensic leads	Technical facts, evidence preservation, containment and recovery records
Communications lead	Coordinated internal, customer, regulatory, and public messaging

In a smaller organization one person may hold several of these. Keep the responsibilities distinct even when the names repeat, otherwise you discover that everyone attended the bridge call and nobody owned the claim calendar.

Notice Early — but Know What Notice Means

One of the fastest ways to manufacture avoidable uncertainty is to wait until the incident is fully investigated before discussing notice. Policies differ: some require notice of a claim, others of a circumstance, event, or loss; some distinguish a hotline contact from formal written notice; the same facts may implicate more than one policy.

So the incident team should escalate a potentially insured event to the policy owner and claim lead early enough for the broker, insurer, and legal advisers to assess the notice position, and a technical debate about whether the event is "really a breach" should never be the reason the insurance workstream never starts. Delay can create an avoidable coverage question under some policy wordings, which is reason enough to escalate the potential claim early and let the responsible advisers assess the notice position.

Early notice does not mean asserting facts you do not yet have. A good initial notice separates what is known, what is reasonably suspected, what is still under investigation, what immediate steps were taken, and who will provide updates. Keep the version actually submitted and the evidence it was sent; record when the organization first became aware of the relevant facts, who made the notice decision, and what wording was relied on.

And keep the lanes separate: notice to an insurer is not notice to a regulator, a customer, an affected individual, a law-enforcement agency, or a contractual counterparty. Each has its own trigger, recipient, owner, and clock, the jurisdictional incident overlay from the cross-country field guide and this claim-response card should meet in the incident plan without being collapsed into a single "notification."

Consent Before Spend: Make the Decision Visible

Cyber incidents create cost fast, forensics, outside counsel, restoration crews, customer notification, credit or identity-protection services, communications advisers, negotiators, surge resources. Often before anyone has a reliable estimate of the loss. Depending on the wording, the policy may require insurer consent, or the use of approved providers, before some of that spend is incurred. You may also already have a trusted incident-response firm on retainer. Those two facts must be reconciled *before* the incident, because engaging a preferred firm without checking the applicable consent or panel requirements can create an avoidable dispute over some or all of the resulting expense, depending on the policy wording and circumstances.

Settle the questions in advance: which providers are pre-approved, and for which services; can you use your retained provider, and by what process; who can request consent out of hours; what happens when action genuinely cannot wait; and how disagreements escalate without stalling the response. During the incident, keep a consent log, request, time, recipient, service, provider, estimated scope, response, conditions, decision. If you must act before consent because harm cannot wait, record the urgency, the alternatives weighed, the authority, and the effort made to reach the carrier. That record does not decide coverage; it preserves the facts someone will later need to evaluate it. What it must not become is a reason to pause containment, the insurer is a stakeholder in the financial workstream, not the incident commander.

Approved Providers and the First Call

Panel firms are useful because they know the carrier's process, rates, and people; your own retained firms are useful because they already know your systems, contracts, and plan. The right answer depends on the policy, the incident, the provider, the jurisdiction, and any conflict, and the readiness failure is discovering the choice for the first time while systems are down. Before the incident, compare your retained legal, forensics, communications, and recovery providers against the applicable panels, seek approval or an agreed exception where appropriate, document who engages whom and under which agreement, check conflicts and independence, clarify how reports and evidence and invoices will be handled, and where practical put the providers through a tabletop.

Be especially clear about the first legal and forensics calls, because how an investigation is structured can shape legal strategy, reporting, and how information moves among the organization, its advisers, and the insurer. Privilege is a legal determination, not a label security can staple to a document; legal should set the working protocol rather than the incident team assuming that copying a lawyer makes every report protected. And the technical team still owes an accurate record, coverage concerns never justify softening language, suppressing a finding, or turning a forensic report into marketing. You need legal discipline and technical truth at the same time.

Run Two Logs from the Beginning

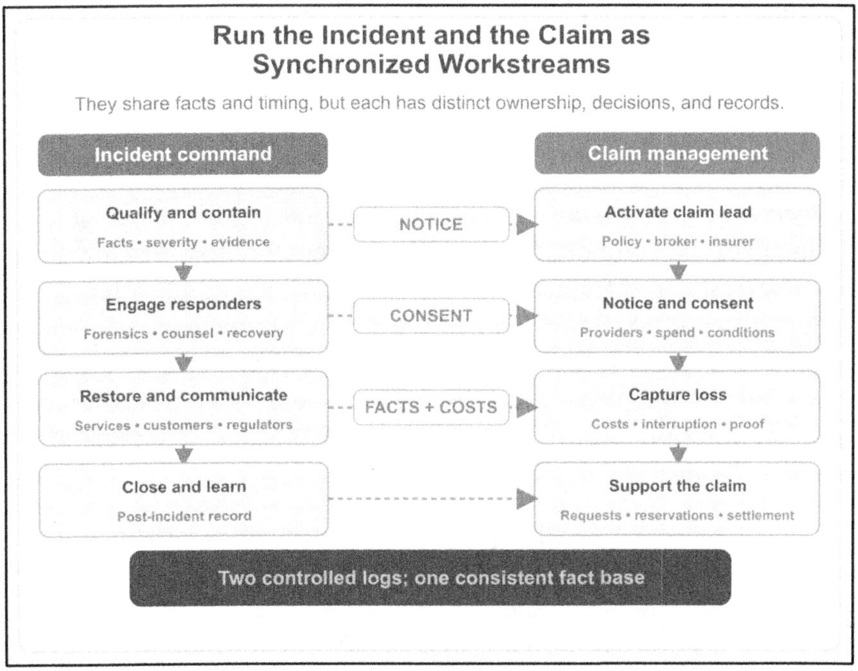

Keep the incident log you already keep, alerts, decisions, containment, evidence, recovery, communications, obligations.

Alongside it, open a claim log that records the financial and contractual story: notice and acknowledgement; insurer, broker, and adviser communications; consent requests and responses; provider engagement and scope; costs incurred and invoices received; affected services and interruption periods; decisions about repair, replacement, workaround, or improvement; information supplied to the insurer; open questions, reservations, and deadlines; other possible policies or recoveries; and eventual payments, denials, or unresolved amounts.

The two logs cross-reference each other rather than compete, and a single chronology of key events keeps times from diverging across the legal, forensic, communications, finance, and insurance records. Words matter here: observed, reported, suspected, confirmed, estimated, and decided are different states, and writing accurately is not the same as writing defensively or hiding bad news. Speculation presented as fact, casual attribution, and premature fault assignment can complicate later legal, regulatory, customer, and insurance review.

Proving Business Interruption Is a Finance Exercise with Technical Inputs

For an incident that materially disrupts operations, business interruption and extra expense can become some of the largest elements of the claimed loss. It is also the head of loss organizations are worst at collecting, because it is discussed at placement and underestimated at claim, and proving it is an accounting exercise nobody rehearsed. You may know revenue fell and still be unable to show how much loss came from the insured event rather than normal variation, another business problem, or a choice made during recovery.

Start the record when disruption begins, not weeks later. Capture the systems, sites, and services affected; when each went down, degraded, was restored, and stabilized; operational capacity before, during, and after; the orders, transactions, or production affected; work shifted to manual processes or alternate sites; revenue delayed versus revenue permanently lost; the additional labor, technology, logistics, and supplier costs; the costs avoided because ordinary operations stopped; customer credits and contractual remedies; the assumptions behind any forecast; and the technical evidence tying the interruption to the event.

Finance owns the loss calculation; technology and the business supply the operational facts; the claim lead keeps the calculation aligned with the policy's process and information requests, and extra expense is far easier to substantiate if incremental costs are captured separately as they are incurred rather than disentangled from business-as-usual spending afterward.

Separate restoration from improvement, too. Rebuilding a server as it was, migrating to a more resilient platform, replacing unsupported technology, and accelerating a planned modernization can all be sensible, but they are not necessarily treated the same way in a claim. Record why the chosen path was necessary, which part restored the prior capability and which part improved it, what alternatives were considered, and who approved it. That discipline helps even when insurance does not respond, because it gives leadership an honest account of the real cost of the incident and the economics of resilience.

Extortion Decisions Need Their Own Governance

An extortion demand applies pressure from several directions at once, and the worst thing you can do is reduce the decision to "will the policy reimburse a payment?" Coverage is one input among many. The organization has to weigh legality and sanctions exposure, safety, the reliability of the attacker's claims, the availability and integrity of backups, the consequences of delay, evidence of data theft, and the plain fact that payment may buy no working decryptor, no deletion, and no silence.

Above all, a payment can be *legally prohibited*: if the party behind the attack is a sanctioned entity or sits in a sanctioned jurisdiction, making or facilitating payment can breach sanctions law, with exposure reaching the organization, its officers, and anyone facilitating it. Sanctions regimes vary by jurisdiction and change over time, so the specifics belong to counsel and current advisories, but the standing rule for this playbook is that no ransom is paid without sanctions screening and legal sign-off, built into the decision rather than bolted on after a number is agreed.

Set the authority before the event: who may recommend and who may authorize a payment; which legal and sanctions checks are mandatory; which insurer notice and consent steps apply; what law-enforcement engagement is expected; how finance and the board enter the decision; and how the decision, the alternatives, and the communications will be documented and controlled. This playbook takes no universal position for or against payment. It insists only that the organization never improvise the authority, legality, and record of so consequential a decision on the attacker's clock.

Third-Party Incidents Create a Proof Problem

When the incident starts at a cloud provider, processor, software supplier, or managed service provider, you may depend on someone else for the very facts the insurer needs. Activate the vendor-incident and contract processes early, and preserve the supplier's notices and timeline, the contractual notification and cooperation requirements, the service-level and availability records, the systems and data affected, the communications about cause and scope, your own mitigation and alternate-service costs, the customer impact, and any incident reports the supplier provides.

Watch for double recovery, too, a supplier credit, an indemnity, another party's insurance, and your own claim can interact, and legal, finance, procurement, and the claim lead need one joined view. The contract cannot manufacture evidence the supplier never kept, which is exactly why cooperation, audit, and record-retention provisions matter before signature. Claim readiness reaches backward into third-party governance.

Expect Questions, Reservations, and Iteration

A claim is rarely one notice followed by one payment. The insurer may ask for facts, documents, invoices, interviews, technical findings, loss calculations, or proof of mitigation; it may acknowledge the claim while reserving its position on some coverage questions; a layered program may produce overlapping requests and differing views. Treat each request as a governed work item, log it, assign an owner, confirm scope and deadline, coordinate the legal, technical, financial, and privacy review, record what was supplied and when, and preserve the submitted version.

A reservation of rights does not necessarily amount to a denial, and it should not be ignored: route it to the policy owner, broker, and coverage adviser, and understand what facts might resolve it. Keep any disagreement professional and evidence-led, and separate the immediate need to respond and recover from the longer coverage conversation. The security leader's contribution throughout is reliable technical evidence, clear causation where it can be established, accurate scope, and a record that does not change depending on who is reading it.

The claim process may also require a formal proof of loss, sworn statement, quantified claim submission, or another structured document within a policy-specific period. Do not treat routine incident updates or invoice sharing as proof that this requirement has been satisfied. The claim lead should have finance, the policy owner, and the appropriate adviser confirm whether a formal submission is required, who is authorized to sign it, which figures remain provisional, and which deadline applies. Preserve the submitted version and the basis for every material amount.

The Minimum Viable Claim-Readiness Kit

A small or mid-sized organization does not need a claims department. It needs a kit people can actually use:

- **A claim-response card** — contacts, notice route, consent requirements, approved providers, policy location, and internal escalation.
- **A named claim lead and alternate** — with authority to coordinate the workstream.
- **A claim log and a decision log** — ready to open alongside the incident log.

- **Dedicated cost codes and an expense tracker** — invoice, provider, date, purpose, approval, service period, and relation to the event.
- **A business-interruption evidence structure** — operational metrics, financial baseline, impact timeline, extra expense, avoided cost, and assumptions.
- **A provider and consent matrix** — retained firms, panel status, engagement route, after-hours contact, and approval state.
- **An extortion-governance card** — decision authority, mandatory legal and sanctions review, insurer and law-enforcement contacts, documentation requirements.
- **A tabletop scenario** — run against at least one material scenario and repeated when the policy or response model changes.

Keep the kit with the incident-response materials, with a resilient offline copy, and test it inside incident exercises rather than in an insurance-only meeting. The test is simple: can the team activate the claim workstream without interrupting containment and recovery?

What Usually Goes Wrong

- **Nobody owns activation.** Finance owns the policy, legal owns counsel, security owns the incident, the broker owns the relationship, everyone owns a piece and nobody starts the claim.
- **Notice waits for certainty.** Escalation is delayed until the investigation is complete, confusing incomplete facts with an inability to notify responsibly.
- **The preferred provider is not approved.** A familiar firm is engaged immediately, and the approval question surfaces only after material cost has piled up.

- **Consent lives in email.** Someone agreed to something, but nobody can establish who, when, for what scope, or under what condition.
- **Invoices prove spend, not purpose.** The costs are real but the descriptions are too vague to tie them to containment, restoration, notification, or interruption.
- **The interruption is reconstructed from memory.** Availability is known approximately, workarounds went undocumented, delayed revenue is treated as lost revenue, and ordinary variation is mixed with incident impact.
- **The incident and claim stories drift apart.** Legal, forensic, finance, communications, and insurance records use different dates, scopes, and descriptions for the same event.
- **Coverage anxiety distorts the investigation.** Teams soften language or avoid documenting a known control weakness, damaging technical truth and creating a larger credibility problem later.
- **The claim closes and nothing changes.** Lessons about provider access, evidence, wording, retention, or recovery cost never reach the incident plan, the risk register, or the next renewal.

Industry Pattern — The Insurance Claim That Lost Its Evidence

> *A company has a serious incident and does many of the hard things well. The team contains the intrusion, engages a forensics firm it trusts, restores the critical service, and keeps customers informed. Weeks later the insurance workstream begins assembling the claim, and the picture sours.*
>
> *The invoices are substantial and genuine, but the proof is weak: the forensics firm was not on the applicable panel and nobody can find written consent for the full scope; several vendors used the same broad invoice description; staff worked nights and weekends, but ordinary payroll and incremental cost were never separated; the service was degraded for days, yet no one preserved the transaction and capacity records needed to show the interruption. The company did not invent the loss. It allowed the evidence of that loss to evaporate while it was busy solving the incident.*
>
> *The lesson is not to let insurance lead the response. It is to run a quiet claim workstream beside the response from the first hour. One person opening the right cost code, preserving approvals, recording operational impact, and keeping the chronology aligned can protect enormous value without distracting the people restoring the business. The organization's claim position was not weakened only by what happened during the incident. It was weakened in the year before it, when nobody had been assigned to prepare the evidence and handoffs the claim would require.*

This playbook is deliberately conceptual. Cyber policies are contracts, and the wording, coverage, conditions, exclusions, notice and consent provisions, available providers, claims practice, and applicable law vary by insurer, policy, market, jurisdiction, and event. Nothing here asserts that a feature is universal or predicts whether a claim will be paid. Build the claim-response card from the organization's actual policy, endorsements, application, submitted clarifications, broker guidance, and insurer instructions, and take qualified legal and insurance advice where privilege, sanctions, regulatory reporting, payment, coverage, settlement, or recovery rights are material. The security leader's job is to make the operating and technical facts accurate, timely, and usable, not to act as coverage counsel or claims adjuster.

What Evidence Should You Expect

A claim-ready organization should be able to produce, without a scramble:

- the current policy record, policy, endorsements, application, clarifications, relevant prior correspondence, insurer and broker contacts, policy owner, and renewal history;
- a verified claim-response card, notice routes, authority, consent conditions, approved providers, other-policy prompts, internal escalation, version date, and resilient storage;
- a practiced activation model, named claim lead and alternate, the role matrix, an exercise record, a contact test, and lessons closed;
- notice and consent records, submitted notices, delivery evidence, acknowledgements, requests, responses, conditions, and decision rationale;
- aligned incident and claim chronologies, technical events, business impact, communications, insurer interactions, key decisions, and changes in known facts;
- provider records, engagements, panel or approval status, scopes of work, conflicts, rates, invoices, deliverables, and approval changes;
- cost and loss evidence, dedicated codes, invoices, payroll or surge-cost records, operational-impact data, business-interruption calculations, assumptions, avoided costs, and supporting technical evidence;
- extortion-decision evidence where applicable, authority, legal and sanctions review, insurer and law-enforcement engagement, alternatives considered, decision, and communications control;

- third-party incident evidence where applicable, supplier notices, contract rights, service impact, cooperation records, mitigation costs, and other potential recoveries;
- a governed request tracker, insurer questions, owners, deadlines, submitted versions, outstanding items, reservations, payments, and recoveries, plus any formal proof-of-loss or structured-submission requirement, its responsible preparer and authorized signatory, its deadline, the submission evidence, and follow-up or amendment status;
- and post-claim learning, changes to the response card, provider arrangements, policy design, renewal representations, controls, risk register, recovery plan, and future exercises.

The evidence should reconcile into one defensible account. It will not be identical for every audience, legal, regulatory, customer, technical, and insurance processes ask different questions, but the underlying facts, timeline, scope, and decisions must agree.

Reality Check

> *Imagine the organization detects ransomware at 2 a.m., and the normal systems are unreliable. The incident commander is containing the spread, legal is assessing obligations, and the executives want to know about recovery. Can someone find the policy and the claim-response card without the affected network? Can the team name the claim lead, give notice through the correct route, check whether its preferred forensics and legal firms are approved, obtain urgent consent, open the right cost codes, and start recording operational impact, all without asking the incident commander to stop running the incident? If the honest answer depends on one person being awake and remembering what happened at renewal, you have insurance. You do not yet have claim readiness.*

What This Means for You as a Security Leader

You do not need to own the insurance program to make the claim operational. You need to make sure the incident machinery and the insurance machinery can meet under pressure. That means knowing who owns the policy, who activates the claim, which actions may require notice or consent, which providers can be engaged, which technical records will later matter, and how the organization will prove operational impact without asking responders to recreate it from memory. It means protecting technical truth while legal, finance, regulatory, customer, and insurance workstreams each use that truth for their own decisions.

The best claim-readiness process is almost invisible during the incident. It does not slow containment, compete with crisis command, or turn every decision into a coverage debate. It runs quietly beside the response: the right notice goes out, approvals are preserved, costs are coded, impact is recorded, questions are owned, and the chronology stays coherent. The policy financed part of the risk. Claim readiness is what protects your ability to actually use that financing when the risk becomes real, which is why it is worth building before the week you need it, and why a stronger claim position begins with treating readiness as an operating capability rather than an insurance form.

Bridge to the M&A, Acquisitions, and Divestitures Playbook

A deal creates a different pressure from an incident; the next playbook follows cyber risk from diligence and deal terms through Day 1 access, integration, and separation.

PLAYBOOK

M&A, Acquisitions, and Divestitures

Governing cyber risk through diligence, Day 1, integration, and separation

The message usually arrives later than it should. "We're acquiring a company, the deal closes in three weeks — can security confirm there are no major issues, and can IT connect the networks on Day 1?" There are several possible answers at that point. "Yes" is rarely an honest one.

By the time it reaches you, the deal team has spent months on financial, tax, legal, operational, and commercial diligence, and security gets a folder: a policy, a penetration-test summary, an insurance certificate, and a spreadsheet of applications. The target's technology leader is understandably guarded about opening sensitive systems to a competitor that might not end up buying. The buyer wants confidence without delay. The integration leaders are already planning shared email, identity, and network access, because ownership changes on Day 1 and everyone assumes the technology should change with it. That last assumption is the dangerous one. **Legal ownership can change at closing. Trust should not.**

An acquisition does not bring only systems. It brings identities, data, products, contracts, customer promises, regulators, suppliers, unresolved incidents, unsupported technology, standing exceptions, technical debt, and a security culture that may be stronger or weaker than the one buying it. One of the most consequential risks is a compromise or incident that began before closing but has not yet been discovered or fully contained. After closing, the buyer may inherit its operational impact, investigation, customer and regulatory consequences, remediation burden, and financial cost. Which entity carries a particular legal obligation or liability depends on the transaction structure, timing, applicable law, contracts, and what each party knew and agreed. A divestiture is the mirror problem: separating that same web without leaving the other party your access, or leaving yourself their data.

The CISO's job here is not to declare the deal safe; nobody can, and certainly not by Friday. It is to turn limited information into a decision the transaction can actually use: what is known and how well it is evidenced; what remains unknown; what could materially change value, timing, legality, customer trust, or continuity; what must happen before closing; what must be protected on Day 1; what can wait for integration; what the organization is consciously accepting; and, if a business is being separated, what a secure exit must look like. That is the playbook, not "approve the acquisition," but make cyber risk visible early enough to change the deal or the integration plan.

M&A Is Not a Larger Vendor Assessment

Third-party assessment asks whether you can rely on another organization while it stays another organization. Acquisition diligence asks what happens when its risk becomes yours, and that changes the questions. You are not only judging whether the target can protect the service it provides you; you may inherit its full estate, people, liabilities, products, customer commitments, regulators, and prior decisions.

Depending on what is transferring and how the transaction is structured, a control weakness may become your remediation, a customer representation may become an obligation you must continue, an unsupported product may become your support problem, a forgotten administrator account may become an access path into the combined organization, and supplier concentration may become your continuity exposure. In a divestiture the dependency runs the other way: the business leaving may still lean on your identity platform, networks, security operations, licenses, and people long after the entity is sold. Use the existing third-party, data, product, resilience, and control work as inputs; the M&A playbook owns the transaction decisions and the movement from one operating model to another.

Get Security into the Deal Without Turning It into a Gate

Security is brought in late because deal teams fear two things, delay and leakage, and both fears are legitimate: transactions run under strict confidentiality, limited access, and compressed timelines. The CISO who responds by demanding a full audit before offering any view will not be invited earlier next time. Earn the earlier seat by offering a proportional process instead: at initial screening, surface material red flags and information gaps; during confirmatory diligence, test the areas most likely to change value, closing conditions, or Day 1 safety; reserve deeper control assessment for when access is lawful, practical, and worth it, and state plainly what each stage can and cannot conclude.

Agree the working arrangements in advance: who may know about the deal, which security people join the restricted team, what may be requested and where it is held, whether clean-team or external-adviser arrangements are needed, how findings are classified and escalated, and who converts a technical finding into a deal decision. The CISO informs the decision; legal, finance, corporate development, the business sponsor, and the authorized governance body own their parts of the transaction. A security finding becomes useful when it is translated into impact, an action, a cost, a condition, or a conscious risk acceptance, not when it is handed over as a list of vulnerabilities with no view on what they mean to the deal.

Start with the Transaction, Not the Questionnaire

Before requesting a single piece of evidence, understand what is actually being bought or separated. Build a transaction cyber brief:

- the deal structure and the entities, assets, or business units involved;
- buyer, seller, target, and any joint-venture or minority relationships;
- countries, regulated sectors, licenses, and authorities in scope;
- products, services, critical operations, intellectual property, and crown-jewel data;
- employees, contractors, customers, and suppliers moving with the deal;
- technology environments, cloud tenants, domains, networks, applications, source repositories, and operational technology in scope;

- the personal, regulated, confidential, or customer data involved;
- known shared services and dependencies;
- the timeline, signing, expected close, any phased transfers;
- the intended operating model after close: standalone, integrated, federated, or temporary;
- expected transition-service arrangements;
- and the business thesis, what value the deal is meant to create.

That last item belongs in a security brief, because a deal done for a product, a customer base, data, a regulated license, engineering talent, or market access carries different crown jewels and different failure modes, and you cannot prioritize diligence without knowing what the buyer is trying to preserve. The brief also keeps scope honest: "we're buying the company" may mean acquiring shares in several entities, selected assets, a product line, customer contracts, IP, or a workforce. The security perimeter does not follow the press release; it follows what legally and operationally moves.

Diligence in Layers

The evidence available before signing is rarely enough to prove that every control operates, so treat diligence as a confidence-building exercise with explicit limits rather than an audit opinion.

The **initial red-flag review** asks only whether anything visible could change appetite for the deal or demand immediate specialist attention: a current or recent material incident; ransomware, extortion, or significant data loss; regulator, customer, or law-enforcement engagement; critical unsupported technology; weak control over privileged access; an inability to identify assets or important data; major or unsupported product vulnerabilities; dependence on one person, supplier, platform, or facility; missing or unreliable backups for critical services; customer promises the target cannot support; or an environment so opaque that the uncertainty itself is material. This pass directs attention; it does not conclude maturity.

Confirmatory diligence then follows the risk:

Workstream	What to establish	Why the deal team cares
Governance and history	Accountability, risk records, audits, incidents, investigations, insurance claims, unresolved findings	Hidden liability, leadership credibility, remediation cost
Assets and architecture	Critical systems, cloud and on-premises estate, external exposure, unsupported technology, network boundaries	Integration complexity, outage and compromise risk
Identity and access	Identity sources, privileged accounts, remote access, service accounts, leavers, shared credentials	Day 1 trust, insider and persistence risk
Detection and response	Logging coverage, alerting, incident plan, forensic capability, retained evidence	Ability to detect inherited compromise and meet obligations
Vulnerability and configuration	Exposure, patching, testing, material findings, exceptions	Near-term remediation and attack-path risk
Data and privacy	Data inventory, ownership, location, transfers, retention, deletion, breaches, rights requests	Legal, customer, migration, and separation constraints

Workstream	What to establish	Why the deal team cares
Product and software	Development lifecycle, source control, build systems, signing keys, open-source components, a product security incident response team (PSIRT), supported life	Product remediation obligations, customer exposure, inherited vulnerability, and trust
Resilience	Critical services, dependencies, backups, restoration tests, recovery objectives	Continuity and integration sequencing
Third parties	Critical suppliers, cloud concentration, outsourcing, sub-processors, change-of-control and exit terms	Consent, continuity, inherited dependency
Contracts and assurance	Customer security commitments, certifications, audits, regulatory obligations, notification terms	Promises and deadlines the buyer may inherit
People and operating model	Key staff, role concentration, outsourced functions, vacancies, culture, retention risk	Ability to operate and integrate the controls

No questionnaire answers all of that; use interviews, architecture views, system extracts, independent reports, incident records, contract summaries, and carefully scoped technical testing where permitted. And some answers cannot be established until the buyer has lawful access and operational visibility, state those as **post-close validation** items with an owner, priority, date, and interim safeguard. Throughout, refuse the three tempting conversions: "not observed" is not "not present," "policy exists" is not "control operates," and "no disclosed incident" is not "no compromise." A claim of no known security incidents is not, by itself, evidence of effective prevention or detection. Establish what the target means by an incident, which reporting threshold it used, what period the answer covers, how events are detected and investigated, and what records support the conclusion.

Unknown Is a Finding

Deal teams want red, amber, or green; M&A diligence needs a fourth state. **Unknown** can mean the evidence was not requested, not provided, not reliable, out of permitted scope, or impossible to establish before close, and those are different reasons with different consequences. Missing evidence about a small internal tool is not the same as missing evidence about production access, customer data, or backups.

For every material unknown, record the open question, why it could not be answered, the consequence if the worst credible answer is true, the decision you can still make despite the uncertainty, the interim safeguard, when and how the answer will be established, and who accepts the exposure until then. This is where a security leader protects the deal without pretending: "we cannot verify privileged-access coverage before close, so Day 1 prohibits direct trust between the environments and validation is a first-week action" is a decision. "Insufficient information" is only a status.

Translate Findings into Deal and Integration Decisions

A technical finding has several possible homes, and naming the right one is most of the value: a **deal-changing issue** material enough for the authorized deal team to reconsider structure, value, timing, or appetite; a **condition before closing** that must be resolved or evidenced first; a matter for **transaction protection** that legal and finance may address through representations, disclosure, indemnity, escrow, holdback, or insurance; a **Day 1 safeguard**; an **integration requirement** for remediation, migration, or convergence after close;

an **accepted inherited risk** retained by the right authority with funding, monitoring, and review; or a **non-issue after analysis** that was tested and found not material.

Security should not draft the legal conclusions from that list. It should explain the scenario, evidence strength, impact, dependencies, urgency, and options so the responsible specialists can convert it into the right instrument. Avoid both failure modes: hiding every issue inside the integration plan where the deal team never sees it, and dramatizing ordinary technical debt as though it were a deal-breaker. The CISO earns trust by telling those two apart.

Signing to Close: Plan Without Pretending You Already Own It

The period between signing and closing is awkward: approvals may be outstanding, the deal may still be restricted, and the buyer needs a safe Day 1 plan without yet having authority to direct the target's operations. Let legal and the deal advisers define the boundary, and inside it prepare the things that make Day 1 safe, named security and incident contacts on both sides, a way to disclose a material incident or control change before close, refreshed diligence for facts that changed after signing, the Day 1 identity/connectivity/data/support decisions, an explicit list of integrations prohibited until validation, the required regulatory and contractual actions, the integration governance model and risk authority, and the evidence to preserve through the transition.

Planning is not control and cooperation is not ownership: do not pressure the target into actions the deal arrangements or the law do not permit. And keep a refresh trigger live, if the target has an incident, loses a critical customer, changes a key supplier, or materially changes its systems before close, the original diligence conclusion may no longer be the decision the buyer is making.

Day 1: Ownership Changes; Trust Does Not

Day 1 is not the day to integrate everything; it is the day to establish authority, visibility, escalation, and safe boundaries. The governing principle is do no harm: whatever you do, do not let the acquisition's unknown risk flow freely into your environment, or yours into theirs, before either is understood.

A minimum Day 1 security plan settles who decides and how the two organizations reach each other in an incident; which privileged accounts exist in the acquired environment and who controls them; which connections are genuinely necessary and how they are restricted and monitored; what assets and security tooling coverage are known and where the blind spots are; which domains, certificates, and internet-facing systems now represent the combined organization; how logs are preserved and when the acquired side invokes the buyer's incident process; which data may move, for what purpose, and under whose approval; which critical services can be restored and by whom; which supplier or license could interrupt operations after the ownership change; and which customer and regulatory promises must continue without a gap.

The principle underneath all of it is to connect business processes before extending technical trust. Shared email, finance consolidation, and executive reporting may be genuinely urgent; flat network access, broad identity federation, mass data movement, and shared administration are not automatically required to achieve them, and they are exactly what you should withhold on Day 1. This matters most because of the inherited-compromise problem: if the target is already compromised, flat network interconnection, broad identity federation, or shared administration can create a path for that compromise to reach the buyer's environment and make containment more difficult. Segment first, observe, validate, and expand trust deliberately, a slow, least-privilege, monitored start costs a little business friction and buys the ability to contain a problem you have not yet found.

Where evidence confidence is low, exposure is material, or threat indicators justify it, conduct a scoped post-close compromise assessment before expanding technical trust. A clean initial scan or an absence of known indicators is useful evidence, but it is not a certificate that the environment has never been compromised.

The First Ninety Days: Discover, Stabilize, Then Converge

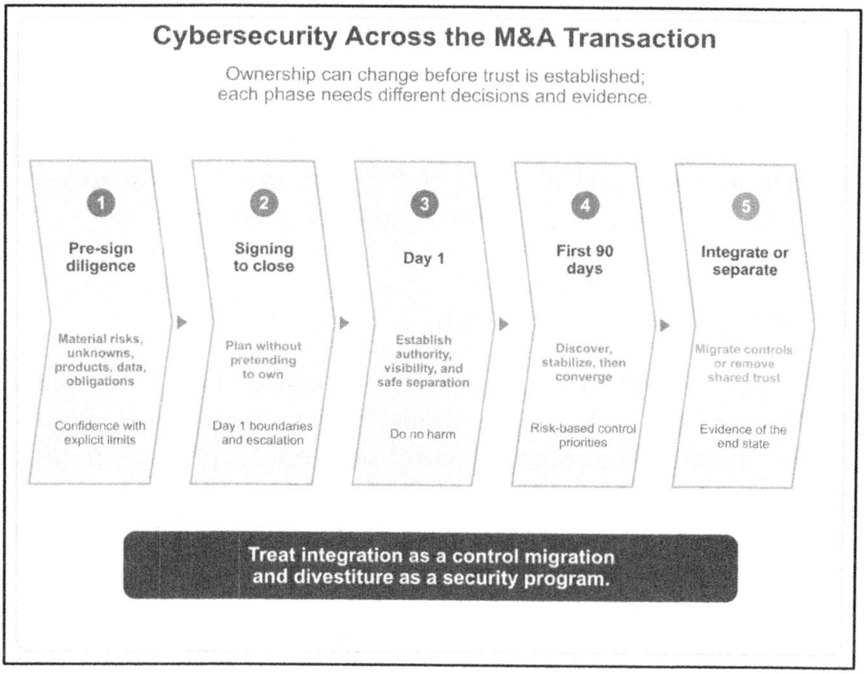

The calendar bends to the risk and the deal, but a staged model helps. In the **first thirty days**, establish reality: validate the asset, identity, data, application, supplier, and external-exposure populations; confirm critical services and recovery dependencies; bring the acquired environment into incident escalation and sufficient monitoring; review privileged access, leavers, remote paths, known incidents, open vulnerabilities, and material exceptions; and reconcile what diligence claimed with what operational access now shows. Do not open by rewriting every policy. Find out which controls actually run.

In the **next thirty**, stabilize material exposure: close the attack paths and control gaps that create immediate combined risk, remove stale privilege, restrict unsafe connectivity, improve endpoint and logging coverage, protect critical backups, and confirm the regulatory, privacy, customer, insurance, and supplier actions the deal triggered, while preserving local capability that works, because replacing a sound acquired control with the buyer's weaker one is regression with a project plan. In the **following thirty**, approve the integration roadmap: decide the target state, sequence the work around business dependencies rather than the urge to make everything look alike, fund it, assign owners, and record which risks remain during transition and who accepts them. Some integrations take far longer than ninety days; the goal by Day 90 is not completion but replacing inherited uncertainty with a governed roadmap, working interim controls, and an honest view of residual risk.

Integration Is a Control Migration

Integration programs love to describe consolidation as though moving from two tools to one automatically reduces risk. Sometimes it does; it can also remove a control before its replacement covers the acquired population. So treat each significant integration as a control migration: define the control objective and both current implementations; establish the full population the target control must cover; preserve evidence from the legacy control; plan the cutover, rollback, exceptions, and monitoring; validate coverage and operation after migration; and retire the old control only once the replacement is proven.

This matters most for identity, endpoint security, logging, vulnerability management, email protection, backups, cloud guardrails, key management, incident response, and secure development. The unified control model from earlier in this volume is what makes this tractable: map both environments to one control objective while keeping their implementations and evidence separate until they genuinely converge. One operating model does not require one tool on the first day, and a parent-company dashboard that turns green because it cannot yet see the acquired estate is not integration, it is a blind spot with good formatting.

People and Culture Are Part of the Control Environment

Acquisitions create key-person risk at exactly the moment key people are most likely to leave. The administrator who understands the legacy identity system, the engineer who owns the build pipeline, the privacy lead who knows where the sensitive data sits, the responder who remembers the last incident, none of them appear in the asset inventory, and losing them can change the risk faster than replacing any product. Identify the roles critical to continuity and integration, the privileged knowledge held by one person, the outsourced and informal responsibilities, the retention risks, and the access changes a role redesign will cause.

And do not assume the acquirer is more mature because it is larger: listen before standardizing, because the target may have better engineering practices, stronger recovery, or more precise asset knowledge, and the integration should carry the best control forward rather than reflexively the buyer's. This is also where monitoring can turn disproportionate, employees in an acquired or separated business are not suspects because ownership changed, so use risk-based access, evidence preservation, and appropriate monitoring under legal, privacy, and HR governance, not a transaction as a warrant for indiscriminate surveillance.

Products, Source Code, and Customer Promises

When the deal includes a technology product, the acquired attack surface does not stop at the corporate network. Establish who owns product-security decisions; the supported versions and end-of-life commitments; the known vulnerabilities and remediation obligations; open disclosure or bug-bounty matters; customer advisories and contractual security promises; the source repositories and who can reach them; the build and deployment systems; the code-signing keys and certificates; the third-party and open-source components; and the PSIRT or equivalent operating model.

Preserve the ability to ship a security fix during integration, a product team forced into a new build environment before its release process is understood can lose precisely the capability customers need most. And review customer assurance on its own terms: certifications and reports have defined entities, systems, and periods, and a transaction can change the scope without extending the assurance, so do not let sales imply that the buyer's certificate instantly covers the acquired product, or the target's report the buyer.

Data Does Not Become Free to Move at Closing

A change of ownership does not make every dataset transferable, combinable, reusable, or indefinitely retainable. Before moving data between environments, establish what data is involved and who owns it, why the combined organization wants to move or use it, the legal/privacy/employment/customer/sector/contractual constraints, the residency and cross-border-transfer requirements, the retention, deletion, and legal-hold obligations, the access and segregation requirements, and whether the data even belongs to an asset or entity that is actually transferring.

Privacy and legal decide the applicable basis and obligations; security makes sure the architecture, access, logging, transfer method, and evidence reflect that decision, the specifics belong to the privacy program and to counsel. Above all, avoid "copy now, classify later," because during a transaction duplicates spread fast into collaboration platforms, migration stores, adviser workspaces, test environments, and devices. The data room itself is sensitive. It holds inventories, vulnerabilities, customer information, IP, and incident history, so govern its access, download, retention, and closure like the crown-jewel store it is.

When an Incident Appears During the Transaction

An incident can surface during diligence, between signing and close, immediately after close, or halfway through integration, and each timing creates different authority, disclosure, insurance, and regulatory questions. With legal and privacy counsel, establish when any applicable notification or reporting periods may have begun, which entity has the relevant obligation, who currently has authority to act, and what the transaction documents require the parties to disclose to one another. The security leader protects people, systems, and evidence; activates the appropriate incident process; determines which entity owns operational response at that moment; escalates to the restricted deal and legal teams; preserves the transaction chronology and what was known when; reassesses the diligence conclusions and Day 1 assumptions; reviews the notification, insurer, customer, and deal implications with the responsible specialists; and keeps investigation facts separate from negotiation positions.

Two failures bracket this: letting deal confidentiality become the reason an incident is not escalated to the people legally required to act, and letting curiosity about the deal widen access to sensitive incident information beyond need. Whether the transaction continues, changes, pauses, or stops is not the CISO's call alone, the CISO's job is to ensure that decision is taken with a truthful account of the incident, the uncertainty, and the exposure being inherited or separated. (An incident that engages the cyber policy also routes into the claim-readiness discipline.)

Divestiture: Separation Is a Security Program

Divestitures are often treated as acquisitions in reverse, but they are harder in one way: you are untangling systems that may have been shared for years. Build a separation inventory covering the entities, people, locations, products, and assets leaving; the applications, cloud tenants, networks, repositories, endpoints, and operational technology; the shared identities, directories, email, domains, DNS, certificates, and collaboration platforms; the privileged and service accounts, secrets, keys, tokens, and remote access; the datasets, backups, archives, logs, legal holds, and records; the security tools, licenses, monitoring, and incident records; the suppliers, sub-processors, contracts, and licenses; the product source, build systems, signing infrastructure, and support obligations; the assurance reports, certifications, and regulatory records; and the shared people or processes needed during transition.

For each item decide whether it transfers, remains, is duplicated, is replaced, is provided temporarily, or is retired, and name the owner on both sides and the evidence that will prove completion. The seller carries two risks at once: leaving the separated business unable to operate securely, and letting it keep access back into the seller. The buyer carries the mirror risk: receiving assets without the data, credentials, evidence, licenses, people, or dependencies needed to run them. Treat separation with the same rigor as integration, plan it as deliberately, and remember that the separation window (access in flux, ownership ambiguous) is exactly when things fall through the cracks.

The Transition-Service Agreement Is a Temporary Operating Model

A transition-service agreement, or TSA, keeps selected services running while separation is completed, and "temporary" routinely lasts longer than anyone planned. Treat it as an operating model with explicit security terms: the services, systems, users, data, and locations in scope; the security responsibility for each control; identity, privileged access, segregation, and joiner-mover-leaver processes; logging, monitoring, incident escalation, and notification; vulnerability, patch, configuration, and change management; backup, restoration, and recovery testing; data use, location, transfer, retention, return, and deletion; supplier and subcontractor dependencies; assurance, audit, and regulator cooperation; service levels and security-escalation paths; who pays for and approves security changes; and the termination, exception, and risk-acceptance authority.

Do not let "the seller will keep providing security" stand as a control description, which security, for which population, using whose tools, with whose analysts watching the alerts, and who patches the system and approves emergency access? Set exit milestones with objective completion evidence, and reopen the risk decision at every extension, because a TSA renewed without reviewing access, data, open findings, and exit blockers is the permanent architecture wearing a temporary label.

Secure Separation and Exit

Separation is not complete when the last user moves; it is complete when shared trust has been removed or explicitly retained under a governed arrangement.

The exit work is concrete:

- disable or transfer user, administrator, service, and emergency accounts;
- remove federation, remote access, network routes, firewall rules, and shared collaboration;
- rotate or revoke passwords, keys, tokens, secrets, certificates, and signing authority;
- separate domains, DNS, email security, and certificate ownership;
- transfer or terminate endpoint, security, cloud, and support licenses;
- remove the departing entity from monitoring or stand up its own;
- transfer the logs, incident records, vulnerability history, and assurance evidence that must move, and preserve the legal holds that must stay;
- return, transfer, archive, or delete data under the approved decision;
- verify backup and replica handling, not just production deletion;
- close the supplier, customer, regulator, and insurer actions;
- test that neither party retains unintended access to the other; and
- obtain accountable sign-off with residual exceptions recorded.

Deletion deserves evidence: "the folder was removed" says nothing about replicas, exports, migration copies, backups, adviser workspaces, or devices, so define what deletion means for each environment and what can realistically be verified, and where retention remains necessary, record the purpose, access, protection, owner, and disposal trigger. Then run a post-separation check after the planned exit, because dormant accounts, forgotten routes, shared secrets, and delayed data copies are usually found only when someone looks after the project has declared success.

The M&A Cyber Risk Register

Do not bury transaction risk in the general enterprise register without a view the integration team can operate. Maintain a transaction cyber risk register: the finding or unknown; the affected entity, system, product, data, or obligation; the evidence and confidence; the credible consequence; the deal / Day 1 / integration / separation classification; the interim safeguard; the action, owner, funding, and milestone; the dependency and decision authority; the risk acceptance and review date; the validation evidence; and closure or transfer into the enterprise risk and control registers. The register must outlive the transaction team. Corporate development moves to the next deal, advisers leave, and integration becomes ordinary operations, so every open cyber item needs a permanent home, owner, and governance forum before that handover happens.

The Minimum Viable M&A Cyber Kit

A small or mid-sized organization can run a disciplined transaction with eight artifacts:

- **A transaction cyber brief** — scope, business thesis, entities, technology, data, products, jurisdictions, timeline, dependencies, and intended operating model.
- **A tiered diligence request** — red-flag questions first, deeper evidence by materiality, with access limits recorded.
- **A findings-and-unknowns record** — evidence strength, consequence, decision, safeguard, owner, and validation plan.

- **A Day 1 security plan** — authority, contacts, trust boundaries, identity, monitoring, incident escalation, data movement, recovery, and critical suppliers.
- **A first-ninety-days roadmap** — discovery, stabilization, target-state decisions, funding, risk acceptance, and validation.
- **A control-migration tracker** — old and new implementations, populations, cutover, exceptions, evidence preservation, and retirement criteria.
- **A separation and TSA register** — shared services, responsibilities, access, data, security operations, exit milestones, and completion evidence.
- **A transaction cyber risk register** — the durable thread from diligence through integration or separation into business-as-usual governance.

These live in controlled documents and workbooks; they need ownership and a transaction cadence that treats cyber findings as decisions rather than attachments, not a specialized platform to hold them.

What Usually Goes Wrong

- **Security arrives after the deal is effectively committed** — asked to validate a decision rather than inform it.
- **The questionnaire becomes the diligence** — policies and yes/no answers accepted without testing scope, operation, evidence, or the target's own unknowns.
- **Unknown is colored green** — missing evidence disappears into an average rating instead of becoming a Day 1 boundary and a validation action.
- **Every finding is a deal-breaker, or none is** — security loses credibility by failing to separate material transaction risk from ordinary remediation.

- **Closing is treated as permission to connect** — broad federation, network access, and data transfer begin before trust boundaries and visibility exist.
- **The buyer's standard automatically wins** — working target controls are removed before the replacement covers the acquired population.
- **Integration is funded; remediation is not** — the business budgets migration and discovers inherited vulnerabilities, unsupported systems, and product obligations need separate investment.
- **Key people leave with the map in their heads** — the plan counts systems and misses the knowledge to operate them.
- **Data moves because ownership changed** — purpose, contracts, residency, retention, and legal holds are considered afterward.
- **The TSA has a date but no exit evidence** — temporary access and shared services are extended because nobody defined completion.
- **The project closes before the risk does** — transaction findings sit in a deal folder with no permanent owner, funding, or governance.

Industry Pattern — The Dashboard That Was Green by Omission

> *A buyer closes an acquisition and moves fast to make the organization feel integrated. Email is connected, broad network routes are opened, administrators are given access across both environments, and the security tooling is scheduled for migration. The work looks efficient, and it is happening before the acquired asset and identity populations are even complete.*
>
> *The first serious review finds that several acquired systems were never enrolled in the buyer's monitoring, old service accounts still hold broad privilege, and the legacy endpoint tool was removed before its replacement reached every device. The combined dashboard is green because it reports the population the buyer knows about. The acquired environment has become less visible at the exact moment it became more trusted, precisely the condition in which an inherited compromise can spread, remain hidden, or become harder to contain.*
>
> *The lesson is not to delay integration indefinitely. It is to separate business integration from technical trust: establish visibility, constrain connectivity, migrate controls population by population, and retire the old control only when the new one proves coverage. Ownership changed at closing. Evidence, not ownership, is what should expand trust.*

This playbook is conceptual. Transaction structures, disclosure duties, regulatory approvals, employee-consultation and competition rules, privacy obligations, insurance effects, tax considerations, contractual remedies, and legal authority all vary by jurisdiction and deal, and nothing here determines whether information may be requested, shared, transferred, retained, deleted, or acted on in a specific transaction. Work from the actual transaction documents, the diligence protocol, applicable law, regulator direction, contracts, and qualified legal, privacy, tax, insurance, financial, and technical advice. Security's job is to supply accurate facts, scenarios, control analysis, evidence confidence, and operational options, not to make the legal conclusions about deal obligations, disclosure, liability, privilege, regulatory approval, employee rights, or transaction structure that sit around them.

What Evidence Should You Expect

A governed M&A cybersecurity process should be able to produce:

- a **transaction cyber brief** — scope, business purpose, entities, jurisdictions, systems, products, data, people, suppliers, timeline, and accountable sponsor;
- **diligence scope and collected evidence** — what access was and was not granted, the findings, the evidence dates, and the stated limits of the conclusion;
- a **findings-and-unknowns record** — materiality, confidence, credible consequence, responsible decision, interim safeguards, post-close validation, and accepted uncertainty;
- **evidence of deal and governance decisions** — that material findings reached the authorized legal, financial, business, and governance owners and changed a term, condition, plan, budget, safeguard, or explicit risk decision where appropriate;
- **signing-to-close preparation** — contacts, incident and change escalation, refreshed diligence, permitted planning boundaries, and required external actions;
- the **Day 1 plan and its verification** — identity, connectivity, monitoring, incident escalation, data movement, recovery, and critical suppliers;
- **integration and control-migration records** — populations, legacy and replacement controls, cutover evidence, validation, and decommissioning;
- **people and knowledge continuity** — critical roles, access changes, knowledge transfer, outsourced dependencies, and retention risk;
- **product and data decisions** where applicable, source and build access, signing authority, PSIRT ownership, customer commitments, and data-transfer, retention, and deletion decisions;

- **transaction incident records** where applicable, facts, chronology, evidence preservation, authority, escalation, and changed conclusions;
- **divestiture and TSA records** where applicable, the separation inventory, responsibility matrix, security terms, exit milestones, and objective completion evidence;
- **secure-separation and exit evidence** — access revocation, credential and key rotation, route removal, data and backup disposition, post-separation testing, and residual exceptions; and
- a **reconciled transaction cyber risk register** — every open item transferred into the enduring enterprise risk, control, obligation, product, or supplier system before the transaction program closes.

The evidence should show more than participation. It should show what security knew, how strongly it knew it, which decision it informed, what stayed uncertain, and who permanently owns the inherited or separated risk.

Reality Check

> *Imagine the deal closes tomorrow. Can you state which identities will trust which systems on Day 1, which networks will connect, which data may move, who can see the security alerts, how an incident is escalated, which critical service cannot yet be restored, and the three unknowns that could most damage the business thesis? Now imagine the business is being sold instead. Can you prove which accounts, routes, data copies, keys, logs, suppliers, and security services will remain shared after close, and name the evidence that will show each one severed at exit? If the answer is "the integration team is working on it," the transaction has activity. It does not yet have a cyber risk decision.*

What This Means for You as a Security Leader

M&A exposes whether the operating model can survive change. The ordinary organization gives you time to establish ownership, build controls, gather evidence, and improve; a transaction compresses all of that while information is restricted, people are unsettled, and commercial momentum is high. Your value is not predicting that nothing will go wrong. It is making uncertainty governable. You tell the deal team which facts are reliable, which unknowns matter, which risks can wait for integration, which boundaries must exist on Day 1, and which issue is serious enough to change the transaction. You keep legal ownership separate from technical trust.

You make sure a control migration does not open a visibility gap, and you carry the open findings into the permanent operating model after the deal team has moved on. On a divestiture you do the reverse without treating separation as deletion by spreadsheet: you know what is shared, decide what transfers, govern the temporary services, remove trust deliberately, and demand evidence that access and data no longer cross the boundary. The mature security leader does not only ask whether the target is secure. The better questions are: what risk are we acquiring, what capability are we preserving, what must be true before we connect, and how will we know the separation is finished?

Part 5 Closing Note: The Tools Are Not the Judgment

The final two playbooks brought the operating model into the moments when ordinary governance is most likely to be outrun. Claim readiness showed how an incident-response organization preserves the financial transfer it bought without letting insurance take over the response. This playbook showed how the same discipline survives a change of ownership, when systems, people, data, products, promises, and unknowns all move faster than the controls around them. That brings the toolkit to its final point, and it is the one Part 5 has been making from the start: a playbook earns its place when it makes judgment repeatable under pressure, the right question asked early, the decision owned, the boundary visible, and the evidence left behind.

Part 5 gathered the applied tools of the operating model and put them to work. It began by insisting that a playbook is a structure to adapt rather than an answer to copy, and that the value a leader brings is the judgment underneath the template, not the template itself.

From there it moved through the artifacts by which a security program is finally read. Board and risk reporting became an exercise in translation, built to prompt a decision rather than display activity, and honest about what the organization does not yet know. The control library and policy index became the governed record beneath that reporting, the place where every claim about a control can be traced to an owner, an implementation, and evidence that it operates. Readiness became the discipline of doing the examiner's work on the organization first, so scope, population, evidence, and the people who must speak to them can withstand examination on their own schedule rather than under outside pressure.

The thirty-, sixty-, and ninety-day plan turned the same discipline inward, toward the first months in a role and the interview that precedes them, where structured entry and visible judgment matter more than reciting a framework. Consulting and advisory work showed the model delivered from outside, under bounded authority and partial context, where scope is a control and the measure of good work is a client left more capable rather than more dependent.

The final two playbooks tested the toolkit in moments when the organization itself is moving. Cyber-insurance claim readiness took a financial transfer out of the policy file and connected it to incident command: notice, consent, approved providers, cost and impact records, truthful technical evidence, and a claim workstream that runs beside the response without taking it over. M&A, acquisitions, and divestitures carried the operating model through a change of ownership: diligence under limited information, unknowns treated as findings, trust constrained on Day 1, controls migrated without losing coverage, and separation proved rather than assumed.

Across all of it, one pattern held. There is a single operating truth in an organization, and these tools are the ways it becomes visible to different audiences and usable in different moments. They carry weight only when a leader supplies the judgment that gives them meaning: a template cannot make the decision, a checklist cannot own the risk, and a playbook cannot replace experience. What they can do is make sure the better question is asked before pressure makes the answer expensive.

Closing Note — From Risk to Trust

If you have read this far, this note is for you, and so, it turns out, was the whole series. Maybe you are an aspiring CISO, still mapping the path in. Maybe you are new to the role, discovering how much of it no certification prepared you for. Maybe you are a fractional or virtual CISO, doing it for several organizations at once. Or maybe you are an IT leader, an infrastructure lead, someone who never asked to carry security accountability but carries it anyway, because it had to land somewhere and it landed on you.

Whichever one you are, you have been doing the job the whole way through these pages because the title was never what made someone a security leader. The work did. The judgment did. The willingness to look at risk honestly and act on it did. There are people with the title who do not really do the job, and people without it who do it every single day. This book was written for the ones who do it, title or not.

From Risk to Trust. The title was always the argument, compressed into four words, a single movement from one to the other. And now that you have reached the end of it, it is worth standing still a moment to see the shape of the journey whole.

Risk is where it begins for all of us. It is the uncomfortable, unglamorous, never-finished work of figuring out what could hurt the organization and what to do about it, the exposures, the gaps, the standing exceptions, the incidents, the trade-offs nobody wants to make. Risk is the raw material of this entire profession. It fills the days. It is the work.

But it was never the point. The point was always what all that risk work is *for*, and that is trust. Trust is what a customer extends when they hand you their data. Trust is what a board grants when it funds your program and backs your judgment. Trust is the quiet assumption a regulator, an auditor, a partner, a colleague makes that you will do what you said, protect what you promised, and tell the truth when something goes wrong. Every framework in this series, every control, every report, every piece of evidence, has been machinery in service of one transformation: taking risk, which is the work, and turning it into trust, which is the job.

That is the arc you actually traveled. You watched risk become controls, and the frameworks resolve onto those controls, and the frameworks, instead of multiplying into an unmanageable pile, collapse into a single operating model. You watched that model become a control library, the library become evidence, and the evidence, finally, become the thing you could stand behind when someone asked you to prove it. Risk in at one end; trust out at the other. That was the machine the whole series was building.

Look back at the distance covered. You may have started out drowning, a different framework for every customer, a fresh scramble for every audit, a pile of obligations in languages you did not speak, and the growing suspicion that no human could hold all of it at once. And you were right: nobody can, not framework by framework. So the answer was to stop trying to.

You learned to build one operating model instead of many, one control universe that many frameworks resolve onto, one obligation register holding what your customers' countries demand, one line of assurance you can follow from a policy all the way down to the evidence that proves it real. Many frameworks, one operating model. That correlation was never a filing trick. It was the only way the modern version of this job is survivable at all.

And the job kept widening as you went, the way it keeps widening in real life. Security stopped being only security. It became privacy, because you are not just protecting systems, you are protecting the people whose data lives inside them. It became cross-border, because your customers and your obligations do not stop politely at your own country's edge. It became resilience and governance and assurance, a role that reaches from the boardroom to the single overlooked service account, from the regulator to the engineer. That breadth can feel like an impossible mandate. It is better understood as the shape of what trust now asks of the people who keep it.

So here is what you carry out of it, not a memorized catalog. You will not remember every control number, and you do not need to; no one is hired to recite them. What you take with you is that you did not just learn *about* security; you learned a way of *thinking* about it. Risk-first. Evidence-led. Honest about the gaps. Able to turn the technical into the language of the people who have to decide. Inclined to build one coherent model rather than drown in many. That way of thinking travels. It moves across frameworks, across countries, across organizations, into rooms where you have nothing to stand on but your own judgment. It is yours now, and no one can take it back.

It would be dishonest to close by pretending any of this gets easy. It does not. Trust is slow to build and quick to lose. Years of careful work, and a single hidden gap, one dishonest answer, one preventable surprise, can spend it all. The frameworks will keep changing. The obligations will keep multiplying. The threats will keep moving, and the budget rarely keeps pace. You will be asked to be certain when you cannot be, to promise what you cannot control, to reassure the person in front of you when the honest answer is the harder one.

You will not always get it right; nobody in this work does. What defines a security leader was never perfection. It is honesty about what is true, judgment about what matters, and the willingness to keep earning trust on the days it would be easier not to. And the days you do the job best are often the days nothing happens and nobody notices, because that is the nature of protecting things. Done well, most of it is invisible.

But there is a quiet dignity in it worth naming at the end. Very few roles come down to something as clean as this one does, once you strip away the tools and the acronyms and the org chart: understand what could go wrong, and earn the standing to do something about it. That is the whole of it, in every organization, at every size, whether or not it is ever written on a door. Everything else is detail.

The series began with risk. It ends, as it was always going to, with trust, because that was the direction of travel the whole time, and it will be every quarter, every audit, every hard conversation, for as long as you do this work.

Now go and earn it.

SERIES CONTENTS

A reference map to the three sibling volumes

Volume IV stands on its own. The contents that follow are a reference map to the three sibling volumes, for when a cross-reference in this book points somewhere you have not read.

Start with the volume that matches the problem in front of you. References to another volume offer deeper grounding; they are never prerequisites for understanding the one in your hands.

Volume I — The CISO Operating Model

Build the leadership foundation: the role, the first months, budgets, frameworks, governance, decision rights, and the language that turns cyber risk into a board conversation.

Part 1 — The CISO Role and Operating Model

1. What the CISO Does and How the Role Has Evolved

2. Reporting Lines, Authority, and Accountability

3. Global CISO, Country CISO, and Business-Unit CISO

4. The First 90 and 180 Days

5. Budgeting, Business Case, and Cyber Risk Appetite

6. The Security Governance Model and the Three Lines of Defense

7. Common CISO Failure Modes

8. Building and Scaling the Security Function

9. Technical Leadership vs Business-Risk Leadership

Part 2 — Cybersecurity Frameworks: Orientation, Selection, and Practical Use

10. Why Frameworks Exist and What Problem Each Solves

11. ISO/IEC 27001 and 27002

12. NIST CSF 2.0

13. NIST SP 800-53 Rev 5

14. SOC 2 Trust Services Criteria

15. CIS Controls v8.1

16. CSA Cloud Controls Matrix (CCM)

17. COBIT 2019

18. ISO 31000 and FAIR

19. Framework Selection — Choosing Your Anchor

20. Running Multiple Frameworks Without Sprawl

Part 3 — Governance and Board Reporting

21. Cybersecurity Governance — Who Owns the Risk

22. Security Steering Committees and Governance Forums

23. Board Reporting and Executive Dashboards

24. Risk Appetite and Policy Governance

25. KRI, KPI, and KCI Model

26. Three Lines of Defense in Practice

27. Communicating Cyber Risk to the Board

Volume I carries the series Introduction.

Volume II — Cyber Risk and Controls

Turn governance into operating protection: identify and express risk, choose treatments, run the register, and operate the control domains through which protection becomes real.

Part 1 — Cyber Risk Management

1. Cyber Risk Management as the Core Discipline

2. Cyber Risk Taxonomy and Classification
3. Inherent, Residual, and Target Risk
4. Risk Treatment, Acceptance, and Exceptions
5. The RCSA Model and Risk Register Design
6. FAIR, ISO 31000, ISO/IEC 27005, and NIST RMF
7. Threat Scenarios and Board-Level Risk Articulation
Part 2 — Cybersecurity Controls and Control Frameworks
8. Cybersecurity Controls as the Operating Layer
9. Identity and Access Management
10. Privileged Access Management
11. Asset Management
12. Vulnerability Management
13. Logging and Monitoring
14. Endpoint Security
15. Network Security
16. Cloud Security
17. Secure Development and DevSecOps
18. Cryptography and Key Management
19. Backup and Recovery
20. Security Awareness and the Human Layer
21. Insider Risk
22. Physical Security
23. Change and Configuration Management
24. Supplier and Third-Party Security Controls

Volume III — Digital Trust and Assurance

Prove the program to people outside it: compliance, audit, and assurance; data security, privacy, and data protection; regulatory and sector-specific requirements; and cloud, DevSecOps, product, and technology security.

Part 1 — Compliance, Audit, and Assurance

1. Compliance Is Not Security

2. How Audits Actually Work

3. Evidence and Control Testing

4. Certification and Attestation in Practice

5. Findings, Nonconformities, and Corrective Action

6. Continuous Assurance

7. Security Testing, Offensive Assurance, and Control Validation

Part 2 — Data Security, Privacy, and Data Protection

8. Data Security and the Information Lifecycle

9. The Privacy Landscape — GDPR, DPDP, ISO 27701, and the NIST Privacy Framework

10. Privacy Governance in Practice

11. Operating Privacy

12. Cross-Border Transfers and Privacy by Design

Part 3 — Regulatory and Sector-Specific Requirements

13. How to Read Any Regulation

14. Financial-Sector Regulation

15. Privacy and Data-Protection Law

16. Resilience, Incident Reporting & Critical Infrastructure

17. Regulating the New Frontier: AI & Cloud

18. Cross-Country Compliance Field Guide

Part 4 — Cloud, DevSecOps, Product, and Technology Security

19. Cloud Governance

20. The Cloud Security Tooling Stack

21. DevSecOps and the Secure Pipeline

22. Containers, Kubernetes, APIs, and Secrets

23. Zero Trust, Secure Access, and the Software Supply Chain

24. Product Security, PSIRT, and the EU Cyber Resilience Act

25. OT, IoT, and Cyber-Physical Security

SOURCES AND FURTHER READING

The principal instruments, and the editions this volume was written against

The entries below identify the principal standards, frameworks, and regulatory instruments this volume draws on, and the editions it was written against. Editions move, and the instruments in this volume move faster than most. Where a requirement matters to a decision, confirm it against the current official text.

Standards and Frameworks

ISO/IEC 27001:2022. The requirements standard for an information security management system. Used in Part 3 as an assurance artifact and in Appendix A's Cross-Framework Mapping; ISO/IEC 27002, rather than 27001, is the ISO control-set anchor in Chapter 18.

ISO/IEC 27002:2022. The guidance companion to the Annex A control set. Its logging, monitoring, threat-intelligence and incident-management controls are used in Chapter 5, and its control set is the ISO anchor mapped in Chapter 18.

ISO/IEC 42001:2023. The international management-system standard for artificial intelligence. Used in Chapter 1 alongside the NIST AI Risk Management Framework and the EU AI Act, as governance machinery rather than as proof of conformity with any regulation.

ISO/IEC 27701:2025. The second edition specifies requirements and guidance for establishing, implementing, maintaining, and continually improving a privacy information management system. It is an independent management-system standard that can be used on its own and remains aligned with ISO/IEC 27001 for organizations that integrate privacy and information-security management. Used in Chapter 19; it replaces the withdrawn ISO/IEC 27701:2019.

ISO/IEC 27031. ICT readiness for business continuity — the bridge between the business continuing to run and what technology has to be ready to do. Used in Chapters 6 and 10. Confirm the current edition.

ISO/IEC 27035. The international incident-management reference, framing incident handling as a governed, repeatable process. Used in Chapter 7. Confirm the current edition.

ISO 22301. The international standard for a business continuity management system. It is not a security standard, and Chapter 6 is explicit about that. Used in Chapters 6 and 10. Confirm the current edition.

NIST Cybersecurity Framework 2.0. Its six functions organize cybersecurity outcomes across the volume. Its Detect and Respond outcomes anchor Chapter 5, its GV.SC category carries third-party risk in Part 3, and it is the spine of the Cross-Framework Mapping in Appendix A.

NIST Artificial Intelligence Risk Management Framework, version 1.0. A voluntary framework for governing and managing AI risk. Used in Chapter 1 with ISO/IEC 42001 and the EU AI Act, and revisited in Chapter 19 as an AI-governance overlay.

NIST's adversarial-machine-learning taxonomy. Named in the front-matter source note as a deeper reference for adversarial machine learning, alongside MITRE ATLAS. This volume names it by subject rather than by publication number, and both taxonomies move quickly — confirm the current edition before relying on their categories.

NIST Special Publication 800-53, Revision 5. The US federal control catalog. One of the anchors mapped in Chapters 18 and 20, and in Appendix A.

NIST Special Publication 800-61, Revision 3, April 2025. Incident handling. Revision 3 supersedes the 2012 guide and is published as a Cybersecurity Framework 2.0 Community Profile — a material change, and Chapters 6 and 7 use the revised structure rather than the older four-phase lifecycle.

NIST Special Publication 800-34. A 2010 US-federal contingency-planning reference. It supports the disaster-recovery and continuity work in Chapters 6 and 10, including the business-impact-analysis and recovery-objective material; confirm the current publication before relying on specifics.

NIST Special Publication 800-84. Test, training and exercise programs, used in Chapter 8 as a vocabulary source for exercises. It dates from 2006 and was written for US federal IT, so pair it with current incident-response and sector guidance.

NIST Special Publication 800-86. Integrating forensic techniques into incident response, used in Chapter 9 for the collection, examination, analysis and reporting discipline. It is a 2006-era reference that predates cloud, SaaS and containers, so supplement it with current platform and provider guidance.

NIST Special Publication 800-161. Cyber supply-chain risk management. Used in Chapter 13, where fourth-party, sub-supplier and component-integrity risk extend the supplier chain. Confirm the current edition before relying on specifics.

NIST Special Publication 800-63-4, July 2025, with SP 800-63A-4 (Identity Proofing and Enrollment) and SP 800-63B-4 (Authentication and Authenticator Management). The Digital Identity Guidelines. Used in Chapter 2 for digital-injection and forged-media attacks against identity proofing, and for account recovery and notification treated as security-sensitive processes. Applied here as leadership principles: nothing in this book implies a private organization must adopt the federal assurance levels.

OWASP GenAI LLM Top 10 2026, released 4 August 2026. Published by the OWASP Foundation. Chapter 2 uses it as a living threat reference rather than reproducing its category structure.

OWASP Top 10 for Agentic Applications, 2026 edition, released December 2025 by the OWASP GenAI Security Project's Agentic Security Initiative. Used in Chapter 2. The chapter's grouping of its entries is the author's own framing rather than the publication's structure. The publication is issued under a Creative Commons Attribution-ShareAlike license — readers who build directly on its material, rather than referring to it as this book does, should observe its license terms. Both OWASP lists are living community documents whose categories and identifiers will change.

MITRE ATT&CK, Enterprise matrix version 19.1. The behavioral vocabulary used in Chapter 5, organized under its tactical objectives. Version 19.1 is the release this chapter was written against; version 19 split the former Defense Evasion tactic into Stealth and Defense Impairment and added or revised techniques, so confirm identifiers and tactic placement against the current release. MITRE ATT&CK® and ATT&CK® are registered trademarks of The MITRE Corporation. The book uses ATT&CK as a behavior and coverage vocabulary, not as a source of incident-frequency, dwell-time, or breach-cost statistics.

MITRE ATLAS. The adversarial-machine-learning knowledge base named in the front-matter source note as a next reference beyond this book's AI threat model.

CIS Critical Security Controls, version 8.1, published by the Center for Internet Security. Its audit log management and network monitoring safeguards are used in Chapter 5, and the control set is one of the anchors mapped in Chapter 18.

Payment Card Industry Data Security Standard, version 4.0.1, PCI Security Standards Council. One of the anchors mapped in Chapter 18, and the standing example in Part 4 of a standard that produces its own validation artifacts.

AICPA Trust Services Criteria, under which SOC 2 examinations are performed. Used in Chapters 14 and 15 from the receiving and producing sides of assurance, and as one of the anchors mapped in Chapter 18. They are criteria, not controls.

Cloud Security Alliance, Cloud Controls Matrix version 4.1, with the Consensus Assessments Initiative Questionnaire (CAIQ) version 4.1 — 283 questions aligned with 207 Cloud Controls Matrix controls across 17 domains — and the CSA STAR registry, whose Level 1 is a self-assessment and Level 2 rests on third-party certification or attestation. Used in Chapters 14, 15, 18 and 20. The Cloud Security Alliance permits narrower use than the other publishers, and this book stays inside it: control identifiers, domain names, and paraphrased intent, with attribution, and nothing further.

Shared Assessments, Standardized Information Gathering (SIG) questionnaire. Used in Chapter 15 as the other standing reference point for maintained questionnaire answers.

COBIT. Named in the Cross-Framework Mapping in Appendix A as a governance anchor. This volume does not work from its text; confirm the current edition and its own wording before relying on it.

CISA, FBI, NSA, and MS-ISAC, #StopRansomware Guide. The public reference used for the ransomware-readiness material in Chapter 8, including data extortion as well as encryption. Confirm the current edition, and pair it with current sanctions, legal, insurer and law-enforcement guidance for any payment decision.

Federal Bureau of Investigation public alert I-120324-PSA, 3 December 2024, Criminals Use Generative Artificial Intelligence to Facilitate Financial Fraud. Used in Chapter 2 for AI-generated text, images, cloned audio and video across romance and investment fraud.

Model Context Protocol and Agent2Agent. Described in Chapter 2 only at the level of what they are for and the trust questions they raise. No protocol version or implementation requirement is pinned, because both are still settling.

Regulations and Supervisory Instruments

Regulation (EU) 2024/1689 — the Artificial Intelligence Act, as amended by Regulation (EU) 2026/1744. Used in Chapters 1 and 19. Its obligations apply in phases rather than on a single date. The prohibited-practice, AI-literacy and general-purpose-AI-model provisions were already applicable when this volume was verified; Regulation (EU) 2026/1744 moved the high-risk obligations to 2 December 2027 for the stand-alone high-risk systems covered by Article 6(2) and Annex III, and to 2 August 2028 for the product-related high-risk systems covered by Article 6(1) and Annex I. Confirm the consolidated text before relying on a date.

Regulation (EU) 2022/2554 — the Digital Operational Resilience Act (DORA), applicable since 17 January 2025. The European Union's operational-resilience regime for the financial sector, and a binding obligation rather than a voluntary framework. Used in Chapters 6 and 19, including its ICT-risk, resilience-testing, third-party and major-incident-reporting duties.

Regulation (EU) 2016/679 — the General Data Protection Regulation (GDPR). Used in Chapter 1 for the extraterritorial pattern the AI Act repeats, and in Chapter 19 where privacy obligations land on the control universe.

The Digital Personal Data Protection Act, 2023, and the Digital Personal Data Protection Rules, 2025 (India). Used in Chapter 19 as the fast-emerging example of a major new market's data-protection law, and described there as operating under phased commencement.

Indian Computer Emergency Response Team (CERT-In) directions. Referenced in the incident-notification discussion in Chapters 9 and 19. Confirm the covered incident, reporting route, current direction and deadline that apply to the organization.

Reserve Bank of India, Securities and Exchange Board of India, and Insurance Regulatory and Development Authority of India instruments. Used in Chapters 6 and 19 as sector overlays that land on a unified control universe. Chapter 19's six-hour example concerns the IRDAI requirement for insurers to report cyber incidents to CERT-In. Volume III covers these regimes in full; this volume treats them as overlays.

Saudi Central Bank (SAMA), Cyber Security Framework. Used in Chapters 6 and 19 as a financial-sector resilience and governance overlay. This volume does not pin an edition; confirm the current instrument, covered entity and effective requirements.

A Note on Method

These entries identify the principal sources and the editions used. The front-matter section A Note on Sources, Method, and Copyright explains this book's relationship to copyrighted standards: it explains and interprets them, and does not reproduce their text or tables.

The cross-framework correlations in this volume — the control universe built in Part 4, the mapping in Chapter 18, and the Cross-Framework Mapping in Appendix A — are the author's own analysis. They are offered as reasoned mappings so that a leader can build one operating model and describe it outward in several languages. They are not an official mapping, and no framework owner has published or endorsed them. Where this book and a standard disagree, the standard wins.

Where this book names a regulation or a supervisory instrument, it does so to show a pattern a leader can recognize and reuse. It is not a complete legal summary, and it does not establish whether an obligation applies to you. Entity scope, national transposition, reporting routes, amendments and effective dates all move. Volume III states the regulatory detail precisely; confirm any of it against the instrument in force on the date it matters, and take qualified legal advice before making a material compliance commitment.

The AI instruments in Part 1 move faster than the rest. The OWASP lists are living community documents, the adversarial-machine-learning taxonomies are revised frequently, and the AI Act's dates have already been amended once. Treat every identifier, category and date in Part 1 as verified at the time of writing and check it before relying on it.

The agent protocols named in this book are described, not specified. The Model Context Protocol and Agent2Agent are covered at the level of what they are for and the trust questions they raise. No version is pinned, because both are still settling, and any version-specific claim should come from the protocol's own documentation.

Several terms used in this book are market categories rather than standards. EDR, SIEM, DLP, CASB and GRC describe product boundaries that vendors and analysts draw differently and revise often. They are used here as orientation, not as a fixed taxonomy, and no vendor or analyst grouping should be treated as an authority on control coverage.

Product behavior and defaults change with version, provider and configuration. Treat any specific feature claim in this book as version-specific, and check it against the documentation for the release you actually run.

GLOSSARY

Terms, abbreviations, and what they are not

Terms are introduced in context throughout the book, where they do their work. This glossary is for lookup and for refreshing — for the reader who met a term four chapters ago and wants it back in one line.

Several entries carry a second sentence saying what the term is not. That is where most of the confusion in this field actually lives.

Frameworks, Standards, and Regulations

AI Act — Regulation (EU) 2024/1689, as amended by Regulation (EU) 2026/1744. The European Union's risk-tiered law for artificial intelligence. It applies in phases, not on a single date.

AI RMF — the NIST Artificial Intelligence Risk Management Framework, version 1.0. A voluntary framework organizing AI risk into four functions: Govern, Map, Measure, Manage. Not a law and not a certification.

ATLAS — MITRE's adversarial machine-learning knowledge base. The AI counterpart to ATT&CK.

ATT&CK — MITRE's knowledge base of observed adversary tactics and techniques. Enterprise matrix version 19.1 is the release this book was written against. It is a vocabulary for describing behavior, not a control framework and not a compliance obligation.

CAIQ — Consensus Assessments Initiative Questionnaire, published by the Cloud Security Alliance. Version 4.1 carries 283 questions aligned to the Cloud Controls Matrix.

CCM — Cloud Controls Matrix. The CSA's cloud-specific control framework, version 4.1, organized across 17 domains.

CERT-In — the Indian Computer Emergency Response Team. India's national incident-reporting authority.

CIS Controls — the CIS Critical Security Controls, version 8.1, published by the Center for Internet Security. A prioritized sequence of safeguards. Ordered for sequencing, not for completeness.

COBIT — Control Objectives for Information and Related Technologies. ISACA's framework for the governance and management of enterprise IT. Used in this volume only as a mapping anchor.

CSA — Cloud Security Alliance. Publisher of the Cloud Controls Matrix, the CAIQ, and the STAR registry.

CSF — the NIST Cybersecurity Framework. Version 2.0 organizes outcomes across six functions: GOVERN, IDENTIFY, PROTECT, DETECT, RESPOND, RECOVER.

DORA — the Digital Operational Resilience Act, Regulation (EU) 2022/2554, applicable since 17 January 2025. The EU's operational-resilience regime for financial entities. A binding obligation, not a voluntary framework.

DPDP — India's Digital Personal Data Protection Act, 2023, and the Digital Personal Data Protection Rules, 2025.

GDPR — Regulation (EU) 2016/679, the General Data Protection Regulation. Its reach extends beyond Europe's borders.

IRDAI — Insurance Regulatory and Development Authority of India. Source of the six-hour incident-reporting requirement that applies to Indian insurers.

ISO 22301 — the international standard for a business continuity management system. It is not a security standard.

ISO/IEC 27001 — the requirements standard for an information security management system. The certifiable one.

ISO/IEC 27002 — the guidance companion to the Annex A control set. Guidance, not requirements: you certify against 27001, not 27002.

ISO/IEC 27031 — ICT readiness for business continuity. The bridge between "the business must keep running" and what technology has to be ready to do.

ISO/IEC 27035 — the international incident-management reference.

ISO/IEC 27701 — the independent management-system standard for a privacy information management system. The 2025 second edition can be used on its own and remains aligned with ISO/IEC 27001.

ISO/IEC 42001 — the international management-system standard for artificial intelligence. Governance machinery, not proof of conformity with the AI Act.

OWASP — the Open Worldwide Application Security Project. Publisher of the OWASP GenAI LLM Top 10 2026 and the Top 10 for Agentic Applications 2026. They are living community documents whose categories and identifiers change.

PCI DSS — the Payment Card Industry Data Security Standard, version 4.0.1.

RBI, SEBI, SAMA — the Reserve Bank of India, the Securities and Exchange Board of India, and the Saudi Central Bank. Sector regulators whose cyber expectations bind the entities they supervise.

SIG — the Standardized Information Gathering questionnaire, published by Shared Assessments.

SOC 2 — an examination in which an independent certified public accountant (CPA) reports on controls at a service organization relevant to selected AICPA Trust Services Criteria. A Type 1 report addresses control design as of a specified date; a Type 2 report also addresses operating effectiveness over a specified period. Either report is scoped to a defined system and criteria, so a clean report may not cover the service or risk you are assessing.

SP 800-xx — NIST Special Publications. This volume uses 800-53 (control catalog), 800-61 (incident handling), 800-34 (contingency planning), 800-84 (exercises), 800-86 (forensics), 800-161 (supply chain), and the 800-63 line (digital identity).

STAR — the CSA's Security, Trust, Assurance and Risk registry. Level 1 is a self-assessment; Level 2 rests on third-party certification or attestation. The level is the whole point.

#StopRansomware Guide — the joint CISA, FBI, NSA and MS-ISAC public reference for ransomware preparation and response.

Trust Services Criteria — the AICPA criteria under which SOC 2 examinations are performed. Criteria, not controls: you choose the controls that meet them.

AI and Emerging Technology Terms

Agentic application — an AI system that plans and takes actions across tools and systems rather than only producing text. The risk shifts from what it says to what it does.

Agent2Agent — an emerging protocol for communication between AI agents. Described in this book at the level of the trust questions it raises; no version is pinned, because it is still settling.

Deepfake — synthetic audio, image, or video created to impersonate a real person.

Fine-tuning — further training of a model on additional data to adapt its behavior. Distinct from inference and from retrieval.

Guardrail — a control placed around a model's inputs or outputs to constrain behavior. A guardrail is a control, not a guarantee.

Hallucination — a fluent, confident output that is factually wrong. The failure mode that matters most, because the system does not crash: it keeps working while being wrong.

Inference — a model producing output from an input, as opposed to being trained.

Jailbreak — an input crafted to bypass a model's safety constraints.

LLM — large language model.

MCP — the Model Context Protocol. A standard for how an AI system connects to tools and data sources. No version is pinned in this book.

Prompt injection — instructions smuggled into content a model reads, causing it to act on the attacker's intent rather than the user's. The manipulation arrives through the model's own input, which is why perimeter controls do not see it.

RAG — retrieval-augmented generation. Supplying a model with retrieved documents at query time so its answer is grounded in your data rather than its training.

Red-teaming — adversarial testing of an AI system to find failure modes before an attacker does.

Shadow AI — AI tools in use across the organization that no one approved, inventoried, or governed.

Operational and Technical Terms

Attestation — an independent practitioner's report on whether specified subject matter or assertions meet stated criteria. It is different from certification, not categorically weaker, and its assurance is bounded by the engagement, criteria, scope, and period or date.

BIA — business impact analysis. The exercise that establishes what the business needs restored, in what order, and how fast.

Blast radius — how far the consequences of a compromise reach before something stops them.

CASB — cloud access security broker. A market category, not a standard.

Concentration risk — the exposure created when many services, or many of your suppliers, depend on the same provider.

Containment — an incident-response activity that limits spread and further harm. Distinct from eradication, which removes the cause, and from recovery, which restores service.

Control universe — the single consolidated set of controls onto which applicable framework requirements and other control requirements are mapped. Regulatory, contractual, and customer duties that are not controls remain in the obligation register rather than being forced into the universe. The central idea of Part 4.

Crosswalk — a mapping that shows which controls in one framework address the same objective as controls in another. The correlations in this book are the author's own analysis, not an official mapping.

DLP — data loss prevention. A market category.

DPIA — data protection impact assessment. Required under GDPR where processing is likely to be high risk.

DPO — data protection officer.

Dwell time — how long an intruder is present before being detected.

EDR — endpoint detection and response. A market category.

Exit planning — the arrangements that let you leave a supplier without losing data, service, or evidence. Increasingly a regulatory obligation rather than good practice.

Forensics — the disciplined collection, examination, analysis and reporting of evidence so findings hold up later.

Fourth party — your supplier's supplier. Your obligations do not stop at the party you contracted with.

GRC — governance, risk and compliance. A market category for tooling.

Immutable backup — a backup that cannot be altered or deleted for a defined period, including by an administrator or an attacker holding administrator credentials.

Legal hold — an instruction to preserve records that may be relevant to litigation or investigation.

Materiality — whether a fact, event, omission, or risk is significant enough to affect a reasonable decision or trigger action under an applicable rule. A context-specific legal and business determination, not a security one.

MFA — multi-factor authentication.

NDA — non-disclosure agreement.

Penetration testing — authorized testing that attempts to exploit weaknesses, as opposed to only identifying them.

Playbook — a prepared, rehearsed sequence for a situation you expect to face. Its value is that it was written before the pressure, not during it.

Privilege — in the legal sense, the protection that can attach to communications with counsel. Relevant to how incident investigations are structured and who directs them.

PSIRT — product security incident response team. Handles vulnerabilities in what you sell, as opposed to what you run.

Right to audit — a contractual right to examine a supplier's controls. A right you never exercise is a clause, not an assurance.

RPO — recovery point objective. How much data you can afford to lose, measured in time.

RTO — recovery time objective. The target time within which a service should be restored. It should sit inside the maximum tolerable downtime, the outer point beyond which disruption becomes unacceptable. RPO and RTO answer different questions and are routinely confused.

SBOM — software bill of materials. An inventory of the components in a piece of software. An inventory, not a security guarantee.

SIEM — security information and event management. A market category.

SLA — service level agreement.

Sub-processor — a third party a processor engages to process personal data on the controller's behalf.

Tabletop exercise — a discussion-based rehearsal of an incident, run against a scenario with injects. It tests decisions and coordination, not technology.

Threat-informed defense — organizing detection and response around observed adversary behavior rather than around tool coverage.

Traceability — the demonstrable line from policy to control to evidence. The proof that the operating model is real rather than declared.

vCISO — a fractional or virtual CISO, engaged part-time or on contract.

Zero trust — an architectural approach that removes implicit trust based on network location. An approach, not a product.

Abbreviations Used in the Quick Reference and Appendix

CSF function codes. GV — Govern. ID — Identify. PR — Protect. DE — Detect. RS — Respond. RC — Recover.

NIST SP 800-53 control families cited in the mapping. AC — Access Control. AT — Awareness and Training. AU — Audit and Accountability. CA — Assessment, Authorization and Monitoring. CM — Configuration Management. CP — Contingency Planning. IA — Identification and Authentication. IR — Incident Response. MP — Media Protection. PE — Physical and Environmental Protection. PM — Program Management. RA — Risk Assessment. SC — System and Communications Protection. SI — System and Information Integrity.

QUICK REFERENCE

A condensed framework reference for rapid review

Reproduced from the earlier quick reference for convenient end-of-book use.

QR · NIST CSF 2.0 — Core at a Glance (Volume I, Part 2 reference)

Function	ID	Purpose (one line)	Cats / Subs
GOVERN	GV	Establishing, communicating, and monitoring the organization's cyber-risk strategy, expectations, and policy	6 / 31
IDENTIFY	ID	Building a current understanding of the organization's cybersecurity risks	3 / 21
PROTECT	PR	Putting safeguards in place to manage the identified cybersecurity risks	5 / 22
DETECT	DE	Finding and analyzing possible attacks and compromises	2 / 11
RESPOND	RS	Taking action on a detected cybersecurity incident	4 / 13
RECOVER	RC	Restoring the assets and operations that a cybersecurity incident disrupted	2 / 8
TOTAL		Govern + Identify + Protect + Detect + Respond + Recover	**22 / 106**

APPENDIX

Cross-Framework Mapping

Appendix A · NIST CSF 2.0 ↔ ISO 27001 / 800-53 / CIS / COBIT / SOC 2 / PCI

Reproduced here for quick reference; the corresponding Cross-Framework Mapping appears in Volume III's Appendix A.

CSF 2.0 Function	ISO/IEC 27001:2022	NIST 800-53 r5 (families)	Other
GOVERN	Clauses 4–6 and 9.3; A.5 organizational controls	PM, PL, RA (program / risk)	COBIT EDM/APO; CIS Govern function
IDENTIFY	A.5.9–A.5.12 asset and classification; 6.1 risk	RA, CM, PM	CIS 1–2; FAIR (risk quantification)
PROTECT	A.5.15–A.5.18 and A.8 technological controls	AC, IA, SC, MP, PE, AT	CIS 3–6, 11–16; PCI DSS Reqs 1–8
DETECT	A.8.15–A.8.16 logging and monitoring	AU, SI, CA	CIS 8, 13; SOC 2 CC7.1–CC7.2
RESPOND	A.5.24–A.5.28 incident management	IR	CIS 17; SOC 2 CC7.3–CC7.5
RECOVER	A.5.29–A.5.30 continuity and ICT readiness	CP	CIS 11 (data recovery); ISO 22301

Made in the USA
Monee, IL
04 November 2026

67376995R00321